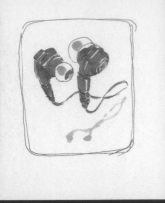

I received earbuds at a New Year's party and remembered that my ears refuse to accept this shape of headphone.

-Tite Kubo

BLEACH is author Tite Kubo's second title. Kubo made his debut with *ZOMBIEPOWDER.*, a four-volume series for *WEEKLY SHONEN JUMP*. To date, *BLEACH* has been translated into numerous languages and has also inspired an animated TV series that began airing in the U.S. in 2006. Beginning its serialization in 2001, *BLEACH* is still a mainstay in the pages of *WEEKLY SHONEN JUMP*. In 2005, *BLEACH* was awarded the prestigious Shogakukan Manga Award in the *shonen* (boys) category.

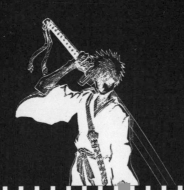

BLEACH
VOL. 71: BABY, HOLD YOUR HAND
SHONEN JUMP Manga Edition

STORY AND ART BY
TITE KUBO

Translation/Joe Yamazaki
Touch-up Art & Lettering/Mark McMurray
Design/Kam Li
Editor/Alexis Kirsch

BLEACH © 2001 by Tite Kubo. All rights reserved. First published
in Japan in 2001 by SHUEISHA Inc., Tokyo. English translation rights
arranged by SHUEISHA Inc.

The stories, characters and incidents mentioned in this publication are
entirely fictional.

Printed in the U.S.A.

Published by VIZ Media, LLC
P.O. Box 77010
San Francisco, CA 94107

10 9 8 7 6 5 4 3 2 1
First printing, November 2017

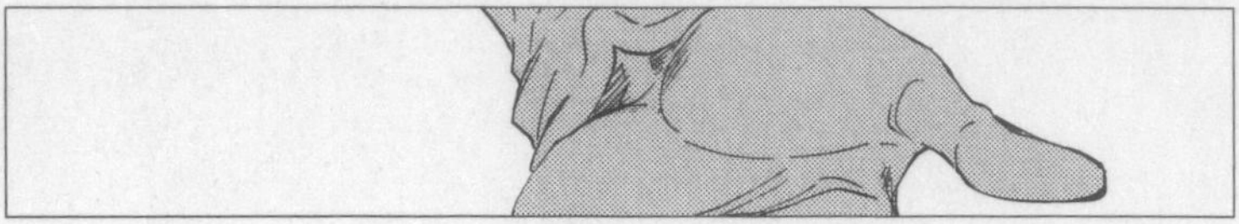

My child's hand, so lost
Wandering, in search of mine
Close but far, I take your hand
Together we will walk, to the end

BLEACH 71

BABY, HOLD YOUR HAND

Shonen Jump Manga

ALL STARS ★

AND

ペルニダ・
パルンカジャス

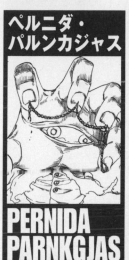

PERNIDA PARNKGJAS

NEMU
KUROTSUCHI

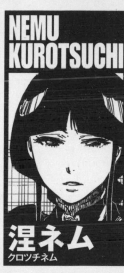

涅ネム
クロツチネム

涅マユリ
クロツチマユリ

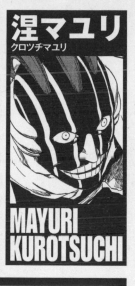

MAYURI KUROTSUCHI

plot

Ichigo Kurosaki meets Soul Reaper Rukia Kuchiki and ends up helping her eradicate Hollows. After developing his powers as a Soul Reaper, Ichigo befriends many humans and Soul Reapers and grows as a person...

After separating from Kyoraku and the others, Bazz-B challenges his old friend Haschwalth but is soon defeated. Meanwhile, Zaraki and Mayuri face off against the Quincy Pernida. Zaraki is knocked out of commission by Pernida's attacks, which rely on using his nerves to incapacitate his opponents. Mayuri reveals that Pernida is Reio's left arm, but is eventually overpowered. Now Nemu has joined the fight, but...

BLEACH

LILLE BARRO

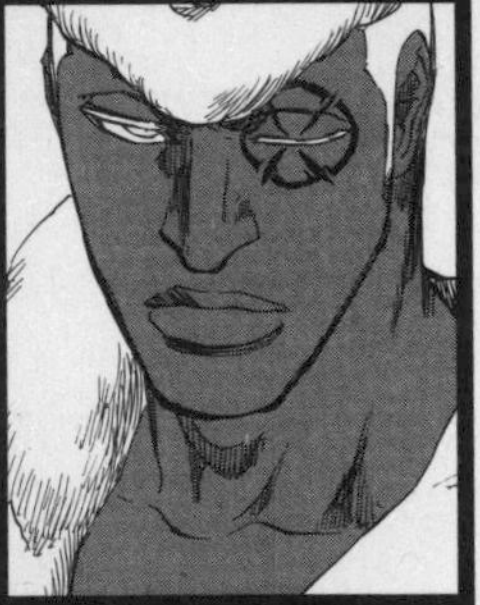

リジェ・バロ

伊勢七緒

イセナナオ

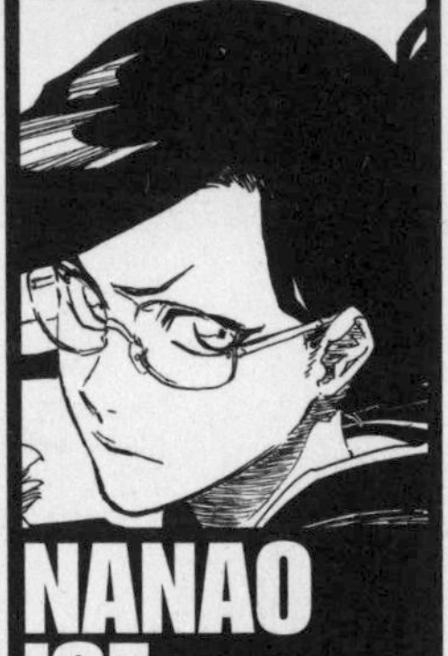

NANAO ISE

SHUNSUI KYORAKU

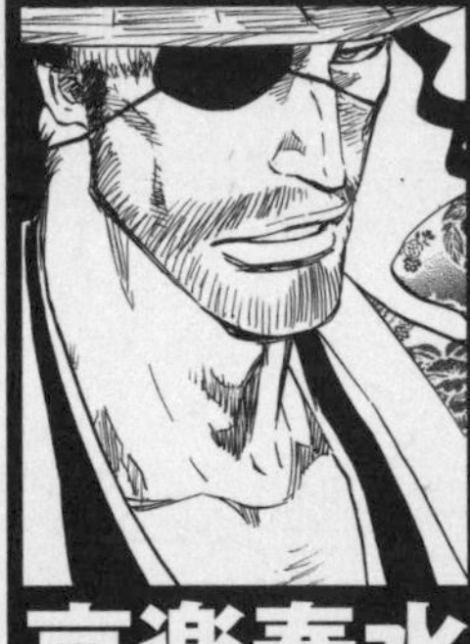

京楽春水

キョウラクシュンスイ

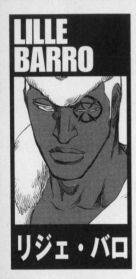

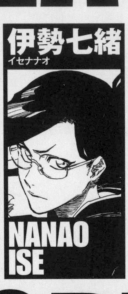

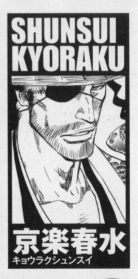

STORIES

BLEACH 71

BABY, HOLD YOUR HAND

CONTENTS

643. BABY, HOLD YOUR HAND 6 [WAITING FOR LOVE] ——————— 7
644. BABY, HOLD YOUR HAND 七 [NEVER ENDING MY DREAM] ——————— 25
645. DON'T CHASE A SHADOW ——————— 43
646. THE SECOND EYE ——————— 61
647. THE THEATRE SUICIDE ——————— 79
648. THE THEATRE SUICIDE SCENE 2 ——————— 97
649. THE THEATRE SUICIDE SCENE 3 ——————— 115
650. THE THEATRE SUICIDE SCENE 4 ——————— 133
651. THE THEATRE SUICIDE SCENE 5 ——————— 151
652. THE THEATRE SUICIDE SCENE 6 ——————— 169

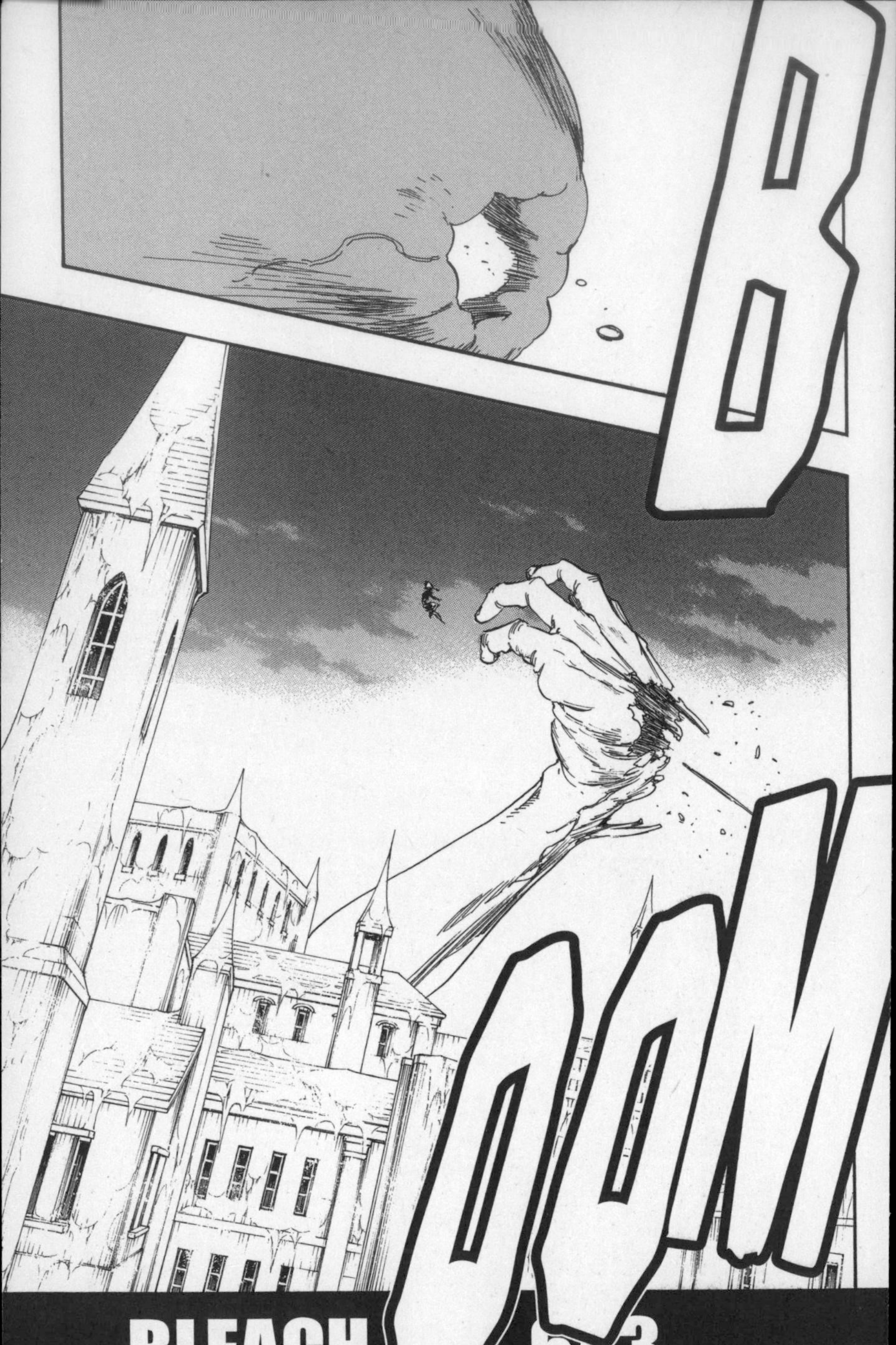
BOOM

BLEACH 643.

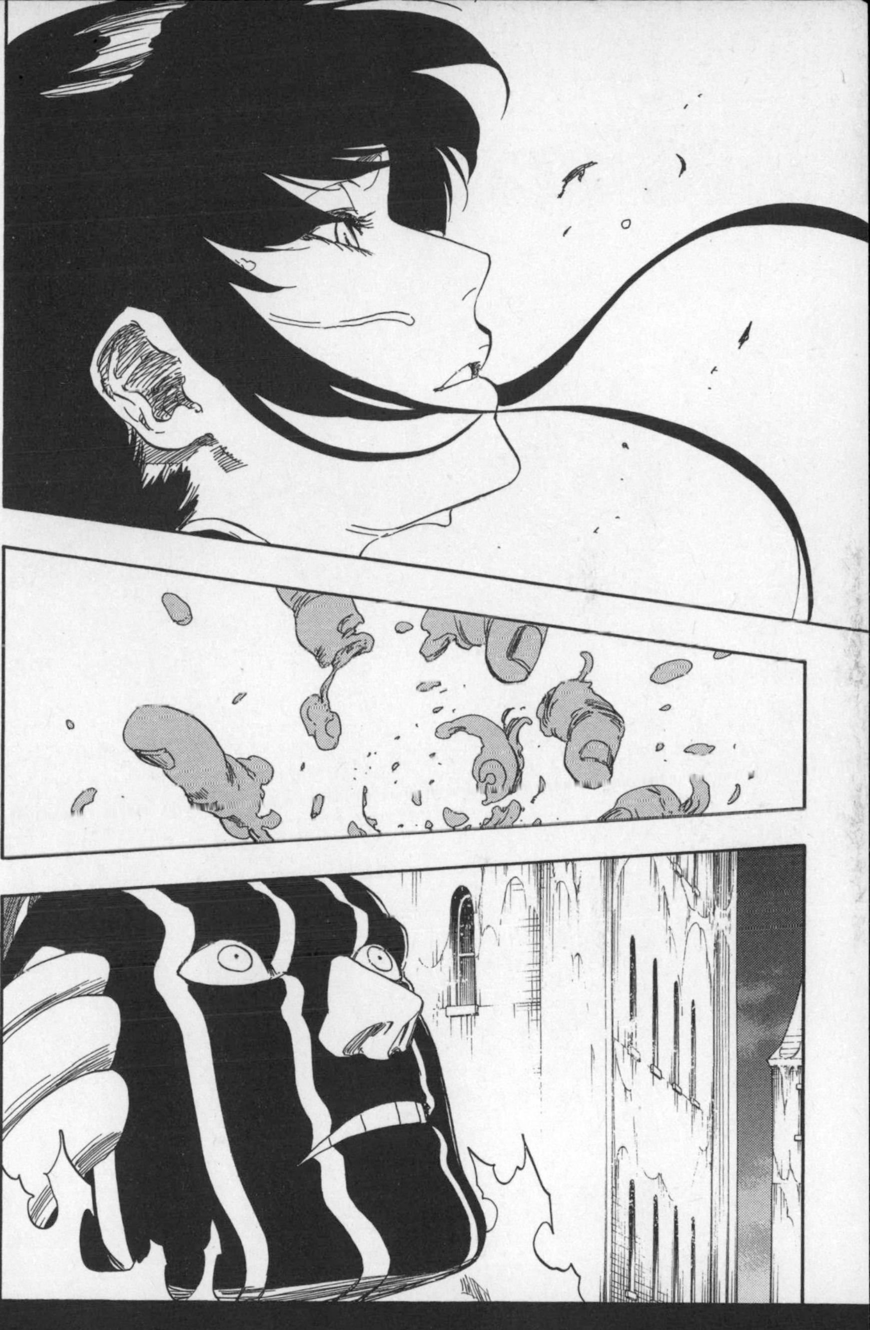

BABY,HOLD YOUR HAND 6

[Waiting for Love]

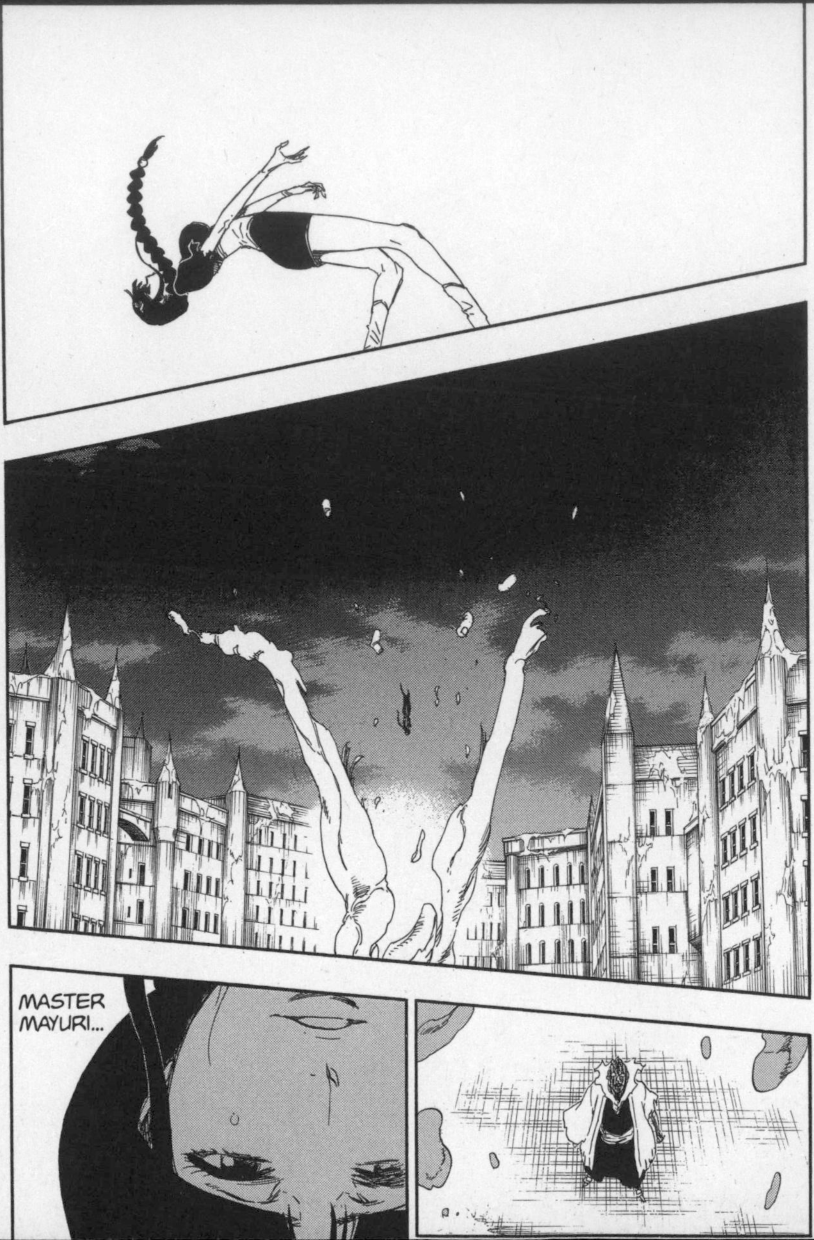
MASTER MAYURI...

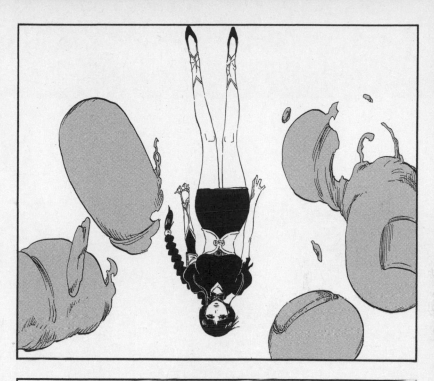

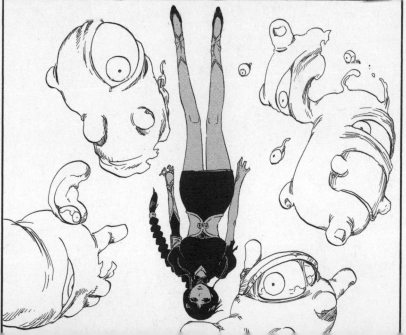

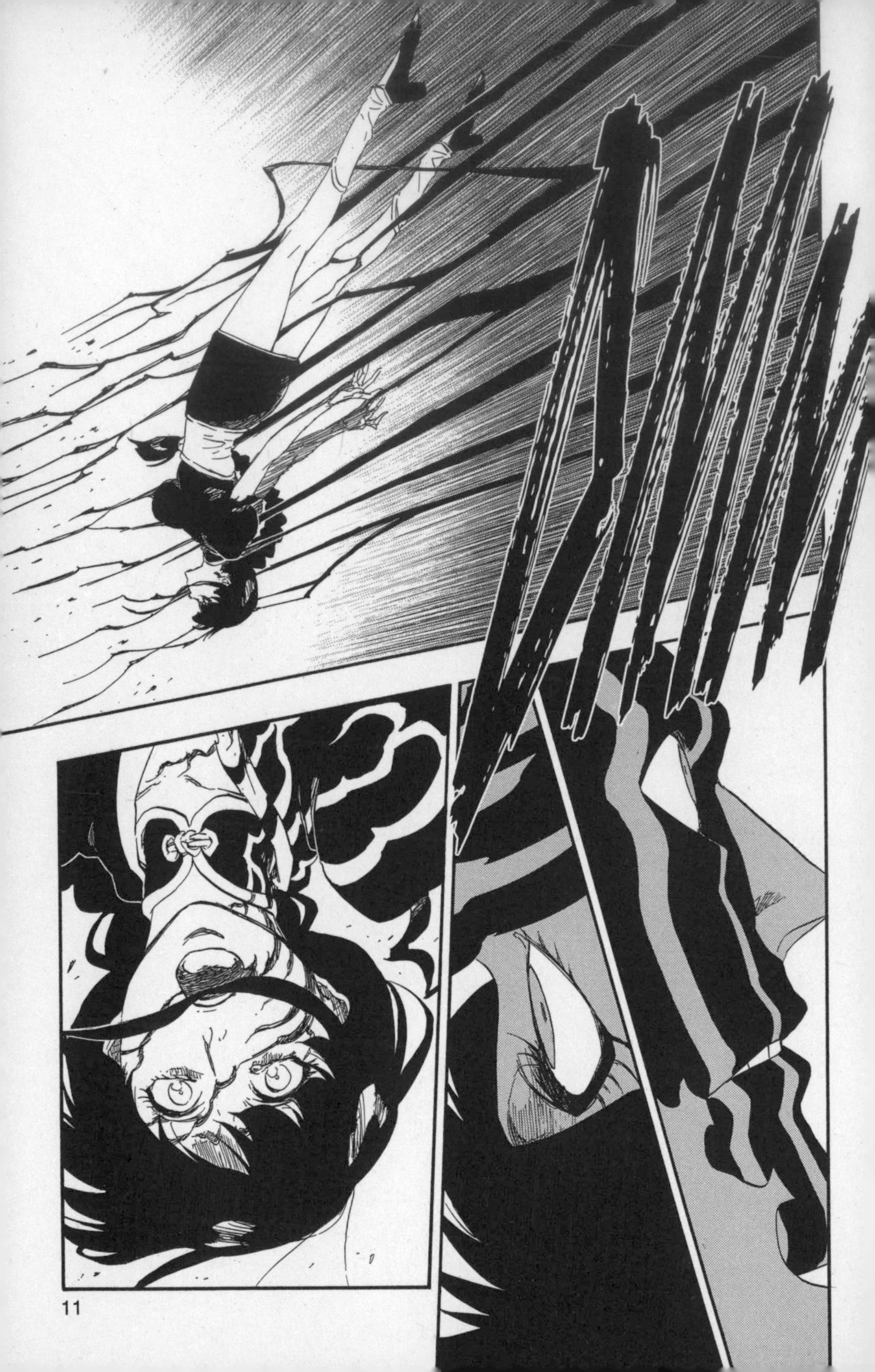

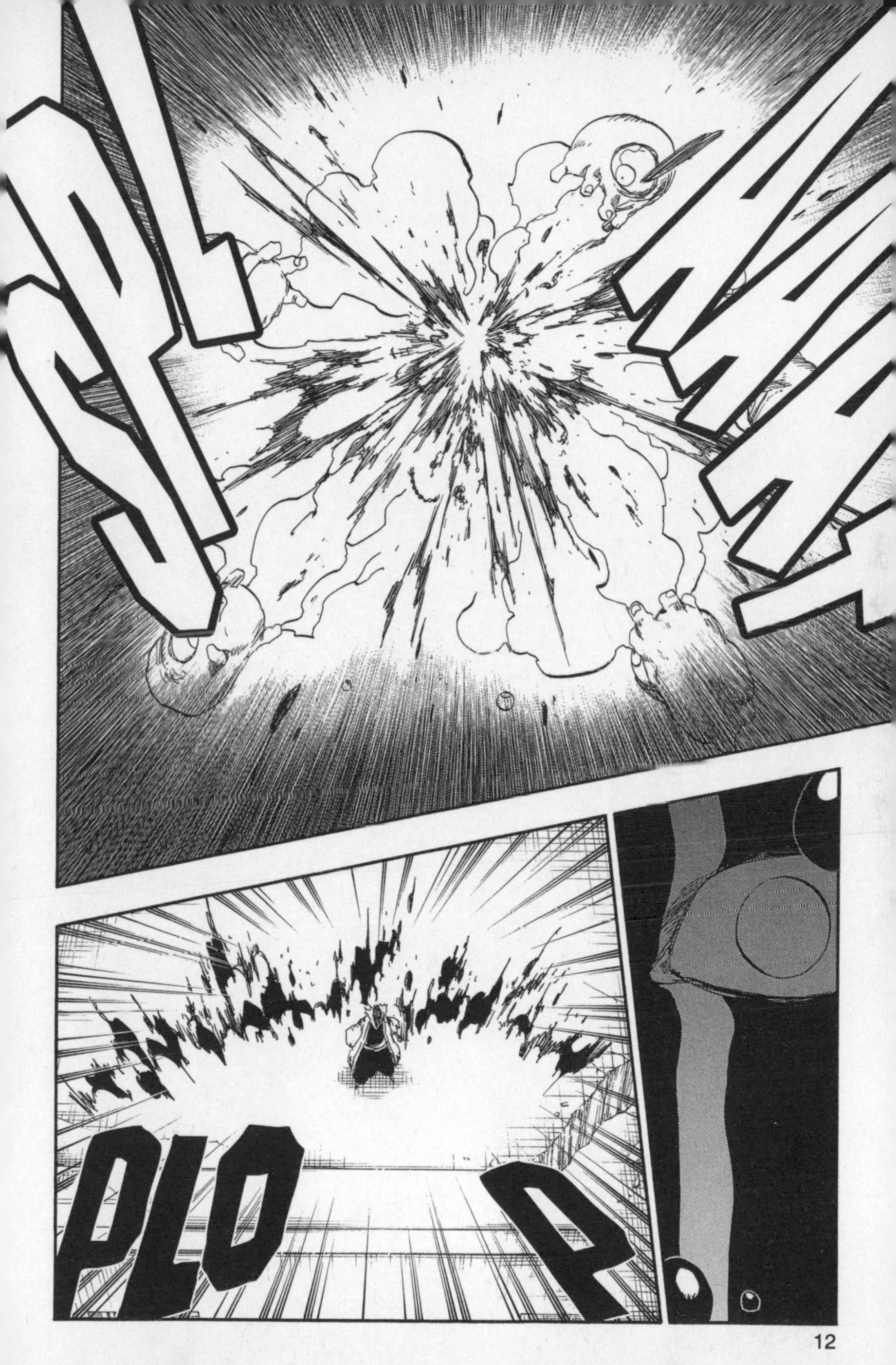
SPLAAA
PLOP!

READ THIS WAY

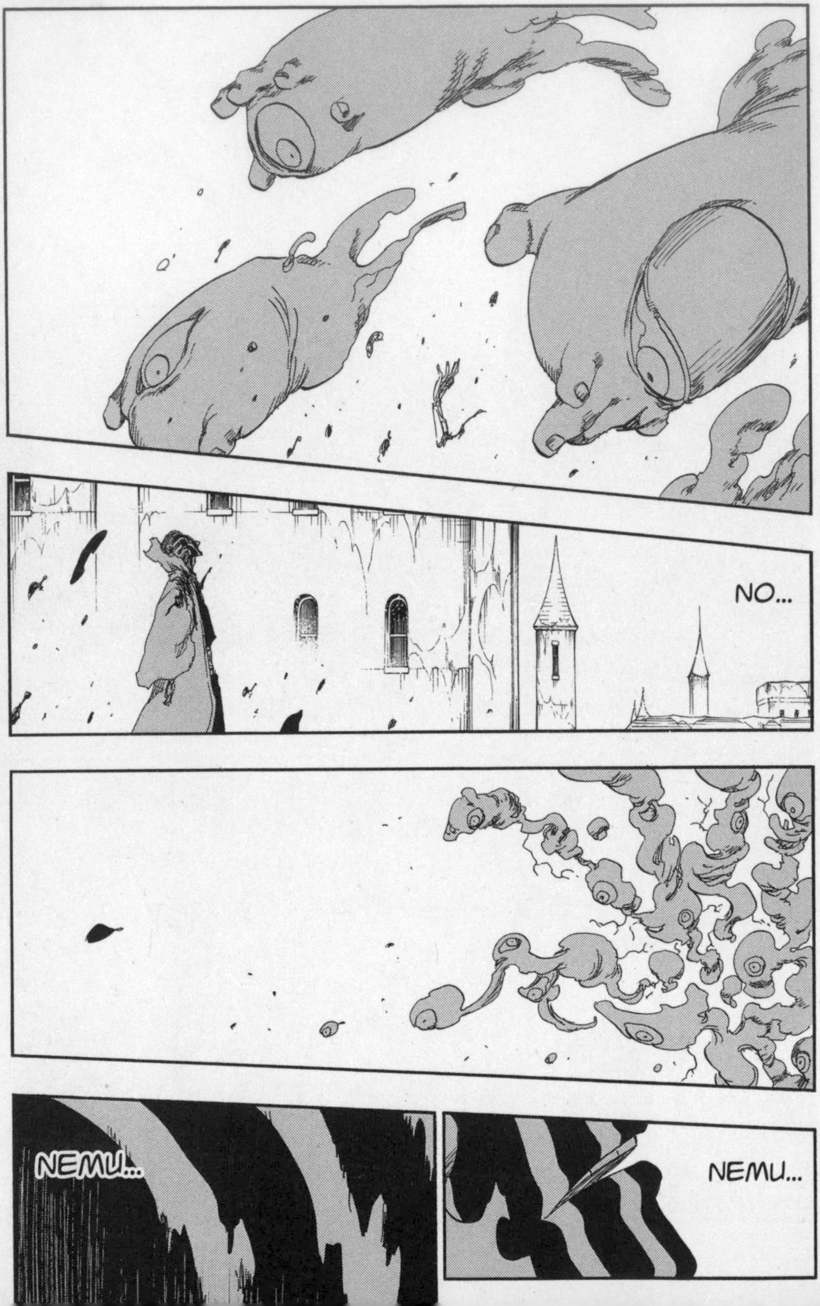
NO...
NEMU...
NEMU...

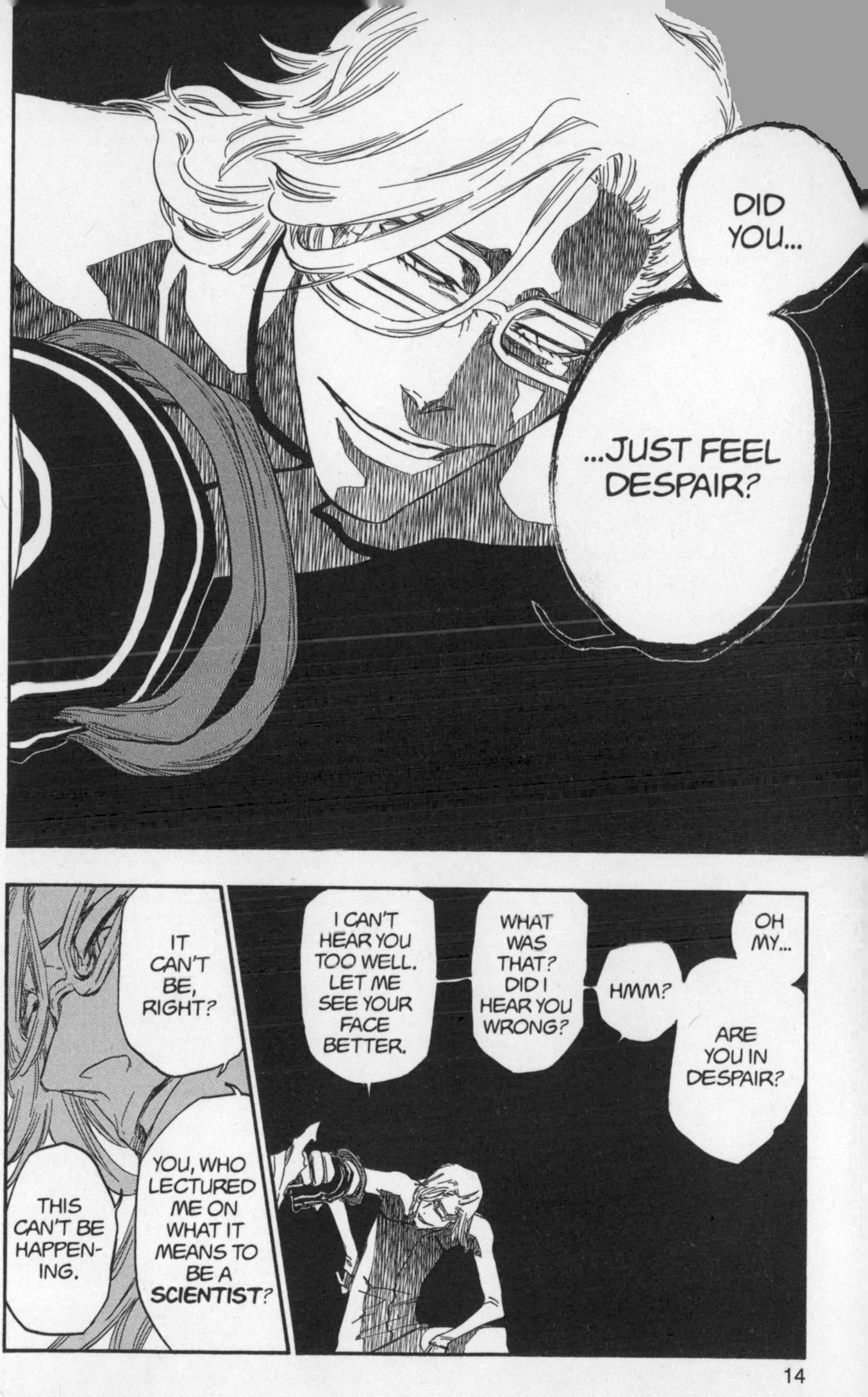

DID YOU...
...JUST FEEL DESPAIR?
OH MY...
HMM?
ARE YOU IN DESPAIR?
WHAT WAS THAT? DID I HEAR YOU WRONG?
I CAN'T HEAR YOU TOO WELL. LET ME SEE YOUR FACE BETTER.
IT CAN'T BE, RIGHT?
YOU, WHO LECTURED ME ON WHAT IT MEANS TO BE A **SCIENTIST**?
THIS CAN'T BE HAPPEN-ING.

READ THIS WAY

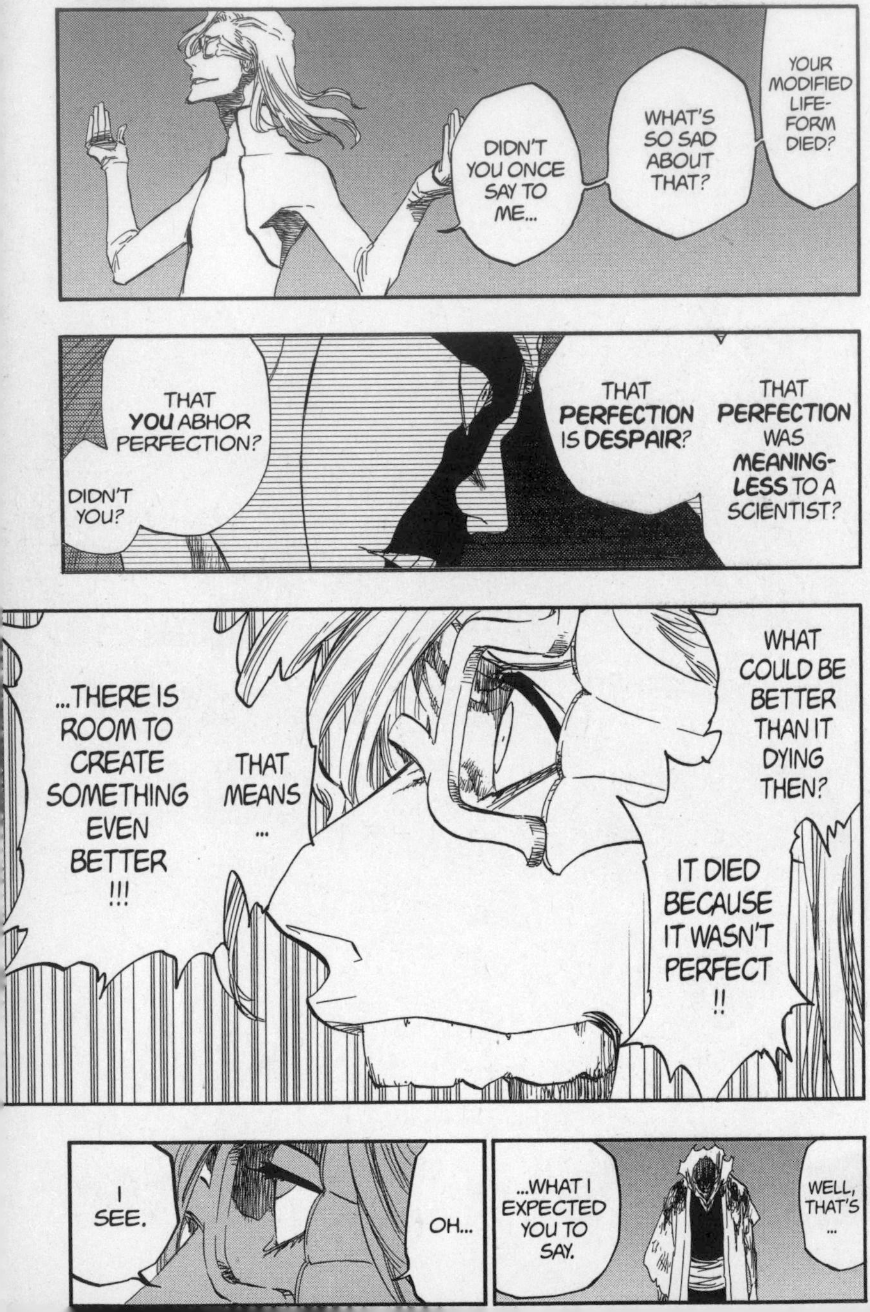
YOUR MODIFIED LIFE-FORM DIED?
WHAT'S SO SAD ABOUT THAT?
DIDN'T YOU ONCE SAY TO ME...
THAT PERFECTION WAS MEANINGLESS TO A SCIENTIST?
THAT PERFECTION IS DESPAIR?
THAT YOU ABHOR PERFECTION?
DIDN'T YOU?
WHAT COULD BE BETTER THAN IT DYING THEN?
IT DIED BECAUSE IT WASN'T PERFECT!!
THAT MEANS...
...THERE IS ROOM TO CREATE SOMETHING EVEN BETTER!!!
WELL, THAT'S...
...WHAT I EXPECTED YOU TO SAY.
OH...
I SEE.

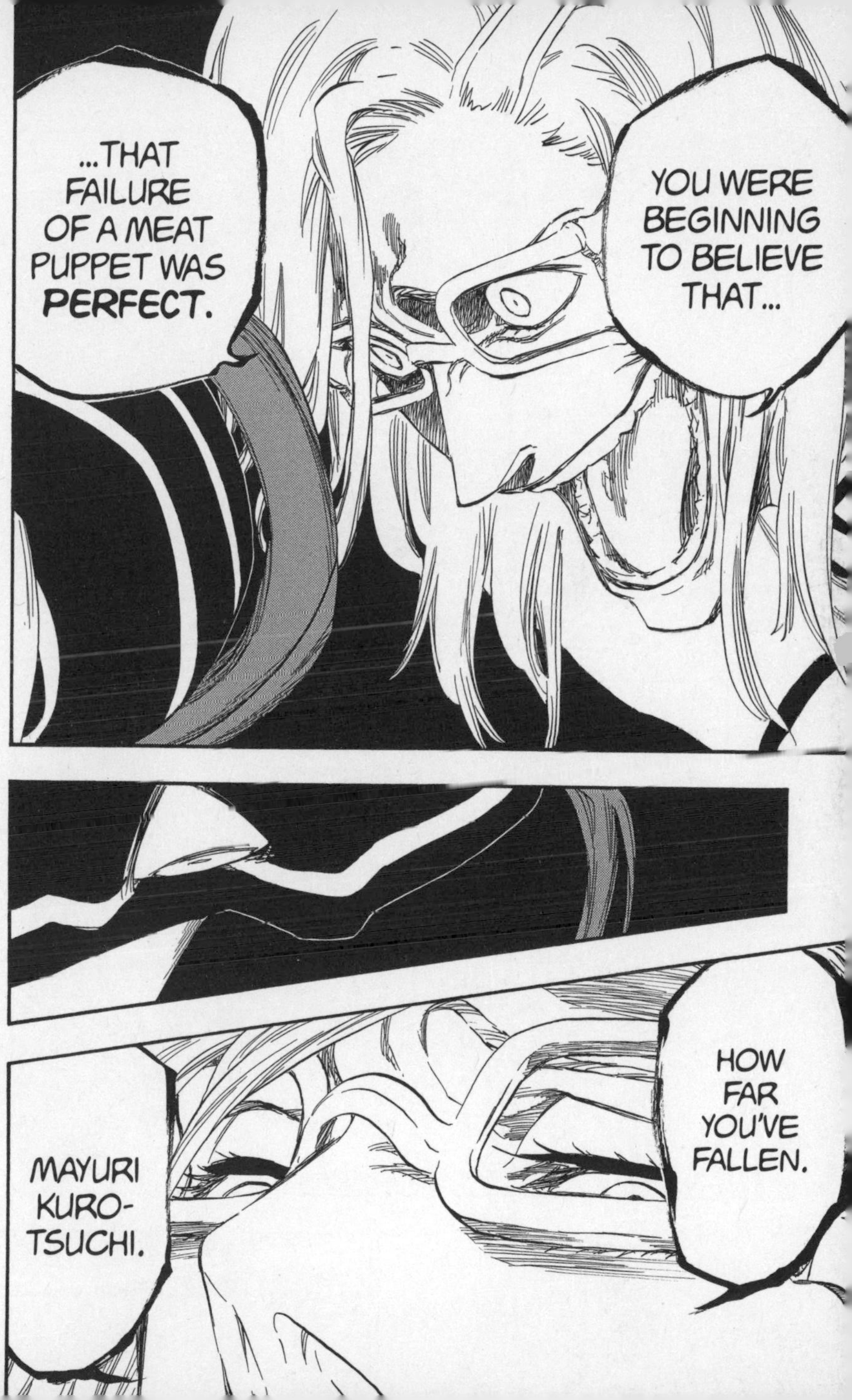
YOU WERE BEGINNING TO BELIEVE THAT...
...THAT FAILURE OF A MEAT PUPPET WAS **PERFECT.**
HOW FAR YOU'VE FALLEN.
MAYURI KURO-TSUCHI.

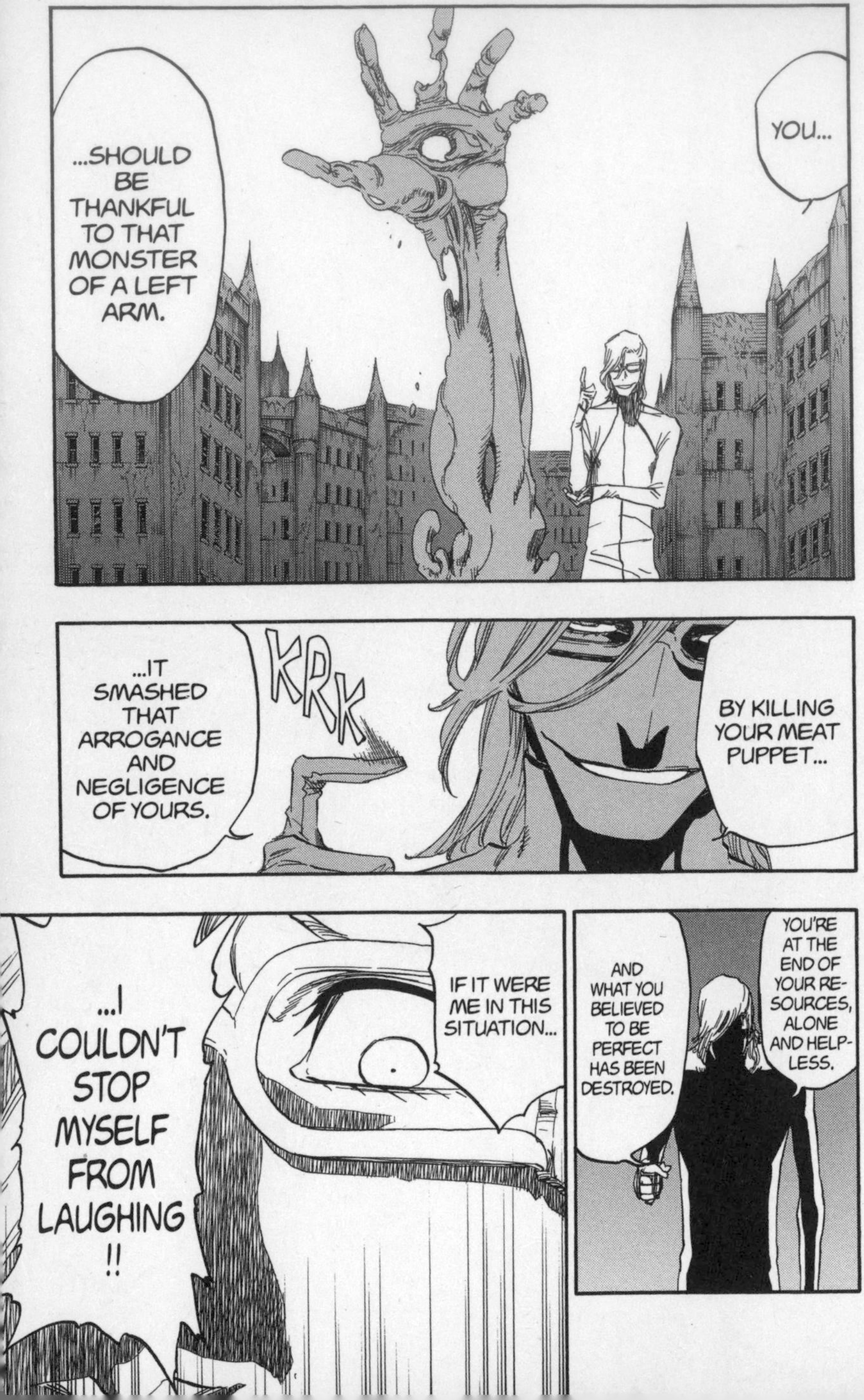
YOU...
...SHOULD BE THANKFUL TO THAT MONSTER OF A LEFT ARM.
BY KILLING YOUR MEAT PUPPET...
KRK
...IT SMASHED THAT ARROGANCE AND NEGLIGENCE OF YOURS.
YOU'RE AT THE END OF YOUR RE-SOURCES, ALONE AND HELP-LESS.
AND WHAT YOU BELIEVED TO BE PERFECT HAS BEEN DESTROYED.
IF IT WERE ME IN THIS SITUATION...
...I COULDN'T STOP MYSELF FROM LAUGHING!!

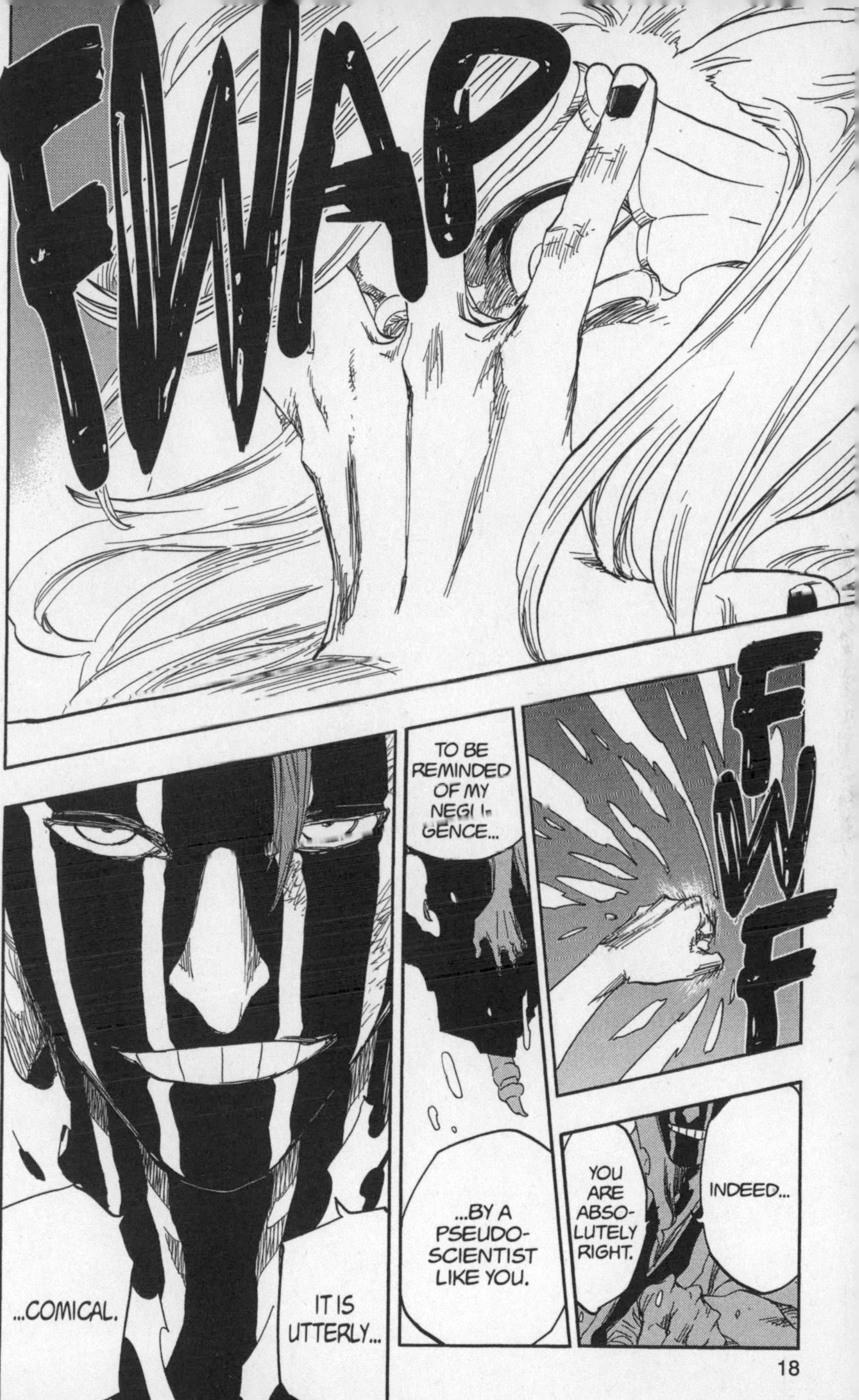
FWAP
FWF
INDEED...
YOU ARE ABSO-LUTELY RIGHT.
TO BE REMINDED OF MY NEGLI-GENCE...
...BY A PSEUDO-SCIENTIST LIKE YOU.
IT IS UTTERLY...
...COMICAL.

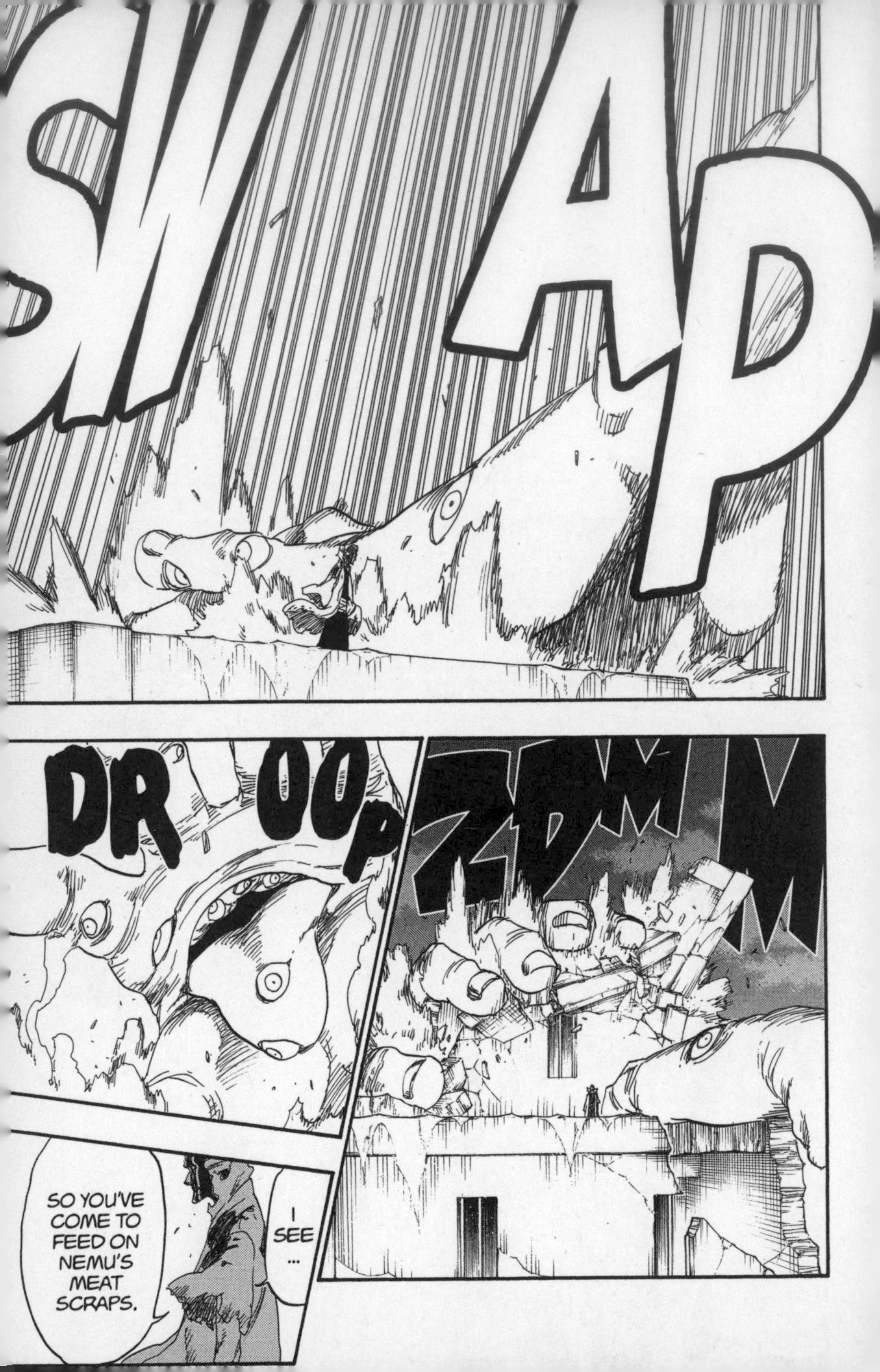
ZDMM
DROOP
I SEE...
SO YOU'VE COME TO FEED ON NEMU'S MEAT SCRAPS.

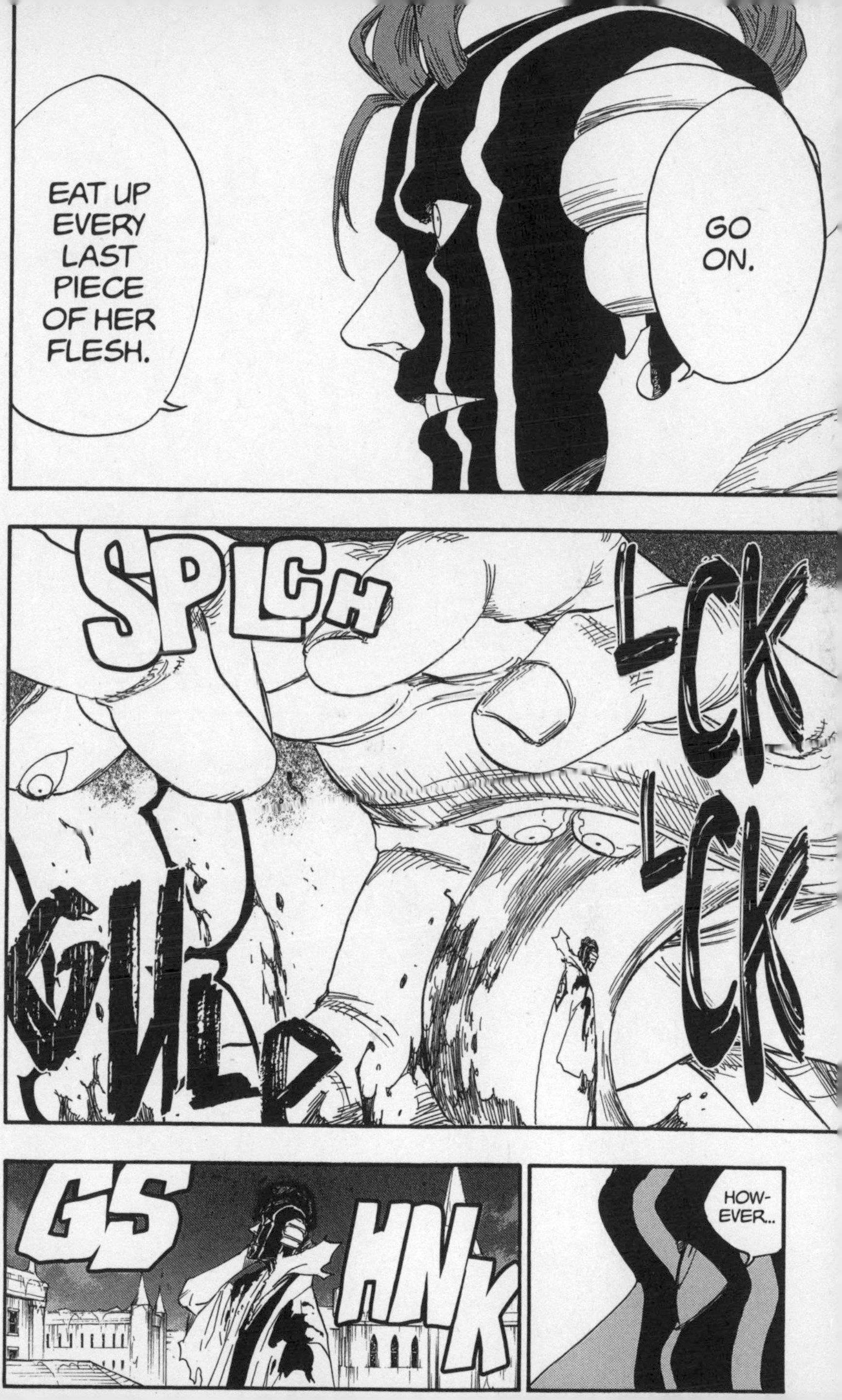
GO ON.
EAT UP EVERY LAST PIECE OF HER FLESH.
LCK LCK
SPLCH
GULP
HOW-EVER..
GS
HNK

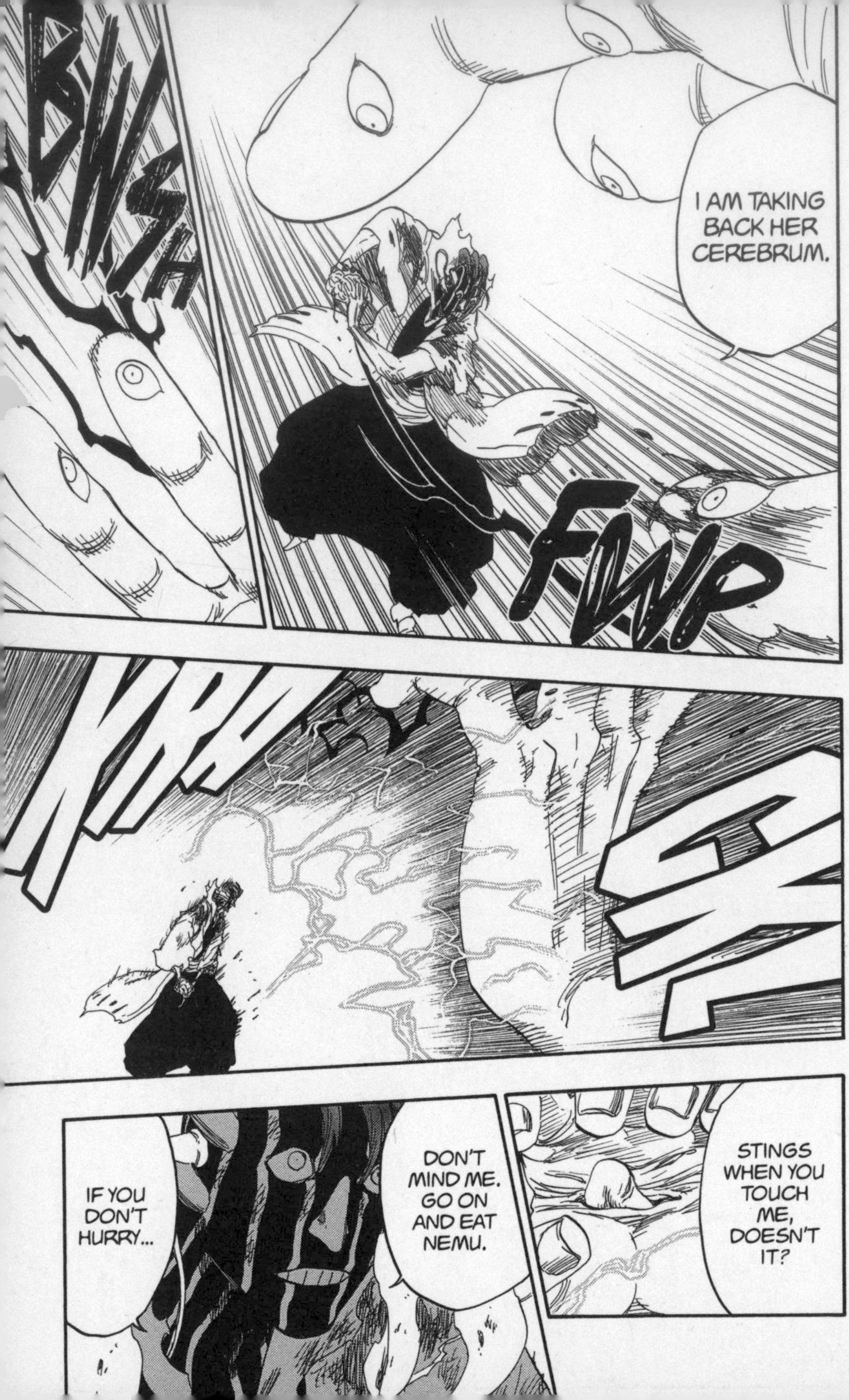
I AM TAKING BACK HER CEREBRUM.
FWP
BWSH
STINGS WHEN YOU TOUCH ME, DOESN'T IT?
DON'T MIND ME. GO ON AND EAT NEMU.
IF YOU DON'T HURRY...

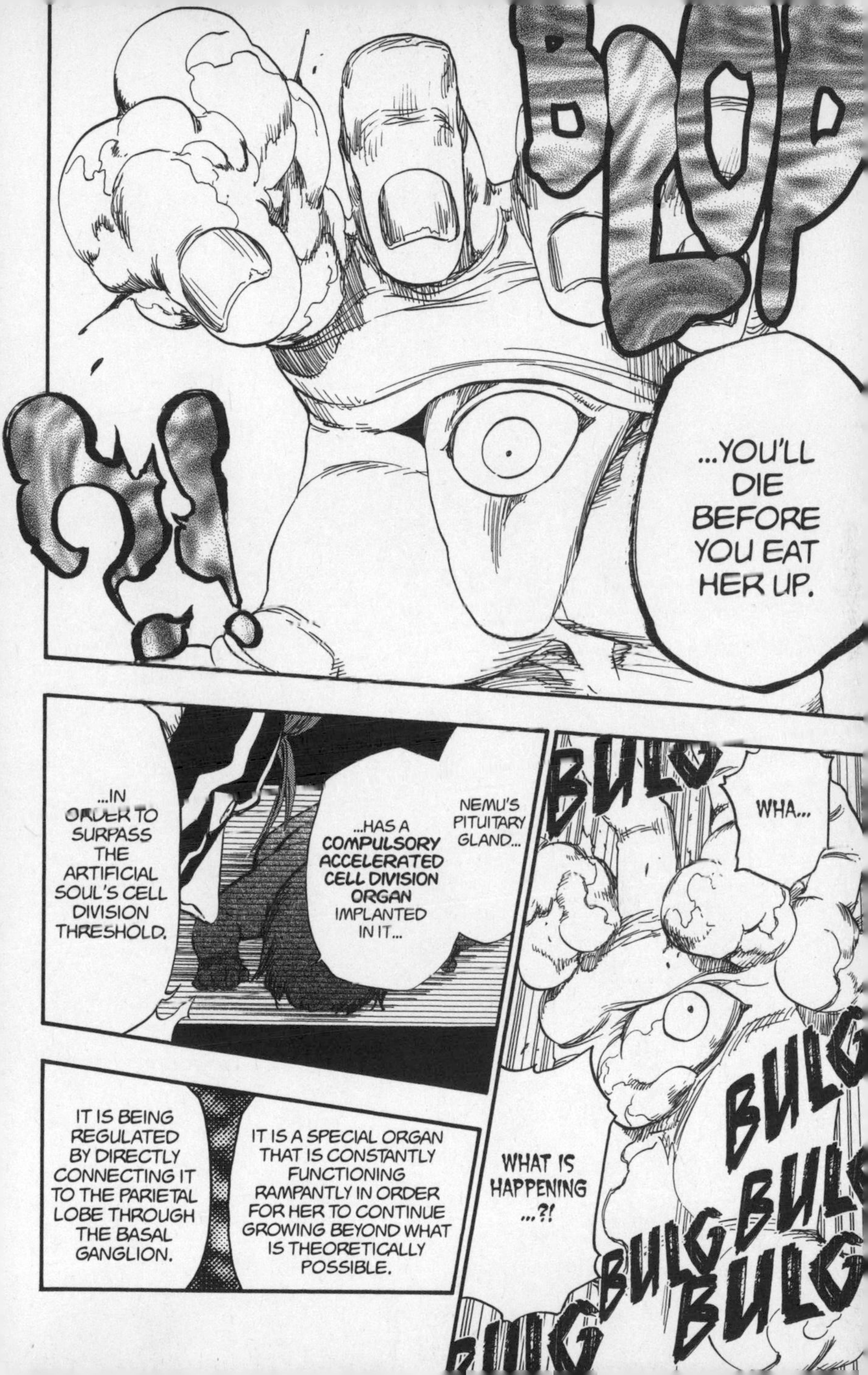
...YOU'LL DIE BEFORE YOU EAT HER UP.
BULG
WHA...
WHAT IS HAPPENING ...?!
BULG
BULG
BULG
BULG
BULG
NEMU'S PITUITARY GLAND...
...HAS A **COMPULSORY ACCELERATED CELL DIVISION ORGAN** IMPLANTED IN IT...
...IN ORDER TO SURPASS THE ARTIFICIAL SOUL'S CELL DIVISION THRESHOLD.
IT IS A SPECIAL ORGAN THAT IS CONSTANTLY FUNCTIONING RAMPANTLY IN ORDER FOR HER TO CONTINUE GROWING BEYOND WHAT IS THEORETICALLY POSSIBLE.
IT IS BEING REGULATED BY DIRECTLY CONNECTING IT TO THE PARIETAL LOBE THROUGH THE BASAL GANGLION.

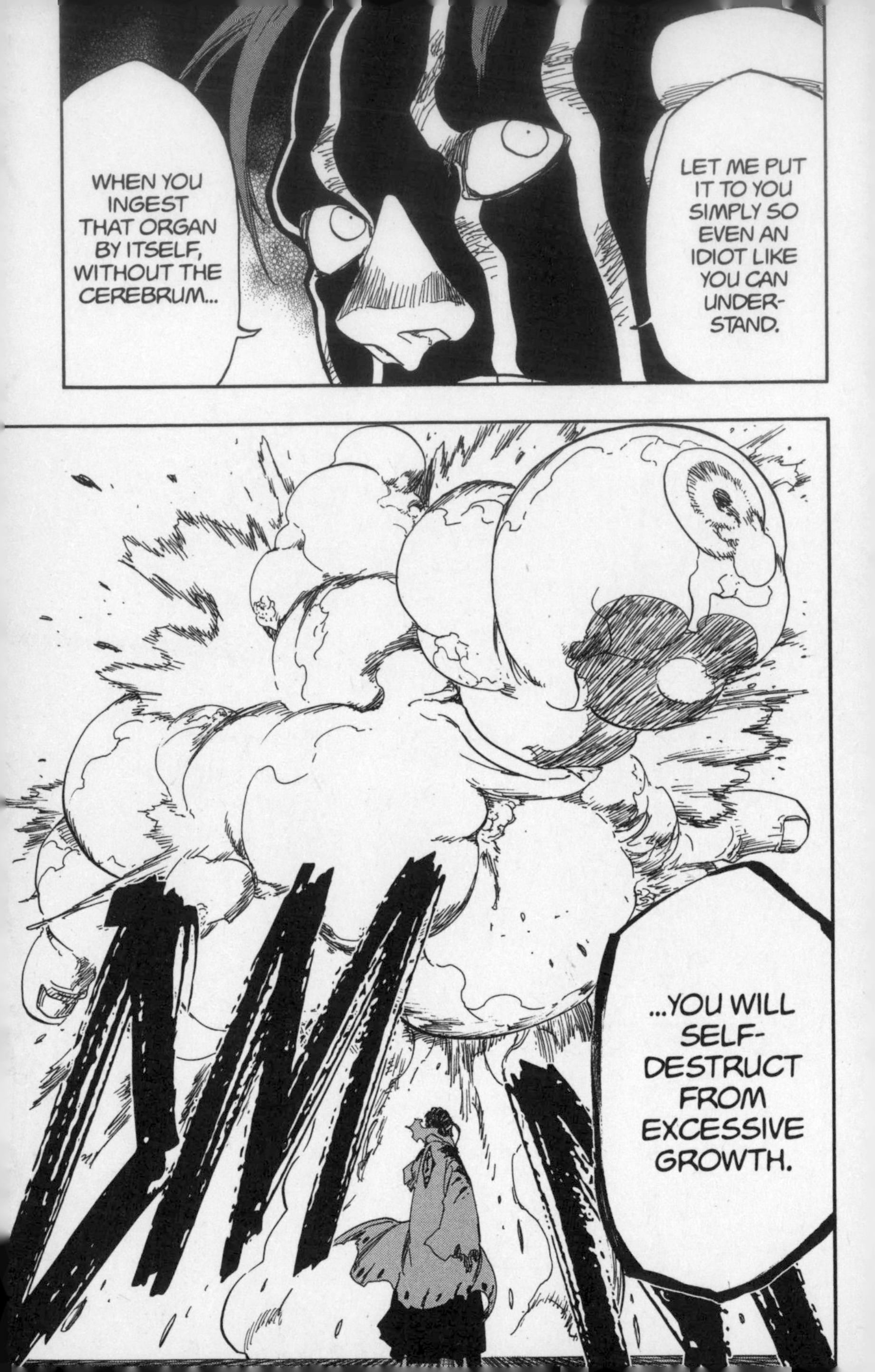
LET ME PUT IT TO YOU SIMPLY SO EVEN AN IDIOT LIKE YOU CAN UNDER-STAND.
WHEN YOU INGEST THAT ORGAN BY ITSELF, WITHOUT THE CEREBRUM...
...YOU WILL SELF-DESTRUCT FROM EXCESSIVE GROWTH.

"I SEEM TO BE DOING WELL," YOU SAY?
DON'T PATRONIZE ME.

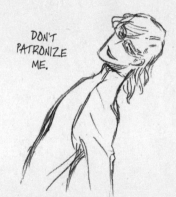

644.BABY,HOLD YOUR HAND 七 (NEVER ENDING MY DREAM)

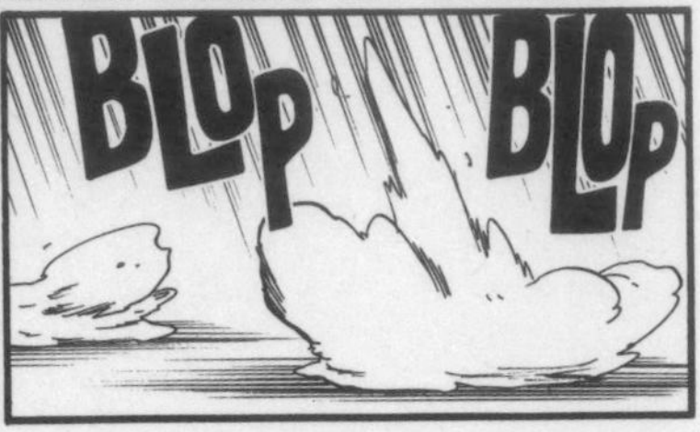
BLOP BLOP

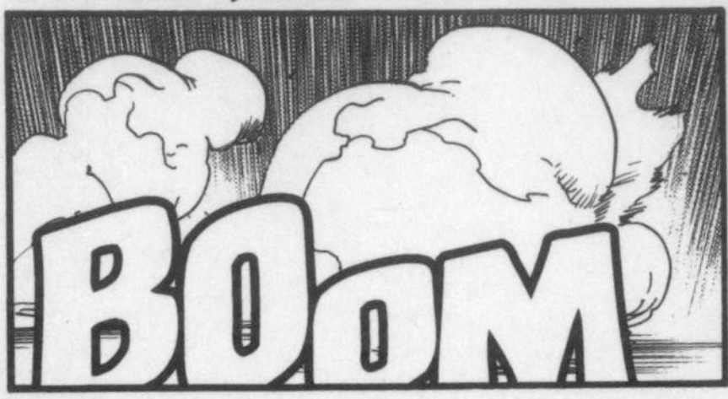
BOOM

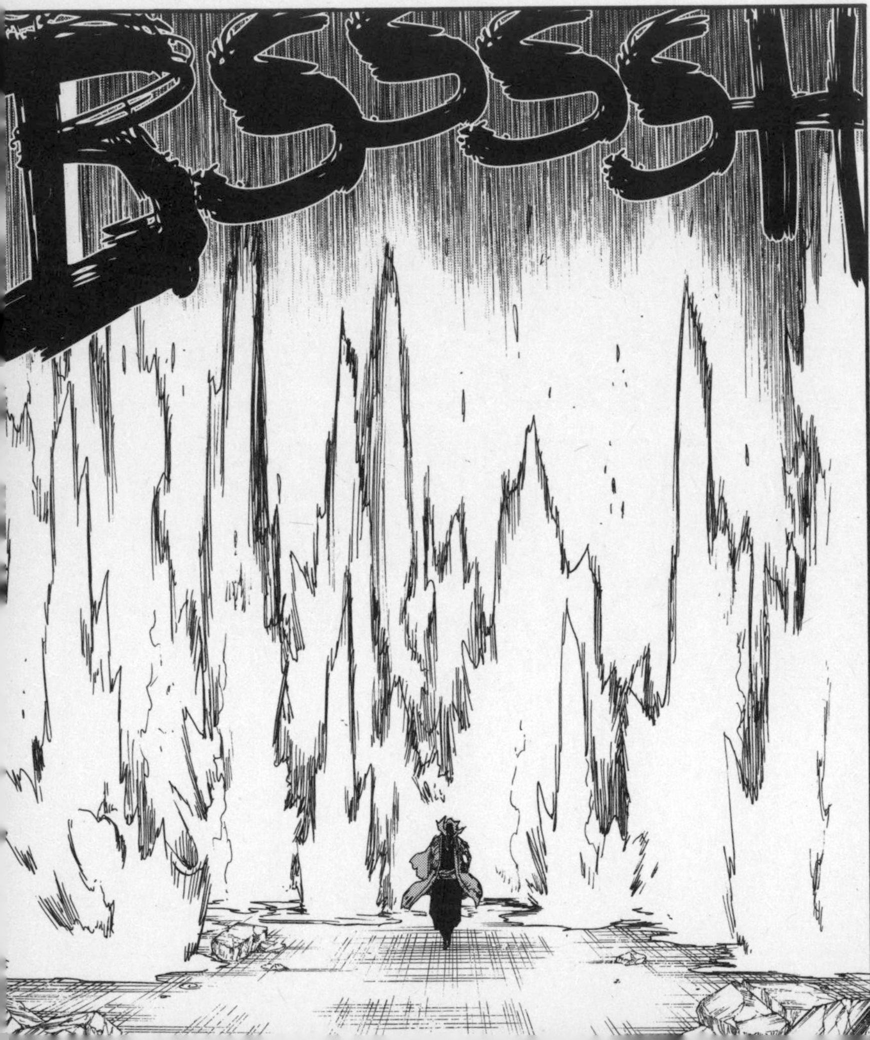
BSSSH

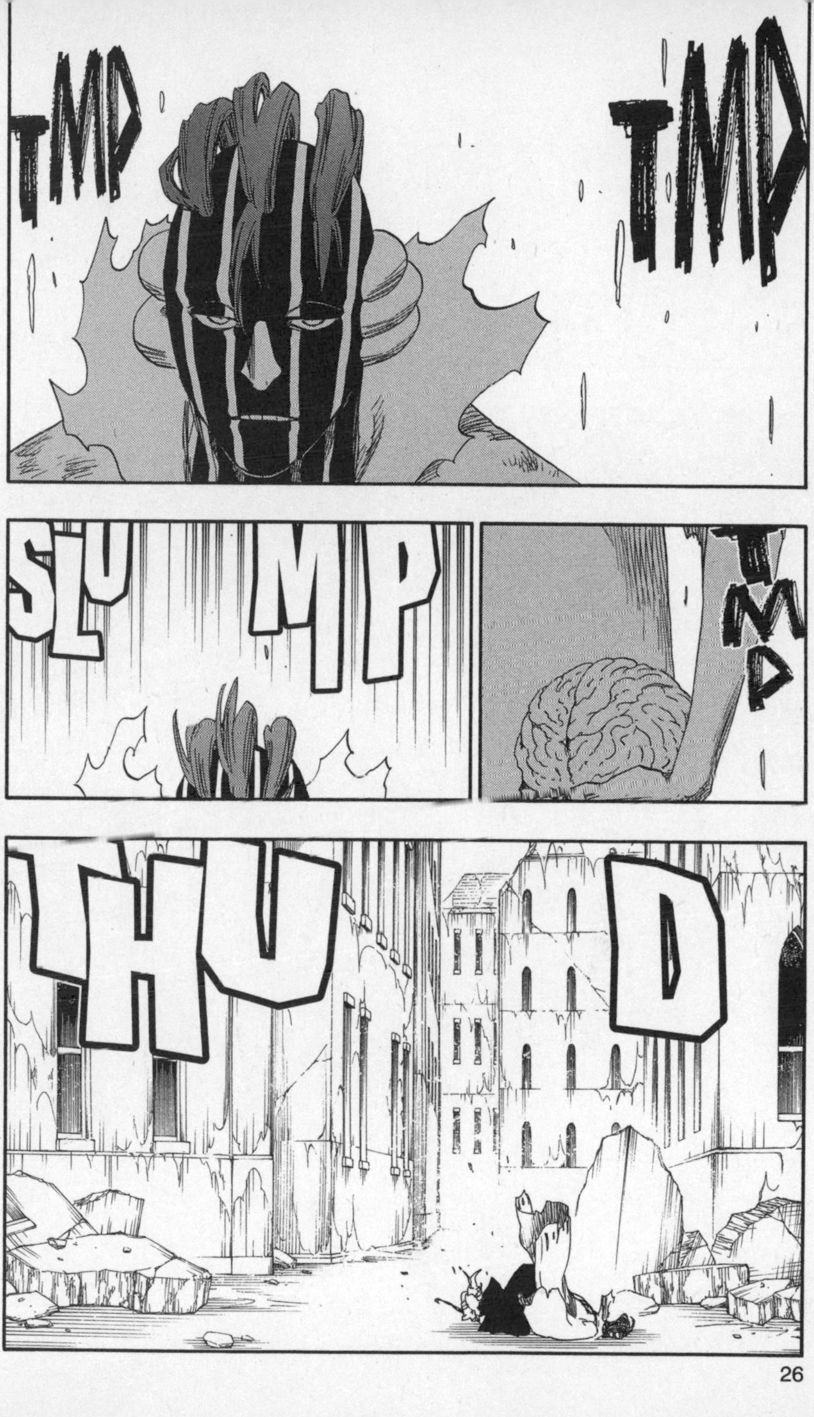
TMP
TMP
TMP
SLUMP
THUD

READ THIS WAY

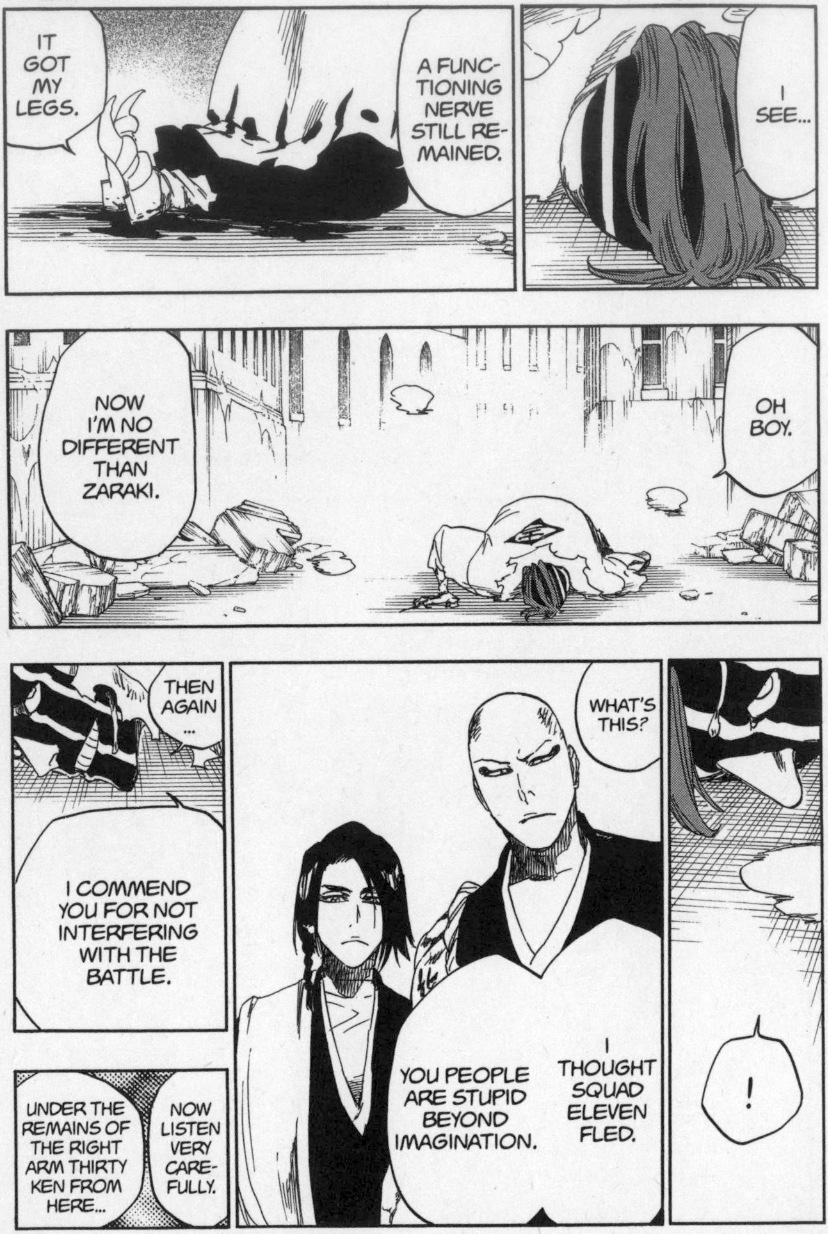
I SEE...
A FUNCTIONING NERVE STILL REMAINED.
IT GOT MY LEGS.
OH BOY.
NOW I'M NO DIFFERENT THAN ZARAKI.
!
WHAT'S THIS?
I THOUGHT SQUAD ELEVEN FLED.
YOU PEOPLE ARE STUPID BEYOND IMAGINATION.
THEN AGAIN...
I COMMEND YOU FOR NOT INTERFERING WITH THE BATTLE.
NOW LISTEN VERY CAREFULLY.
UNDER THE REMAINS OF THE RIGHT ARM THIRTY KEN FROM HERE...

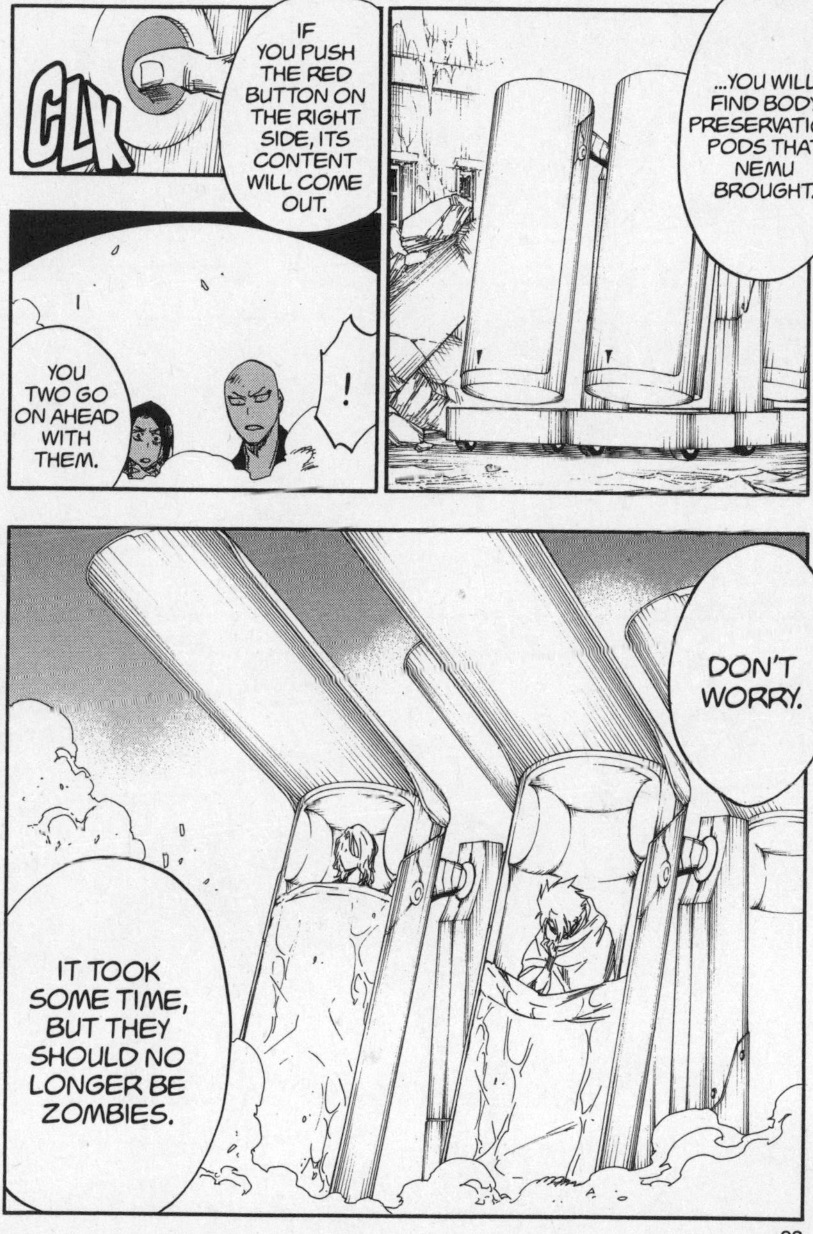
...YOU WILL FIND BODY PRESERVATION PODS THAT NEMU BROUGHT.
CLK
IF YOU PUSH THE RED BUTTON ON THE RIGHT SIDE, ITS CONTENT WILL COME OUT.
!
YOU TWO GO ON AHEAD WITH THEM.
DON'T WORRY.
IT TOOK SOME TIME, BUT THEY SHOULD NO LONGER BE ZOMBIES.

READ THIS WAY

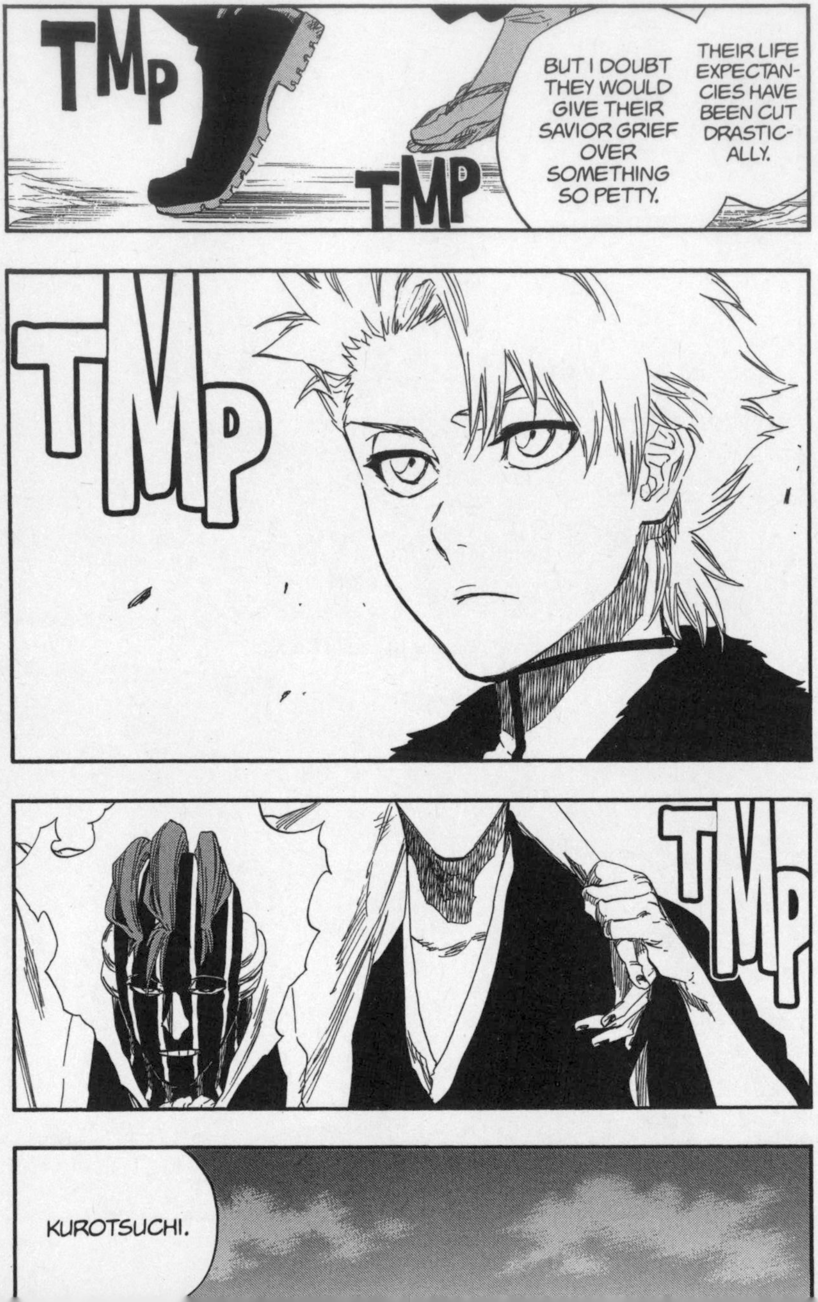
THEIR LIFE EXPECTANCIES HAVE BEEN CUT DRASTICALLY.
BUT I DOUBT THEY WOULD GIVE THEIR SAVIOR GRIEF OVER SOMETHING SO PETTY.
TMP
TMP
TMP
TMP
KUROTSUCHI.

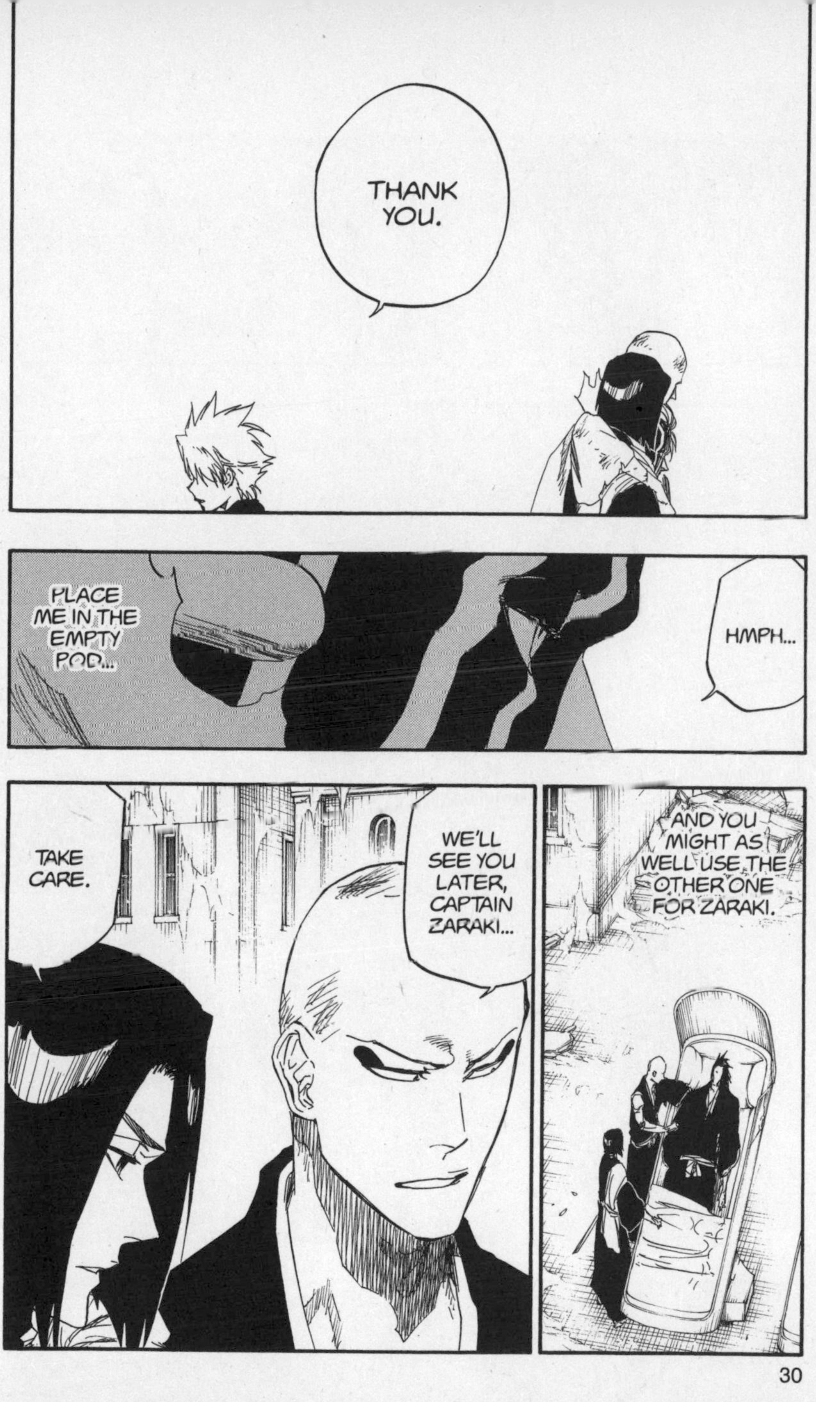
THANK YOU.
HMPH...
PLACE ME IN THE EMPTY POD...
AND YOU MIGHT AS WELL USE THE OTHER ONE FOR ZARAKI.
WE'LL SEE YOU LATER, CAPTAIN ZARAKI...
TAKE CARE.

READ THIS WAY

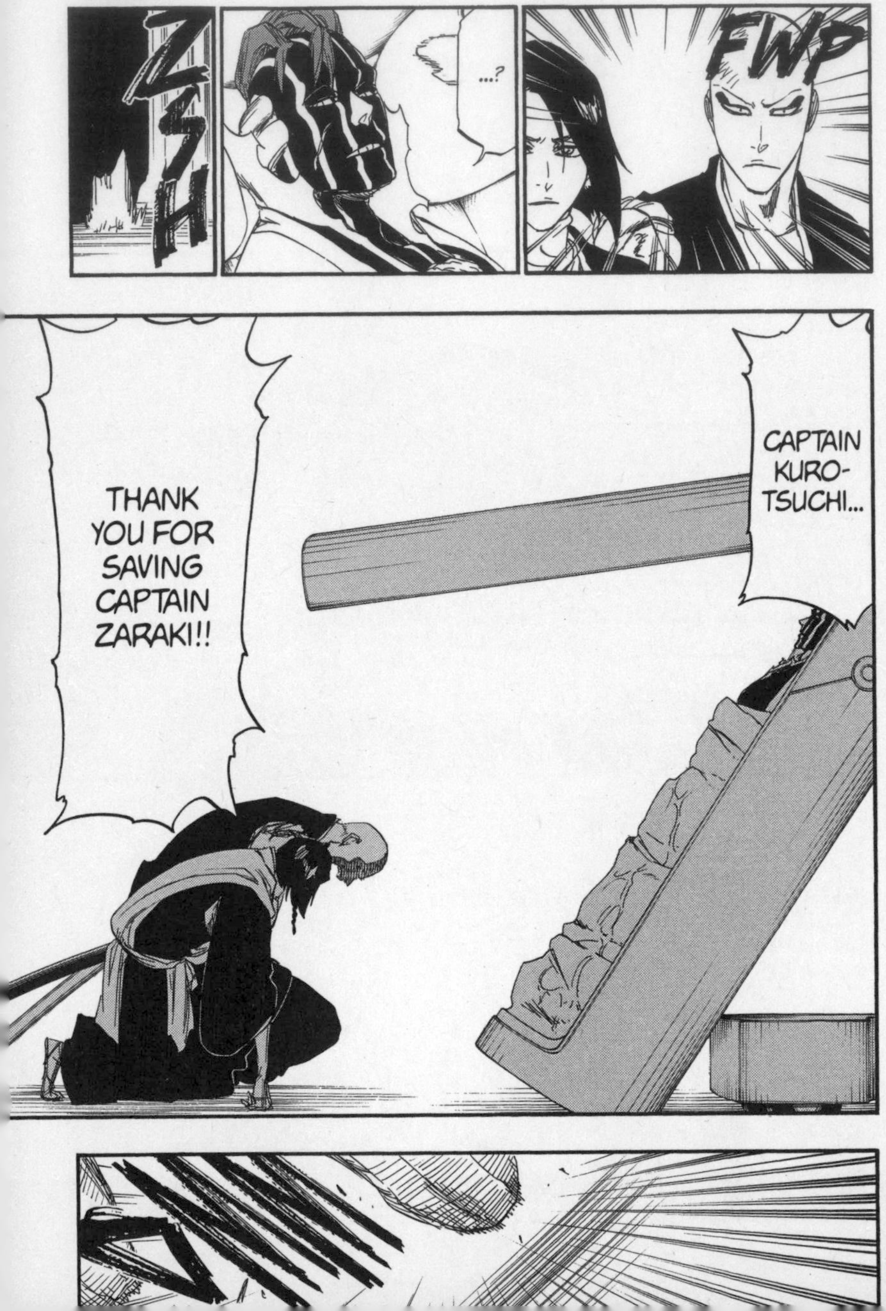
FWP
...?
ZZH
CAPTAIN KURO-TSUCHI...
THANK YOU FOR SAVING CAPTAIN ZARAKI!!

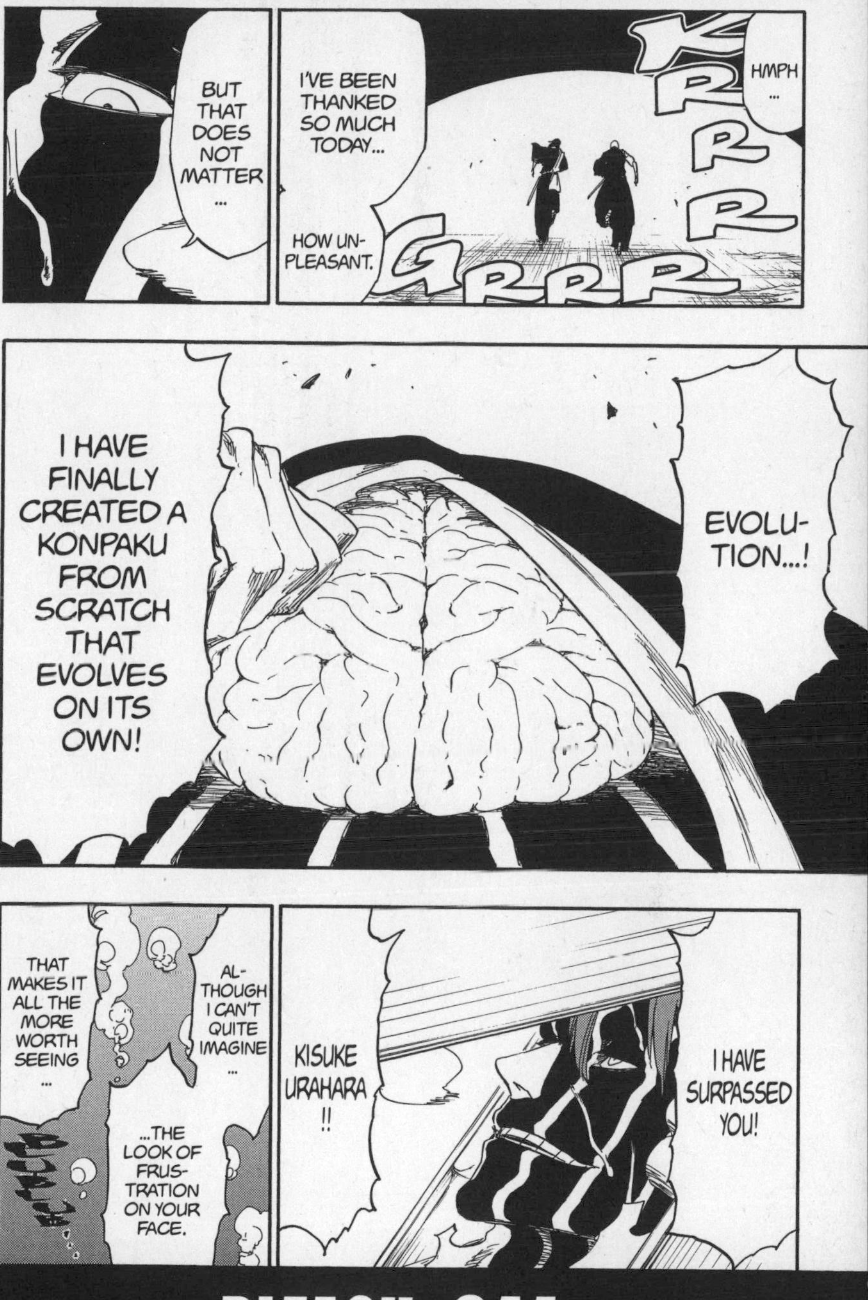

HMPH ...
KRRR
I'VE BEEN THANKED SO MUCH TODAY...
HOW UN-PLEASANT.
GRRR
BUT THAT DOES NOT MATTER ...
EVOLU-TION...!
I HAVE FINALLY CREATED A KONPAKU FROM SCRATCH THAT EVOLVES ON ITS OWN!
I HAVE SURPASSED YOU!
KISUKE URAHARA !!
AL-THOUGH I CAN'T QUITE IMAGINE ...
...THE LOOK OF FRUS-TRATION ON YOUR FACE.
THAT MAKES IT ALL THE MORE WORTH SEEING ...

BLEACH 644.

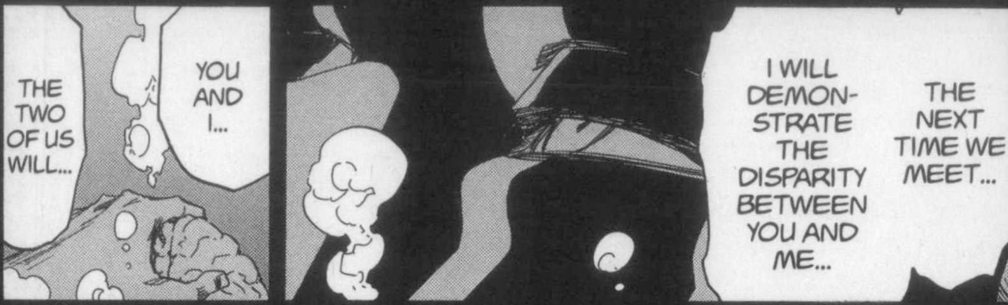
THE NEXT TIME WE MEET...
I WILL DEMON-STRATE THE DISPARITY BETWEEN YOU AND ME...
YOU AND I...
THE TWO OF US WILL...

BABY, HOLD YOUR HAND 七

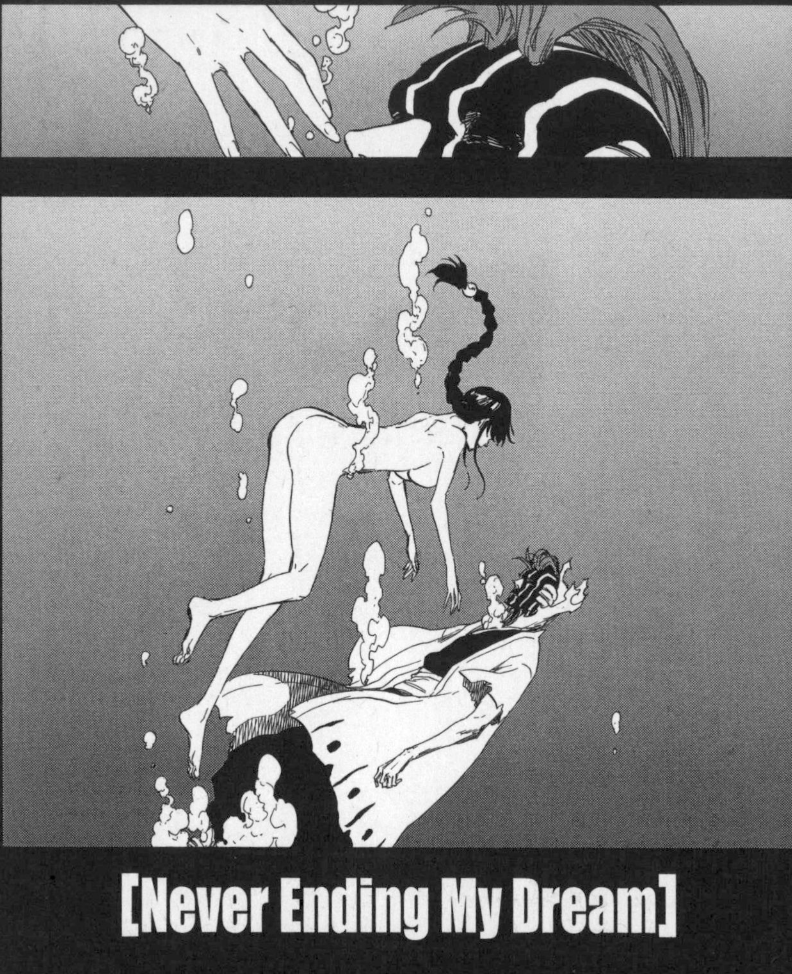

[Never Ending My Dream]

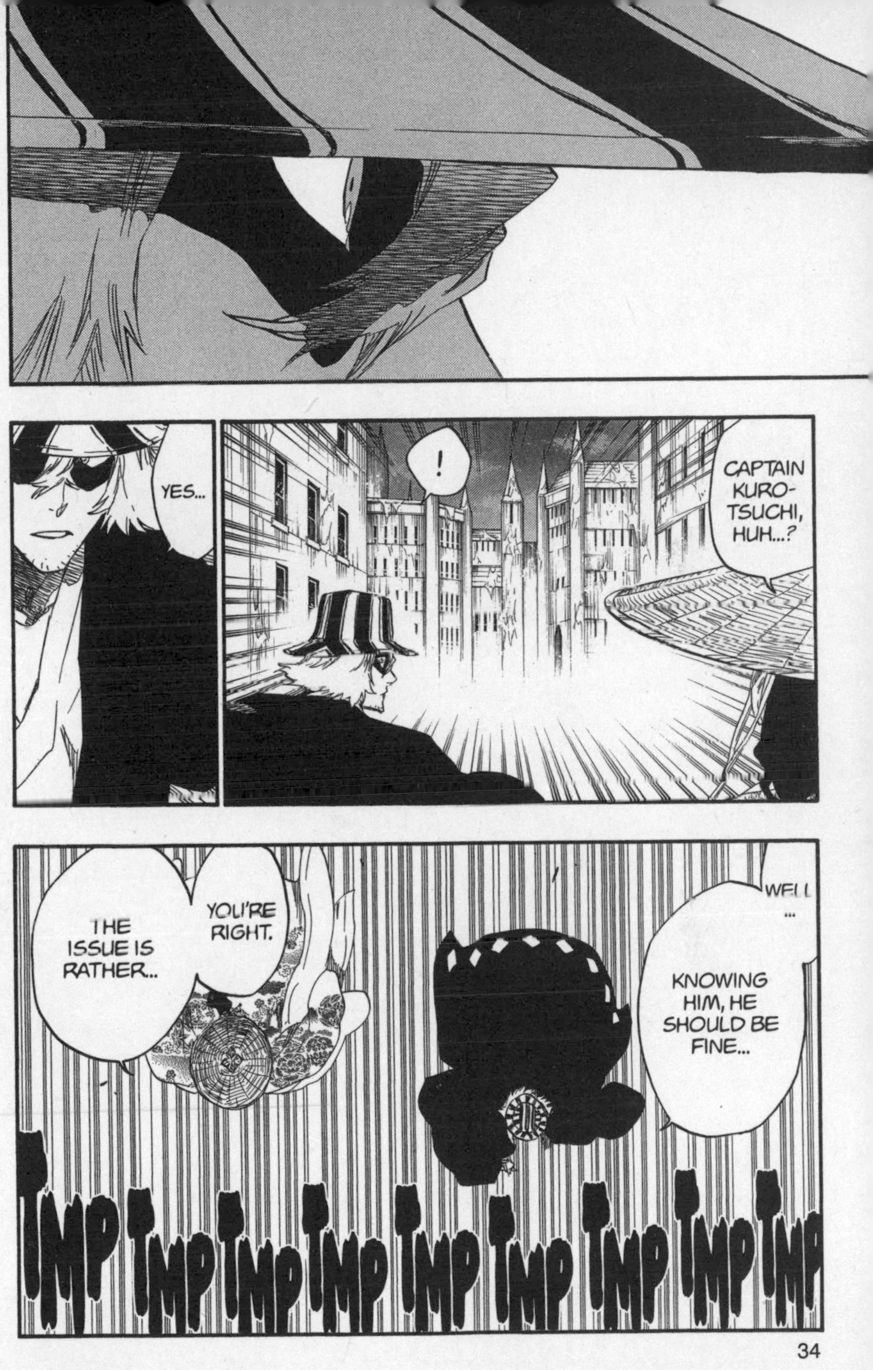
CAPTAIN KURO-TSUCHI, HUH...?
!
YES...
WELL ...
KNOWING HIM, HE SHOULD BE FINE...
YOU'RE RIGHT.
THE ISSUE IS RATHER...
TMP TMP TMP TMP TMP TMP TMP TMP TMP TMP

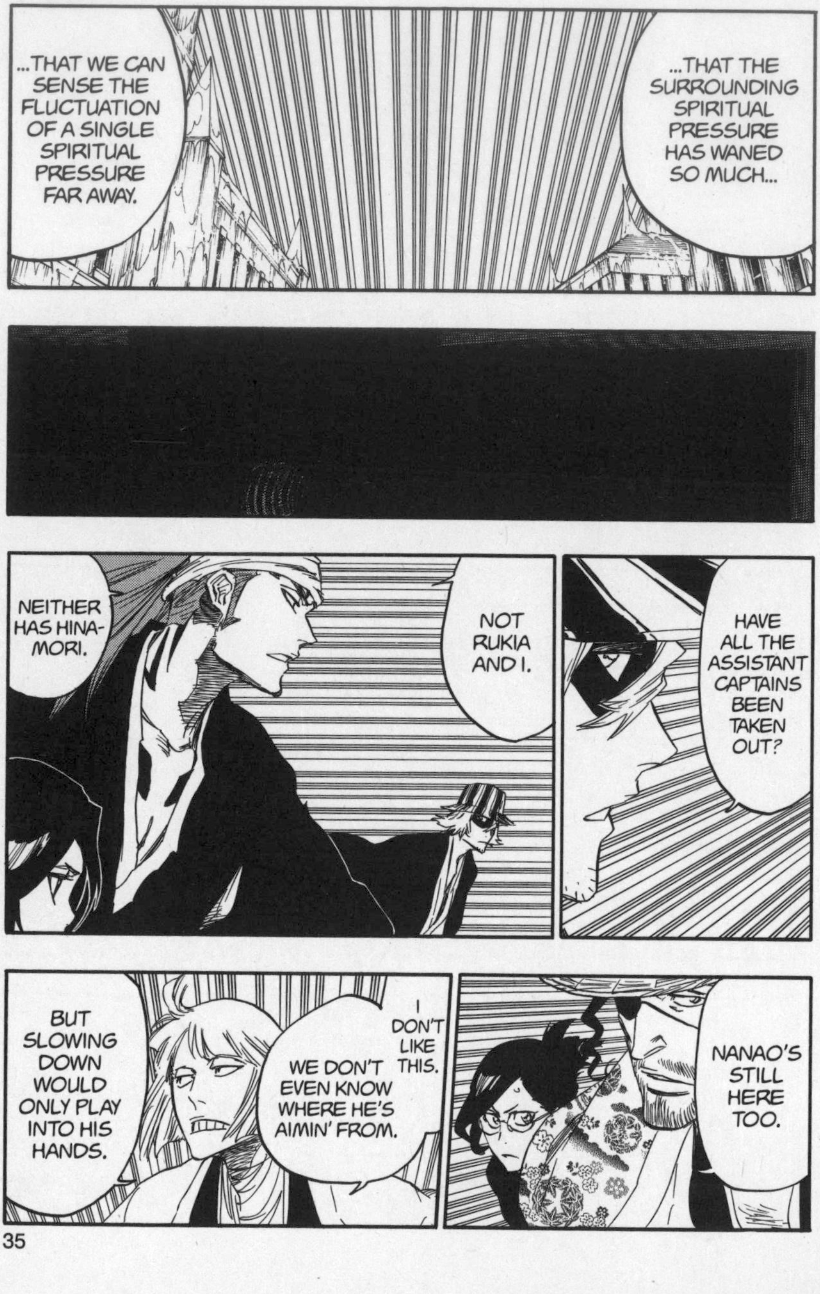
...THAT THE SURROUNDING SPIRITUAL PRESSURE HAS WANED SO MUCH...
...THAT WE CAN SENSE THE FLUCTUATION OF A SINGLE SPIRITUAL PRESSURE FAR AWAY.
HAVE ALL THE ASSISTANT CAPTAINS BEEN TAKEN OUT?
NOT RUKIA AND I.
NEITHER HAS HINAMORI.
NANAO'S STILL HERE TOO.
I DON'T LIKE THIS.
WE DON'T EVEN KNOW WHERE HE'S AIMIN' FROM.
BUT SLOWING DOWN WOULD ONLY PLAY INTO HIS HANDS.

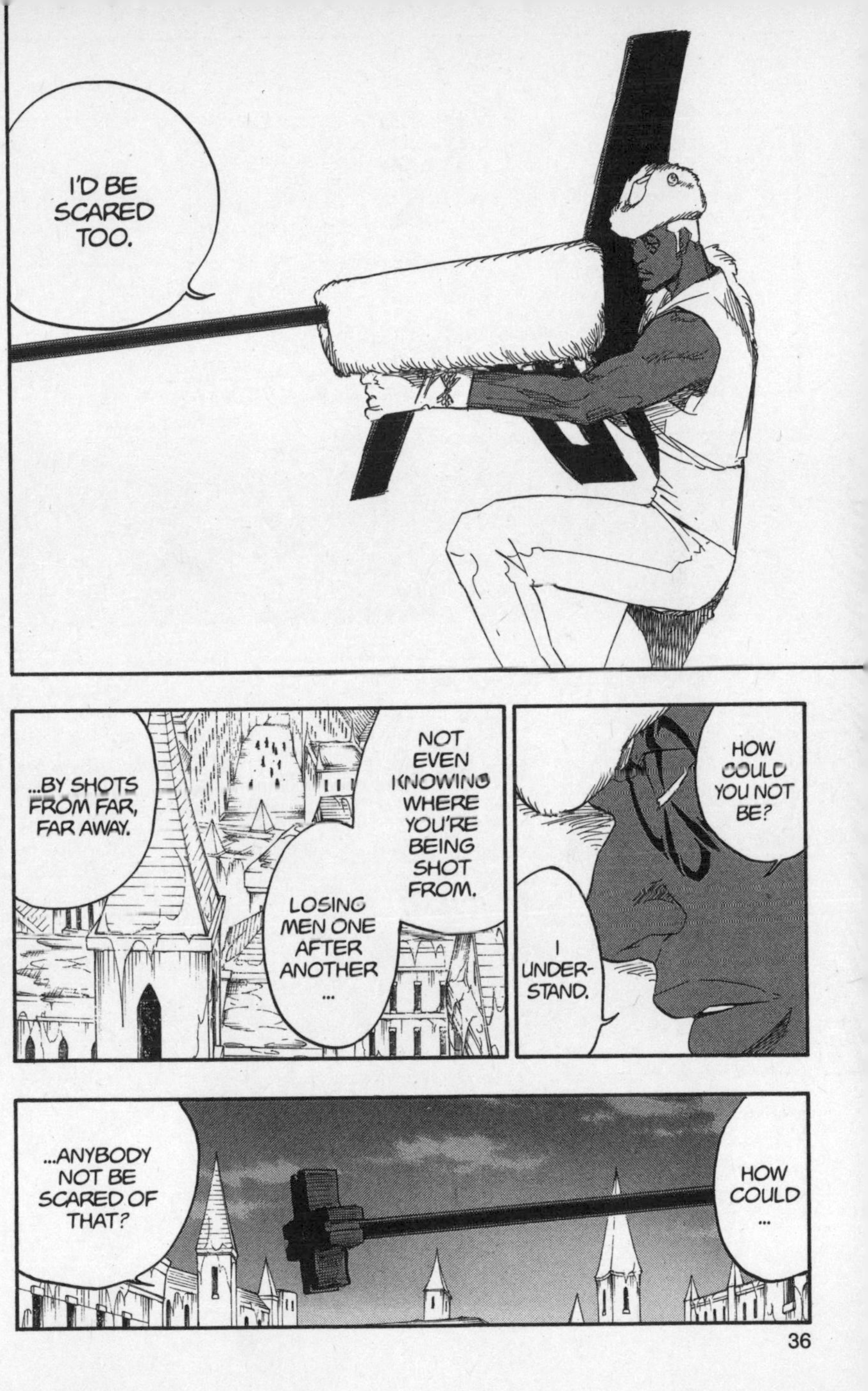
I'D BE SCARED TOO.
HOW COULD YOU NOT BE?
I UNDERSTAND.
NOT EVEN KNOWING WHERE YOU'RE BEING SHOT FROM.
LOSING MEN ONE AFTER ANOTHER...
...BY SHOTS FROM FAR, FAR AWAY.
HOW COULD...
...ANYBODY NOT BE SCARED OF THAT?

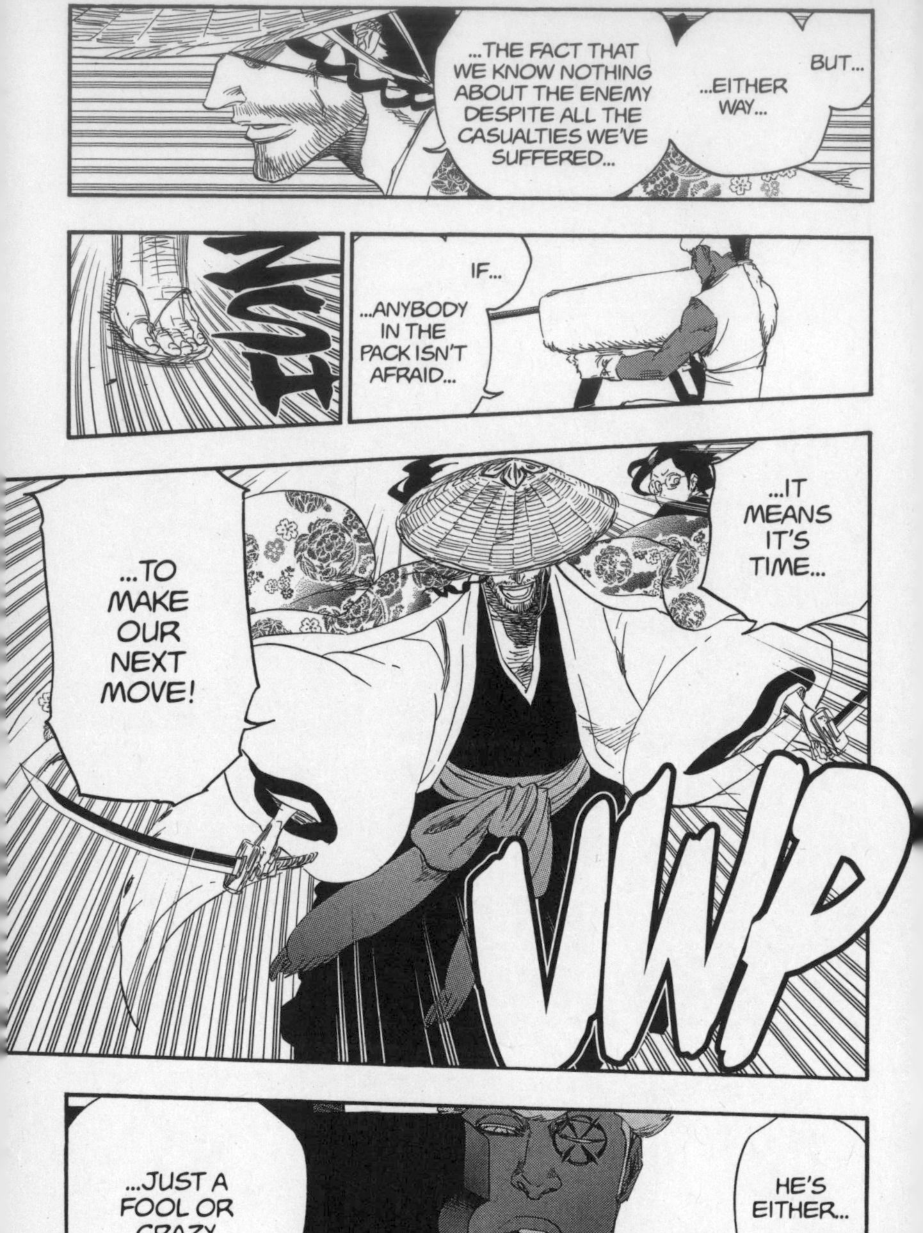
BUT...
...EITHER WAY...
...THE FACT THAT WE KNOW NOTHING ABOUT THE ENEMY DESPITE ALL THE CASUALTIES WE'VE SUFFERED...
IF...
...ANYBODY IN THE PACK ISN'T AFRAID...
WSH
...IT MEANS IT'S TIME...
...TO MAKE OUR NEXT MOVE!
VWP
HE'S EITHER...
...JUST A FOOL OR CRAZY.

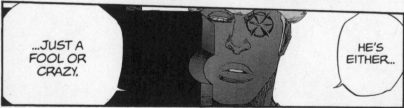

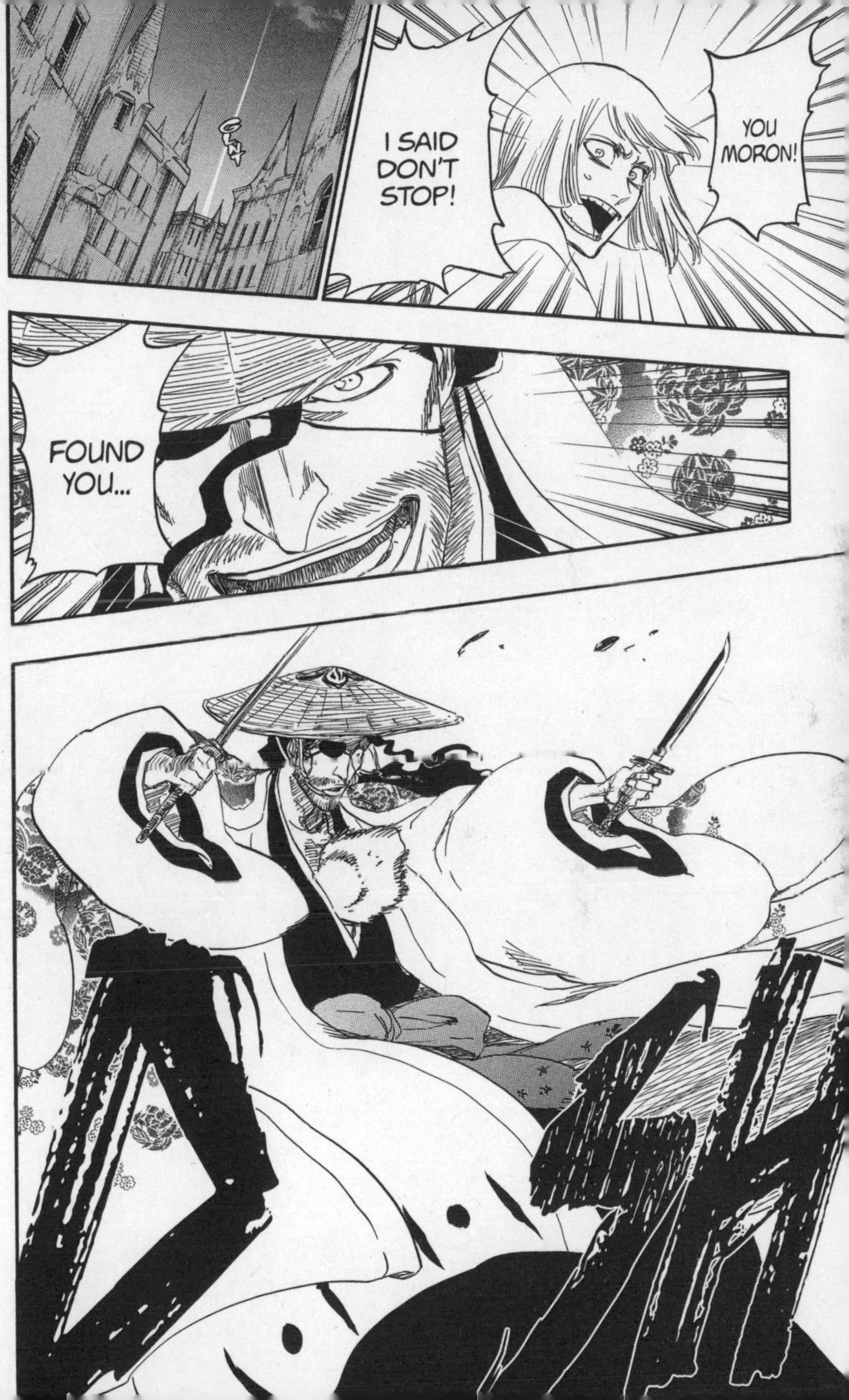
YOU MORON!
I SAID DON'T STOP!
GLNT
FOUND YOU...

READ THIS WAY

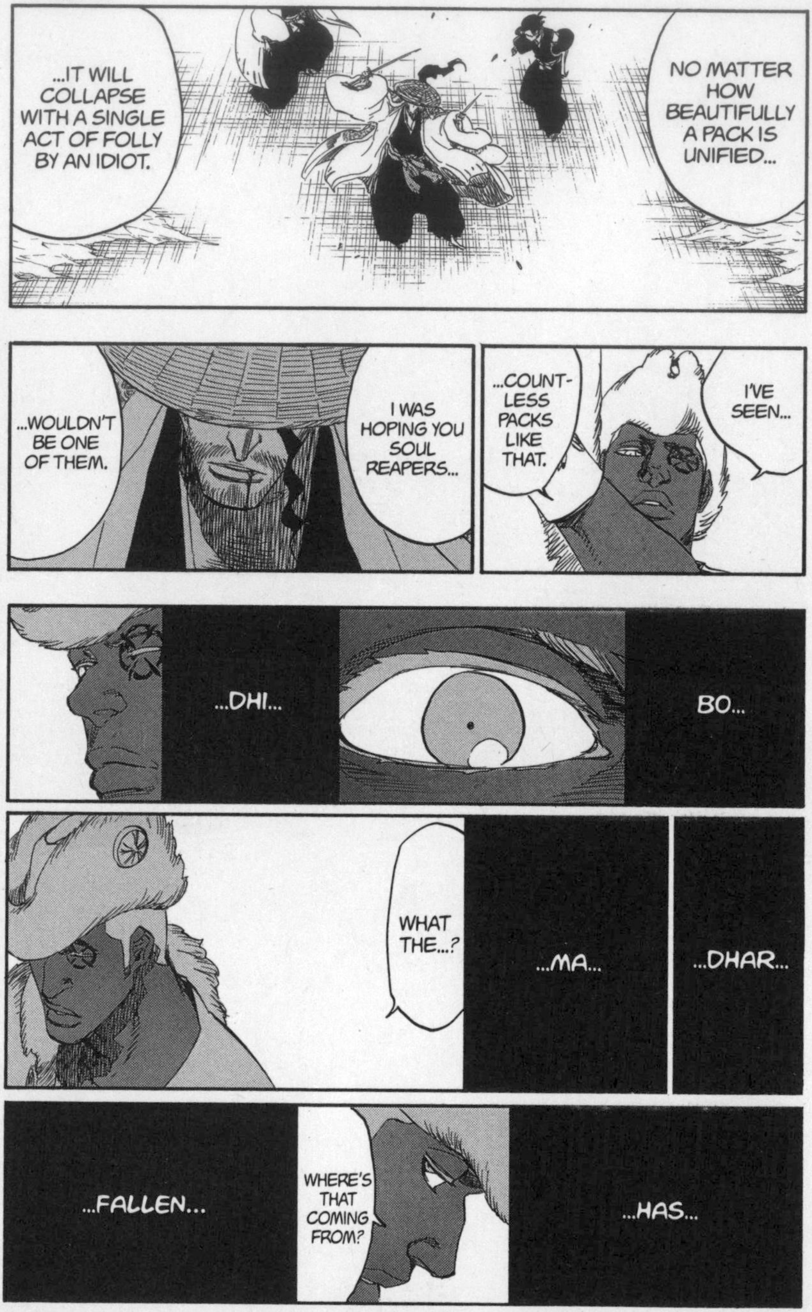

NO MATTER HOW BEAUTIFULLY A PACK IS UNIFIED...
...IT WILL COLLAPSE WITH A SINGLE ACT OF FOLLY BY AN IDIOT.
I'VE SEEN...
...COUNT-LESS PACKS LIKE THAT.
I WAS HOPING YOU SOUL REAPERS...
...WOULDN'T BE ONE OF THEM.
BO...
...DHI...
...DHAR...
...MA...
WHAT THE...?
...HAS...
WHERE'S THAT COMING FROM?
...FALLEN...

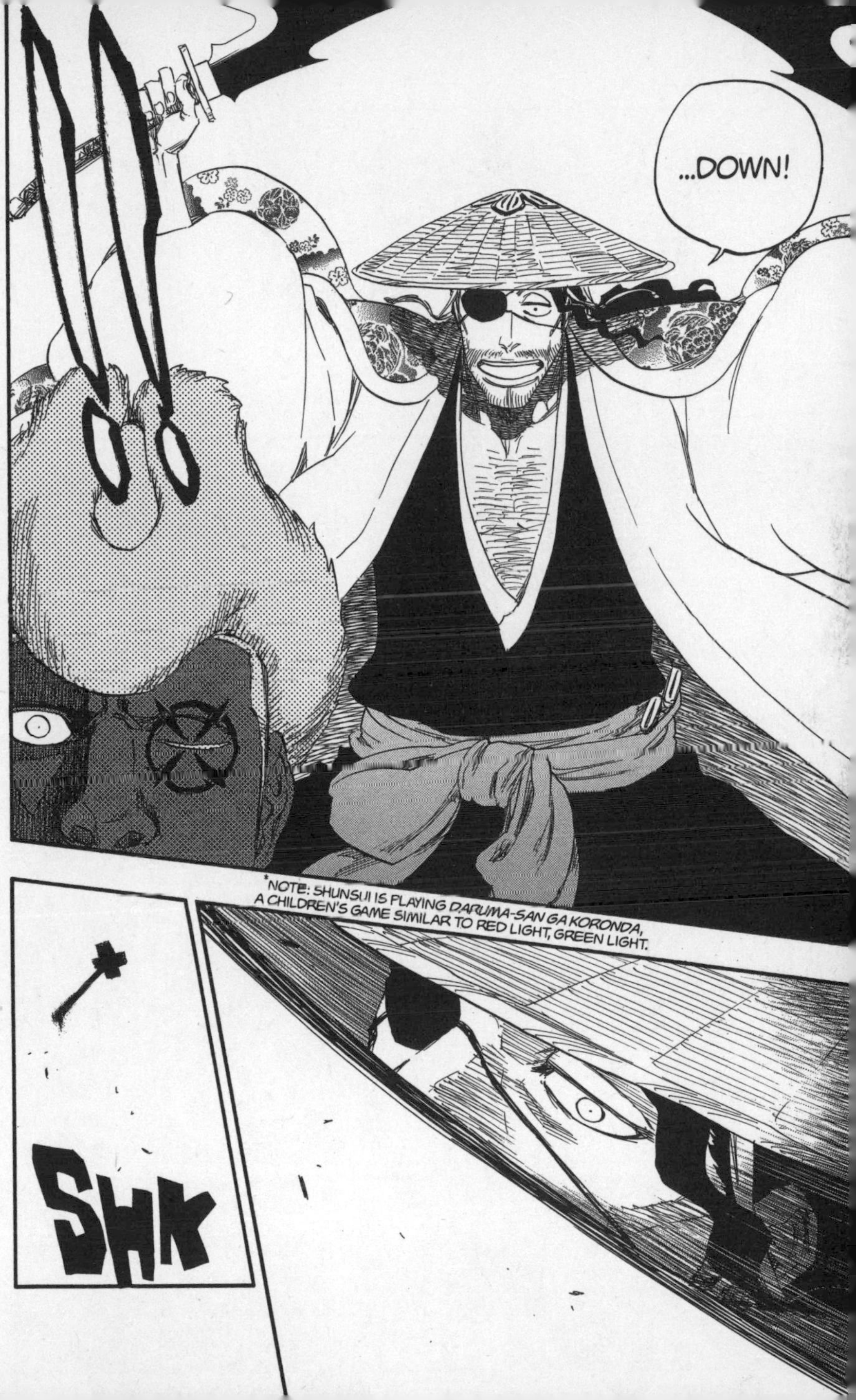
...DOWN!
*NOTE: SHUNSUI IS PLAYING *DARUMA-SAN GA KORONDA*, A CHILDREN'S GAME SIMILAR TO RED LIGHT, GREEN LIGHT.
SHK

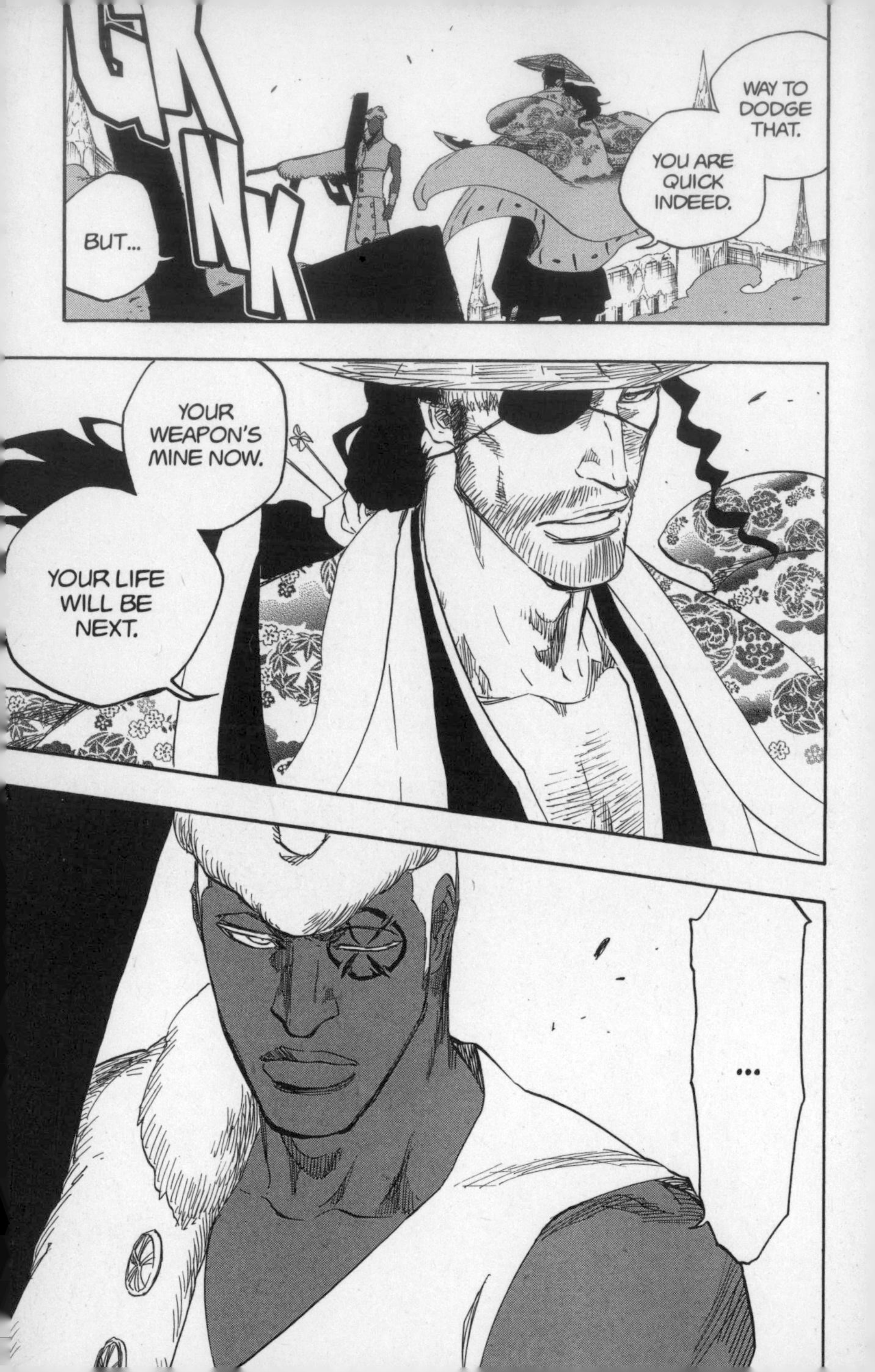
WAY TO DODGE THAT.
YOU ARE QUICK INDEED.
BUT...
YOUR WEAPON'S MINE NOW.
YOUR LIFE WILL BE NEXT.
...

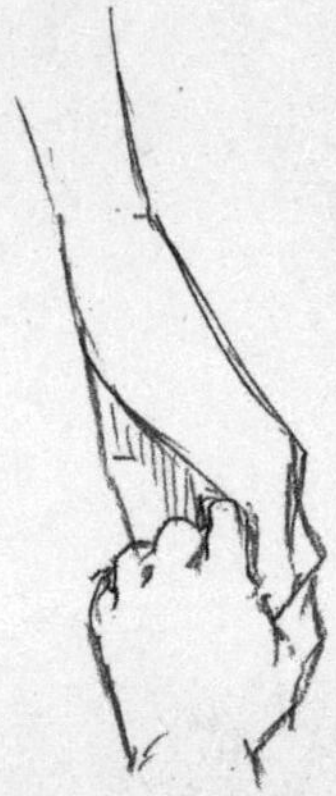

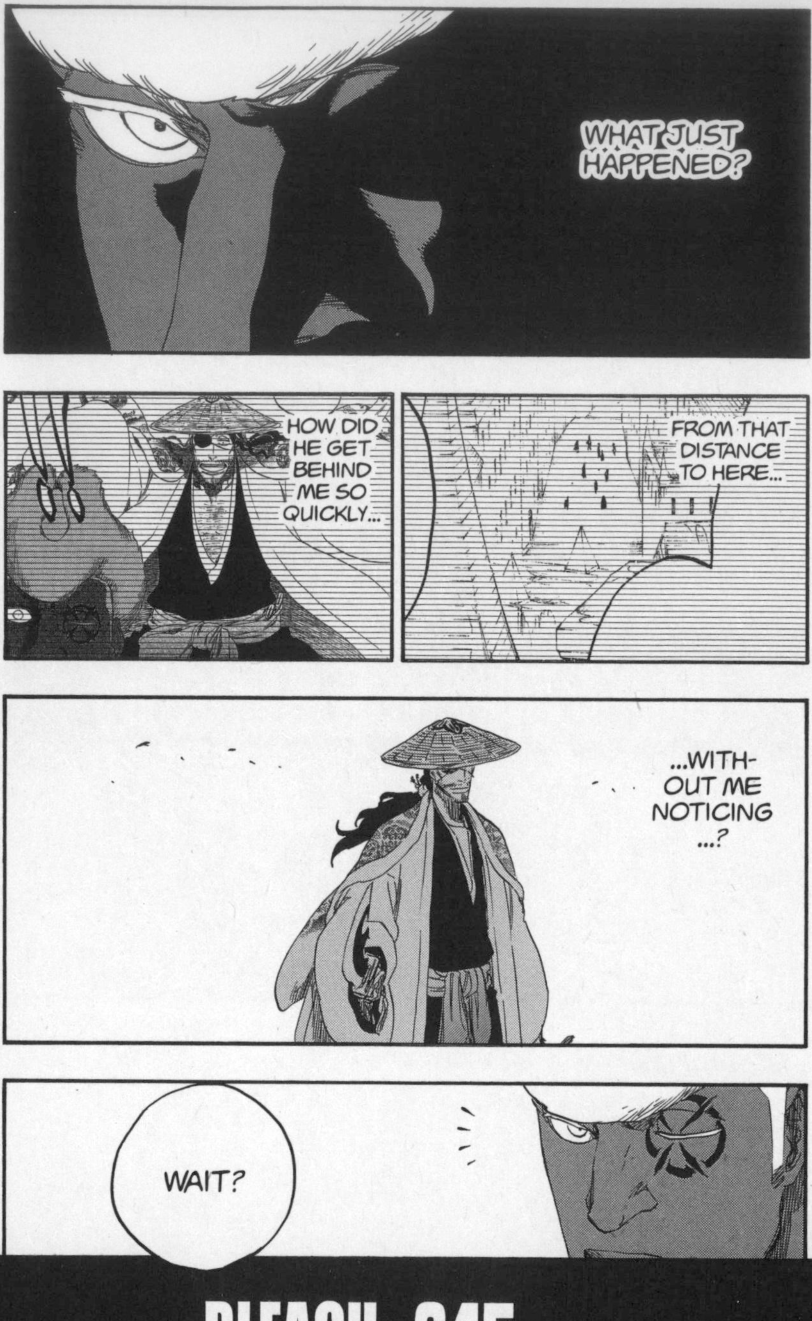
WHAT JUST HAPPENED?
FROM THAT DISTANCE TO HERE...
HOW DID HE GET BEHIND ME SO QUICKLY...
...WITH-OUT ME NOTICING ...?
WAIT?

BLEACH 645.

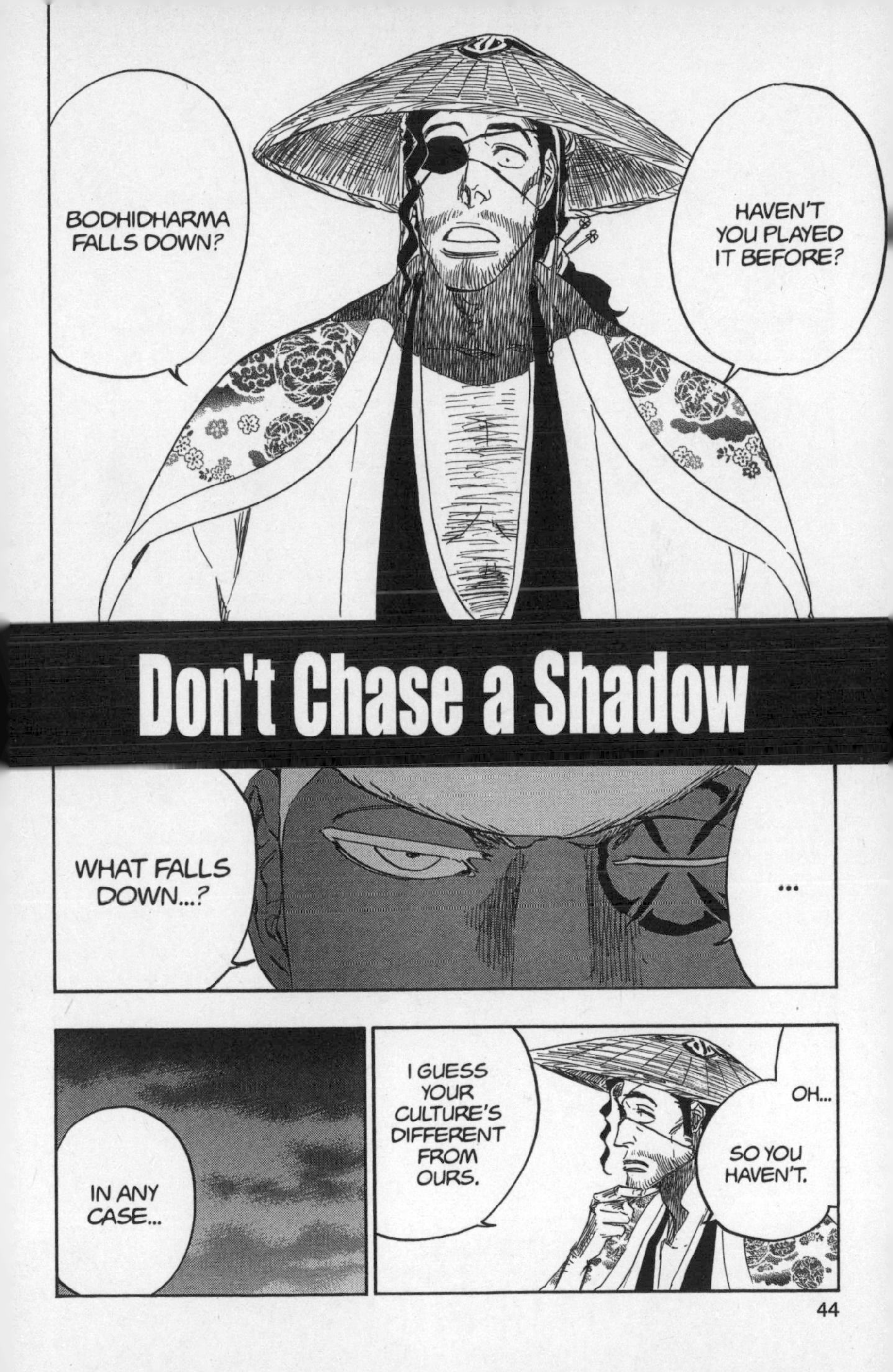
HAVEN'T YOU PLAYED IT BEFORE?
BODHIDHARMA FALLS DOWN?
Don't Chase a Shadow
...
WHAT FALLS DOWN...?
OH...
SO YOU HAVEN'T.
I GUESS YOUR CULTURE'S DIFFERENT FROM OURS.
IN ANY CASE...

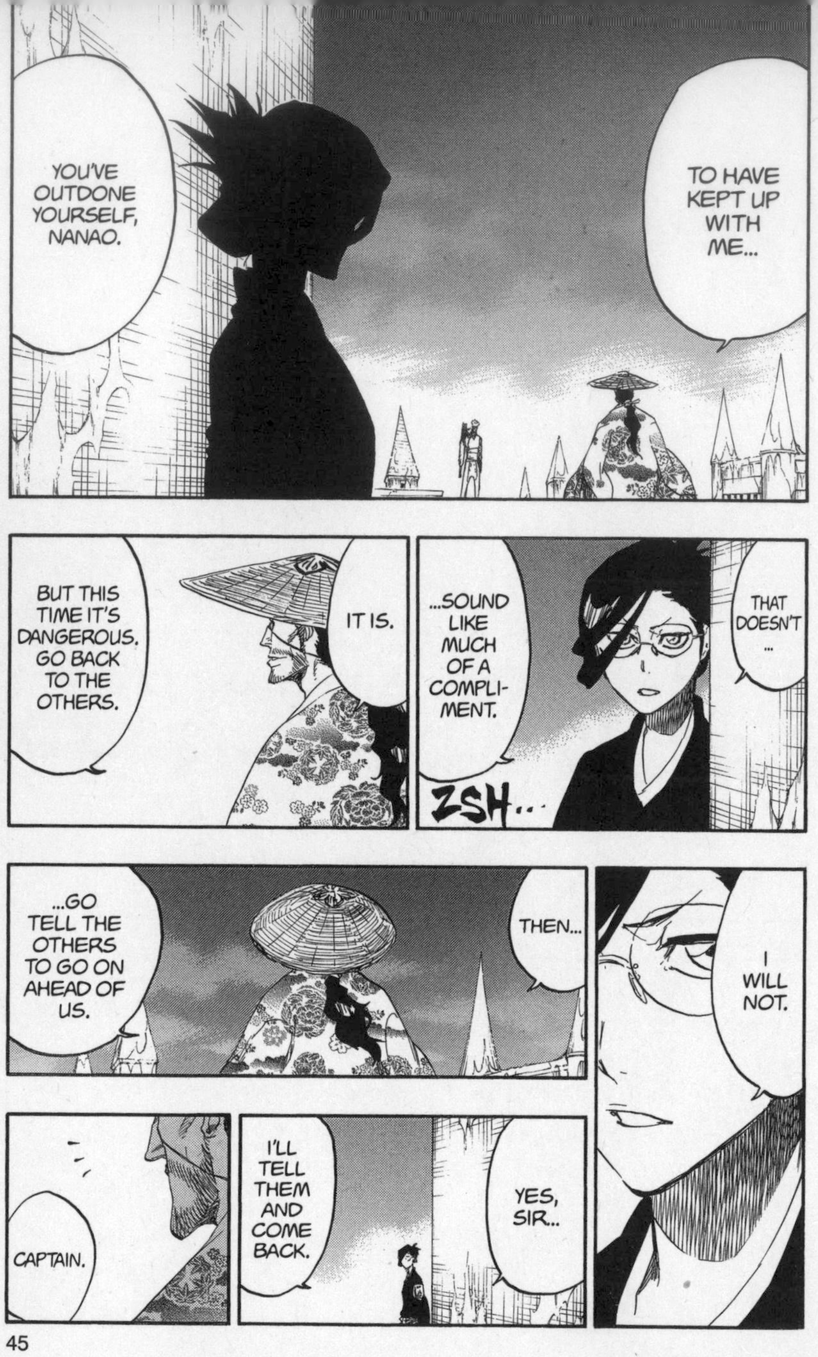
TO HAVE KEPT UP WITH ME...
YOU'VE OUTDONE YOURSELF, NANAO.
THAT DOESN'T ...
...SOUND LIKE MUCH OF A COMPLIMENT.
ZSH...
IT IS.
BUT THIS TIME IT'S DANGEROUS. GO BACK TO THE OTHERS.
I WILL NOT.
THEN...
...GO TELL THE OTHERS TO GO ON AHEAD OF US.
YES, SIR...
I'LL TELL THEM AND COME BACK.
CAPTAIN.

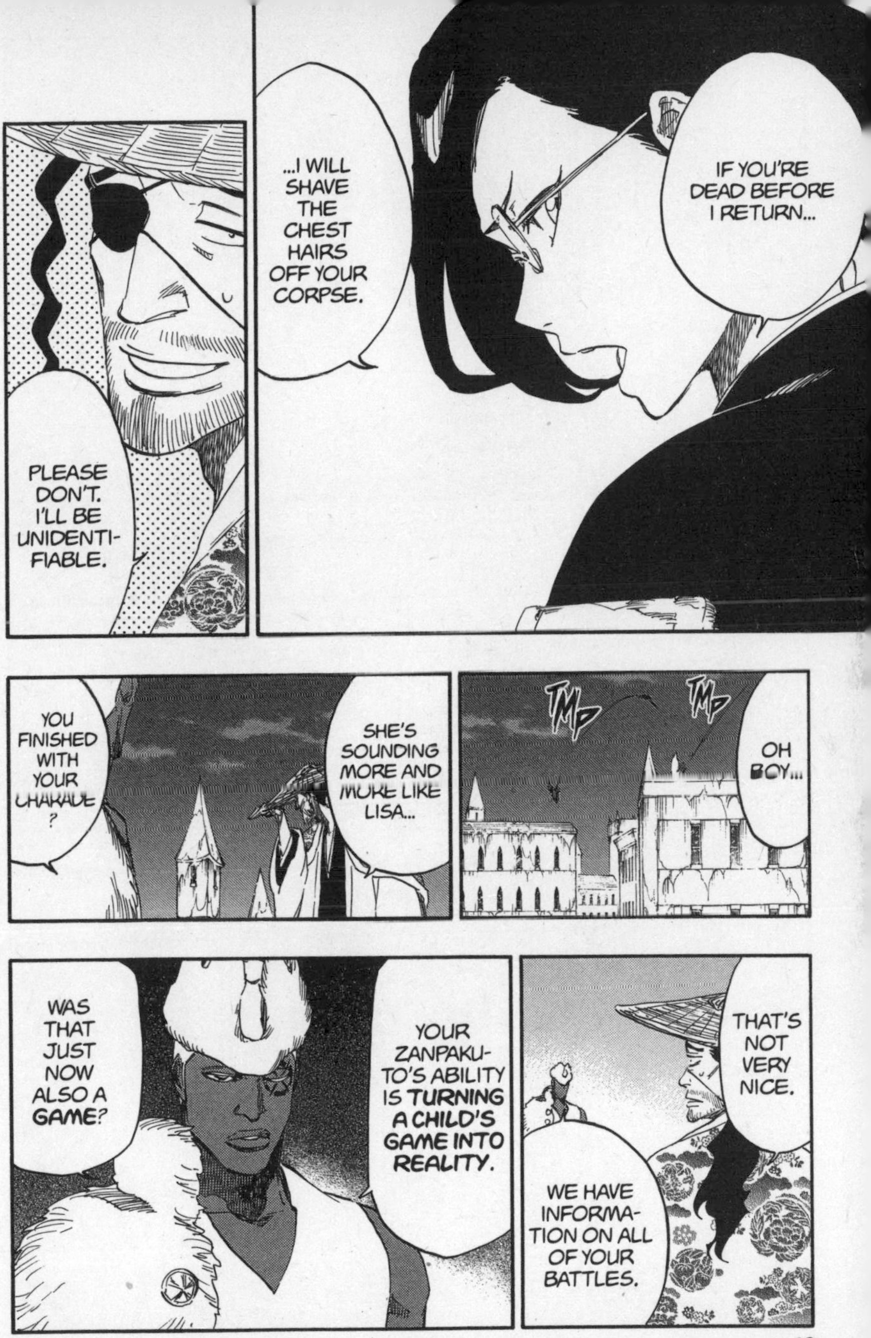
IF YOU'RE DEAD BEFORE I RETURN...
...I WILL SHAVE THE CHEST HAIRS OFF YOUR CORPSE.
PLEASE DON'T. I'LL BE UNIDENTI-FIABLE.
TMP
TMP
OH BOY...
SHE'S SOUNDING MORE AND MORE LIKE LISA...
YOU FINISHED WITH YOUR CHARADE?
THAT'S NOT VERY NICE.
WE HAVE INFORMATION ON ALL OF YOUR BATTLES.
YOUR ZANPAKU-TO'S ABILITY IS **TURNING A CHILD'S GAME INTO REALITY**.
WAS THAT JUST NOW ALSO A **GAME**?

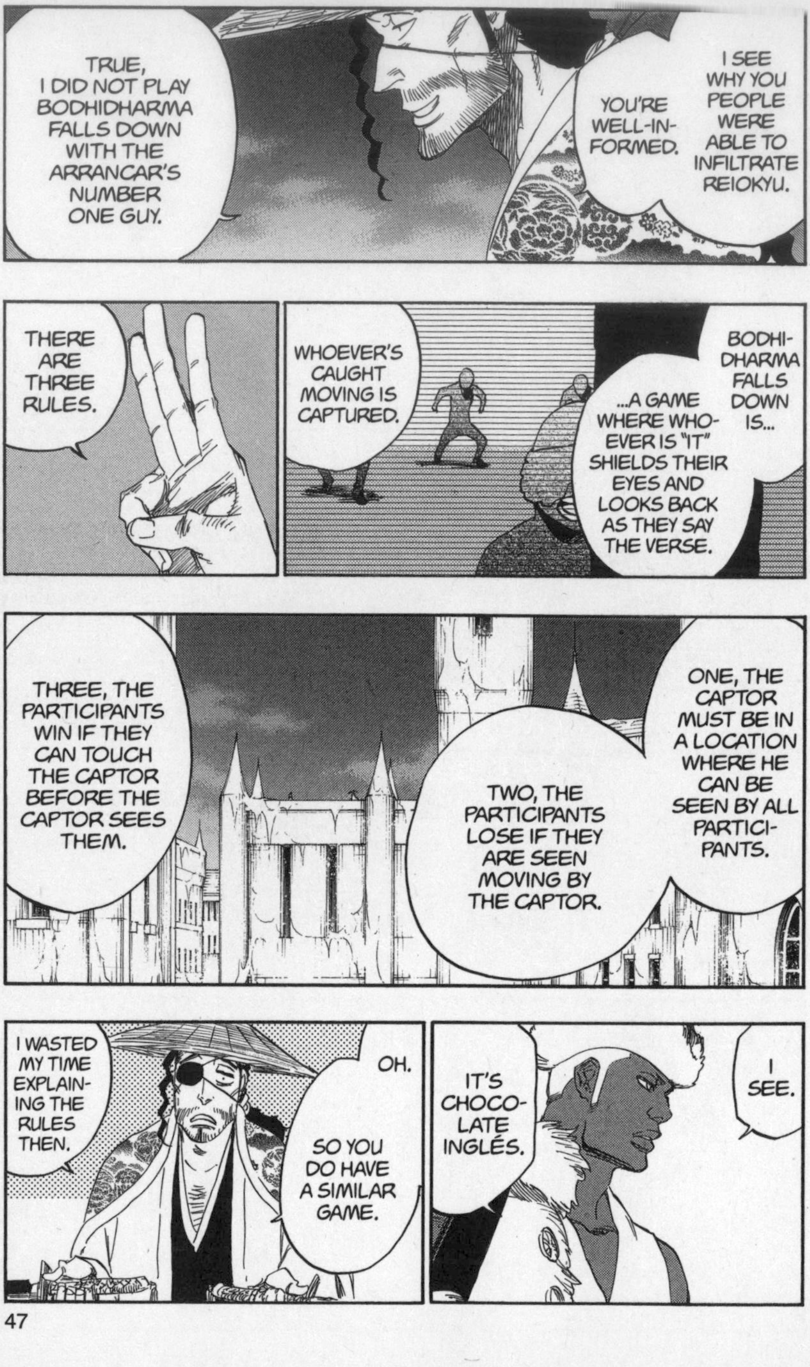
YOU'RE WELL-INFORMED.
I SEE WHY YOU PEOPLE WERE ABLE TO INFILTRATE REIOKYU.
TRUE, I DID NOT PLAY BODHIDHARMA FALLS DOWN WITH THE ARRANCAR'S NUMBER ONE GUY.
BODHIDHARMA FALLS DOWN IS...
...A GAME WHERE WHOEVER IS "IT" SHIELDS THEIR EYES AND LOOKS BACK AS THEY SAY THE VERSE.
WHOEVER'S CAUGHT MOVING IS CAPTURED.
THERE ARE THREE RULES.
ONE, THE CAPTOR MUST BE IN A LOCATION WHERE HE CAN BE SEEN BY ALL PARTICIPANTS.
TWO, THE PARTICIPANTS LOSE IF THEY ARE SEEN MOVING BY THE CAPTOR.
THREE, THE PARTICIPANTS WIN IF THEY CAN TOUCH THE CAPTOR BEFORE THE CAPTOR SEES THEM.
I SEE.
IT'S CHOCOLATE INGLÉS.
OH.
SO YOU DO HAVE A SIMILAR GAME.
I WASTED MY TIME EXPLAINING THE RULES THEN.

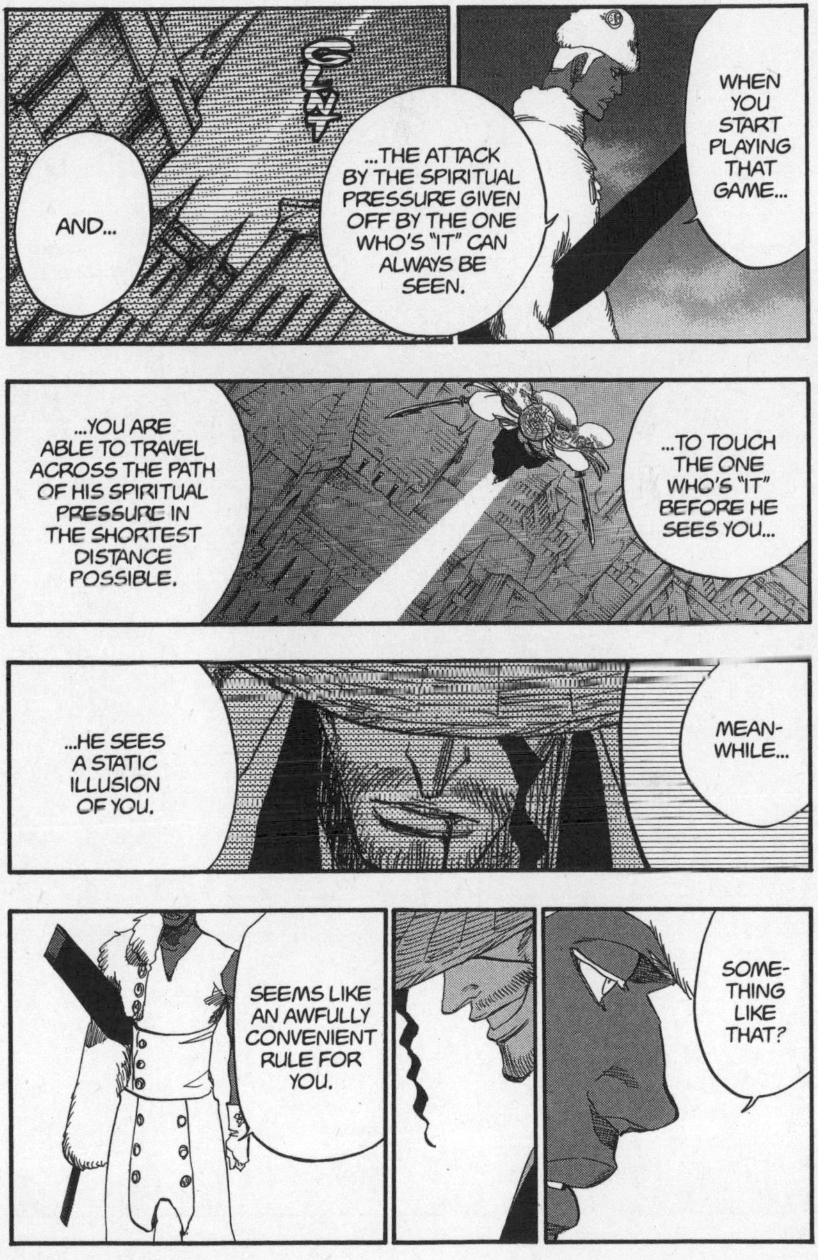
WHEN YOU START PLAYING THAT GAME...
...THE ATTACK BY THE SPIRITUAL PRESSURE GIVEN OFF BY THE ONE WHO'S "IT" CAN ALWAYS BE SEEN.
AND...
...TO TOUCH THE ONE WHO'S "IT" BEFORE HE SEES YOU...
...YOU ARE ABLE TO TRAVEL ACROSS THE PATH OF HIS SPIRITUAL PRESSURE IN THE SHORTEST DISTANCE POSSIBLE.
MEAN-WHILE...
...HE SEES A STATIC ILLUSION OF YOU.
SOME-THING LIKE THAT?
SEEMS LIKE AN AWFULLY CONVENIENT RULE FOR YOU.

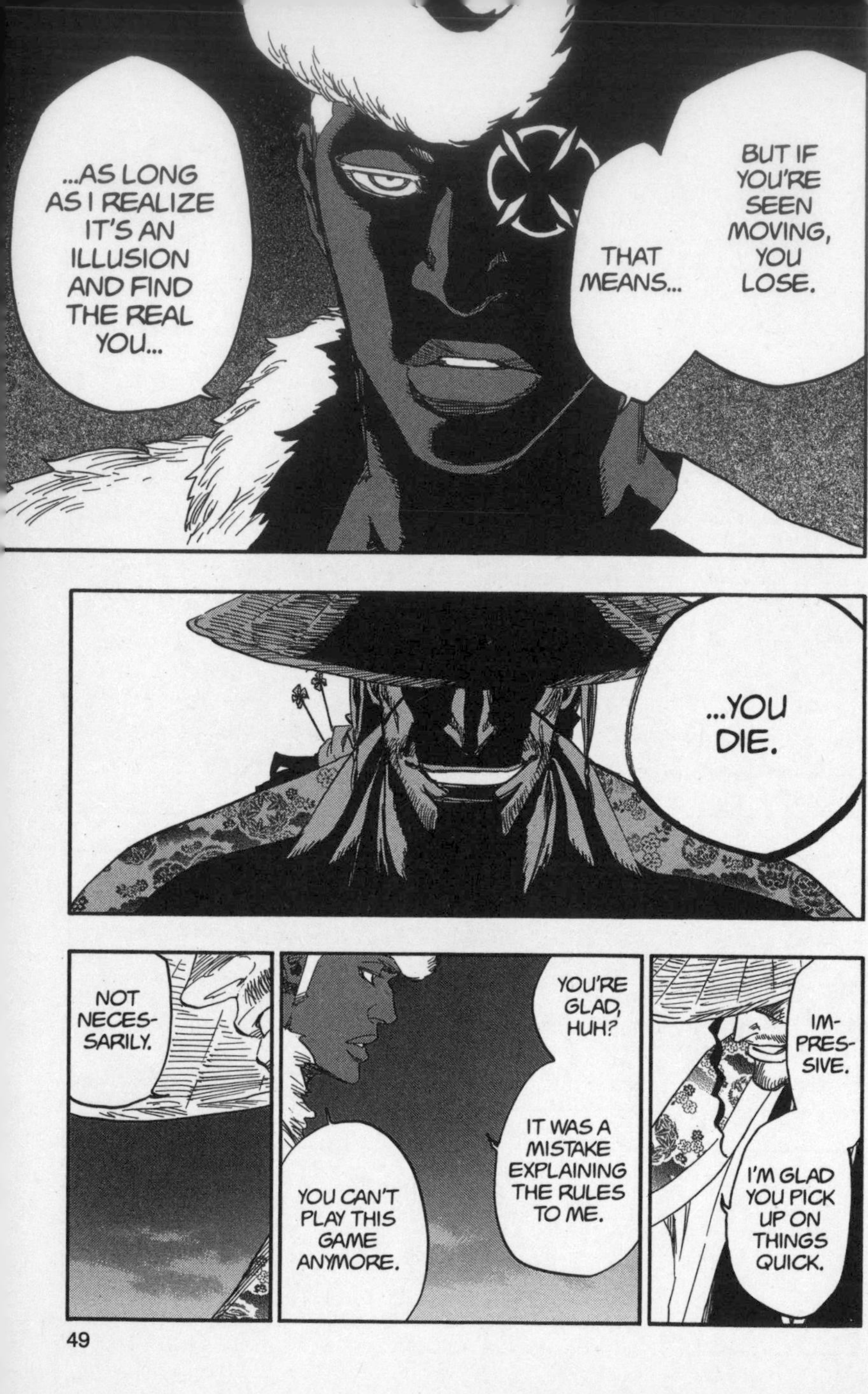
BUT IF YOU'RE SEEN MOVING, YOU LOSE.
THAT MEANS...
...AS LONG AS I REALIZE IT'S AN ILLUSION AND FIND THE REAL YOU...
...YOU DIE.
IM-PRES-SIVE.
I'M GLAD YOU PICK UP ON THINGS QUICK.
YOU'RE GLAD, HUH?
IT WAS A MISTAKE EXPLAINING THE RULES TO ME.
YOU CAN'T PLAY THIS GAME ANYMORE.
NOT NECES-SARILY.

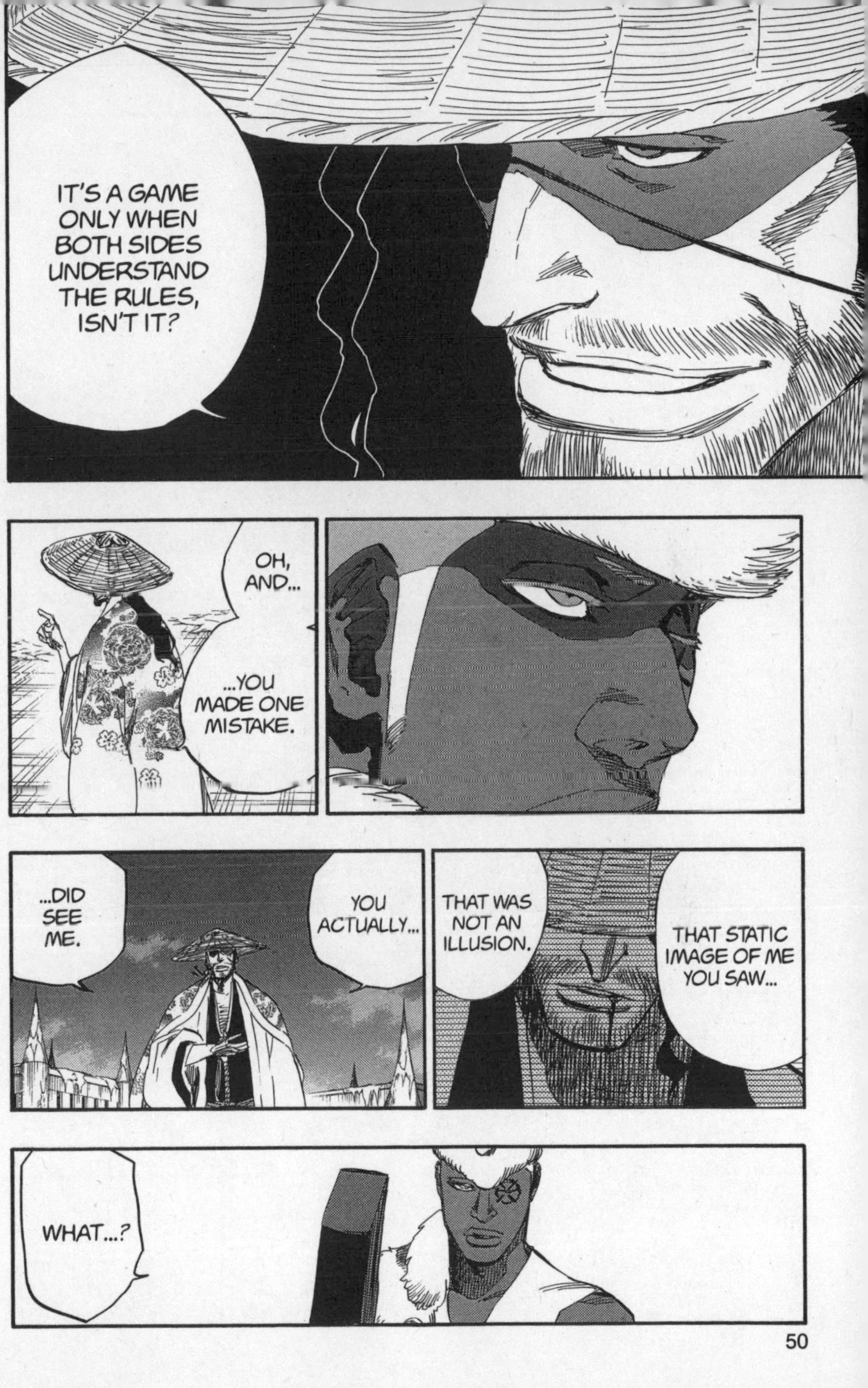
IT'S A GAME ONLY WHEN BOTH SIDES UNDERSTAND THE RULES, ISN'T IT?
OH, AND...
...YOU MADE ONE MISTAKE.
THAT STATIC IMAGE OF ME YOU SAW...
THAT WAS NOT AN ILLUSION.
YOU ACTUALLY...
...DID SEE ME.
WHAT...?

READ THIS WAY

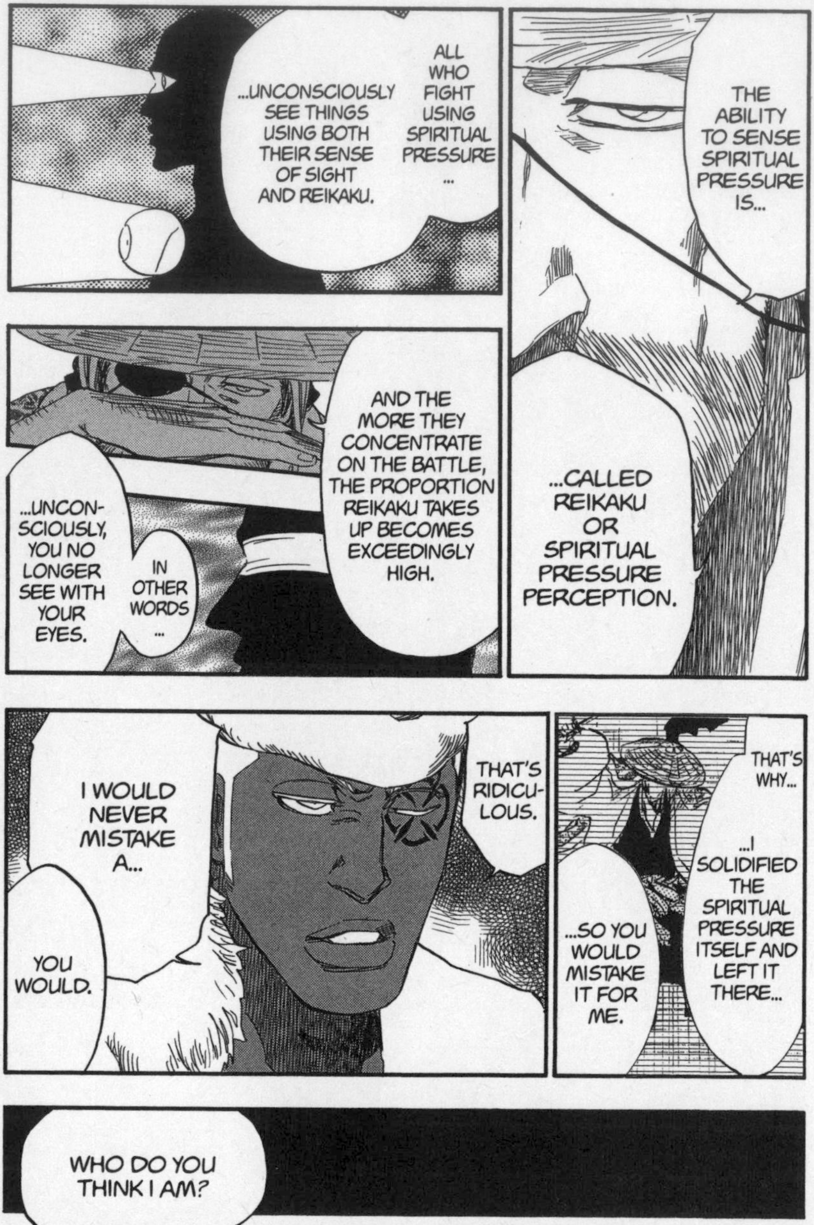
THE ABILITY TO SENSE SPIRITUAL PRESSURE IS...
...CALLED REIKAKU OR SPIRITUAL PRESSURE PERCEPTION.
ALL WHO FIGHT USING SPIRITUAL PRESSURE...
...UNCONSCIOUSLY SEE THINGS USING BOTH THEIR SENSE OF SIGHT AND REIKAKU.
AND THE MORE THEY CONCENTRATE ON THE BATTLE, THE PROPORTION REIKAKU TAKES UP BECOMES EXCEEDINGLY HIGH.
IN OTHER WORDS...
...UNCONSCIOUSLY, YOU NO LONGER SEE WITH YOUR EYES.
THAT'S WHY...
...I SOLIDIFIED THE SPIRITUAL PRESSURE ITSELF AND LEFT IT THERE...
...SO YOU WOULD MISTAKE IT FOR ME.
THAT'S RIDICULOUS.
I WOULD NEVER MISTAKE A...
YOU WOULD.
WHO DO YOU THINK I AM?

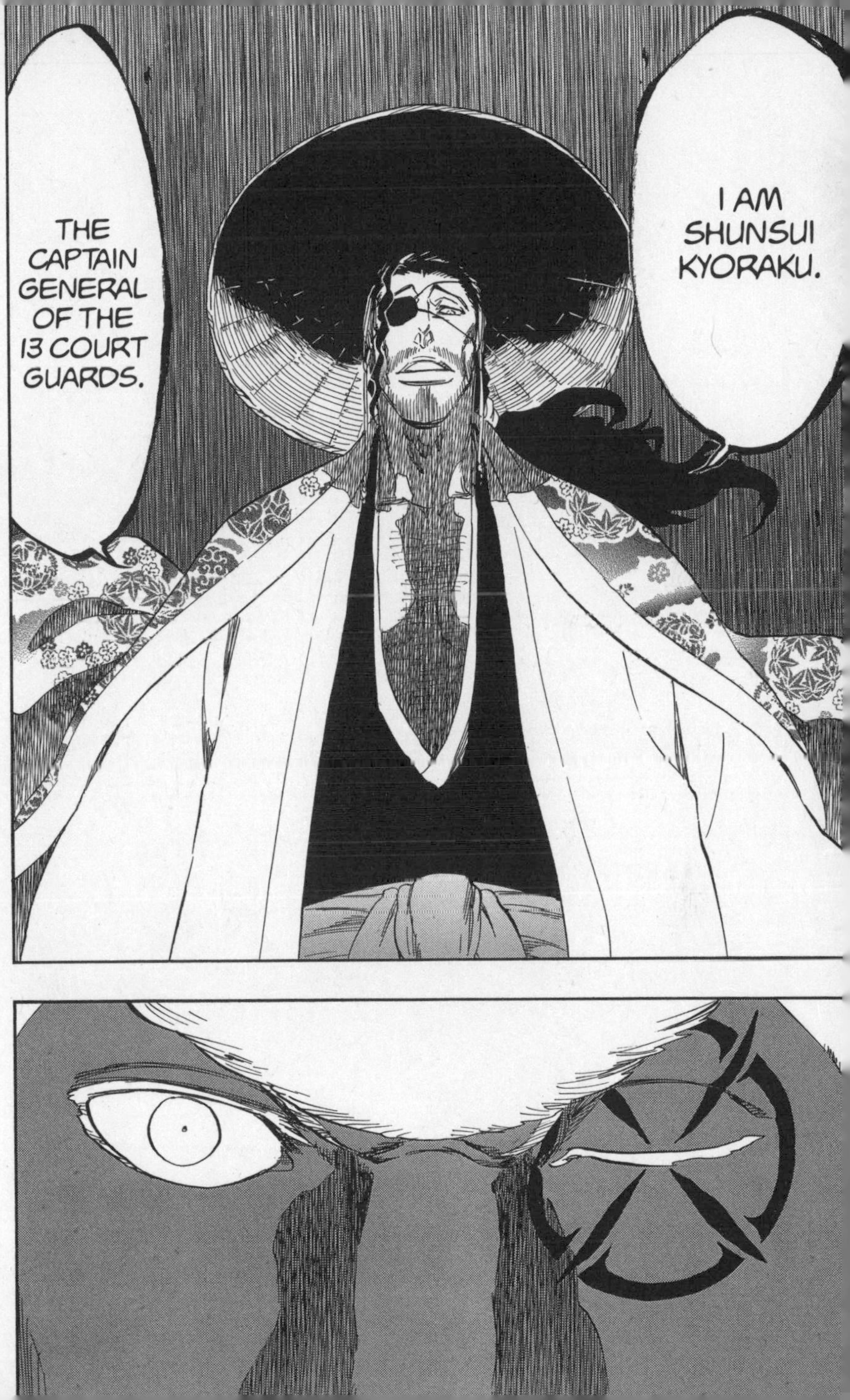
I AM SHUNSUI KYORAKU.
THE CAPTAIN GENERAL OF THE 13 COURT GUARDS.

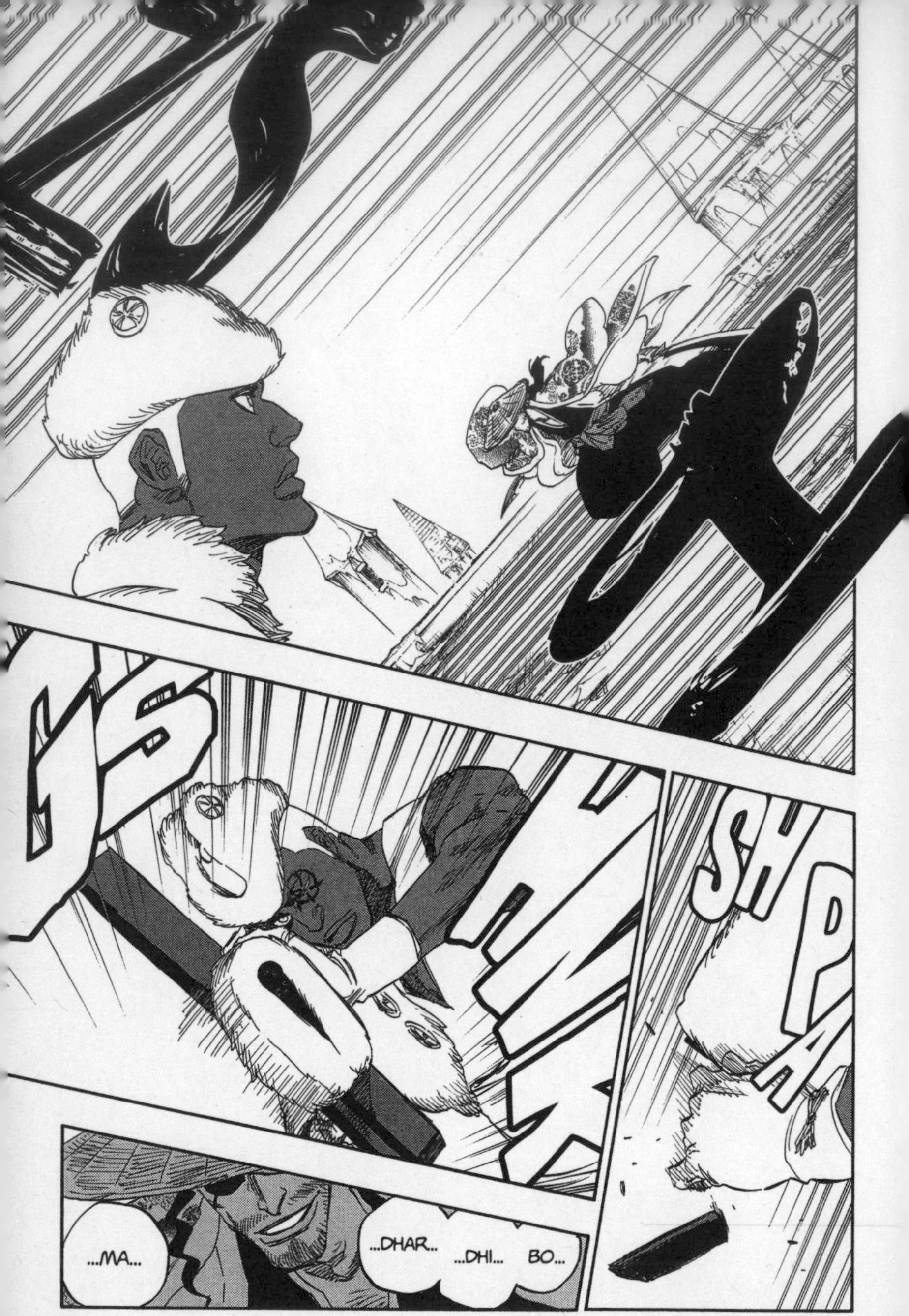
...DHAR... ...DHI... BO...
...MA...

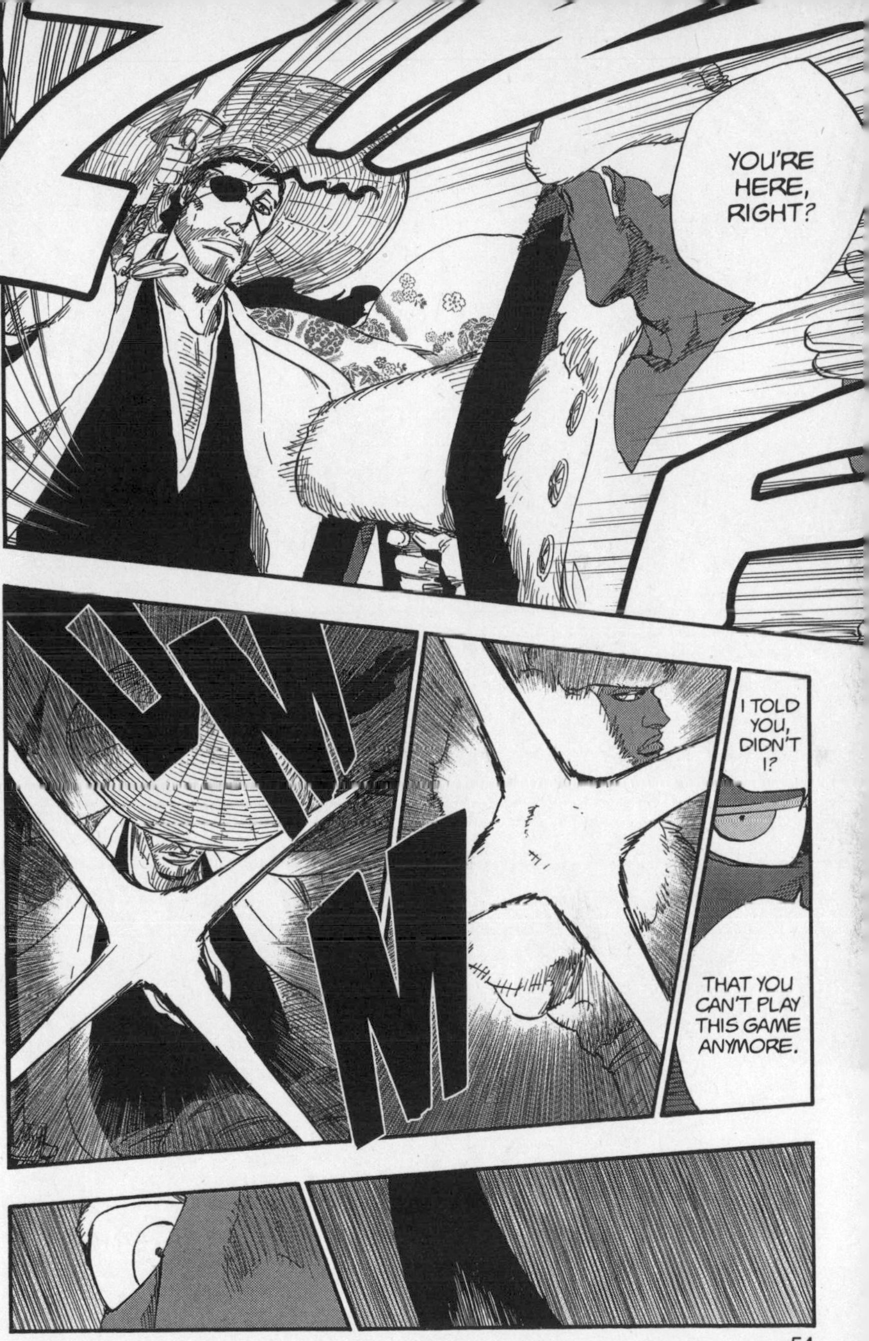
YOU'RE HERE, RIGHT?
I TOLD YOU, DIDN'T I?
THAT YOU CAN'T PLAY THIS GAME ANYMORE.

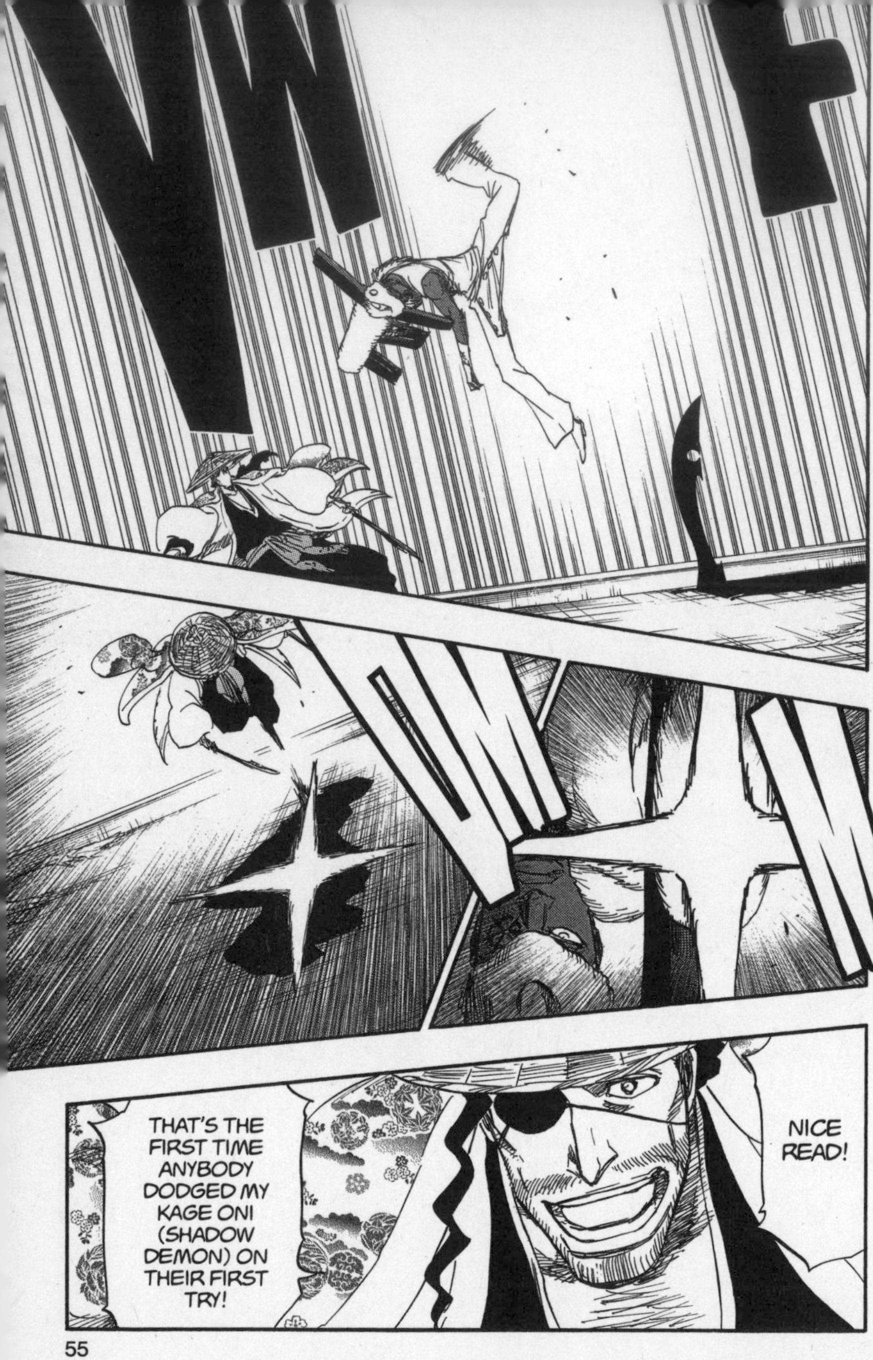
NICE READ!
THAT'S THE FIRST TIME ANYBODY DODGED MY KAGE ONI (SHADOW DEMON) ON THEIR FIRST TRY!

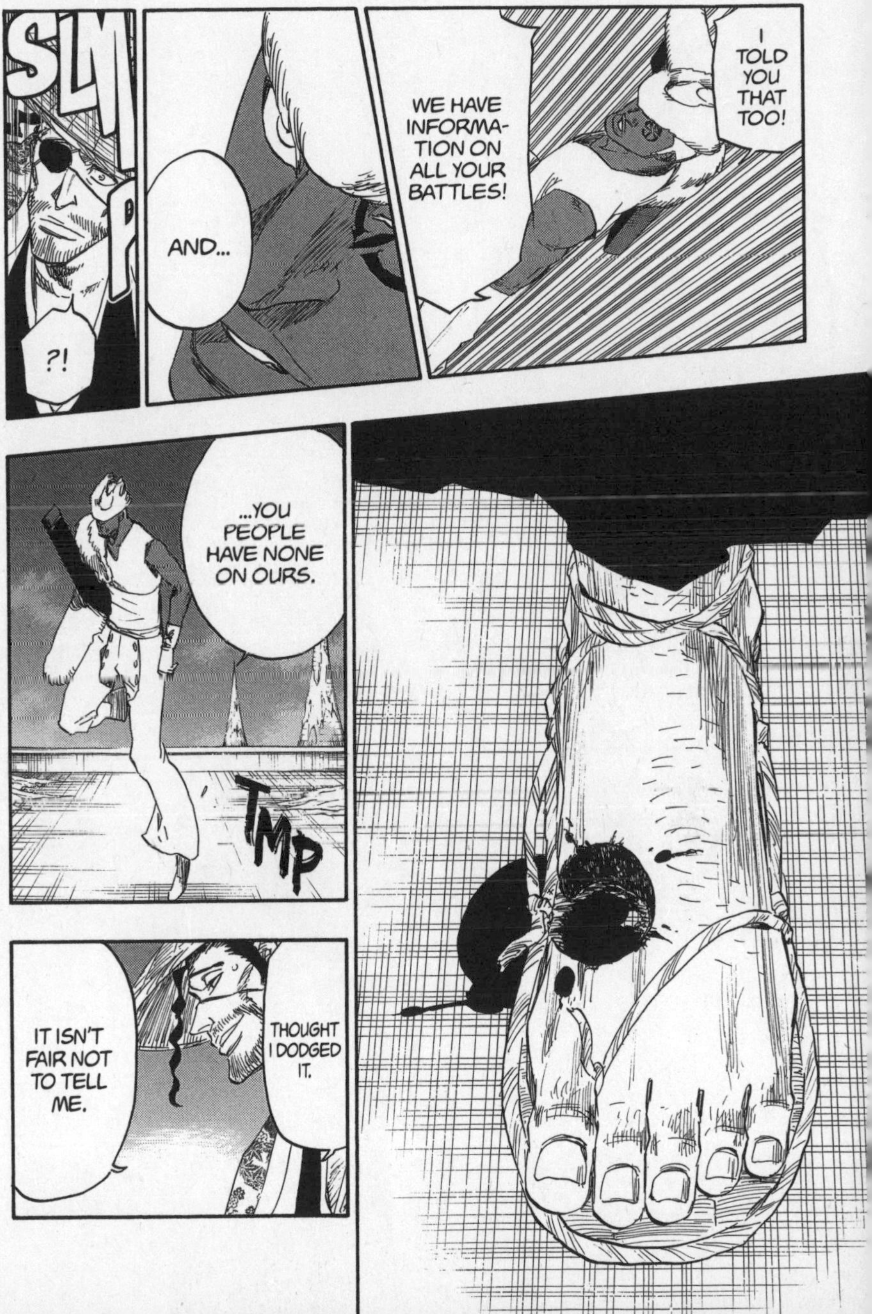
I TOLD YOU THAT TOO!
WE HAVE INFORMATION ON ALL YOUR BATTLES!
AND...
SLMP
?!
...YOU PEOPLE HAVE NONE ON OURS.
TMP
THOUGHT I DODGED IT.
IT ISN'T FAIR NOT TO TELL ME.

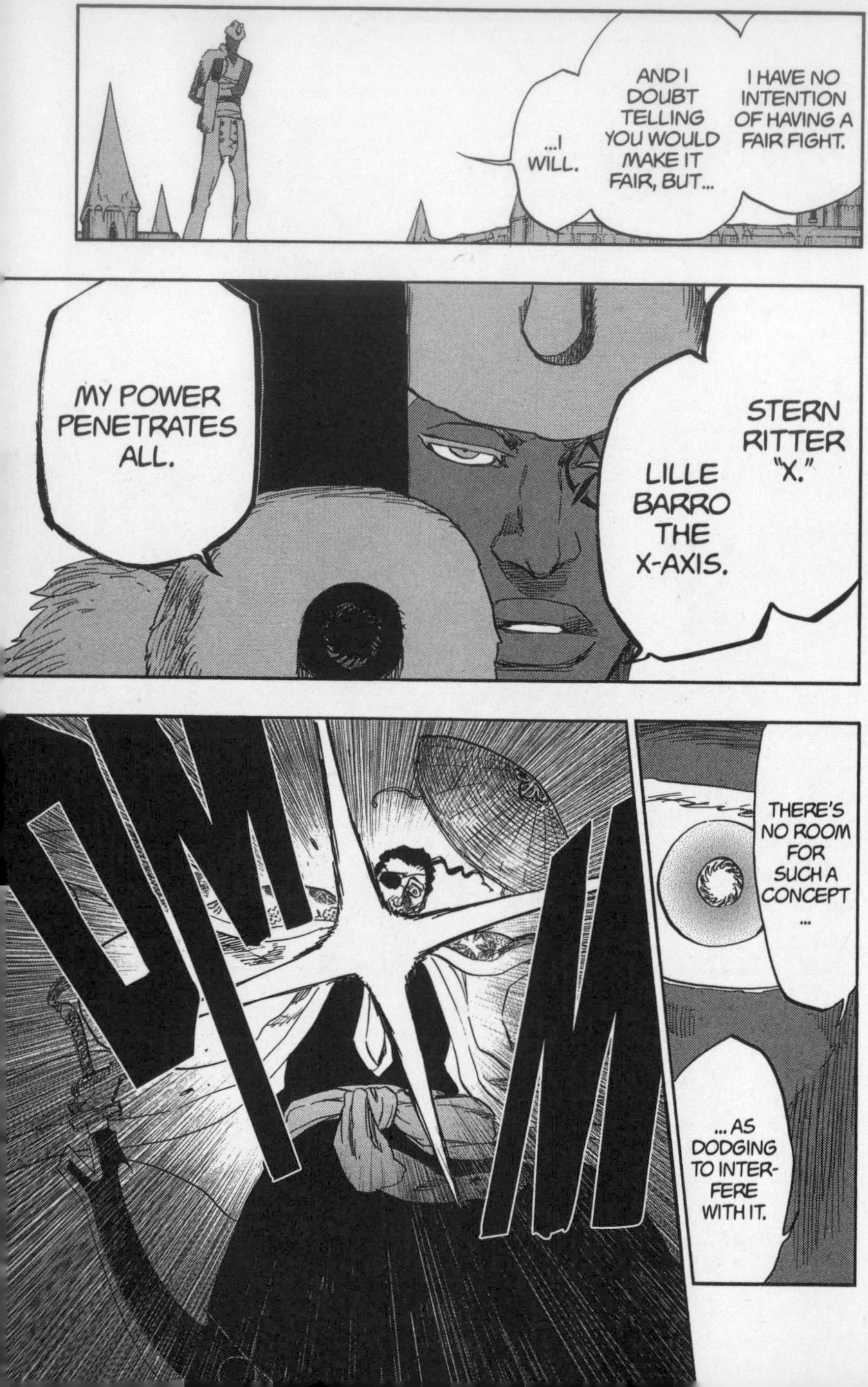
I HAVE NO INTENTION OF HAVING A FAIR FIGHT.
AND I DOUBT TELLING YOU WOULD MAKE IT FAIR, BUT...
...I WILL.
STERN RITTER "X."
LILLE BARRO THE X-AXIS.
MY POWER PENETRATES ALL.
THERE'S NO ROOM FOR SUCH A CONCEPT ...
...AS DODGING TO INTER-FERE WITH IT.

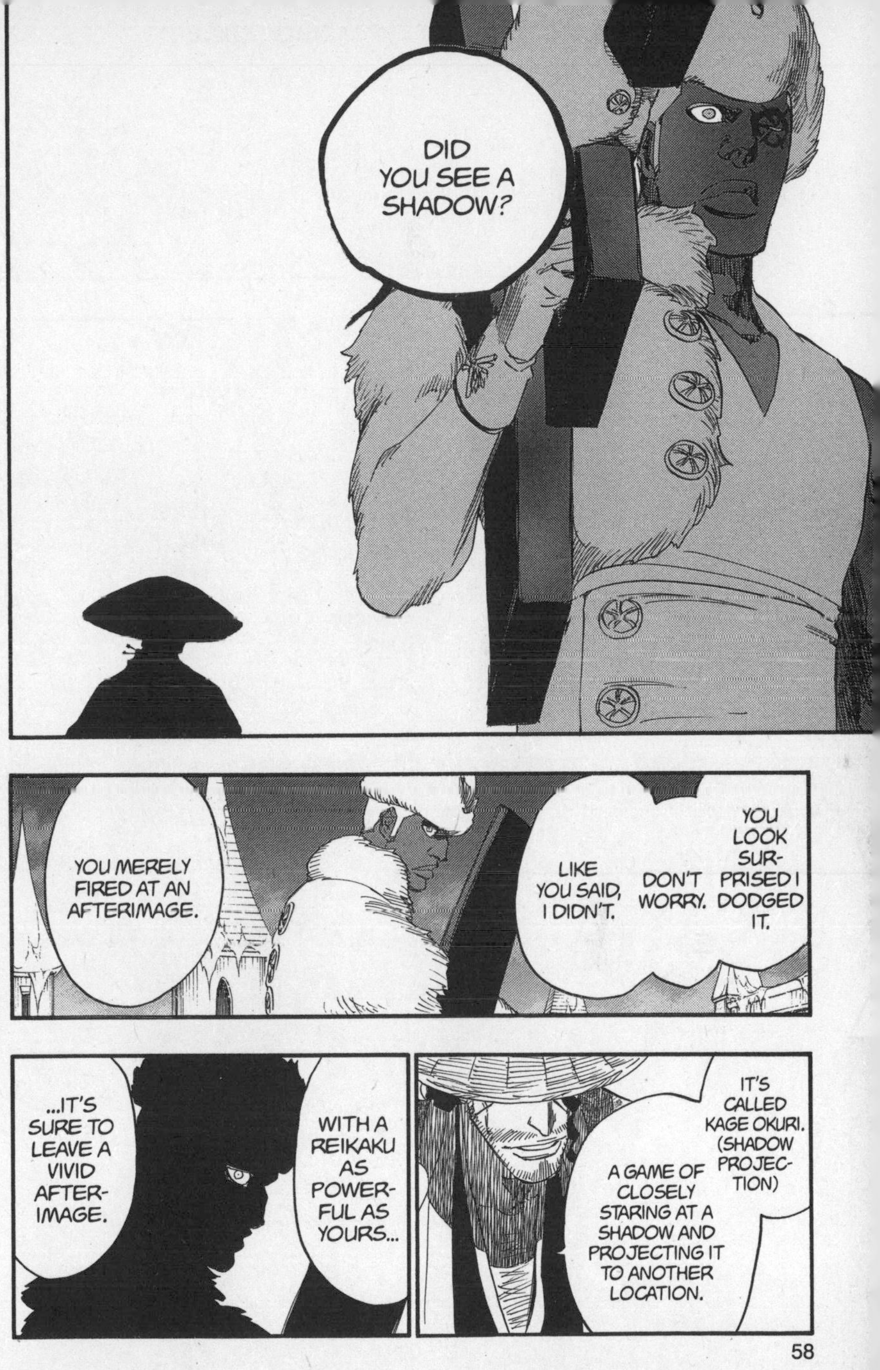
DID YOU SEE A SHADOW?
YOU LOOK SURPRISED I DODGED IT.
DON'T WORRY.
LIKE YOU SAID, I DIDN'T.
YOU MERELY FIRED AT AN AFTERIMAGE.
IT'S CALLED KAGE OKURI. (SHADOW PROJECTION)
A GAME OF CLOSELY STARING AT A SHADOW AND PROJECTING IT TO ANOTHER LOCATION.
WITH A REIKAKU AS POWERFUL AS YOURS...
...IT'S SURE TO LEAVE A VIVID AFTERIMAGE.

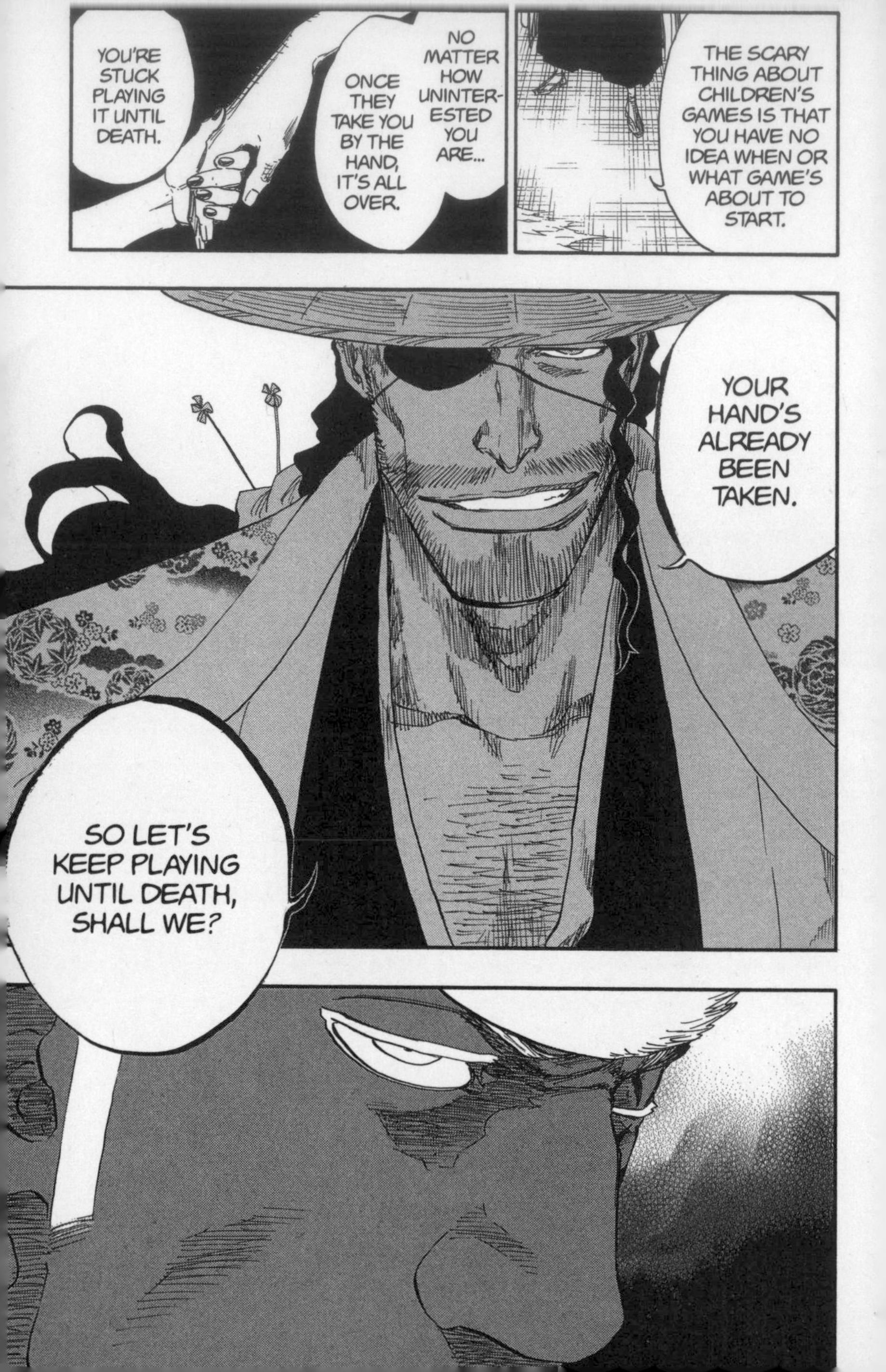
THE SCARY THING ABOUT CHILDREN'S GAMES IS THAT YOU HAVE NO IDEA WHEN OR WHAT GAME'S ABOUT TO START.
NO MATTER HOW UNINTER-ESTED YOU ARE...
ONCE THEY TAKE YOU BY THE HAND, IT'S ALL OVER.
YOU'RE STUCK PLAYING IT UNTIL DEATH.
YOUR HAND'S ALREADY BEEN TAKEN.
SO LET'S KEEP PLAYING UNTIL DEATH, SHALL WE?

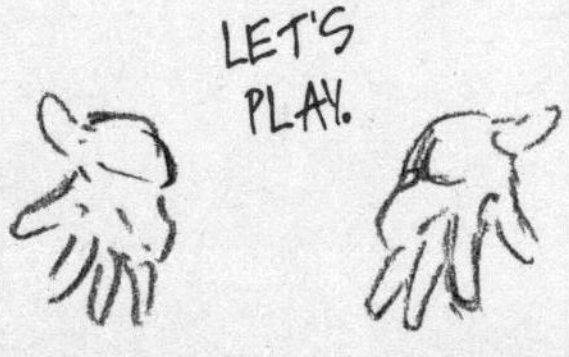
LET'S
PLAY.

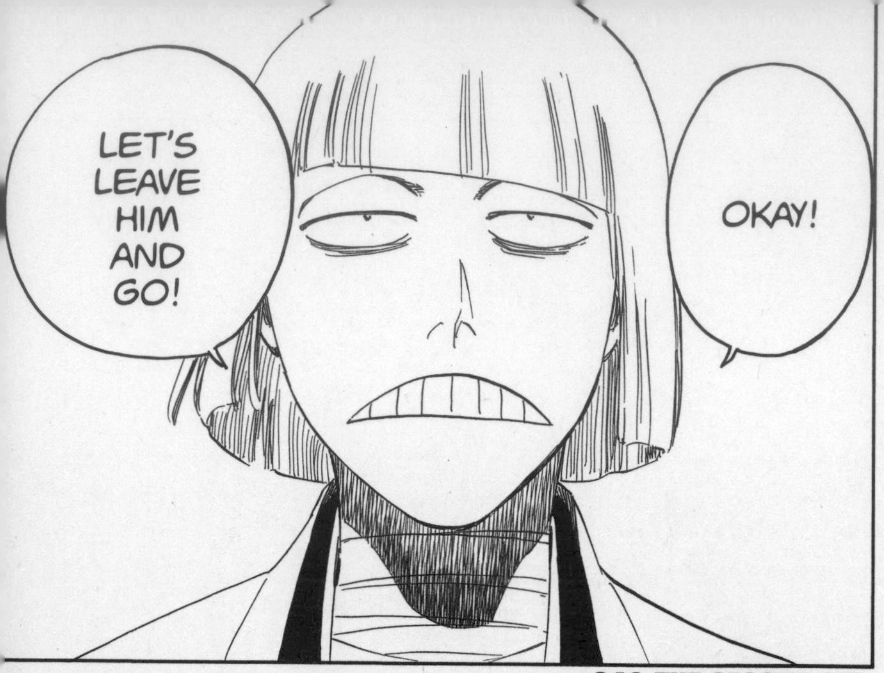
OKAY!
LET'S LEAVE HIM AND GO!

646. THE SECOND EYE

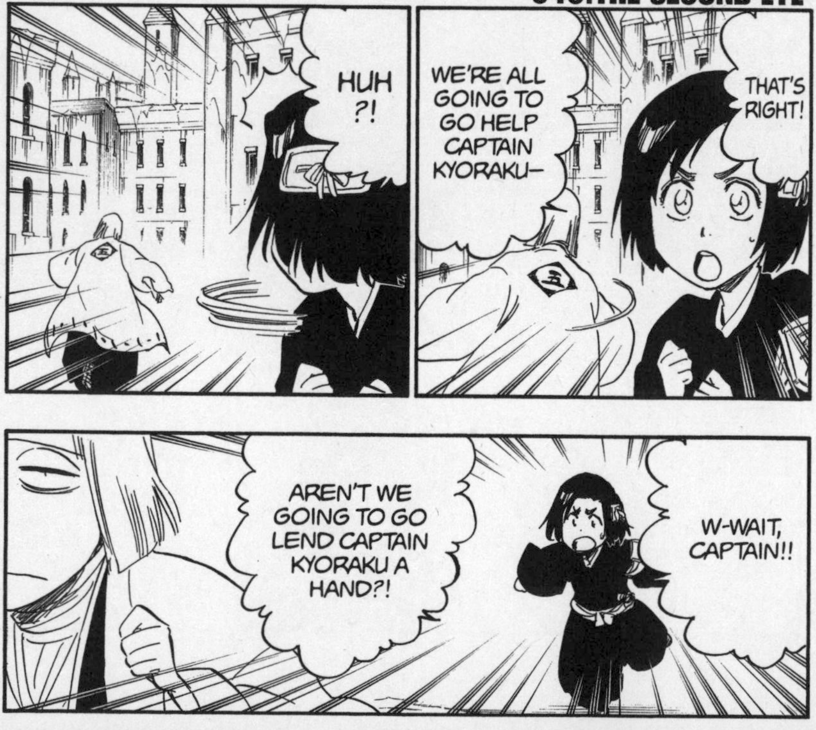
THAT'S RIGHT!
WE'RE ALL GOING TO GO HELP CAPTAIN KYORAKU–
HUH ?!
W-WAIT, CAPTAIN!!
AREN'T WE GOING TO GO LEND CAPTAIN KYORAKU A HAND?!

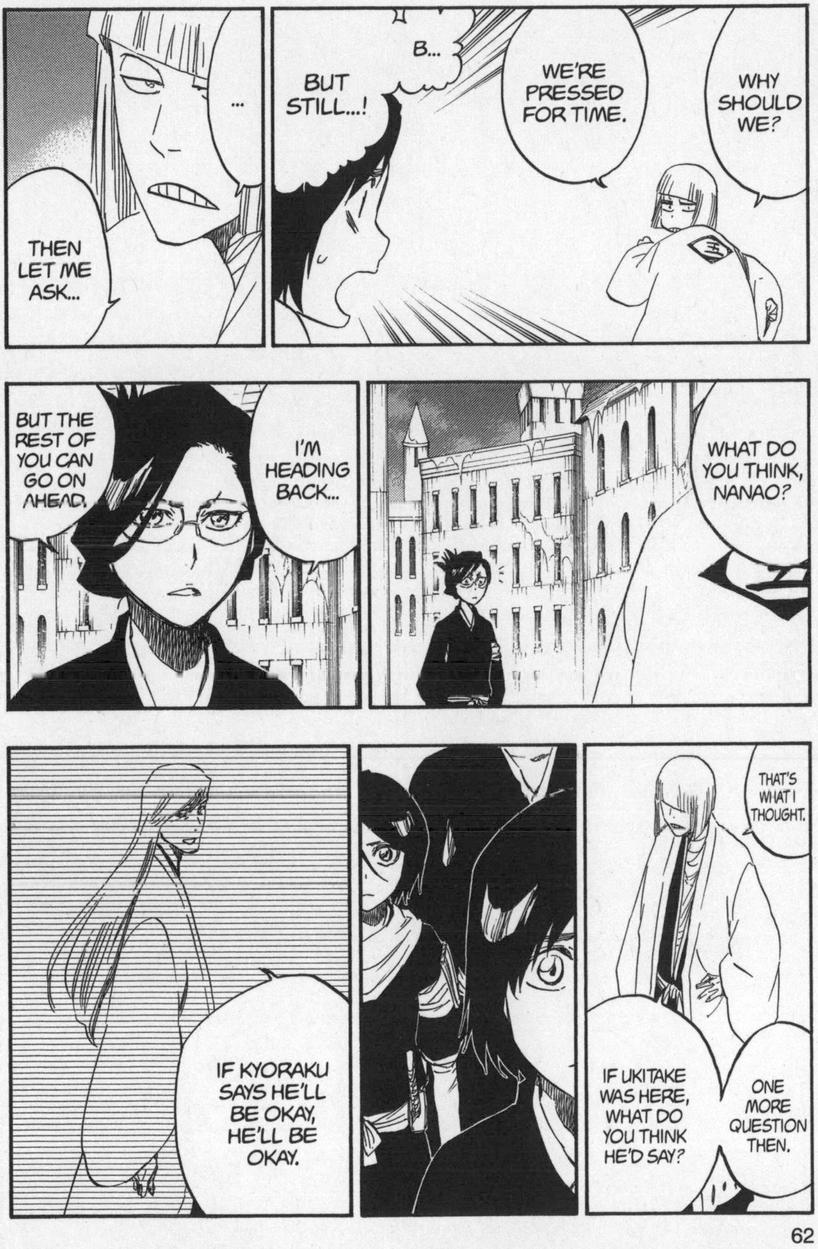
WHY SHOULD WE?
WE'RE PRESSED FOR TIME.
B...
BUT STILL...!
...
THEN LET ME ASK...
WHAT DO YOU THINK, NANAO?
I'M HEADING BACK...
BUT THE REST OF YOU CAN GO ON AHEAD.
THAT'S WHAT I THOUGHT.
ONE MORE QUESTION THEN.
IF UKITAKE WAS HERE, WHAT DO YOU THINK HE'D SAY?
IF KYORAKU SAYS HE'LL BE OKAY, HE'LL BE OKAY.

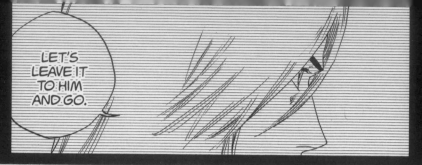

LET'S
LEAVE IT
TO HIM
AND GO.

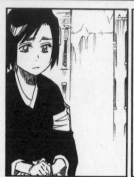

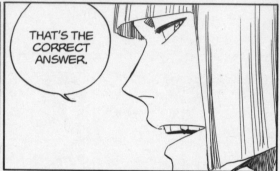

THAT'S THE
CORRECT
ANSWER.

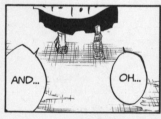

AND...

OH...

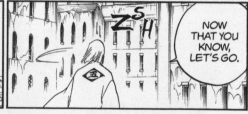

ZSH

NOW
THAT YOU
KNOW,
LET'S GO.

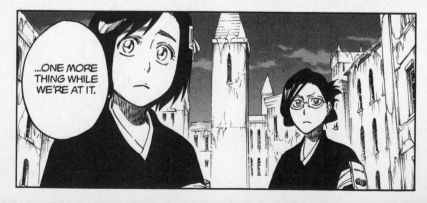

...ONE MORE
THING WHILE
WE'RE AT IT.

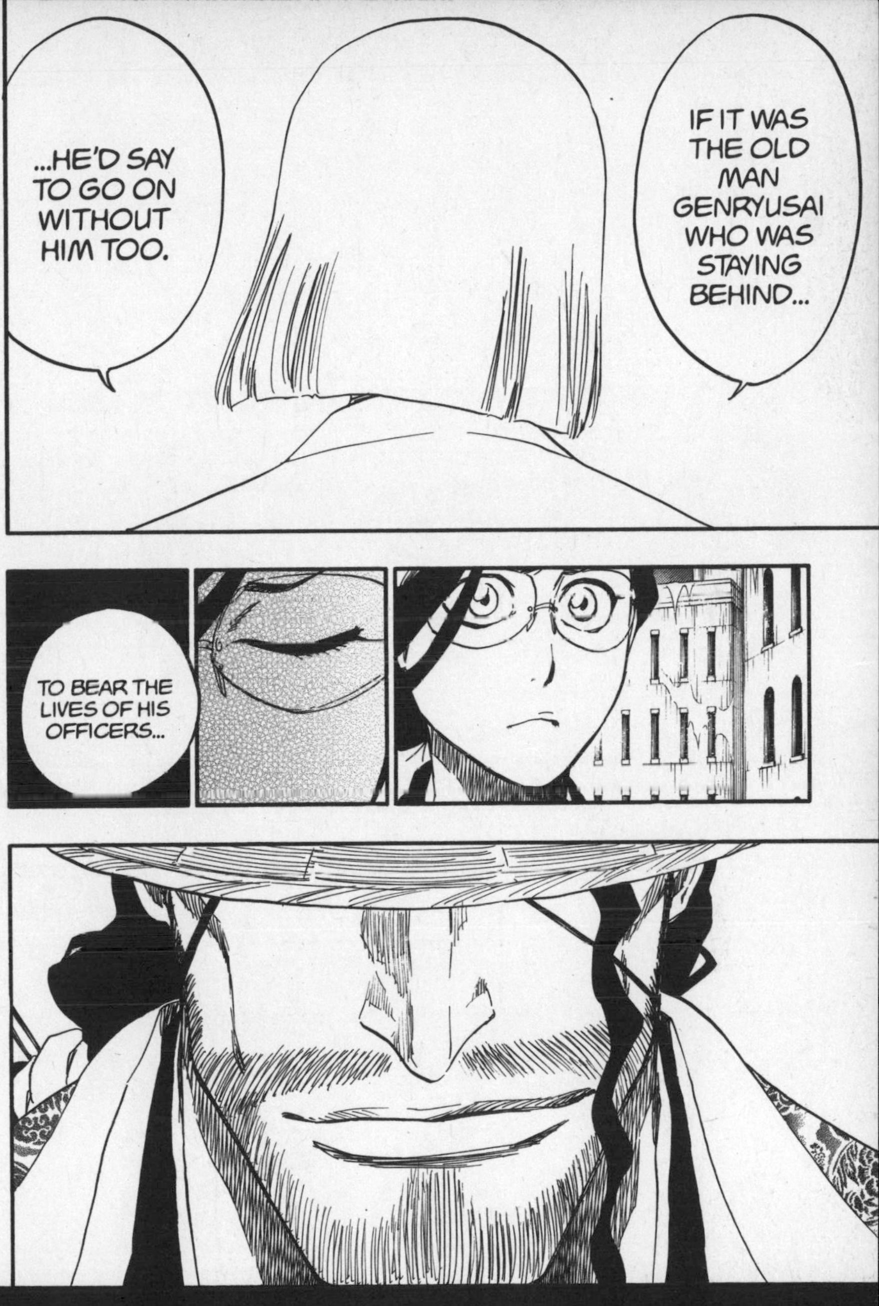
IF IT WAS THE OLD MAN GENRYUSAI WHO WAS STAYING BEHIND...
...HE'D SAY TO GO ON WITHOUT HIM TOO.
TO BEAR THE LIVES OF HIS OFFICERS...

BLEACH 646.

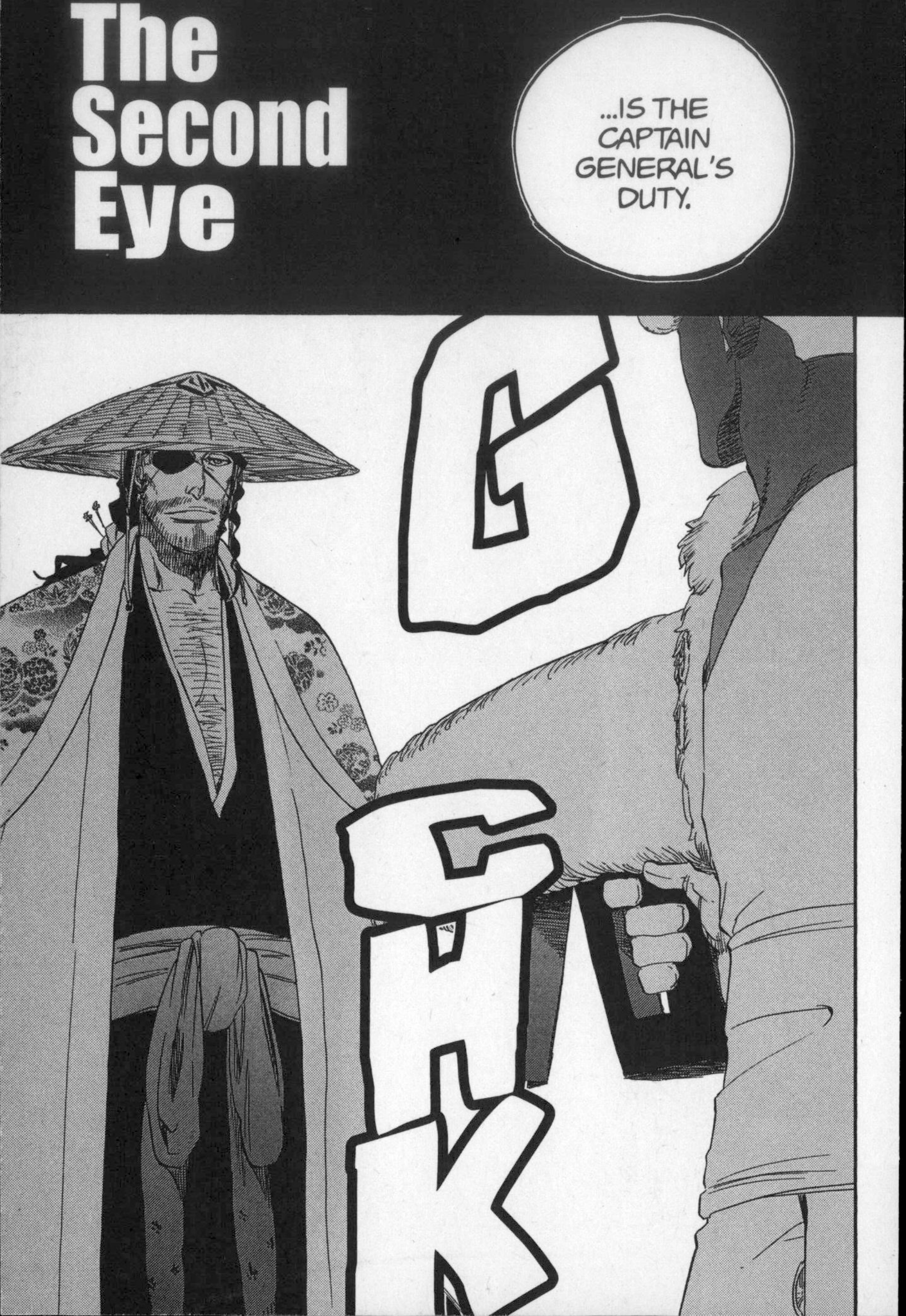
The Second Eye
...IS THE CAPTAIN GENERAL'S DUTY.
GCHK

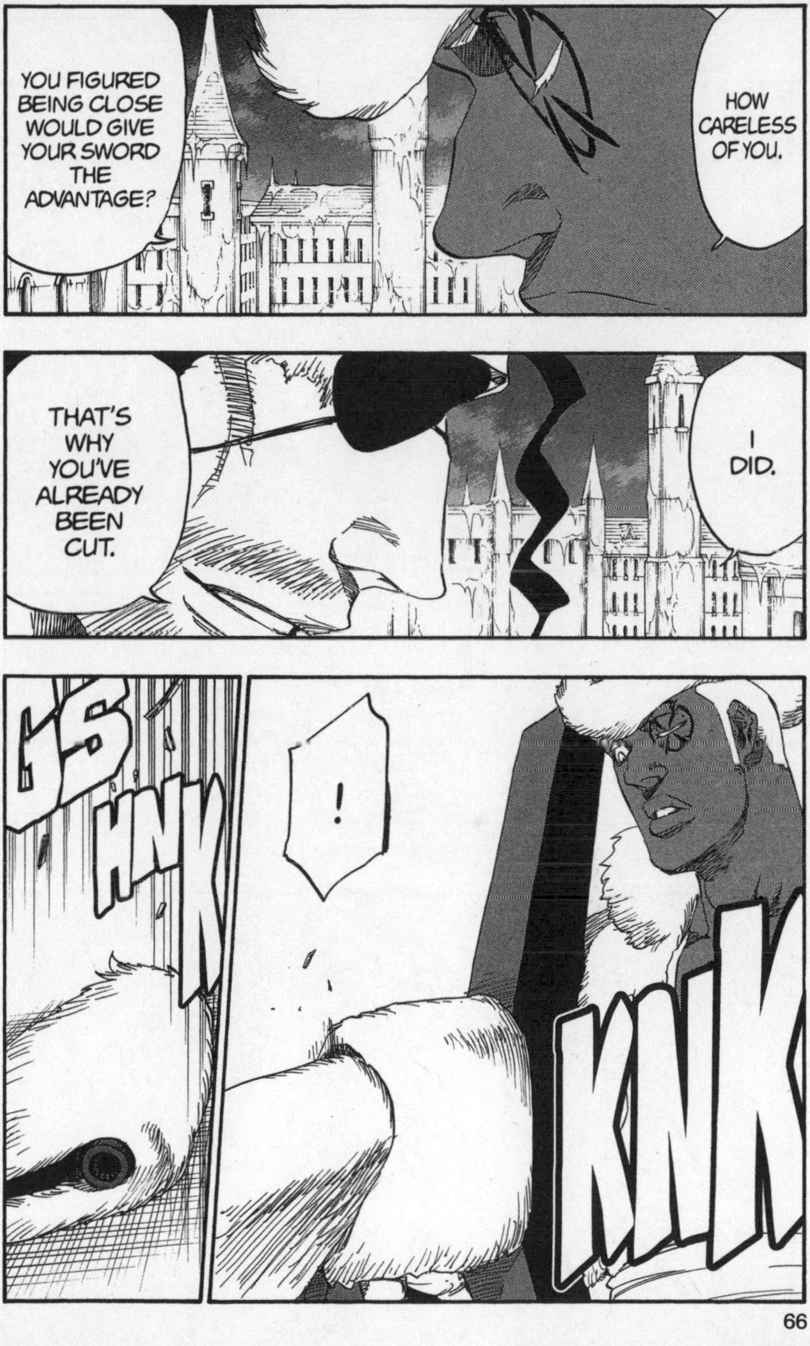
HOW CARELESS OF YOU.
YOU FIGURED BEING CLOSE WOULD GIVE YOUR SWORD THE ADVANTAGE?
I DID.
THAT'S WHY YOU'VE ALREADY BEEN CUT.
!
KNK
SHNK

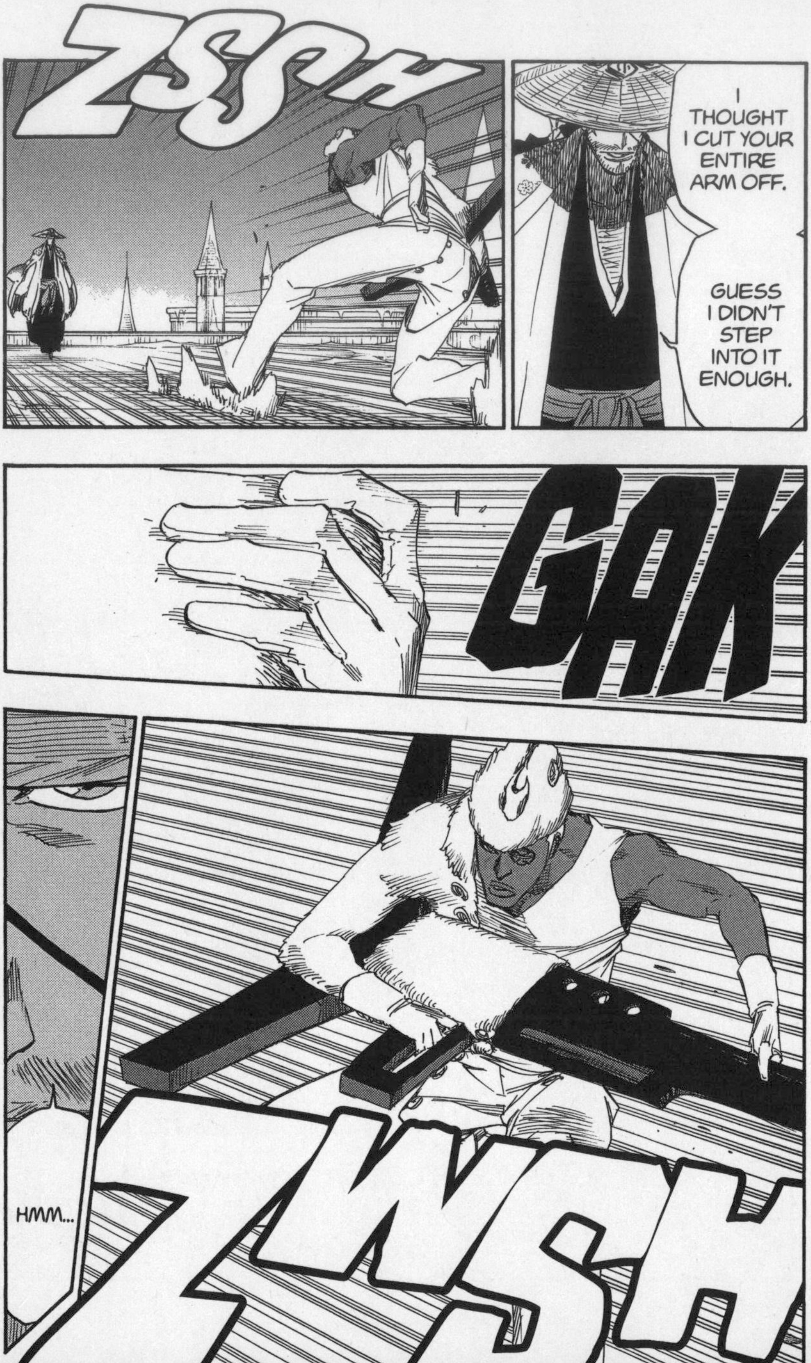
I THOUGHT I CUT YOUR ENTIRE ARM OFF.
GUESS I DIDN'T STEP INTO IT ENOUGH.
ZSSH
GAK
ZWSH
HMM...

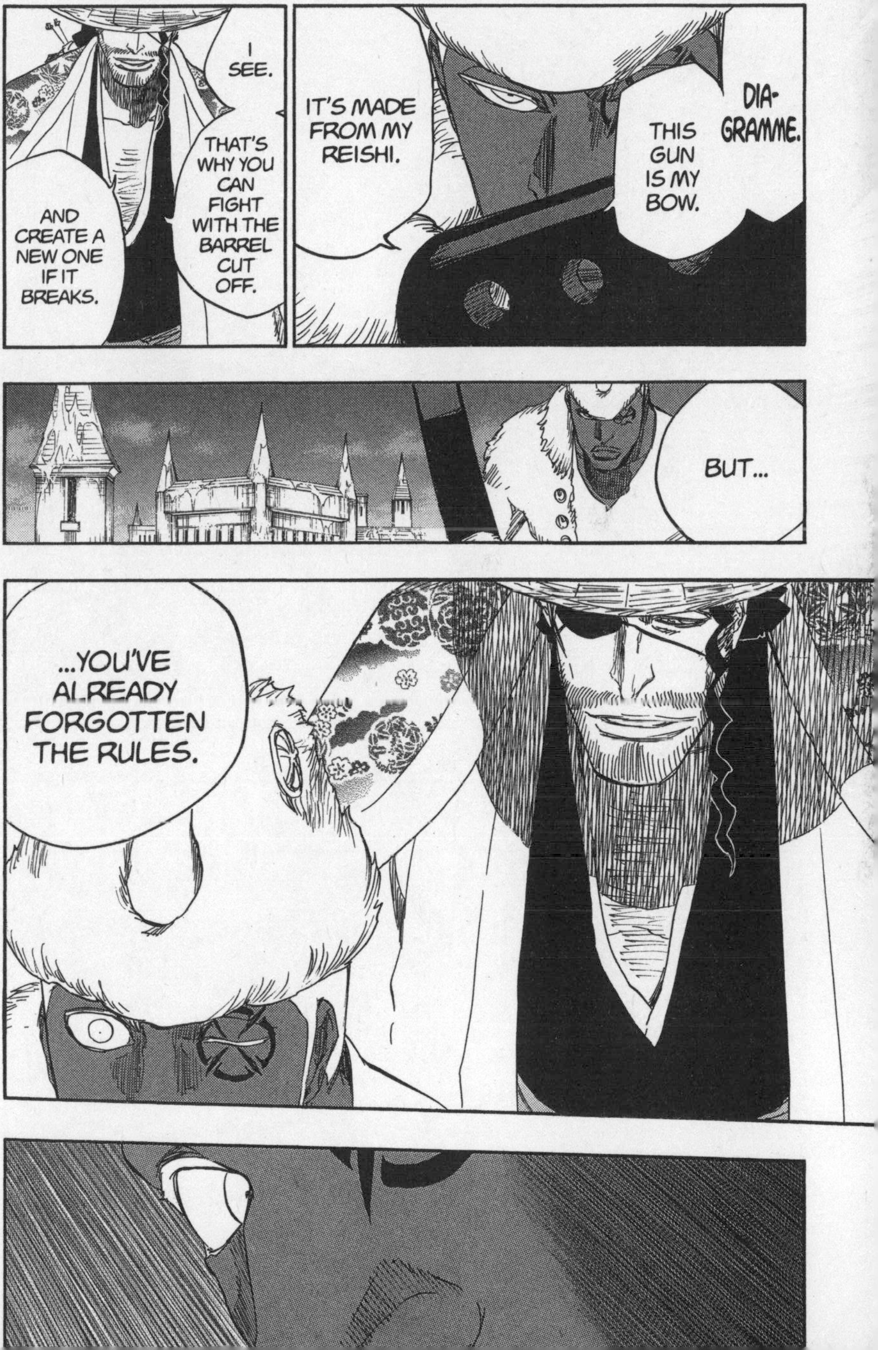
DIA-GRAMME.
THIS GUN IS MY BOW.
IT'S MADE FROM MY REISHI.
I SEE.
THAT'S WHY YOU CAN FIGHT WITH THE BARREL CUT OFF.
AND CREATE A NEW ONE IF IT BREAKS.
BUT...
...YOU'VE ALREADY FORGOTTEN THE RULES.

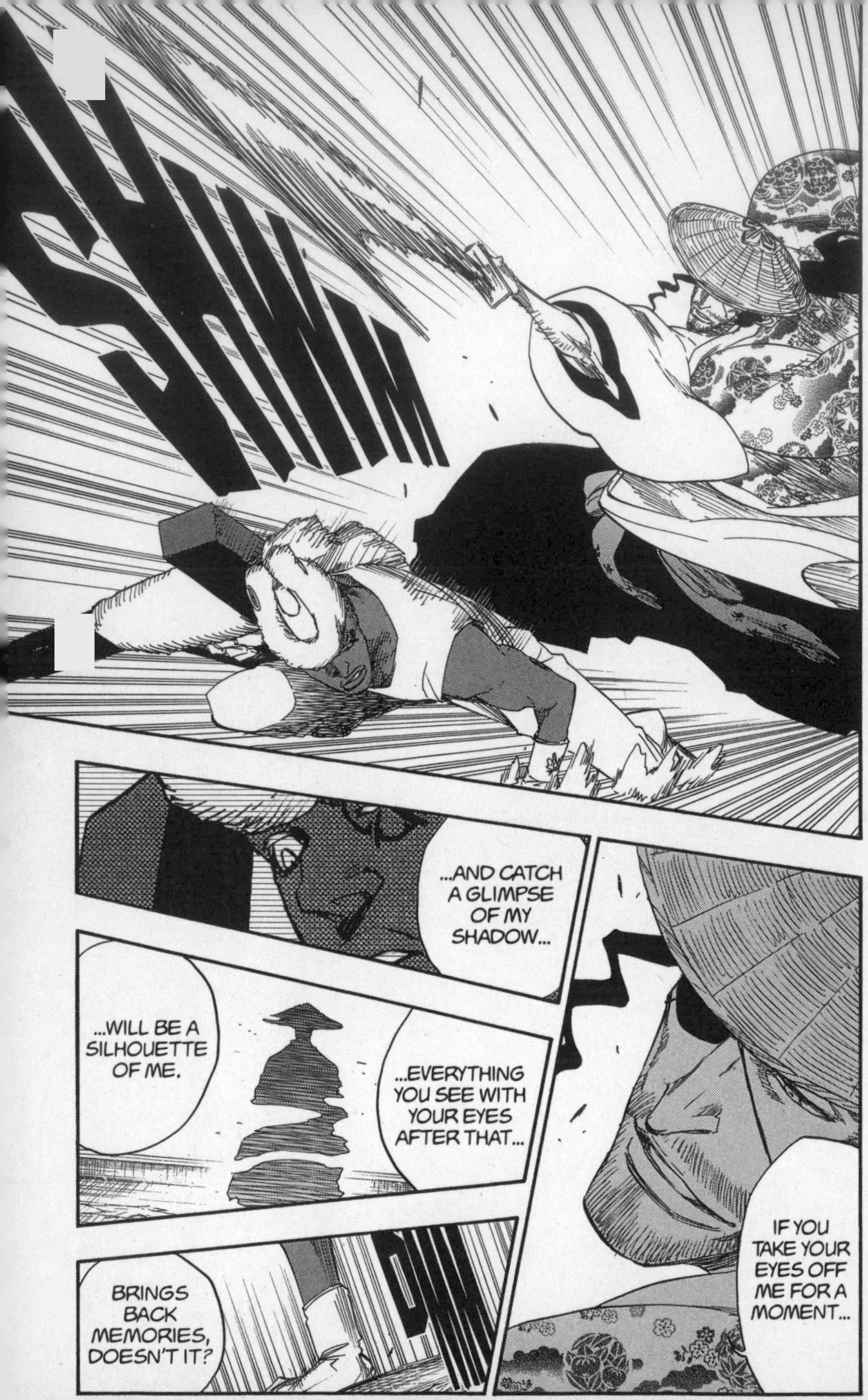
IF YOU TAKE YOUR EYES OFF ME FOR A MOMENT...
...AND CATCH A GLIMPSE OF MY SHADOW...
...EVERYTHING YOU SEE WITH YOUR EYES AFTER THAT...
...WILL BE A SILHOUETTE OF ME.
BRINGS BACK MEMORIES, DOESN'T IT?

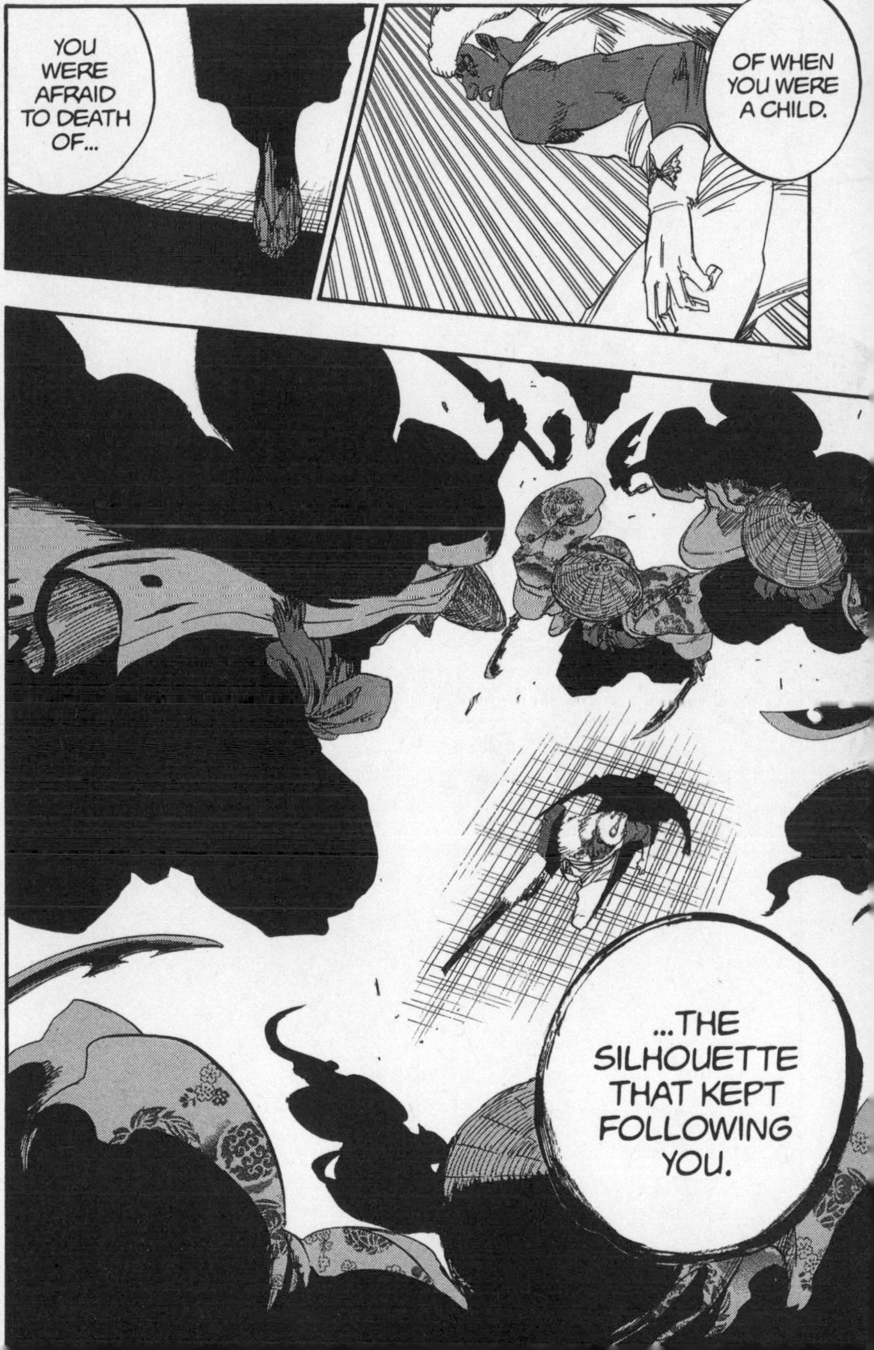
OF WHEN YOU WERE A CHILD.
YOU WERE AFRAID TO DEATH OF...
...THE SILHOUETTE THAT KEPT FOLLOWING YOU.

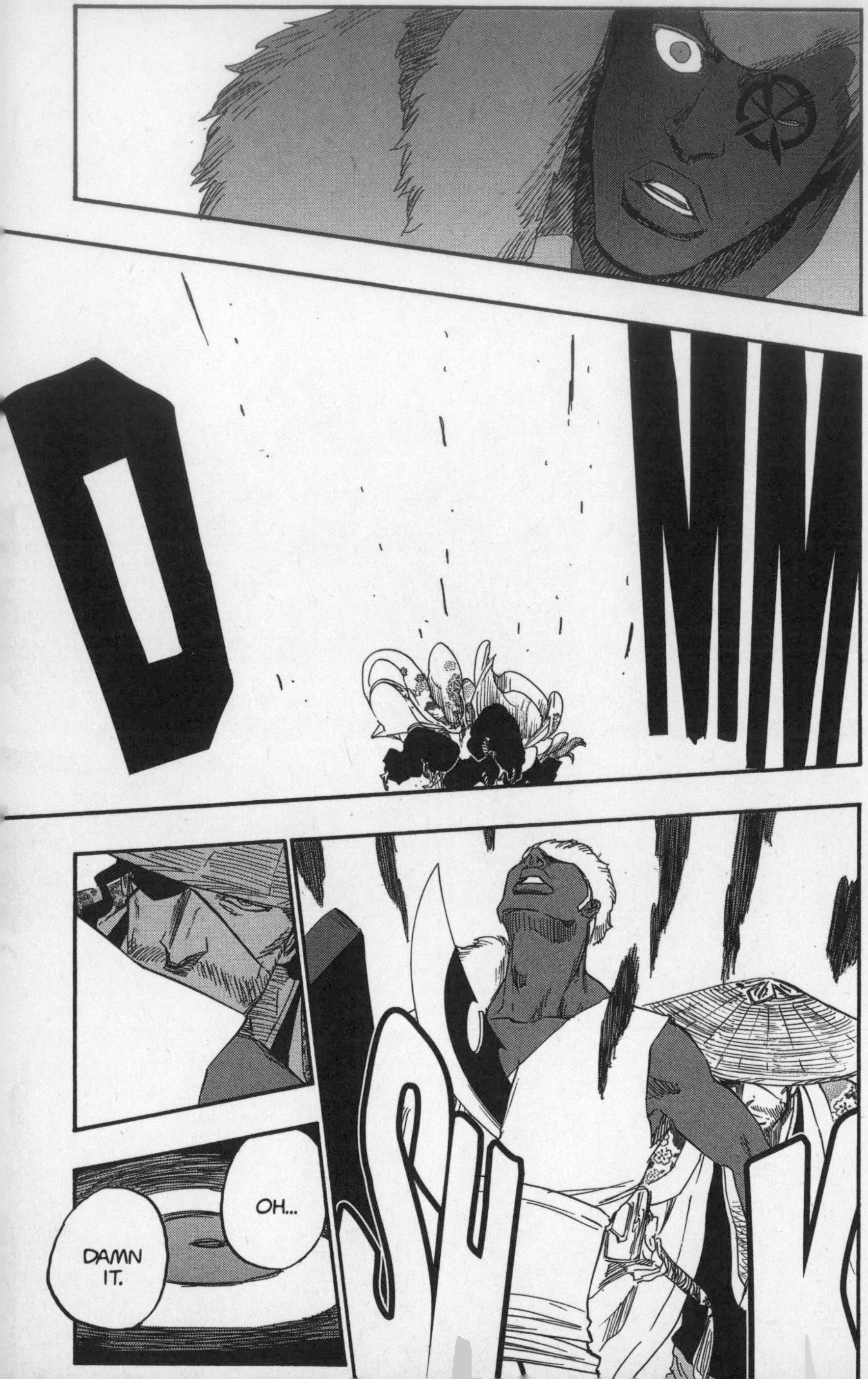
DOMM
OH...
DAMN IT.

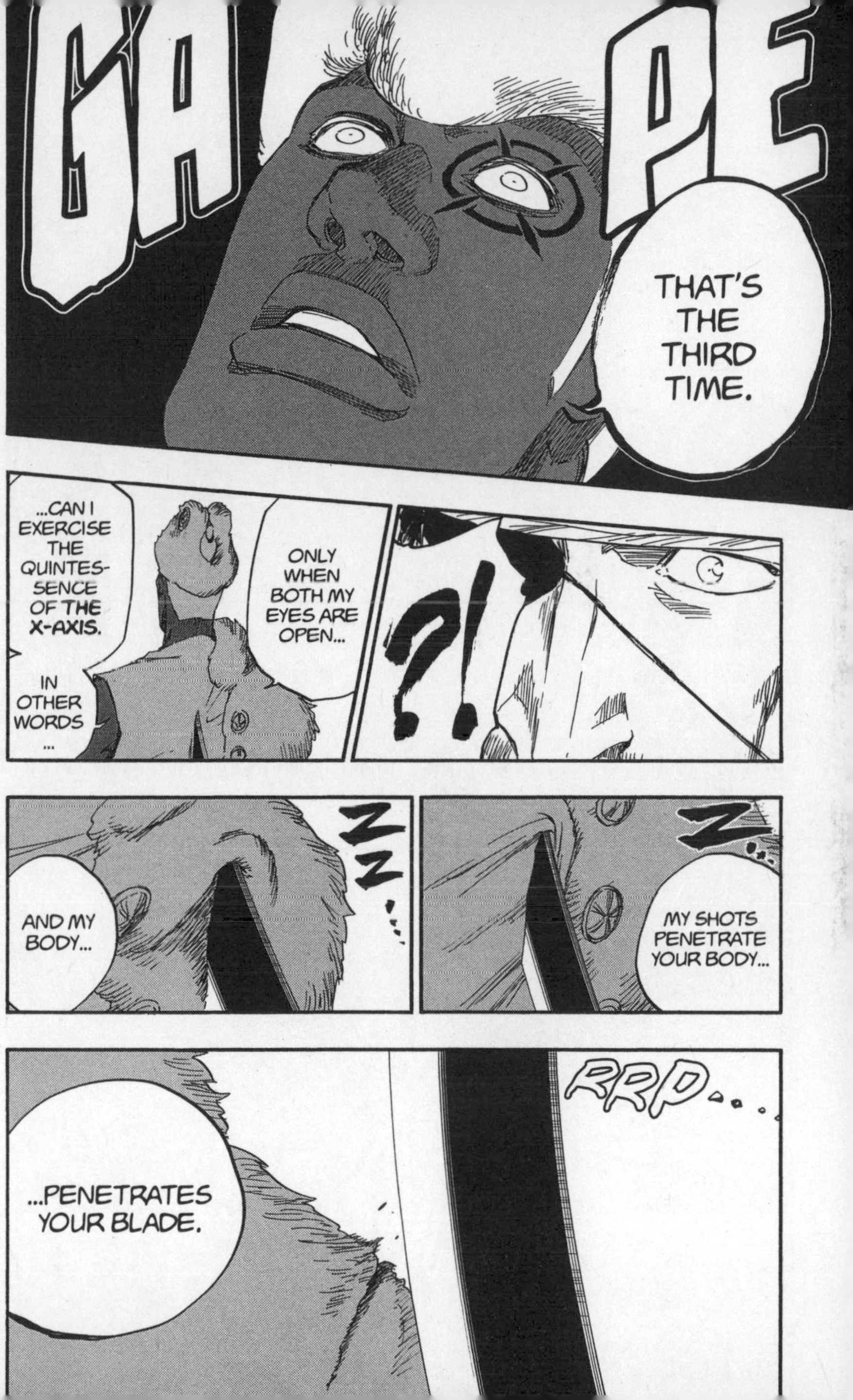
GA PE
THAT'S THE THIRD TIME.
?!
ONLY WHEN BOTH MY EYES ARE OPEN...
...CAN I EXERCISE THE QUINTESSENCE OF THE X-AXIS.
IN OTHER WORDS...
Z...
MY SHOTS PENETRATE YOUR BODY...
ZZ...
AND MY BODY...
RRP...
...PENETRATES YOUR BLADE.

READ THIS WAY

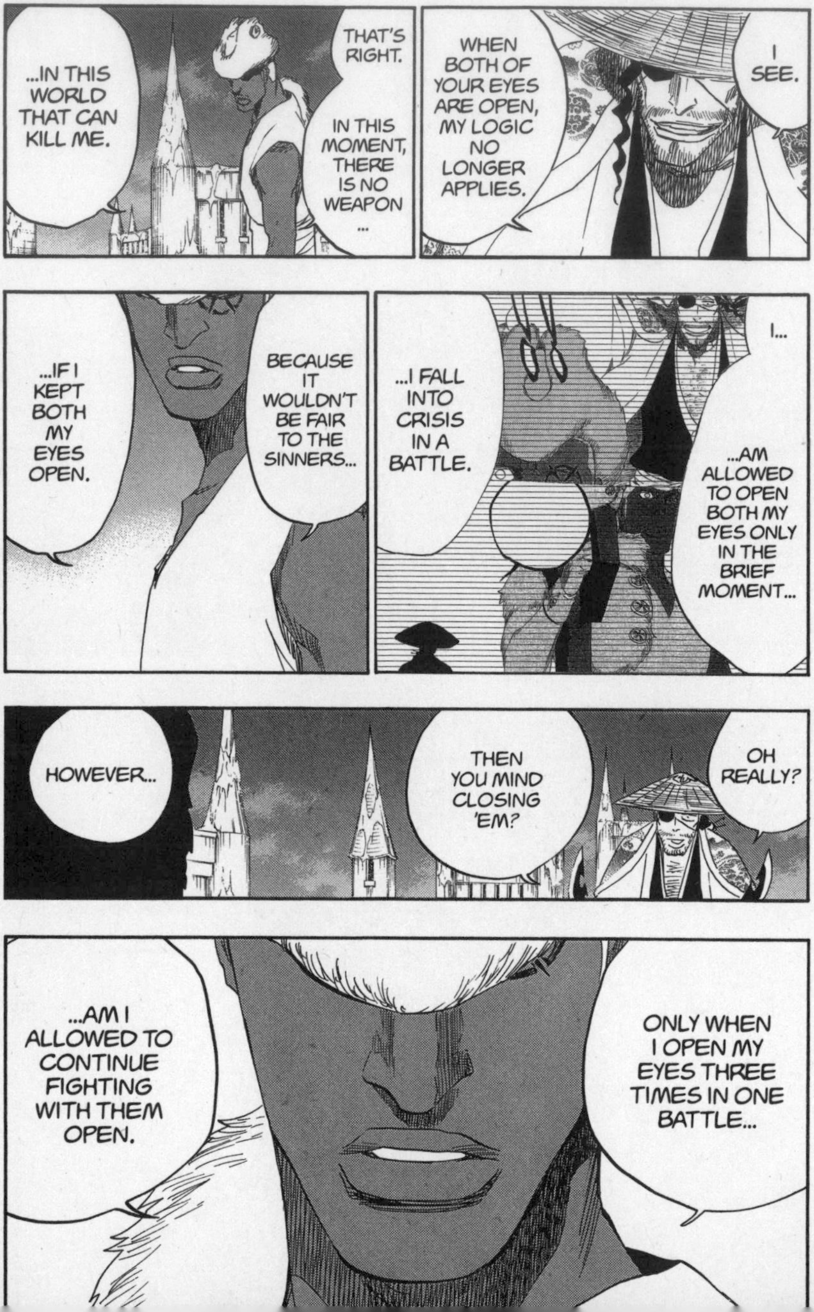
I SEE.
WHEN BOTH OF YOUR EYES ARE OPEN, MY LOGIC NO LONGER APPLIES.
THAT'S RIGHT.
IN THIS MOMENT, THERE IS NO WEAPON...
...IN THIS WORLD THAT CAN KILL ME.
I...
...AM ALLOWED TO OPEN BOTH MY EYES ONLY IN THE BRIEF MOMENT...
...I FALL INTO CRISIS IN A BATTLE.
BECAUSE IT WOULDN'T BE FAIR TO THE SINNERS...
...IF I KEPT BOTH MY EYES OPEN.
OH REALLY?
THEN YOU MIND CLOSING 'EM?
HOWEVER...
ONLY WHEN I OPEN MY EYES THREE TIMES IN ONE BATTLE...
...AM I ALLOWED TO CONTINUE FIGHTING WITH THEM OPEN.

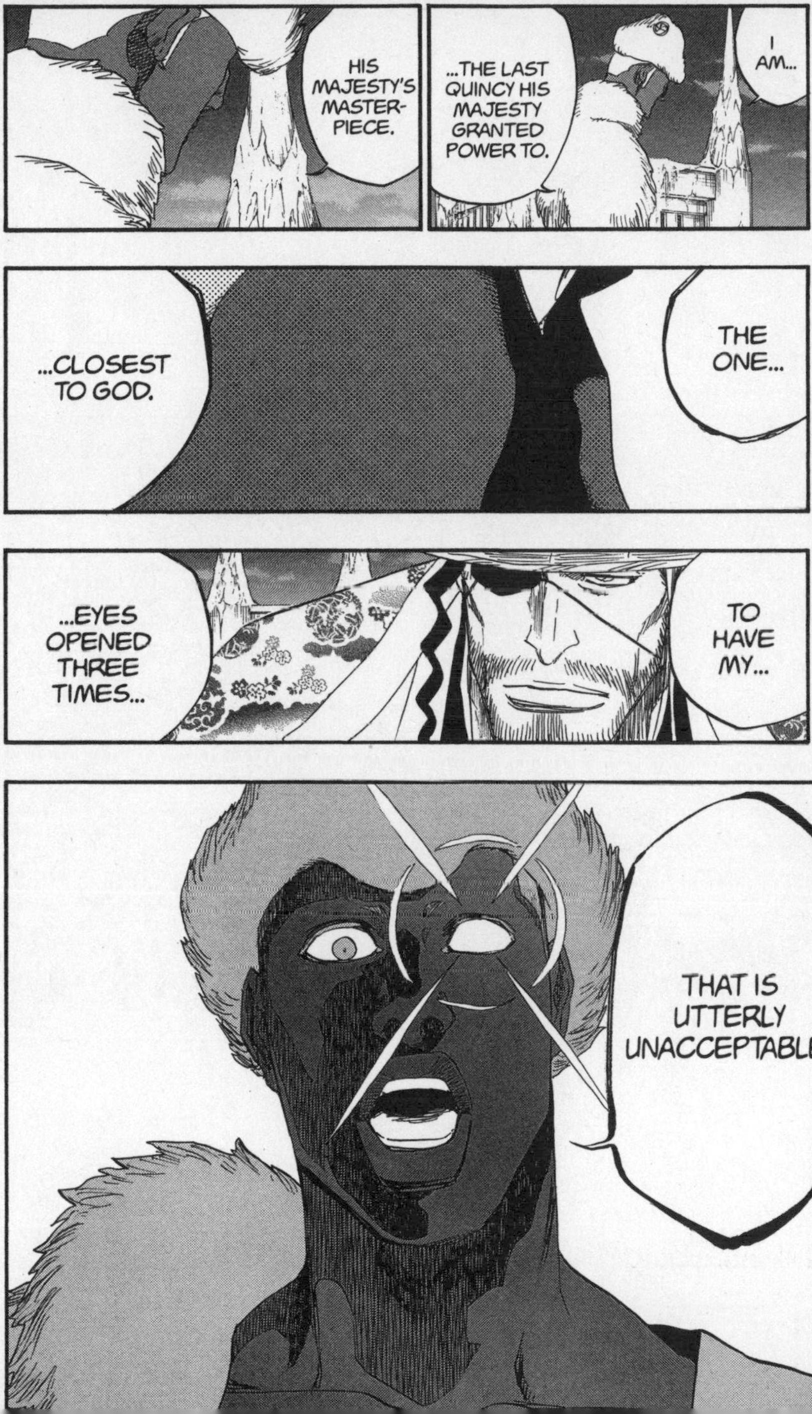
I AM...
...THE LAST QUINCY HIS MAJESTY GRANTED POWER TO.
HIS MAJESTY'S MASTER-PIECE.
THE ONE...
...CLOSEST TO GOD.
TO HAVE MY...
...EYES OPENED THREE TIMES...
THAT IS UTTERLY UNACCEPTABLE.

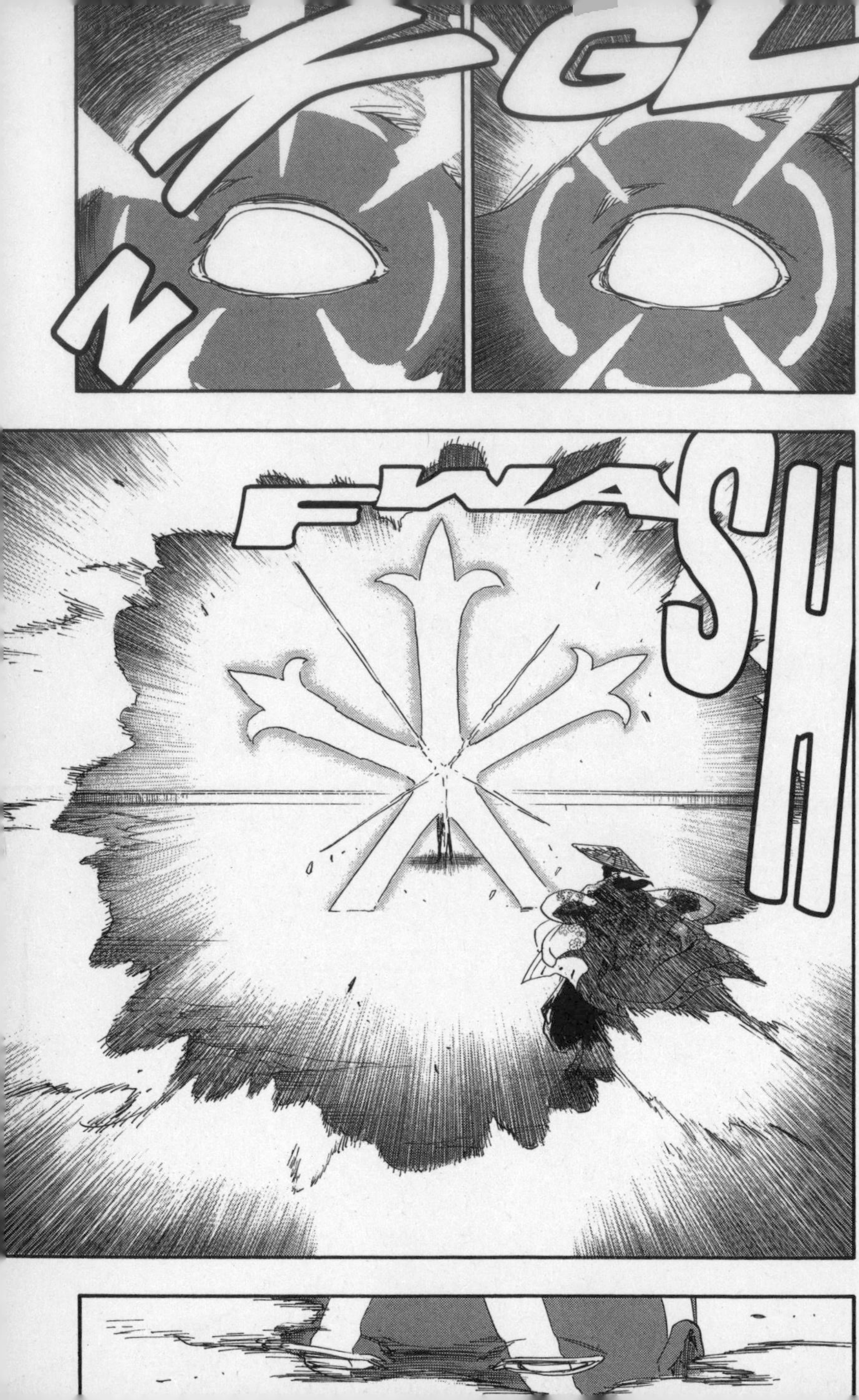
FWASH

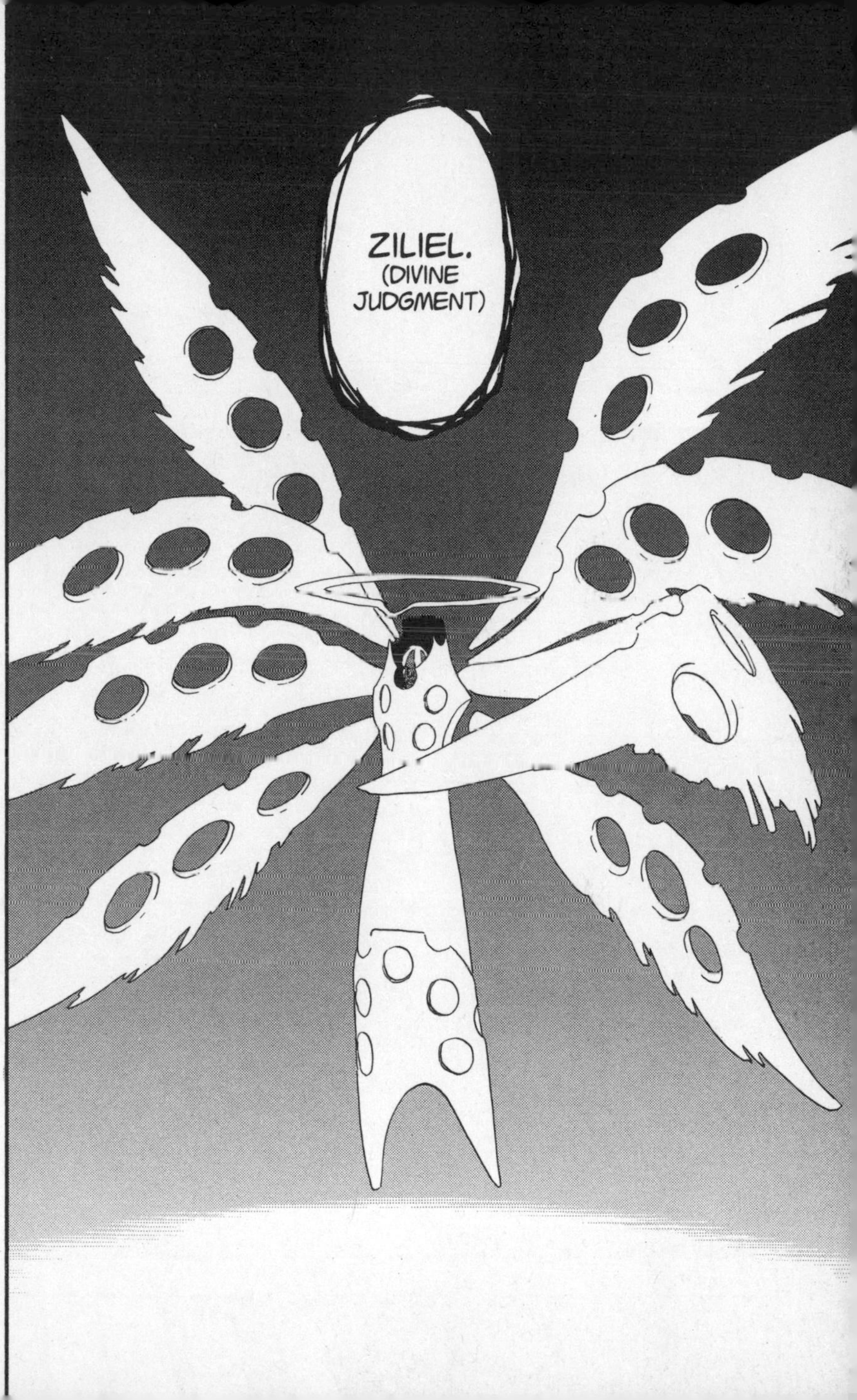
ZILIEL.
(DIVINE JUDGMENT)

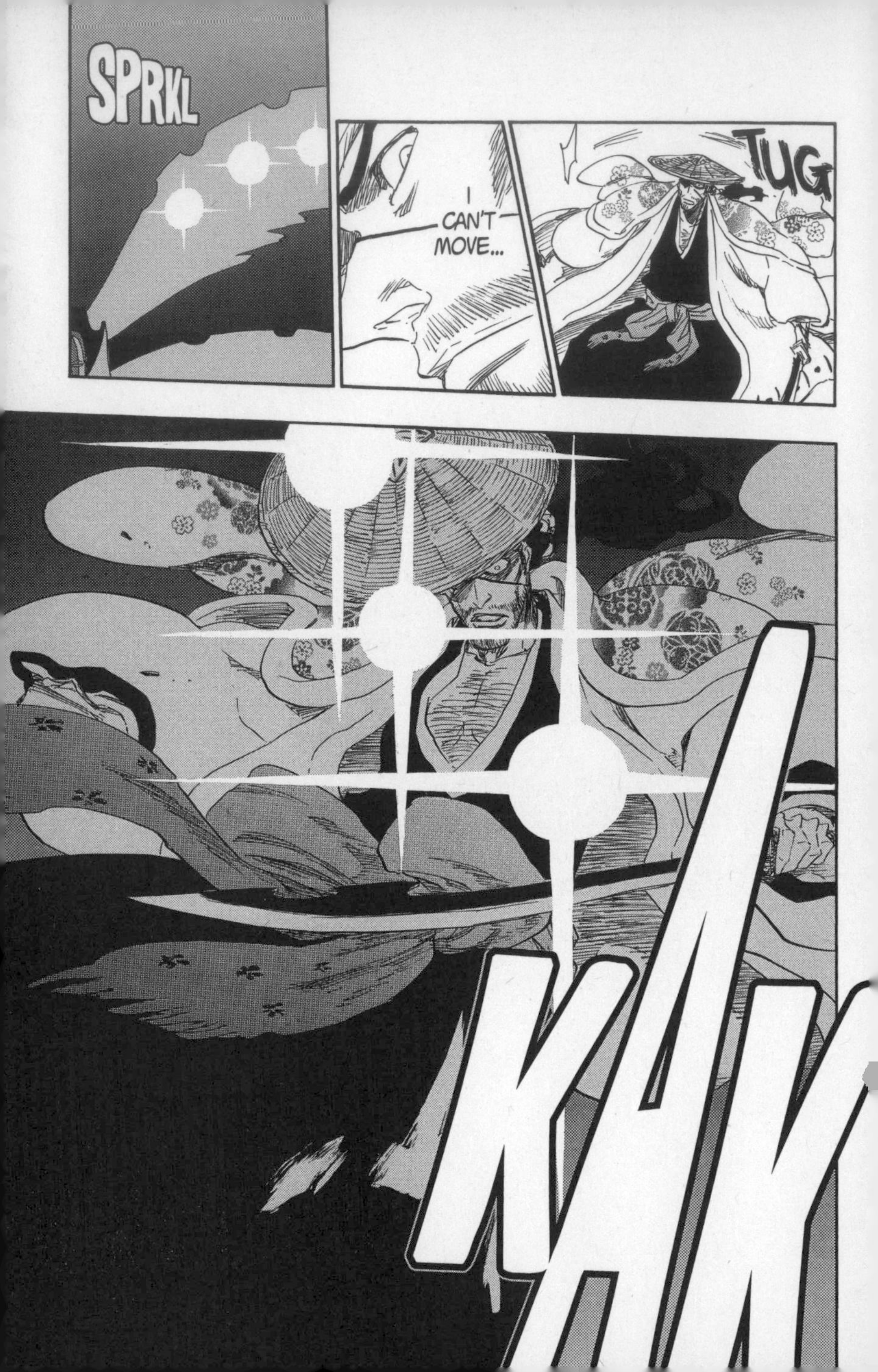
TUG
I CAN'T MOVE...
SPRKL
KAN

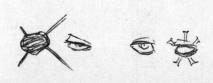

647. THE THEATRE SUICIDE

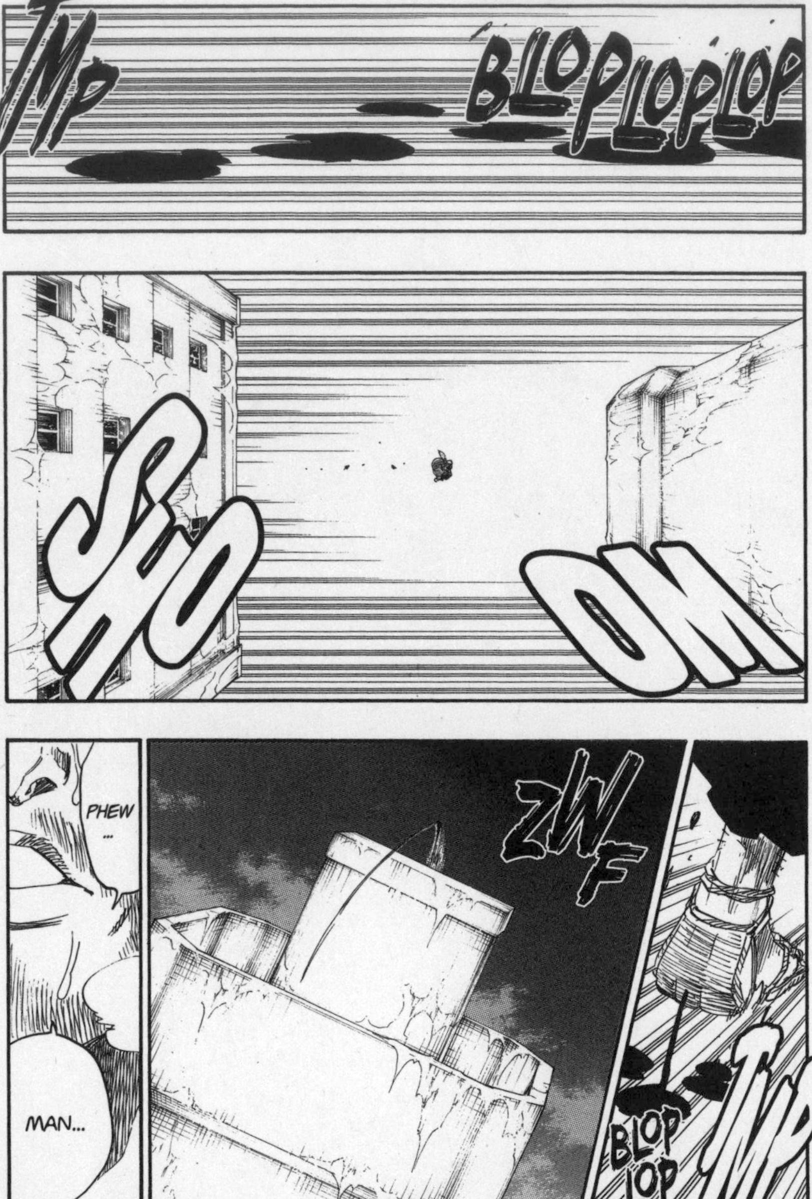
BLOPLOPLOP
TMP
SHOOM
TMP
BLOP LOP
ZWF
PHEW...
MAN...

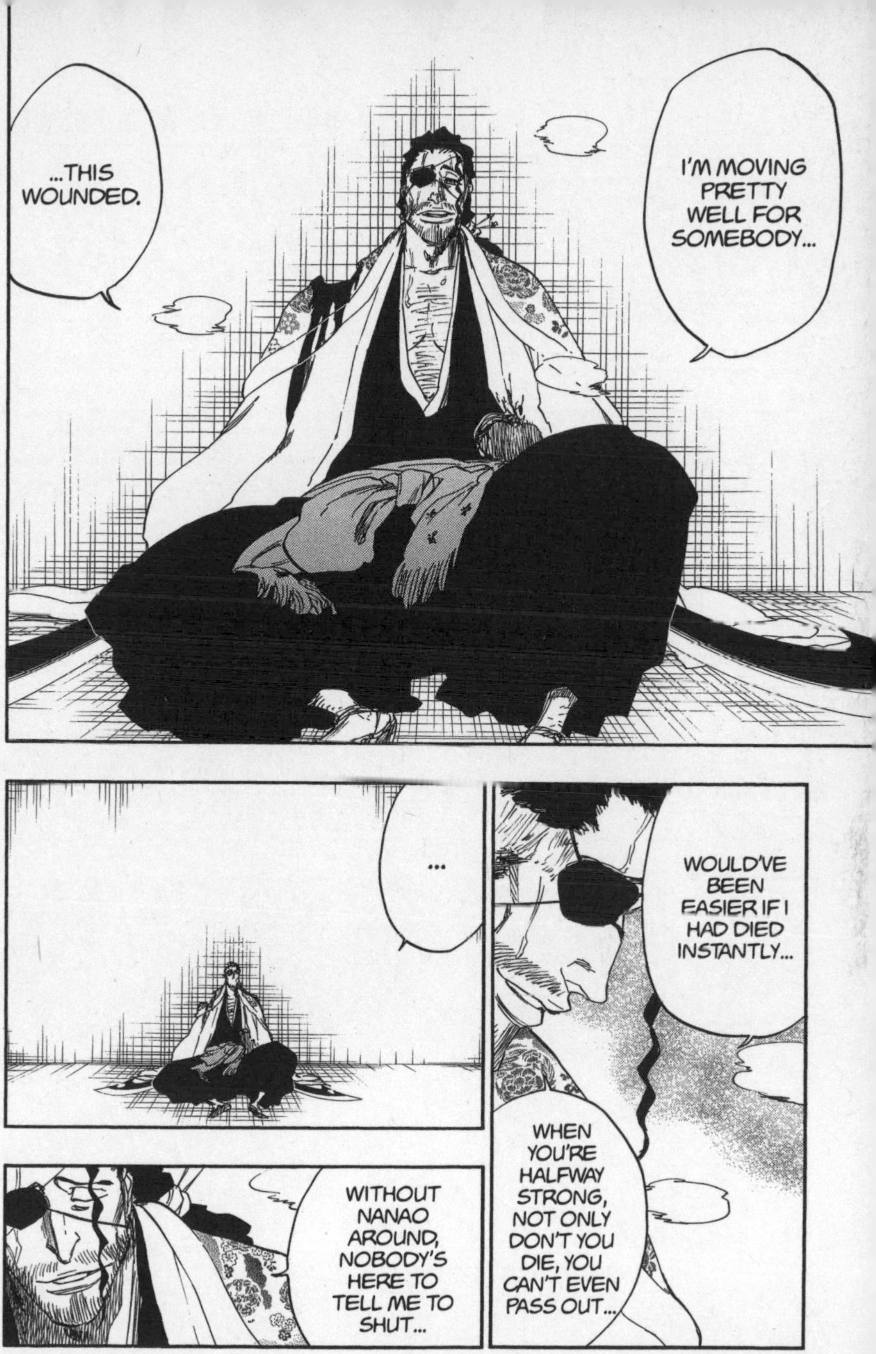
I'M MOVING PRETTY WELL FOR SOMEBODY...
...THIS WOUNDED.
WOULD'VE BEEN EASIER IF I HAD DIED INSTANTLY...
WHEN YOU'RE HALFWAY STRONG, NOT ONLY DON'T YOU DIE, YOU CAN'T EVEN PASS OUT...
...
WITHOUT NANAO AROUND, NOBODY'S HERE TO TELL ME TO SHUT...

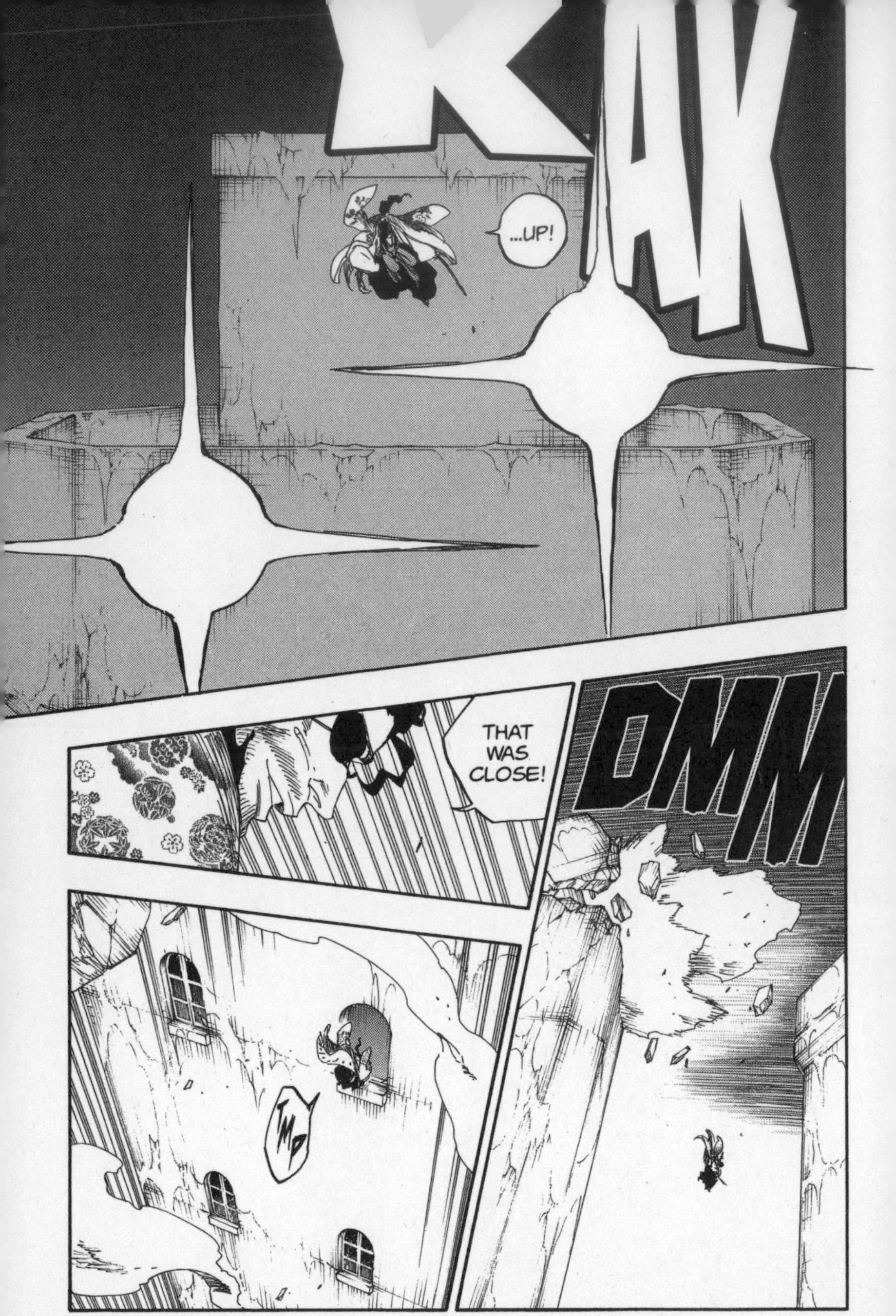
KAK
...UP!
DMM
THAT WAS CLOSE!
TMP

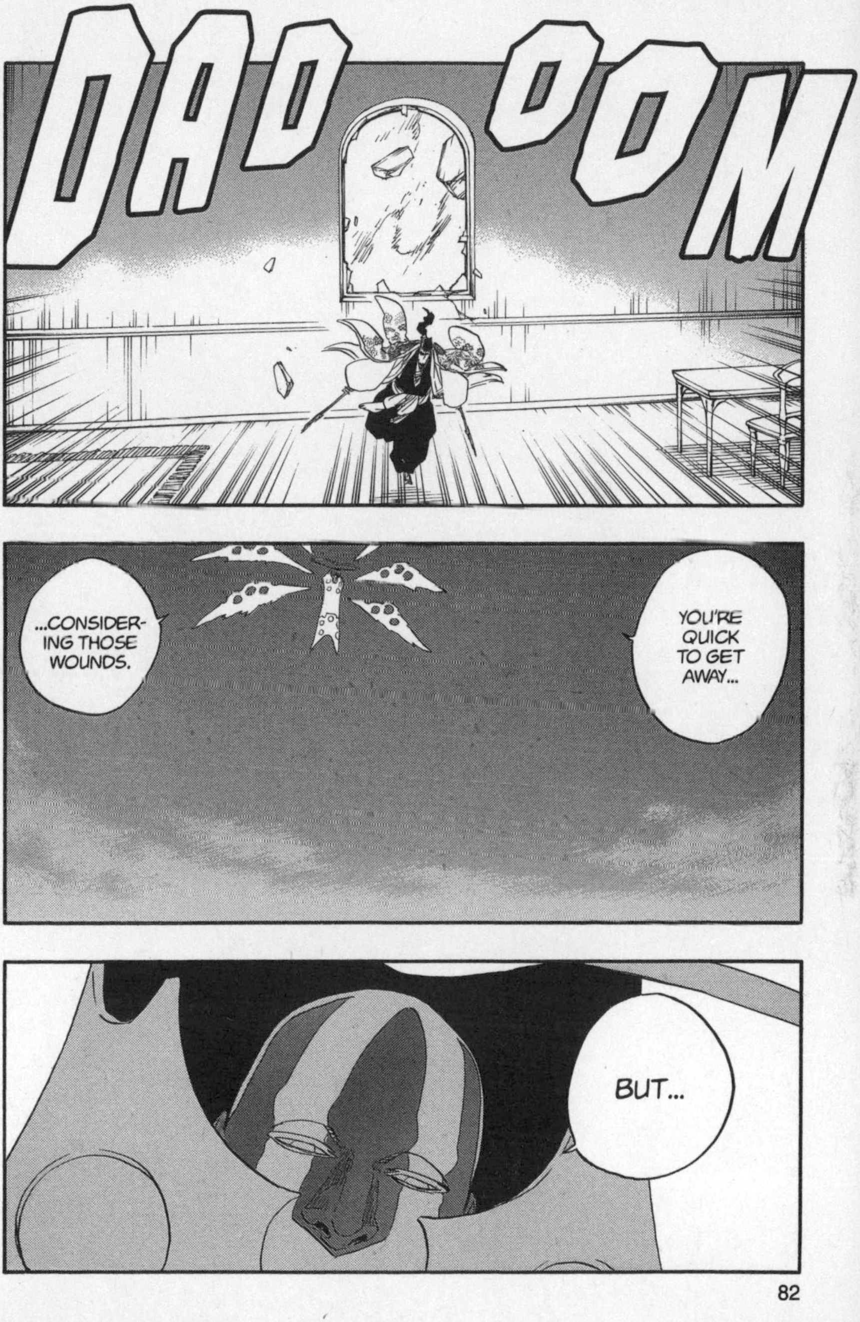
DADOOM
YOU'RE QUICK TO GET AWAY...
...CONSIDERING THOSE WOUNDS.
BUT...

READ THIS WAY

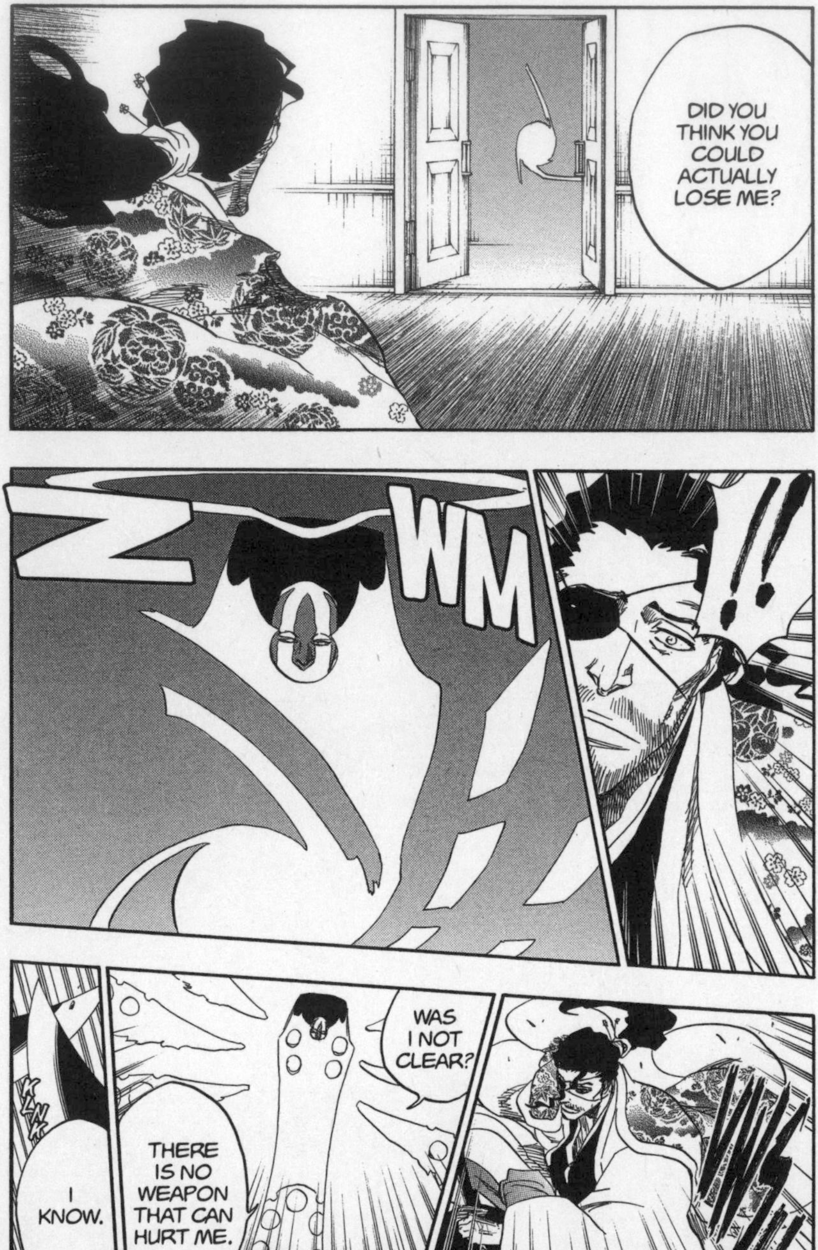

DID YOU THINK YOU COULD ACTUALLY LOSE ME?
!!
ZWM
WAS I NOT CLEAR?
THERE IS NO WEAPON THAT CAN HURT ME.
I KNOW.

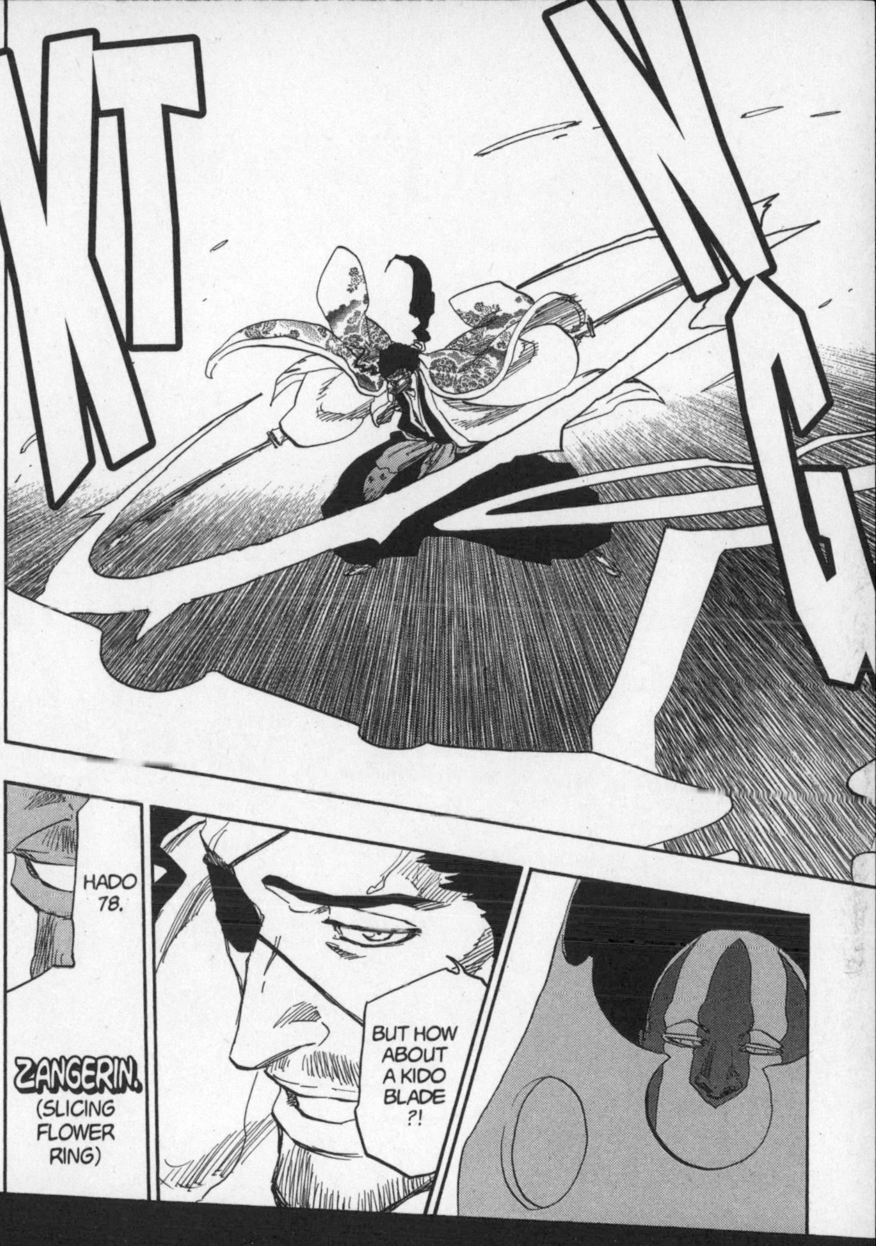
KTNG
BUT HOW ABOUT A KIDO BLADE ?!
HADO 78.
ZANGERIN.
(SLICING FLOWER RING)

BLEACH 647.

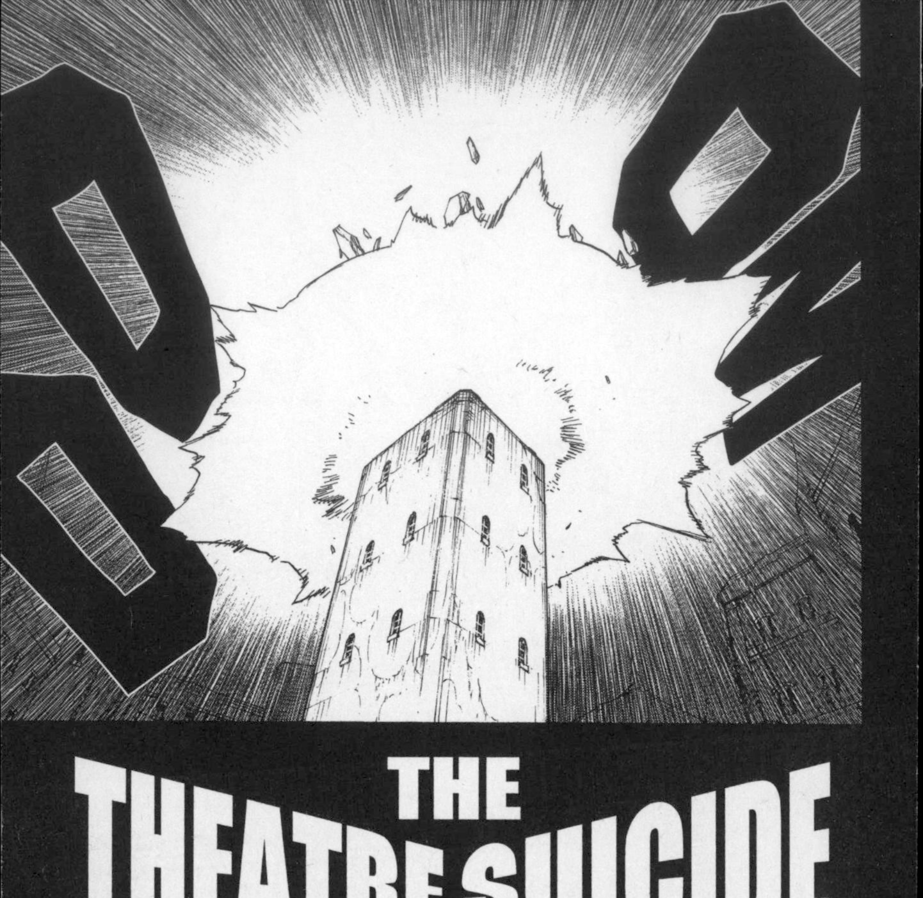

THE THEATRE SUICIDE

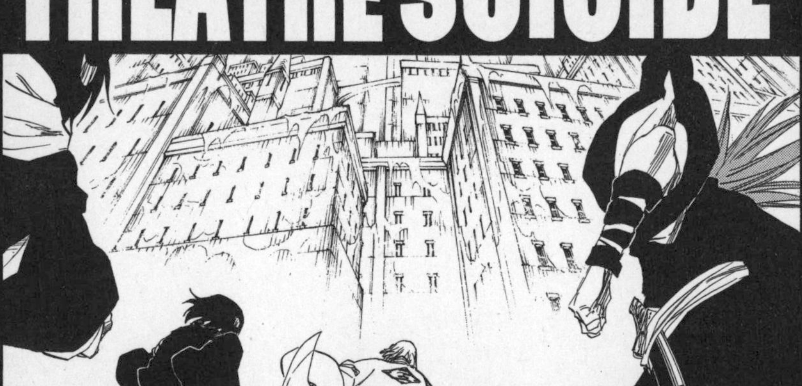

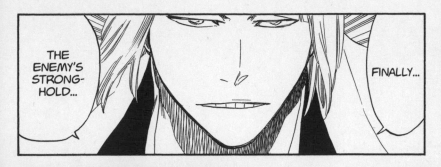

THE ENEMY'S STRONG-HOLD...

FINALLY...

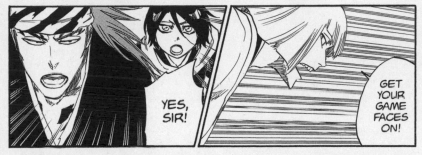

YES, SIR!

GET YOUR GAME FACES ON!

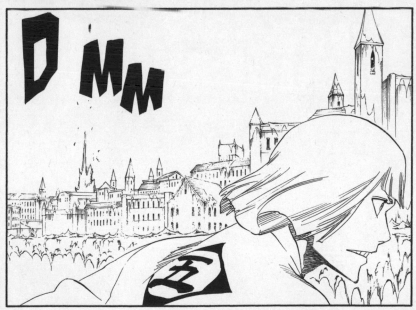

D MM

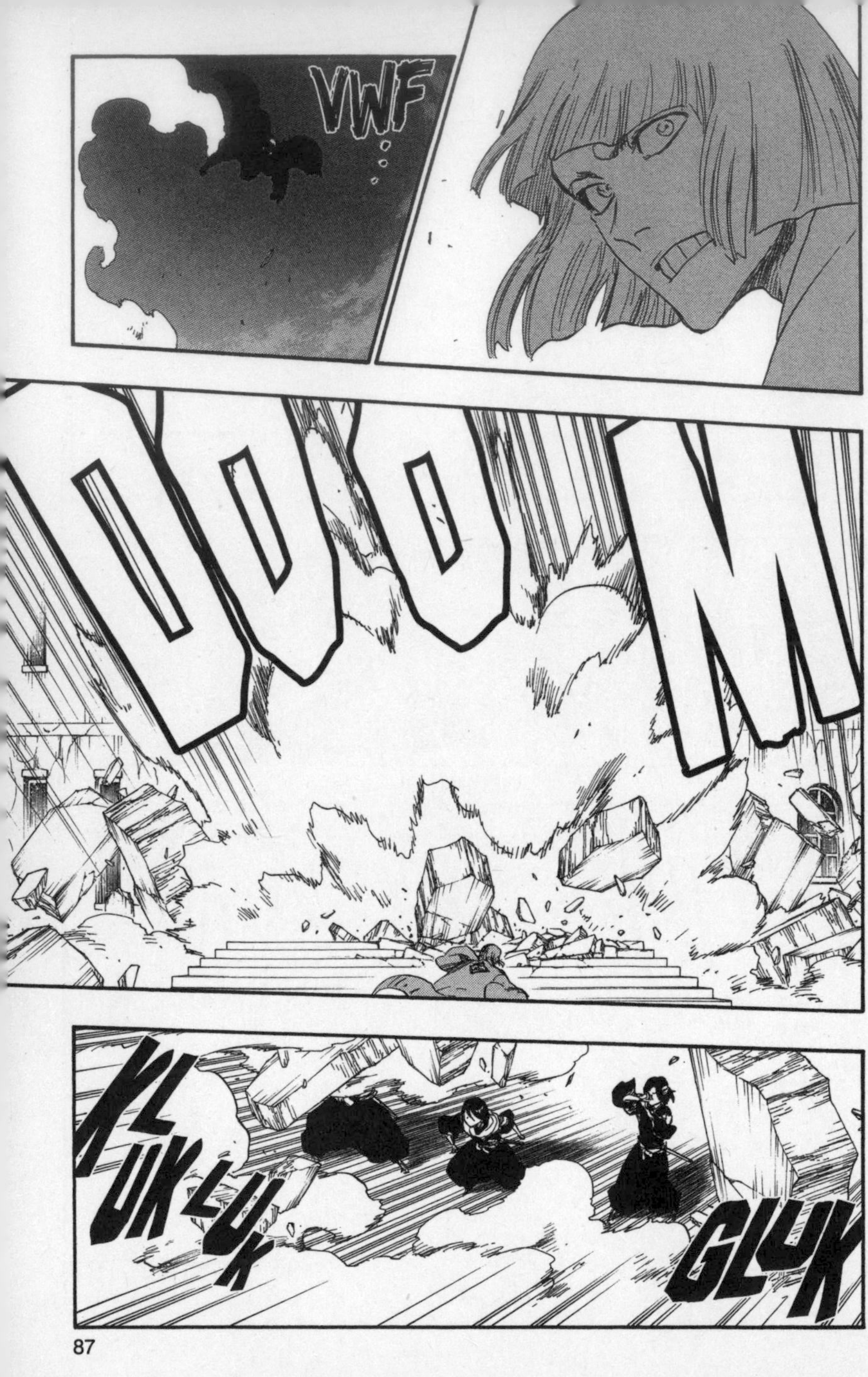
VWF
GLUK
KLUK KLUK

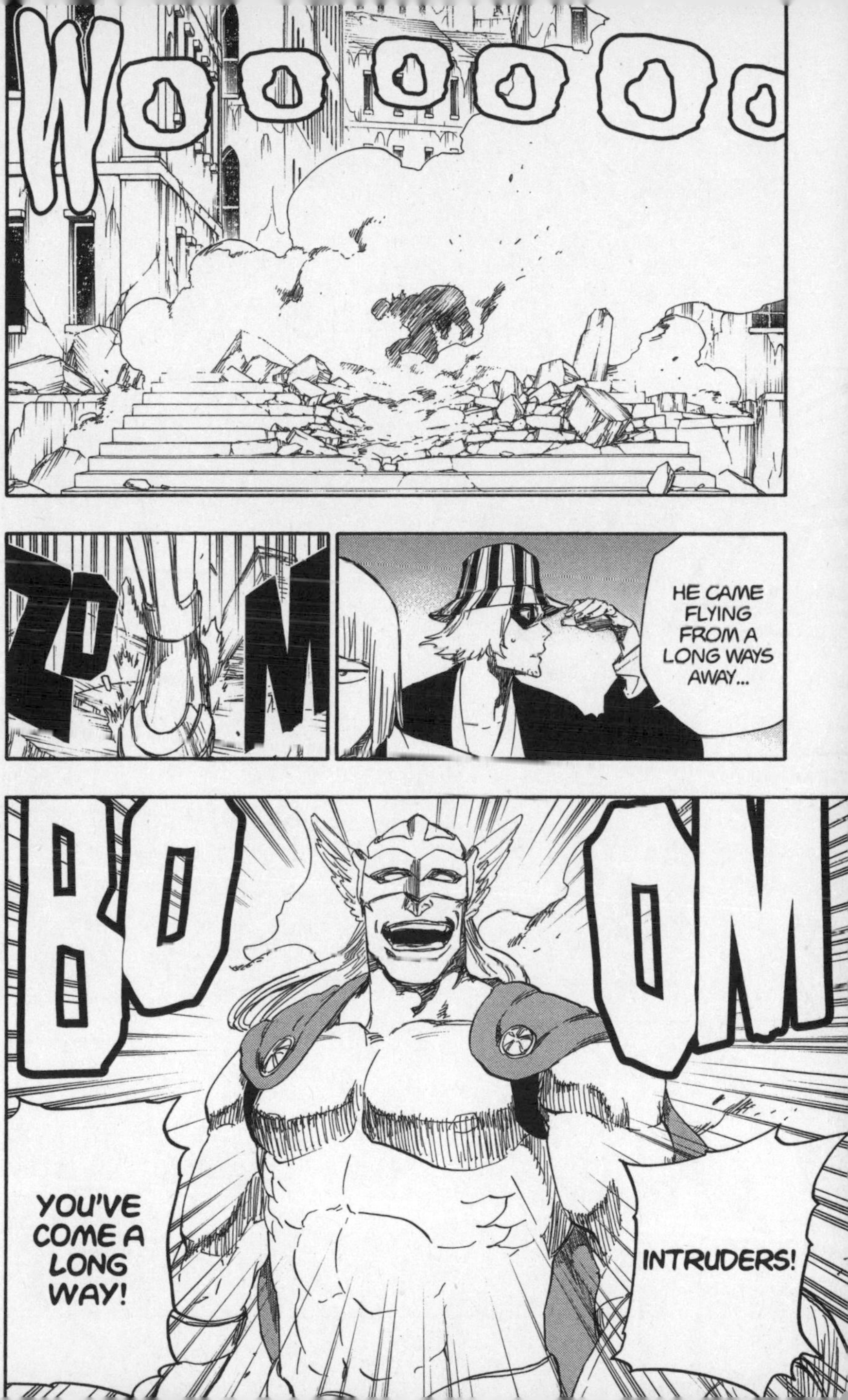
WOOOOOO
HE CAME FLYING FROM A LONG WAYS AWAY...
BOOM
YOU'VE COME A LONG WAY!
INTRUDERS!

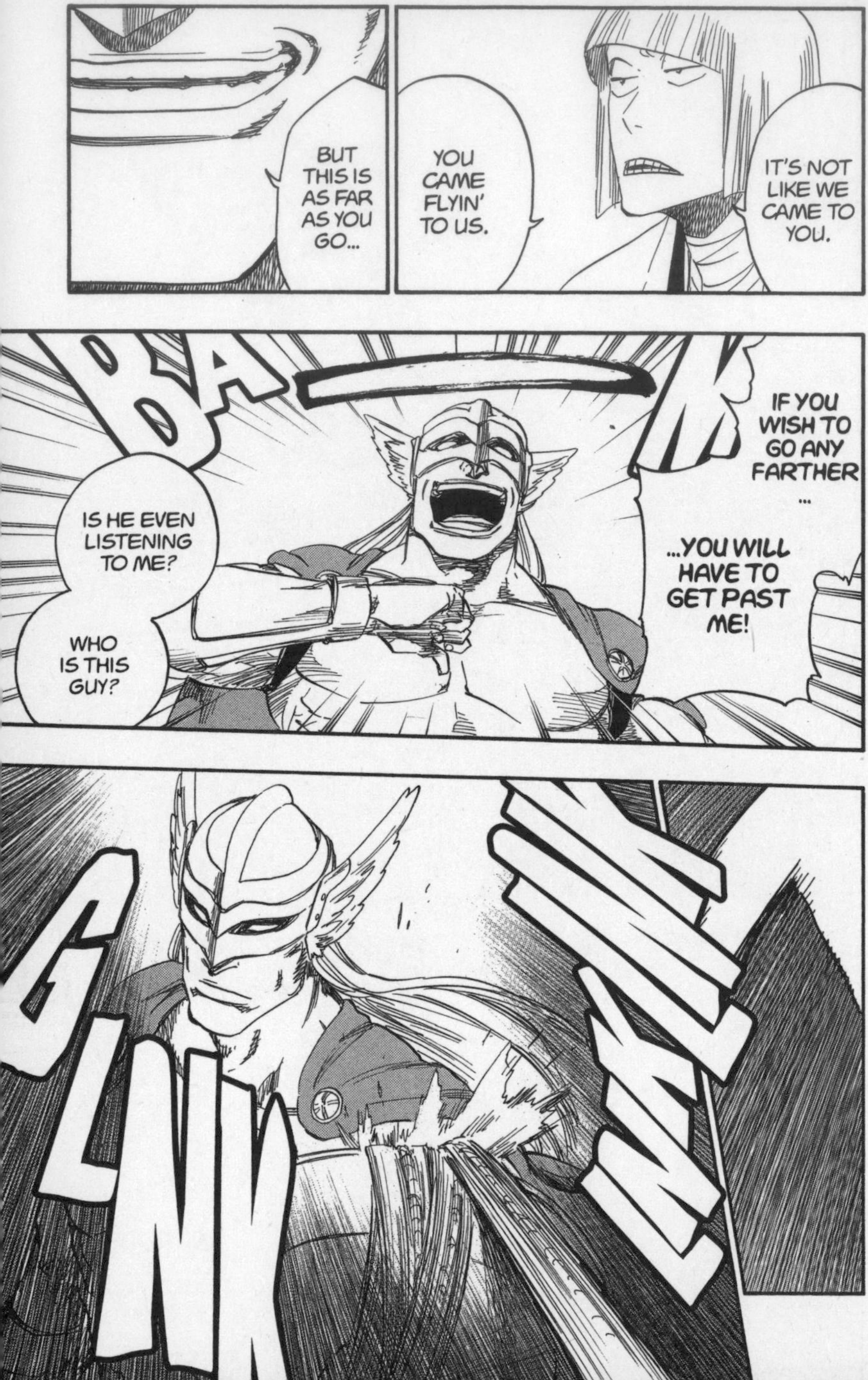
IT'S NOT LIKE WE CAME TO YOU.
YOU CAME FLYIN' TO US.
BUT THIS IS AS FAR AS YOU GO...
BA—K
IF YOU WISH TO GO ANY FARTHER ...
...YOU WILL HAVE TO GET PAST ME!
IS HE EVEN LISTENING TO ME?
WHO IS THIS GUY?

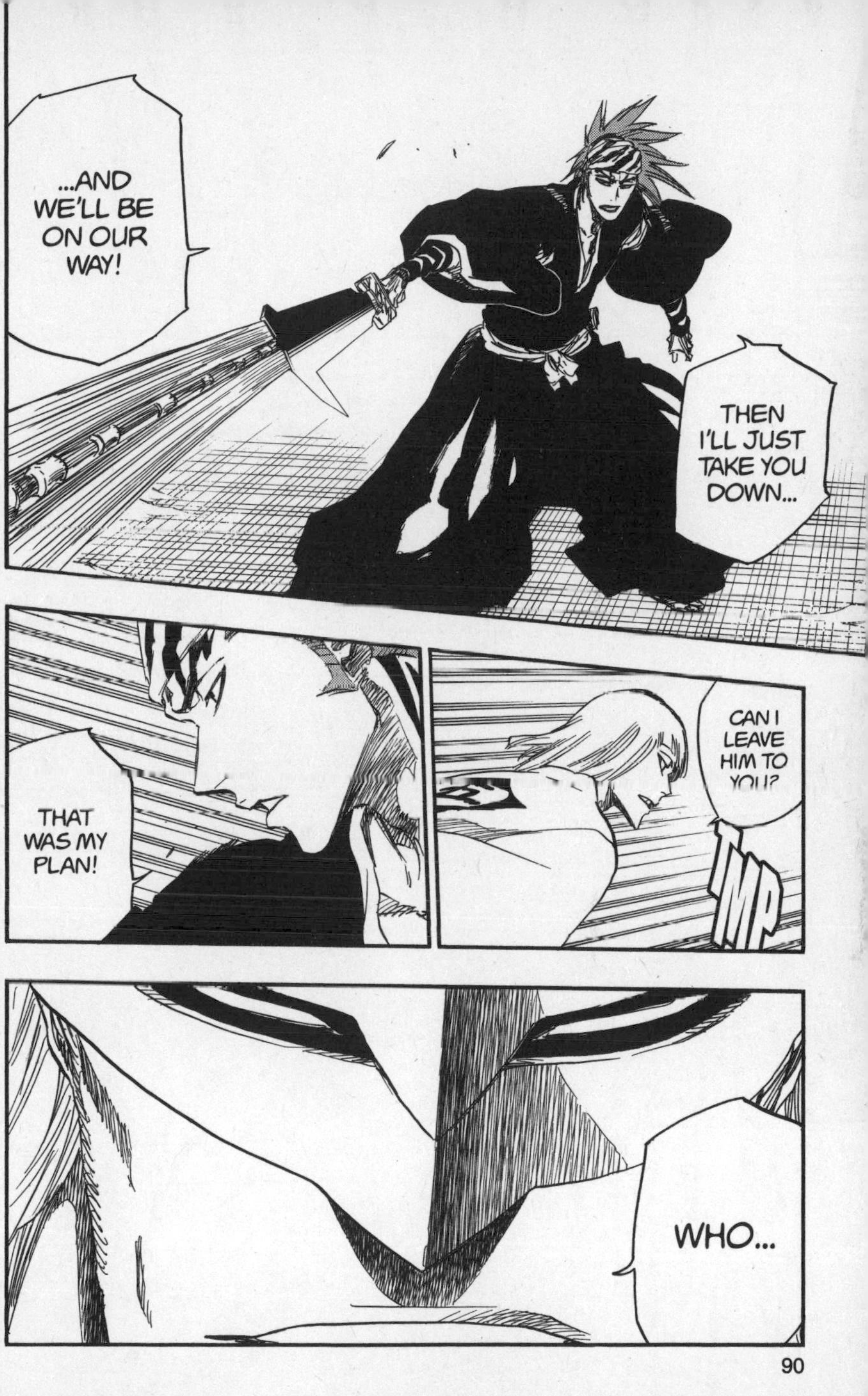
THEN I'LL JUST TAKE YOU DOWN...
...AND WE'LL BE ON OUR WAY!
CAN I LEAVE HIM TO YOU?
TMP
THAT WAS MY PLAN!
WHO...

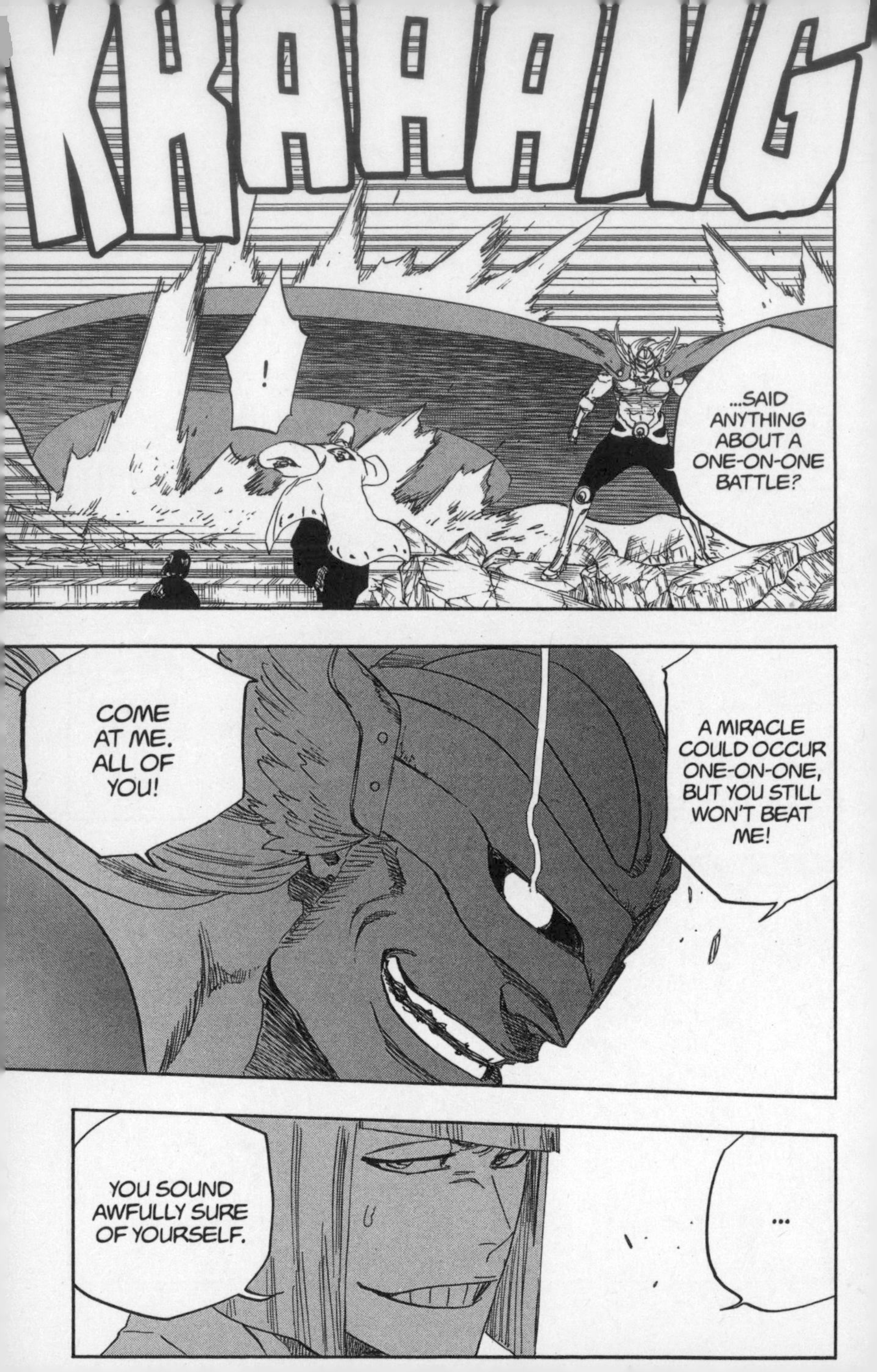
KRAAANG
...SAID ANYTHING ABOUT A ONE-ON-ONE BATTLE?
!
A MIRACLE COULD OCCUR ONE-ON-ONE, BUT YOU STILL WON'T BEAT ME!
COME AT ME. ALL OF YOU!
...
YOU SOUND AWFULLY SURE OF YOURSELF.

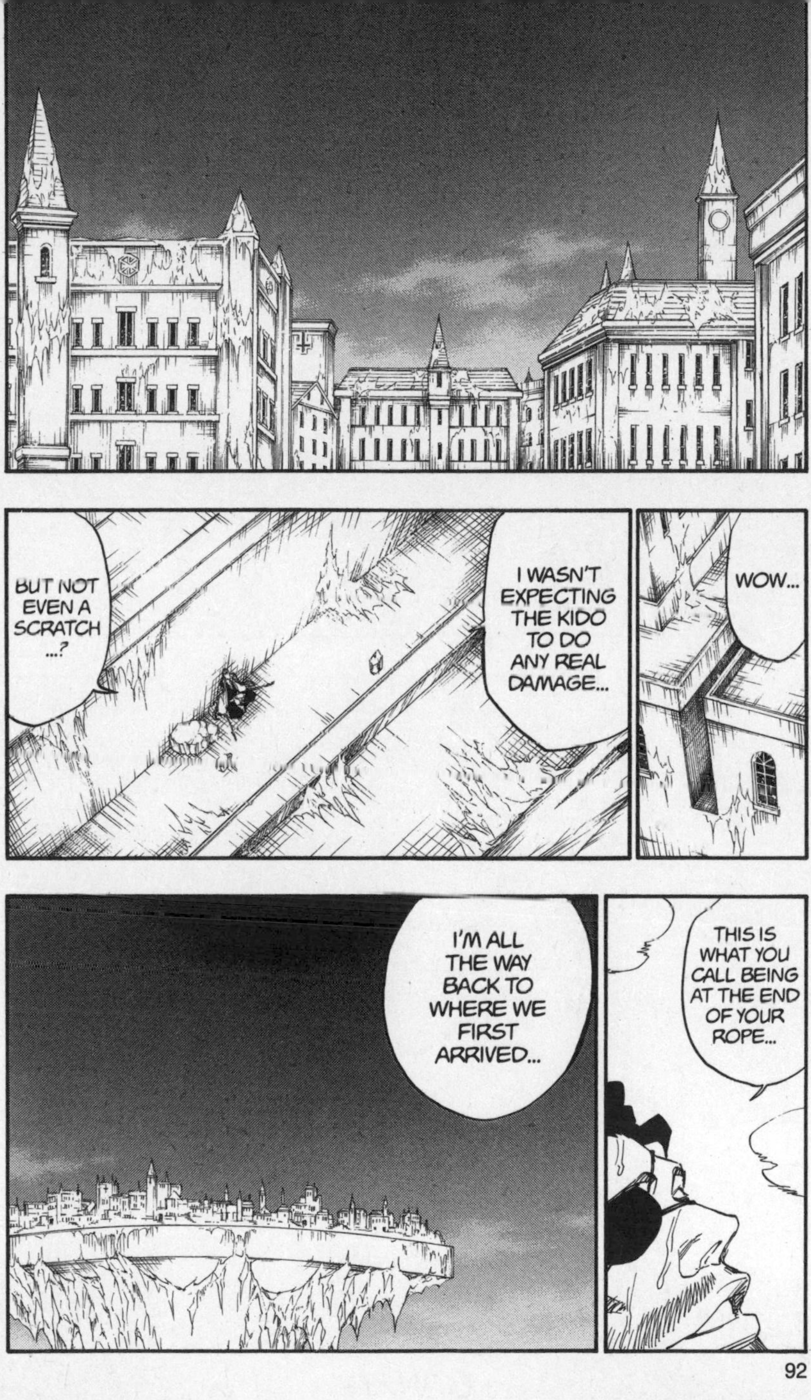
WOW...
I WASN'T EXPECTING THE KIDO TO DO ANY REAL DAMAGE...
BUT NOT EVEN A SCRATCH ...?
THIS IS WHAT YOU CALL BEING AT THE END OF YOUR ROPE...
I'M ALL THE WAY BACK TO WHERE WE FIRST ARRIVED...

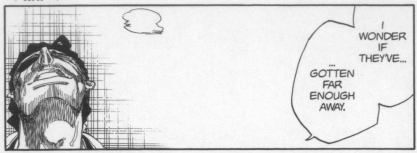

I WONDER IF THEY'VE...

...GOTTEN FAR ENOUGH AWAY.

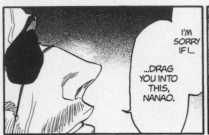

I'M SORRY IF I...

...DRAG YOU INTO THIS, NANAO.

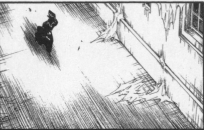

GGHK...

TIME TO MAKE THE NEXT MOVE FROM THE END OF THE ROPE.

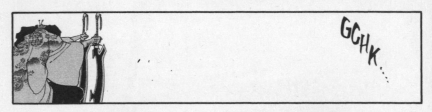

WELL...

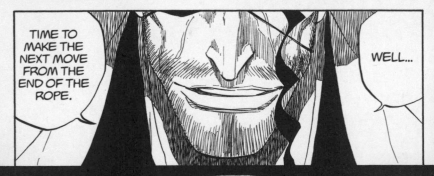

BANKAI.

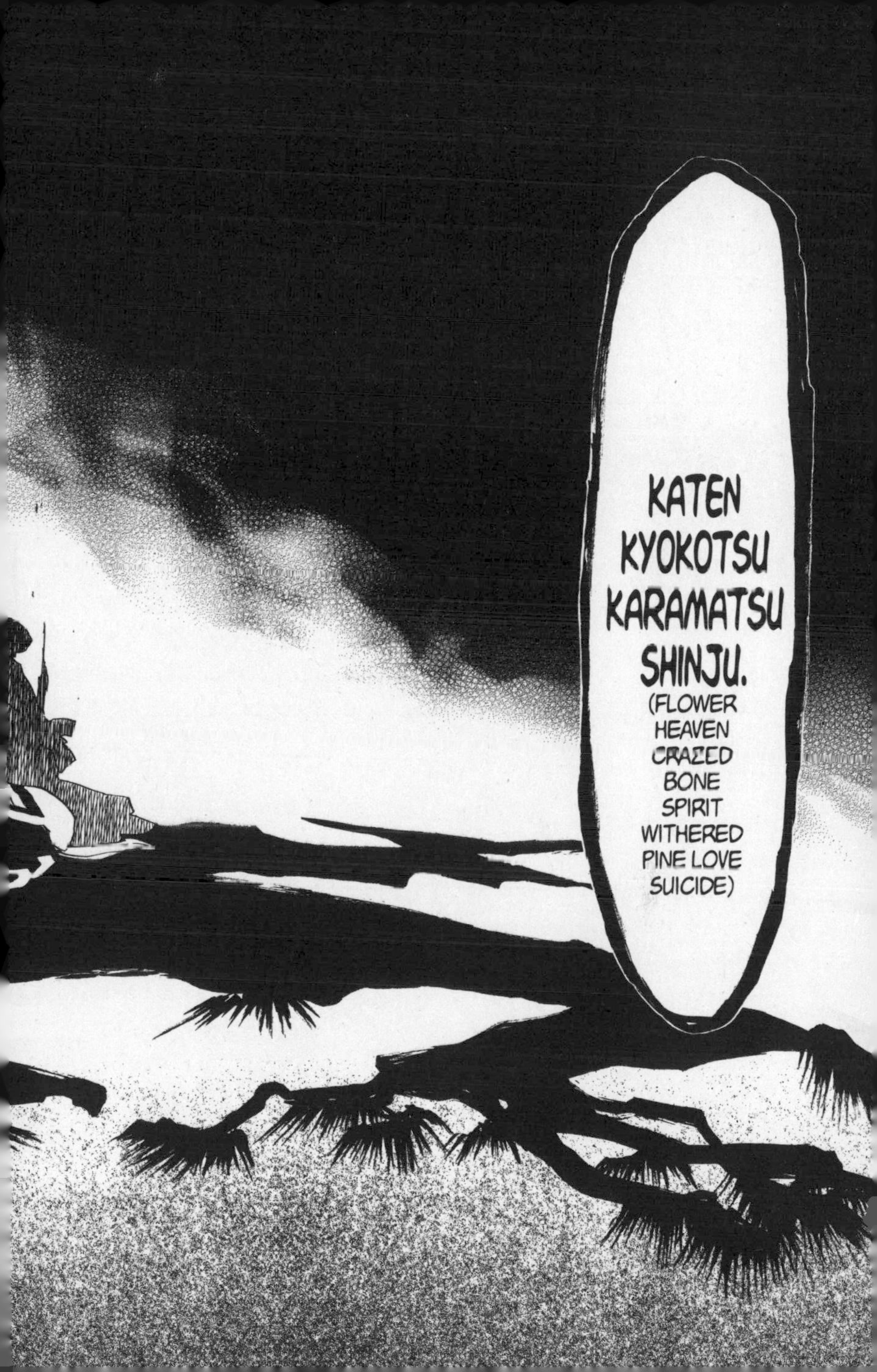
KATEN KYOKOTSU KARAMATSU SHINJU.
(FLOWER HEAVEN CRAZED BONE SPIRIT WITHERED PINE LOVE SUICIDE)

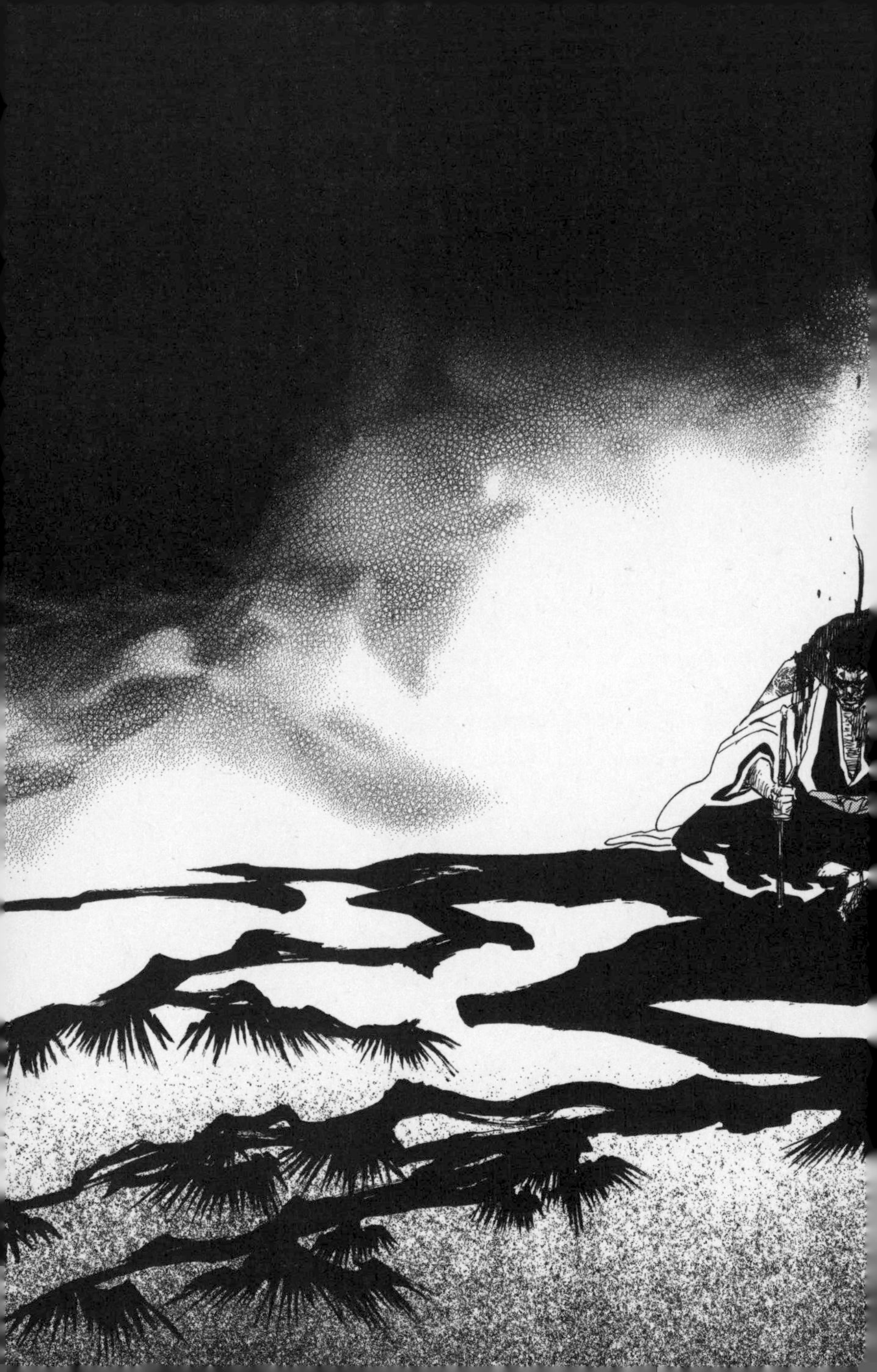

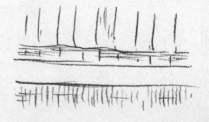

648. THE THEATRE SUICIDE SCENE 2

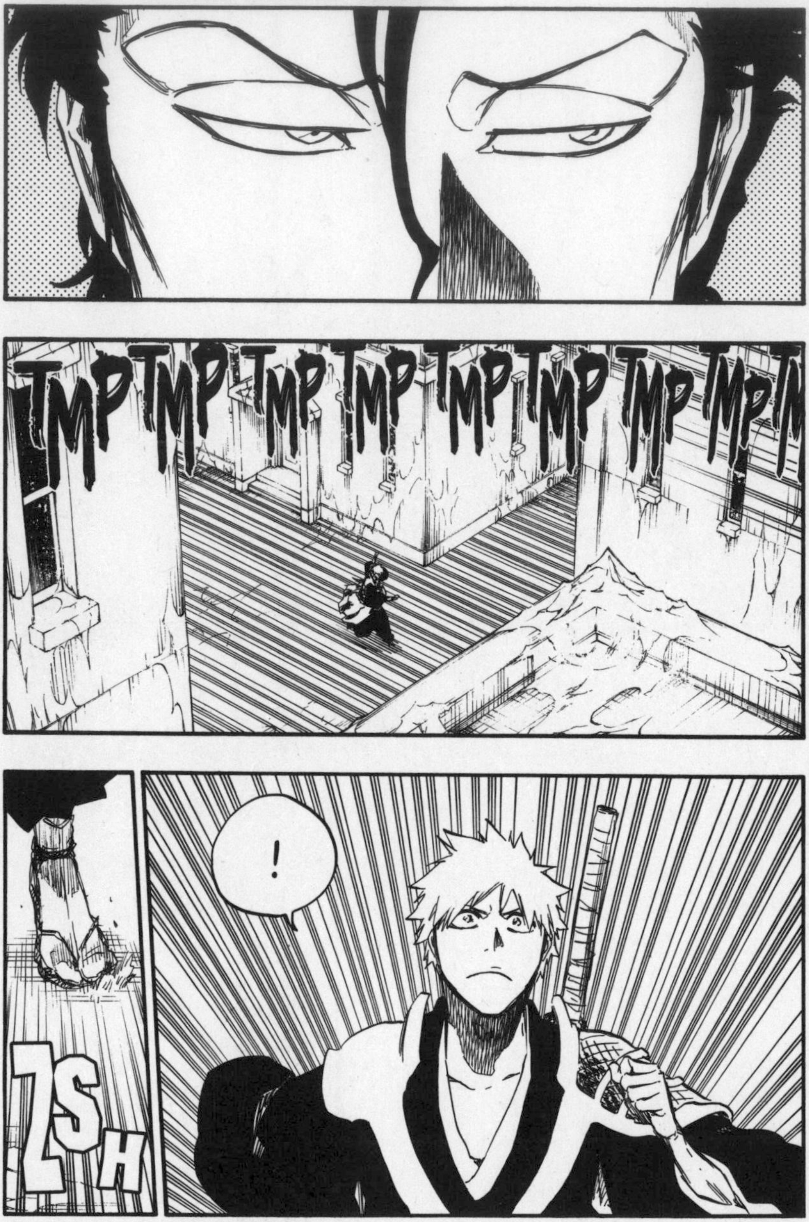
TMP TMP TMP TMP TMP TMP TMP TMP
!
ZSH

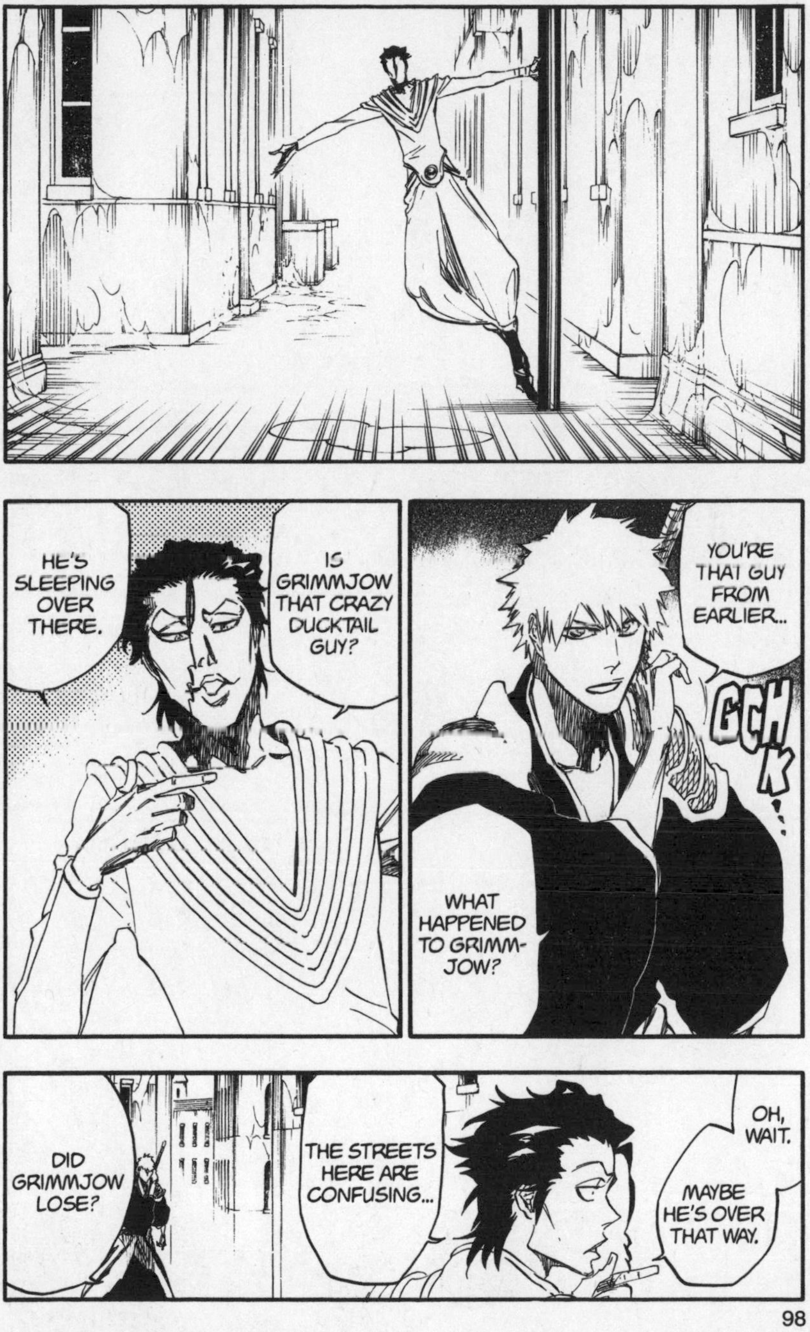
YOU'RE THAT GUY FROM EARLIER...
GCHK
WHAT HAPPENED TO GRIMMJOW?
IS GRIMMJOW THAT CRAZY DUCKTAIL GUY?
HE'S SLEEPING OVER THERE.
OH, WAIT.
MAYBE HE'S OVER THAT WAY.
THE STREETS HERE ARE CONFUSING...
DID GRIMMJOW LOSE?

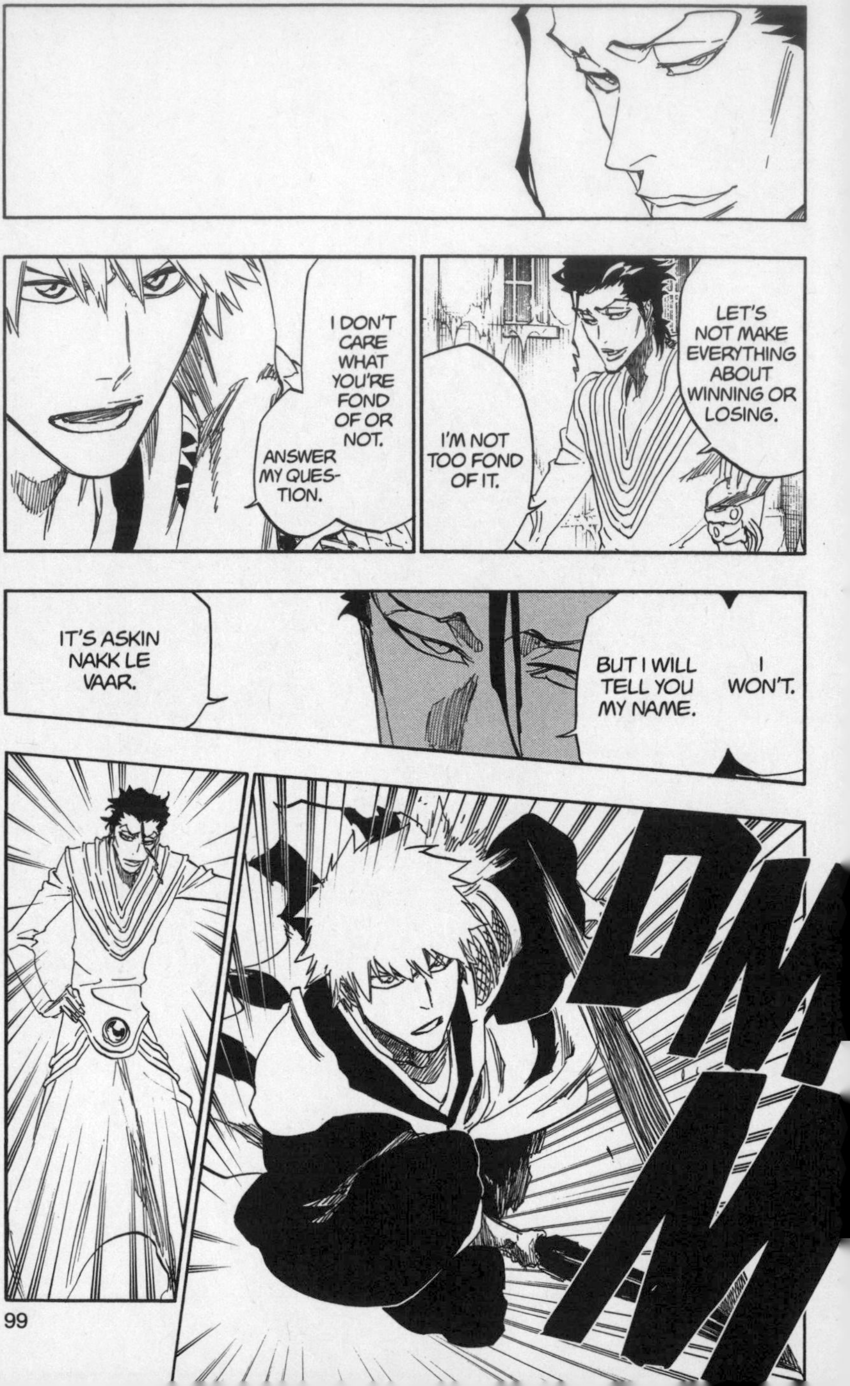
LET'S NOT MAKE EVERYTHING ABOUT WINNING OR LOSING.
I'M NOT TOO FOND OF IT.
I DON'T CARE WHAT YOU'RE FOND OF OR NOT.
ANSWER MY QUES-TION.
I WON'T.
BUT I WILL TELL YOU MY NAME.
IT'S ASKIN NAKK LE VAAR.

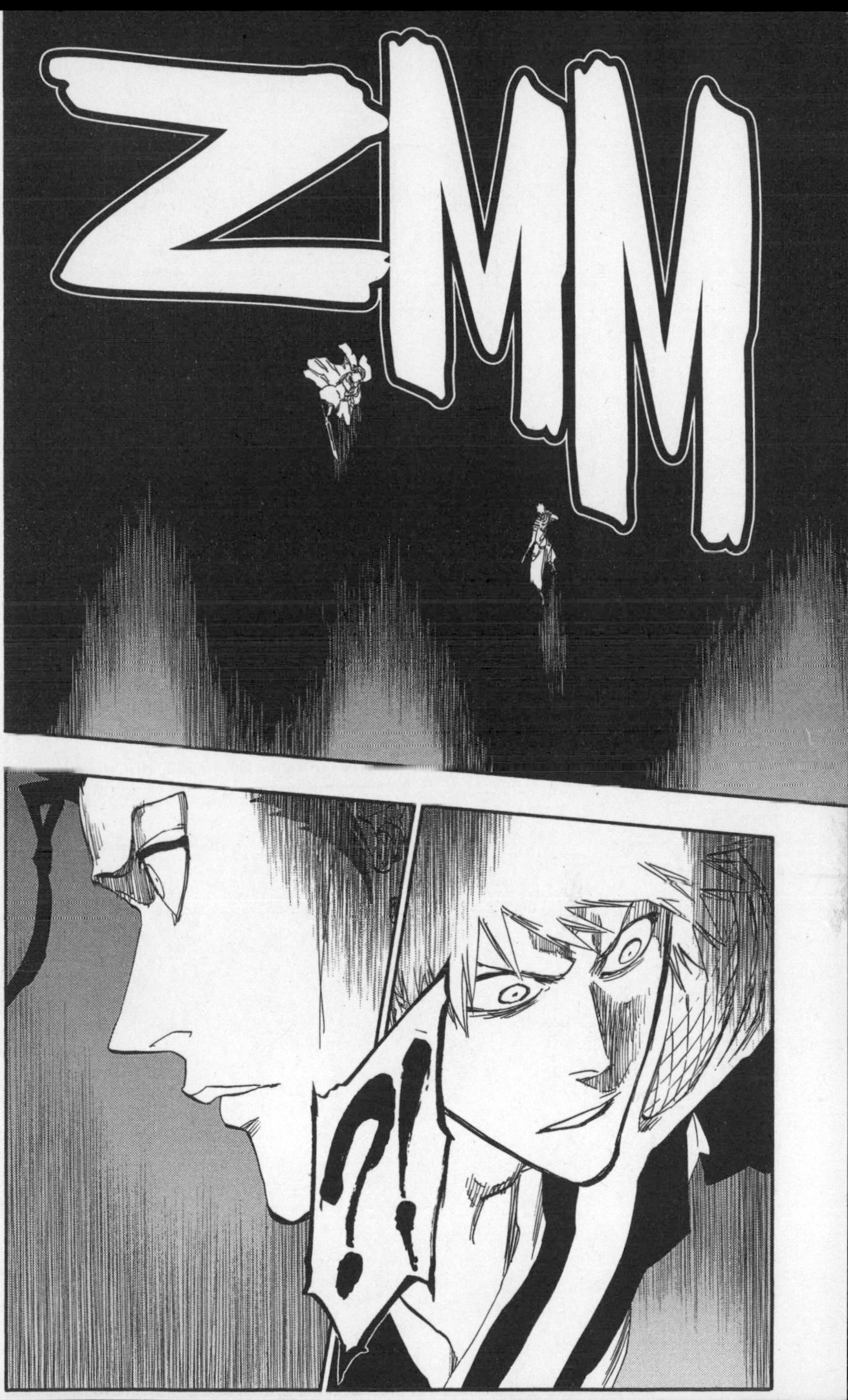
ZMM

READ THIS WAY

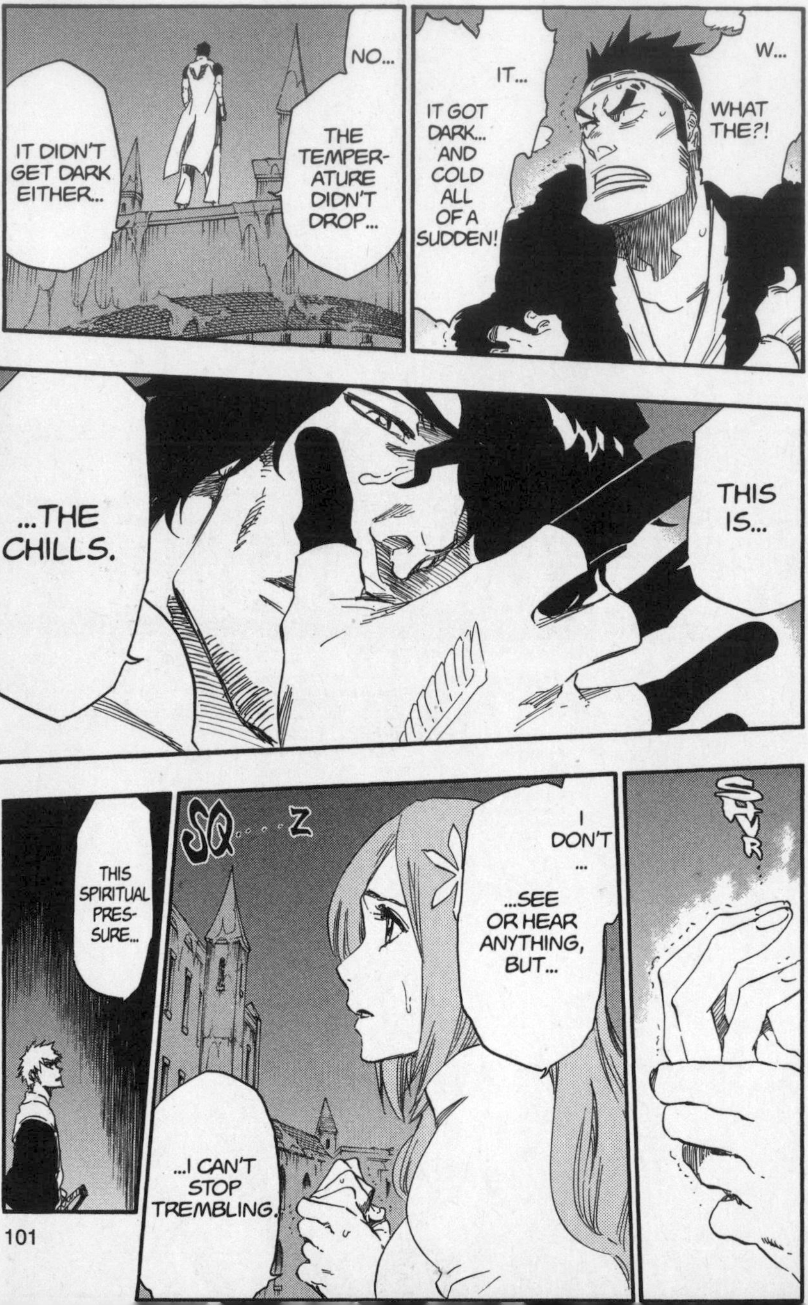
W...
WHAT THE?!
IT...
IT GOT DARK... AND COLD ALL OF A SUDDEN!
NO...
THE TEMPERATURE DIDN'T DROP...
IT DIDN'T GET DARK EITHER...
THIS IS...
...THE CHILLS.
SHVR
I DON'T...
...SEE OR HEAR ANYTHING, BUT...
...I CAN'T STOP TREMBLING.
SQ...Z
THIS SPIRITUAL PRESSURE...

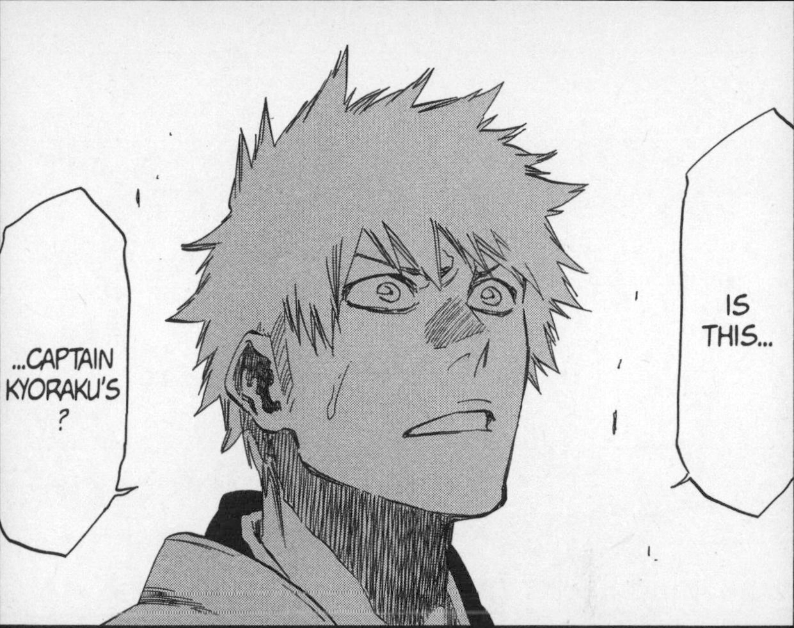
IS THIS...
...CAPTAIN KYORAKU'S?

THE THEATRE SUICIDE SCENE 2

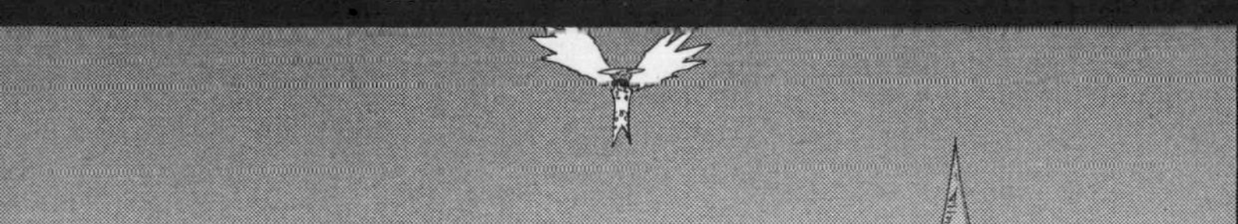

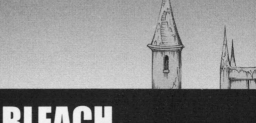

BLEACH 648.

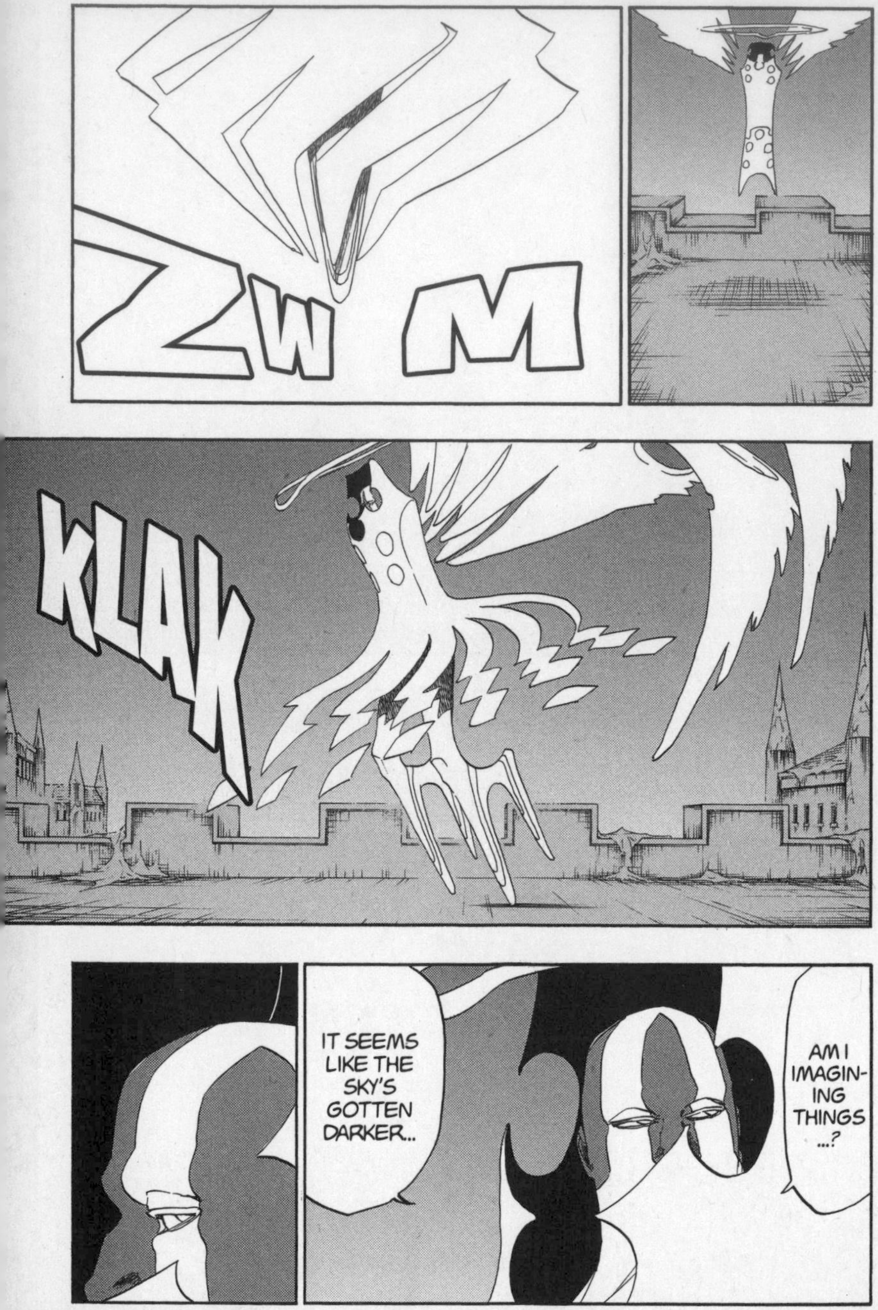
ZWM
KLAK
AM I IMAGINING THINGS ...?
IT SEEMS LIKE THE SKY'S GOTTEN DARKER...

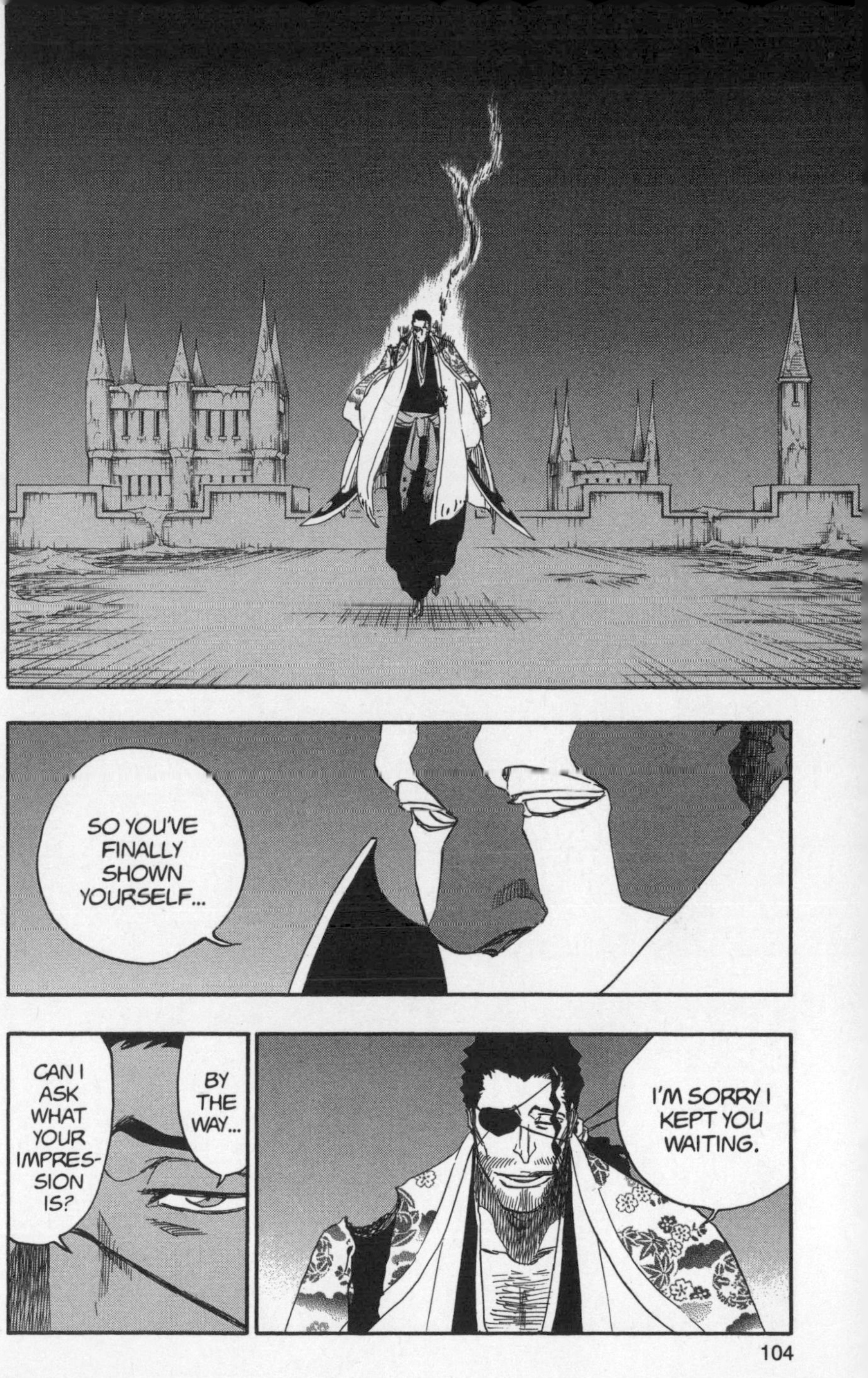
SO YOU'VE FINALLY SHOWN YOURSELF...
I'M SORRY I KEPT YOU WAITING.
BY THE WAY...
CAN I ASK WHAT YOUR IMPRESSION IS?

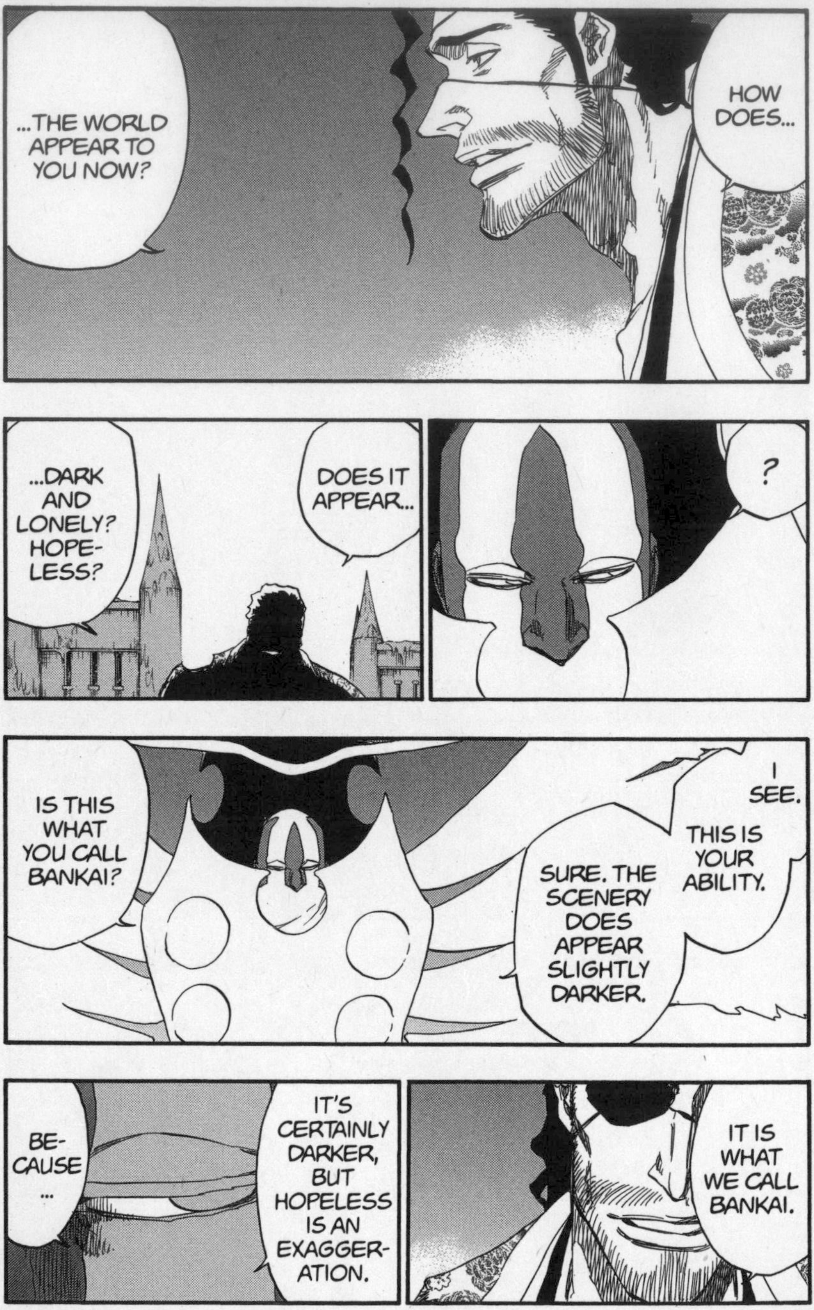
HOW DOES...
...THE WORLD APPEAR TO YOU NOW?
?
DOES IT APPEAR...
...DARK AND LONELY? HOPELESS?
I SEE.
THIS IS YOUR ABILITY.
SURE. THE SCENERY DOES APPEAR SLIGHTLY DARKER.
IS THIS WHAT YOU CALL BANKAI?
IT IS WHAT WE CALL BANKAI.
IT'S CERTAINLY DARKER, BUT HOPELESS IS AN EXAGGERATION.
BECAUSE...

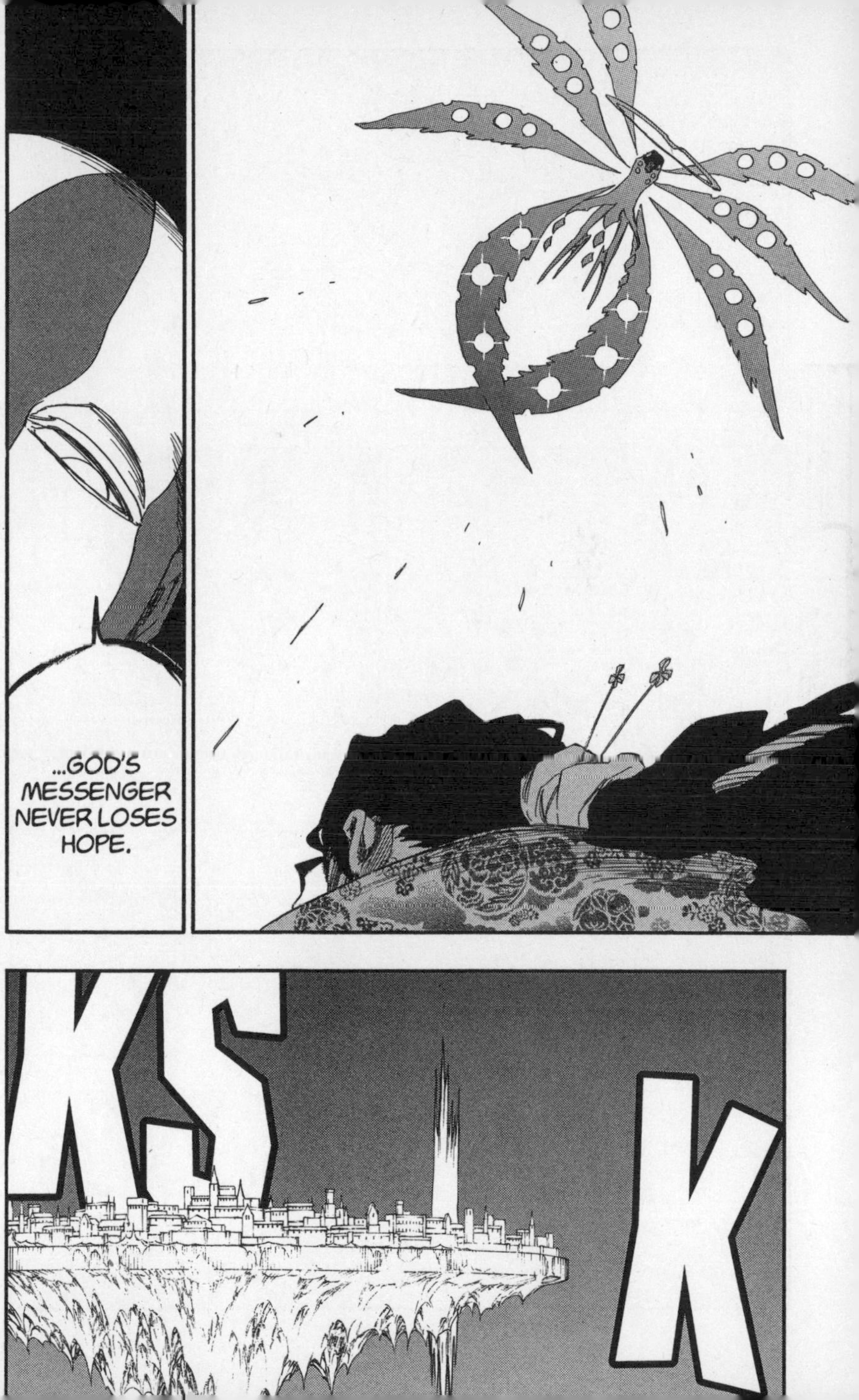
...GOD'S MESSENGER NEVER LOSES HOPE.
KSSK

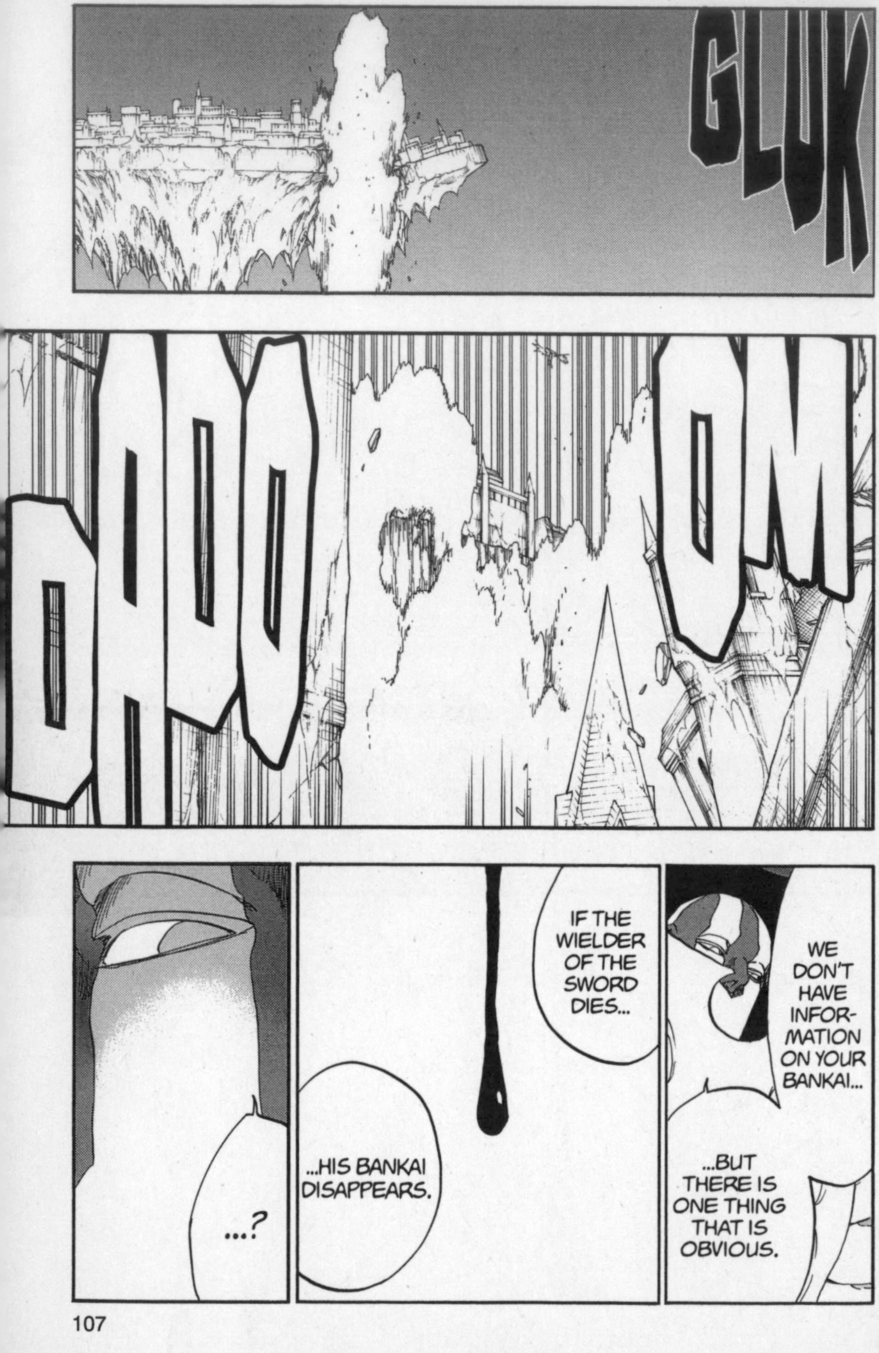
GLUK
WE DON'T HAVE INFOR-MATION ON YOUR BANKAI...
...BUT THERE IS ONE THING THAT IS OBVIOUS.
IF THE WIELDER OF THE SWORD DIES...
...HIS BANKAI DISAPPEARS.
...?

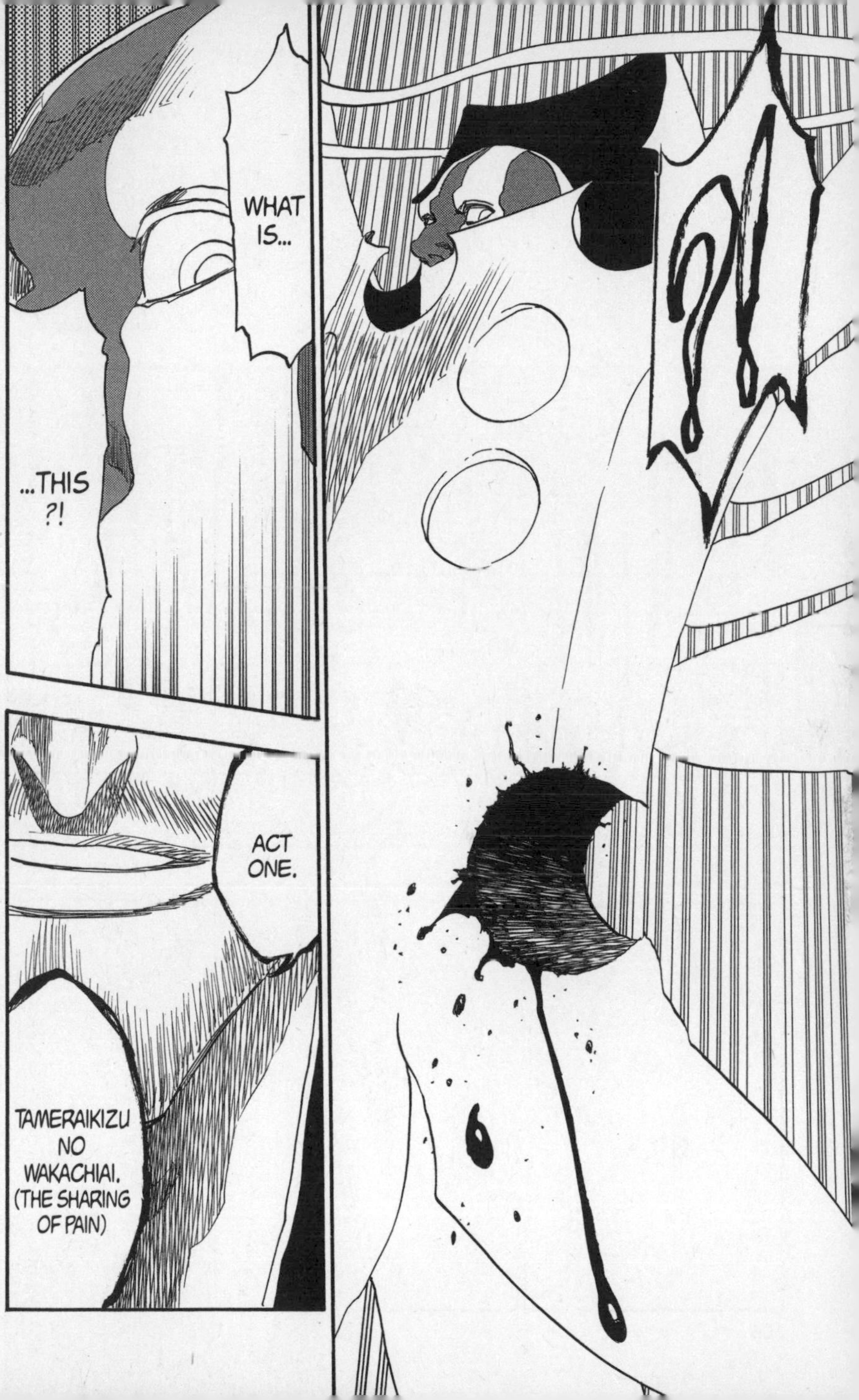
?!
WHAT IS...
...THIS ?!
ACT ONE.
TAMERAIKIZU NO WAKACHIAI. (THE SHARING OF PAIN)

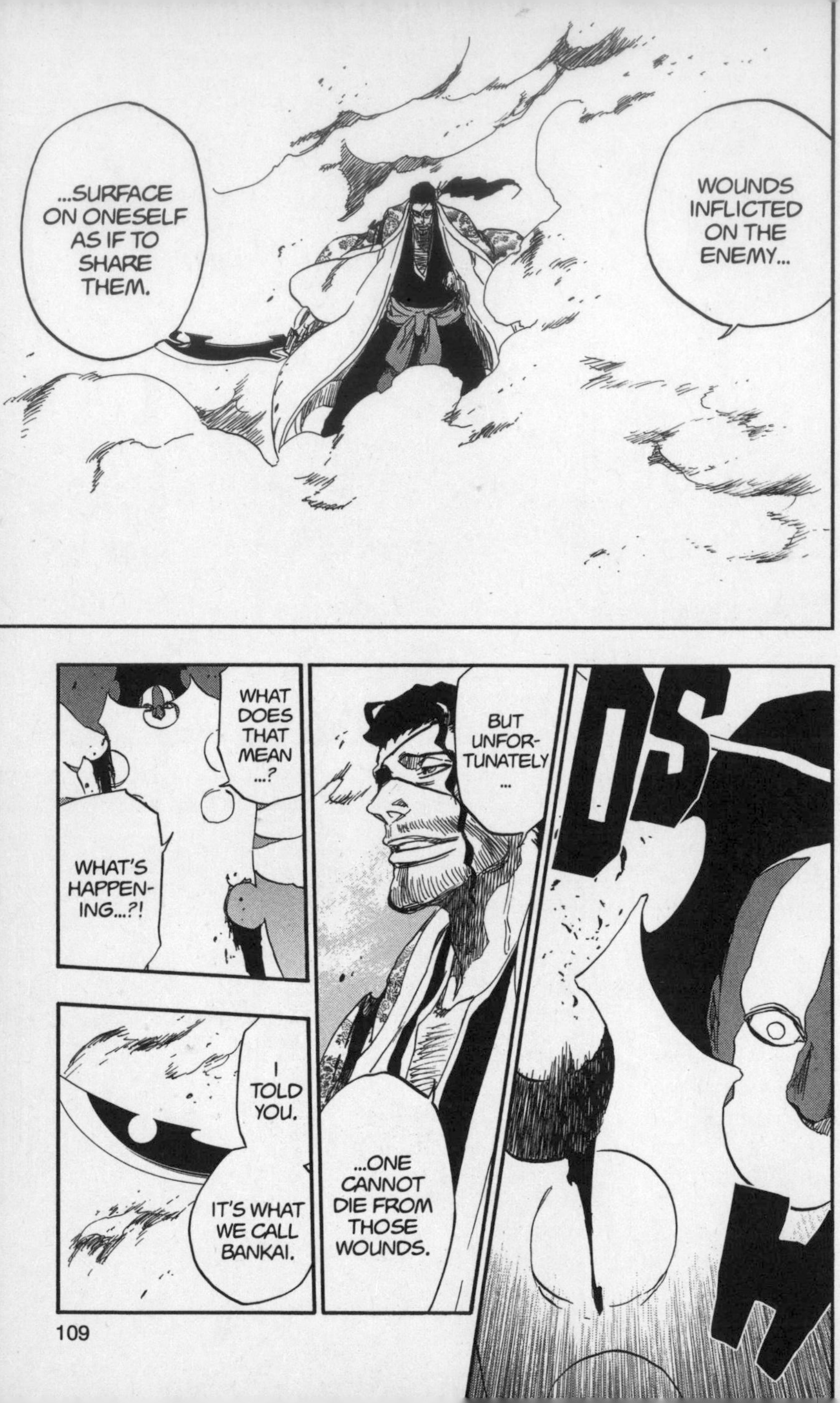
WOUNDS INFLICTED ON THE ENEMY...
...SURFACE ON ONESELF AS IF TO SHARE THEM.
BUT UNFORTUNATELY...
...ONE CANNOT DIE FROM THOSE WOUNDS.
WHAT DOES THAT MEAN...?
WHAT'S HAPPENING...?!
I TOLD YOU.
IT'S WHAT WE CALL BANKAI.

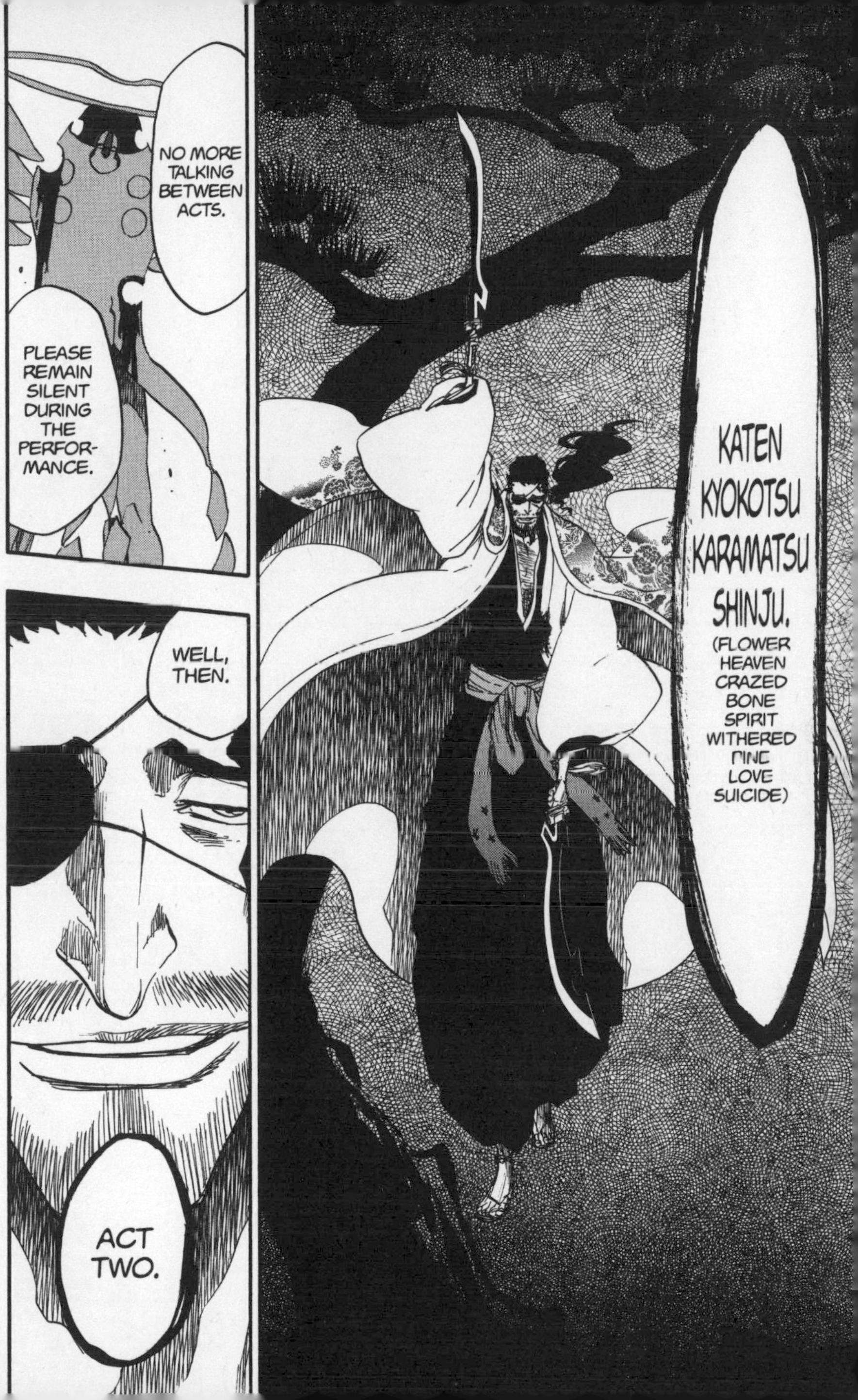
KATEN KYOKOTSU KARAMATSU SHINJU.
(FLOWER HEAVEN CRAZED BONE SPIRIT WITHERED PINE LOVE SUICIDE)
NO MORE TALKING BETWEEN ACTS.
PLEASE REMAIN SILENT DURING THE PERFORMANCE.
WELL, THEN.
ACT TWO.

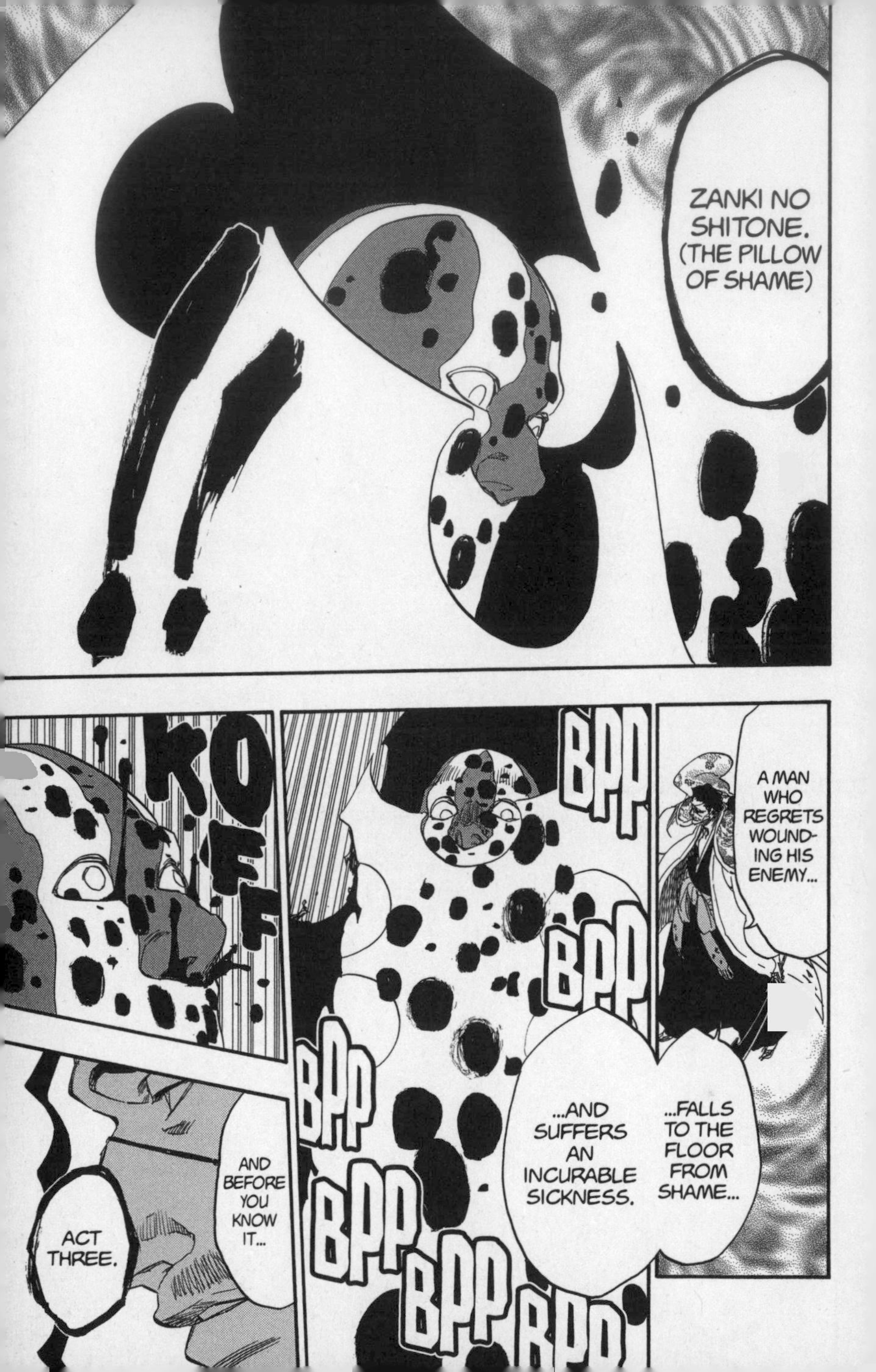
ZANKI NO SHITONE. (THE PILLOW OF SHAME)
A MAN WHO REGRETS WOUND-ING HIS ENEMY...
...FALLS TO THE FLOOR FROM SHAME...
...AND SUFFERS AN INCURABLE SICKNESS.
BPP
BPP
BPP
BPP
BPP
KOFF
AND BEFORE YOU KNOW IT...
ACT THREE.

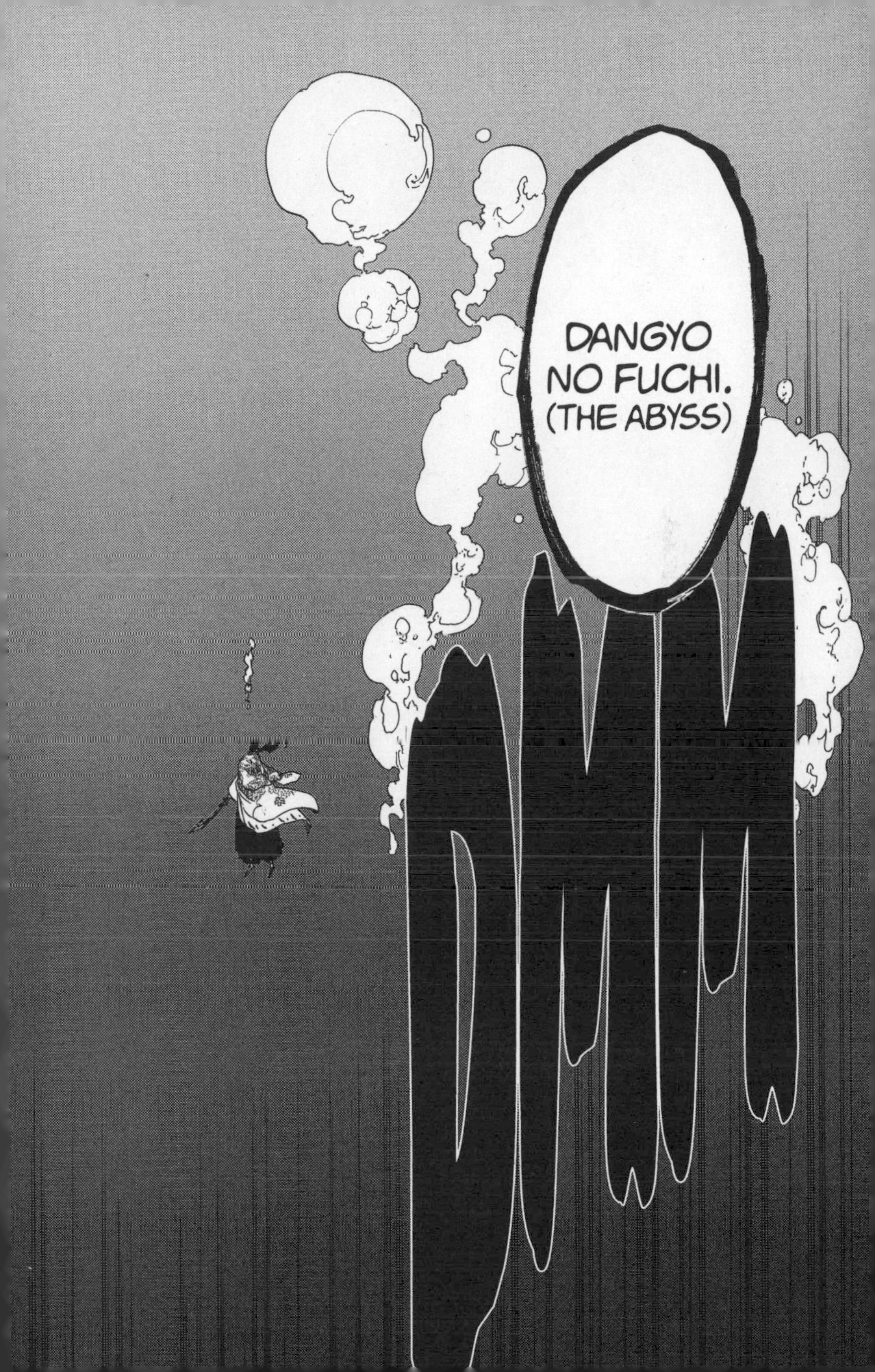
DANGYO NO FUCHI. (THE ABYSS)

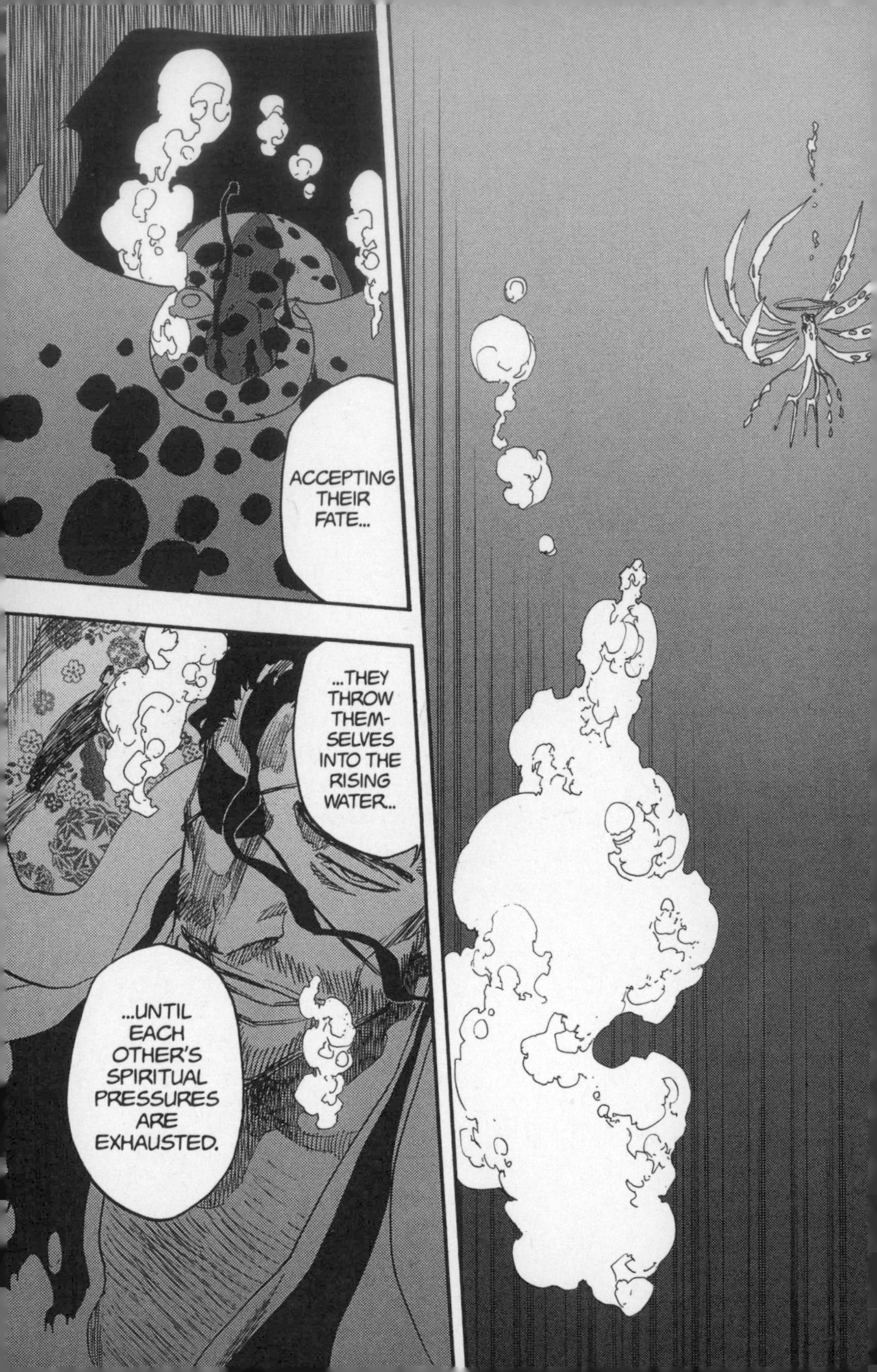
ACCEPTING THEIR FATE...
...THEY THROW THEM-SELVES INTO THE RISING WATER...
...UNTIL EACH OTHER'S SPIRITUAL PRESSURES ARE EXHAUSTED.

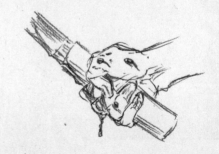

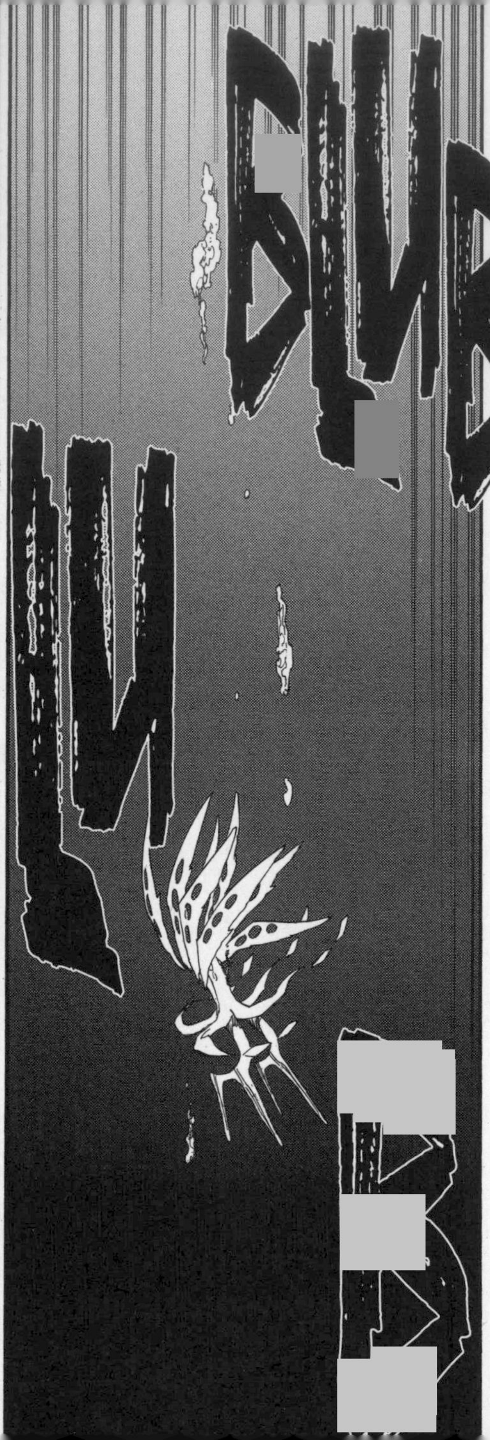

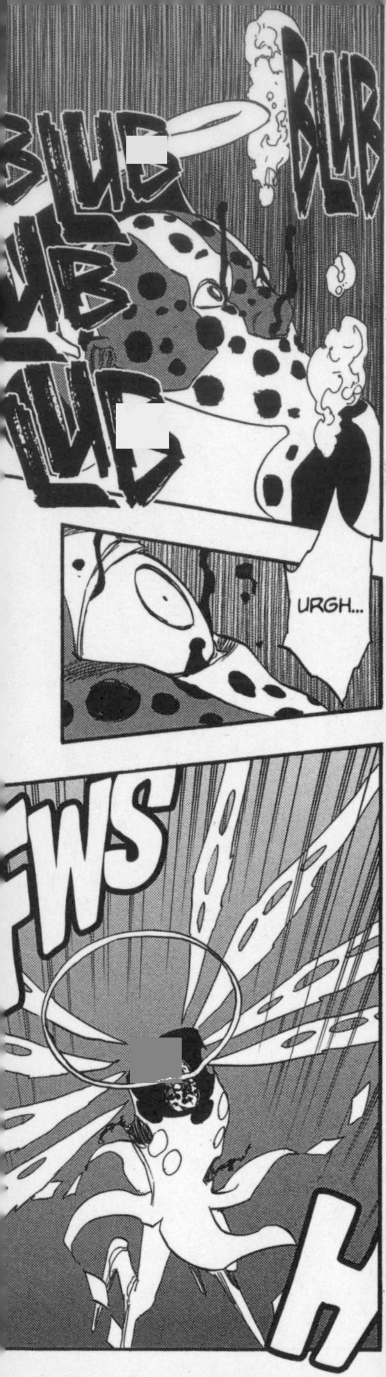
BLUB
URGH...

649.THE THEATRE SUICIDE SCENE 3

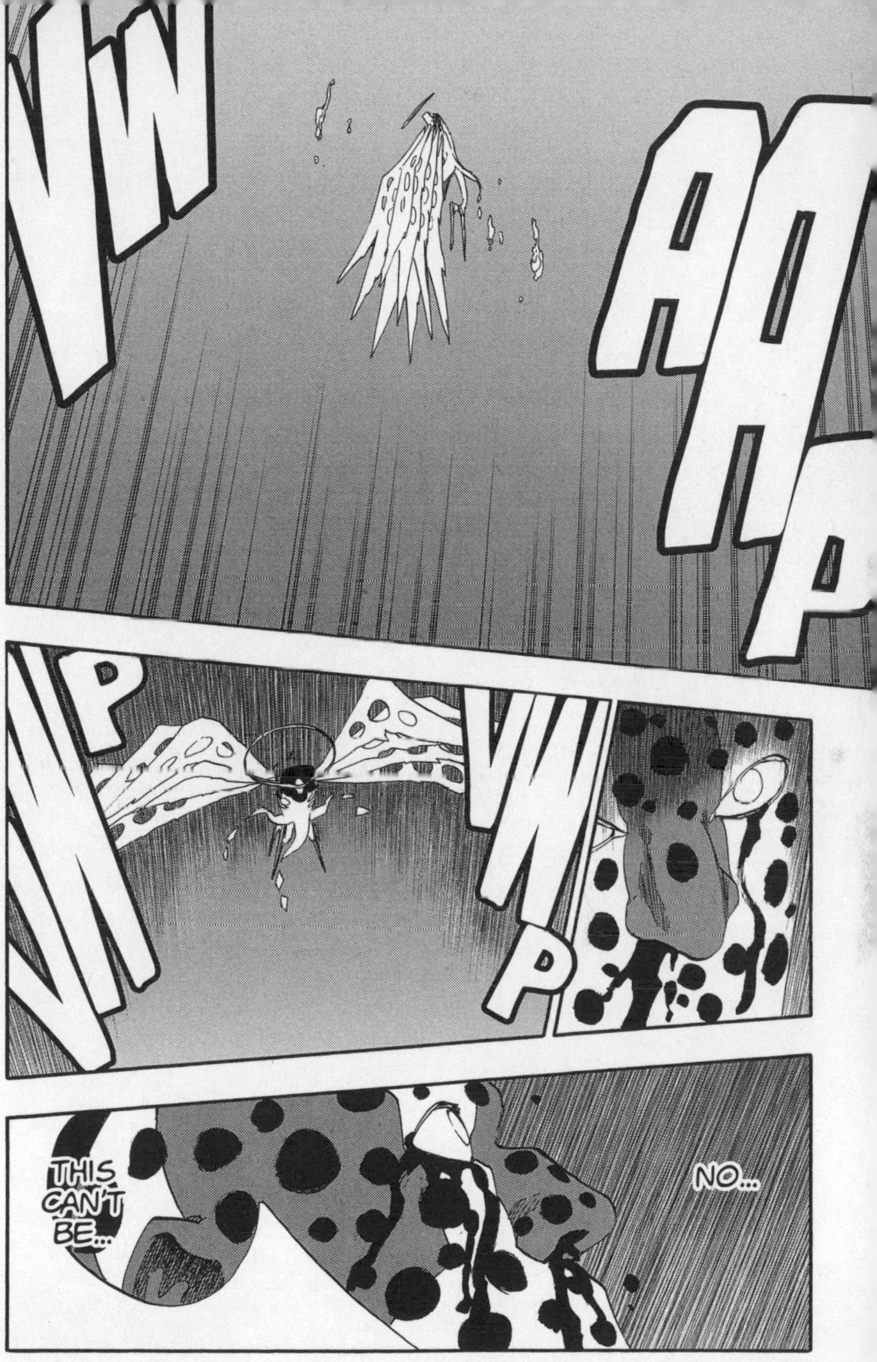
NO...
THIS CAN'T BE...

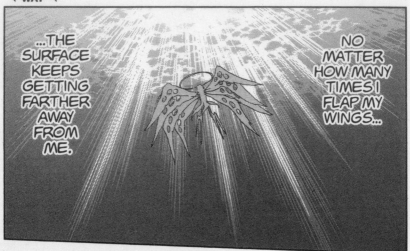

READ THIS WAY

NO MATTER HOW MANY TIMES I FLAP MY WINGS...
...THE SURFACE KEEPS GETTING FARTHER AWAY FROM ME.
OF COURSE.
WE THREW OURSELVES INTO THE WATER, REMEMBER?
FLAP YOUR WINGS ALL YOU WANT, BUT WHAT'S DONE IS DONE.
ALTHOUGH...
...IT'S NOT THAT I DON'T KNOW HOW YOU FEEL.

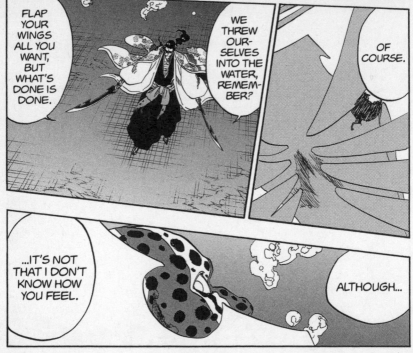

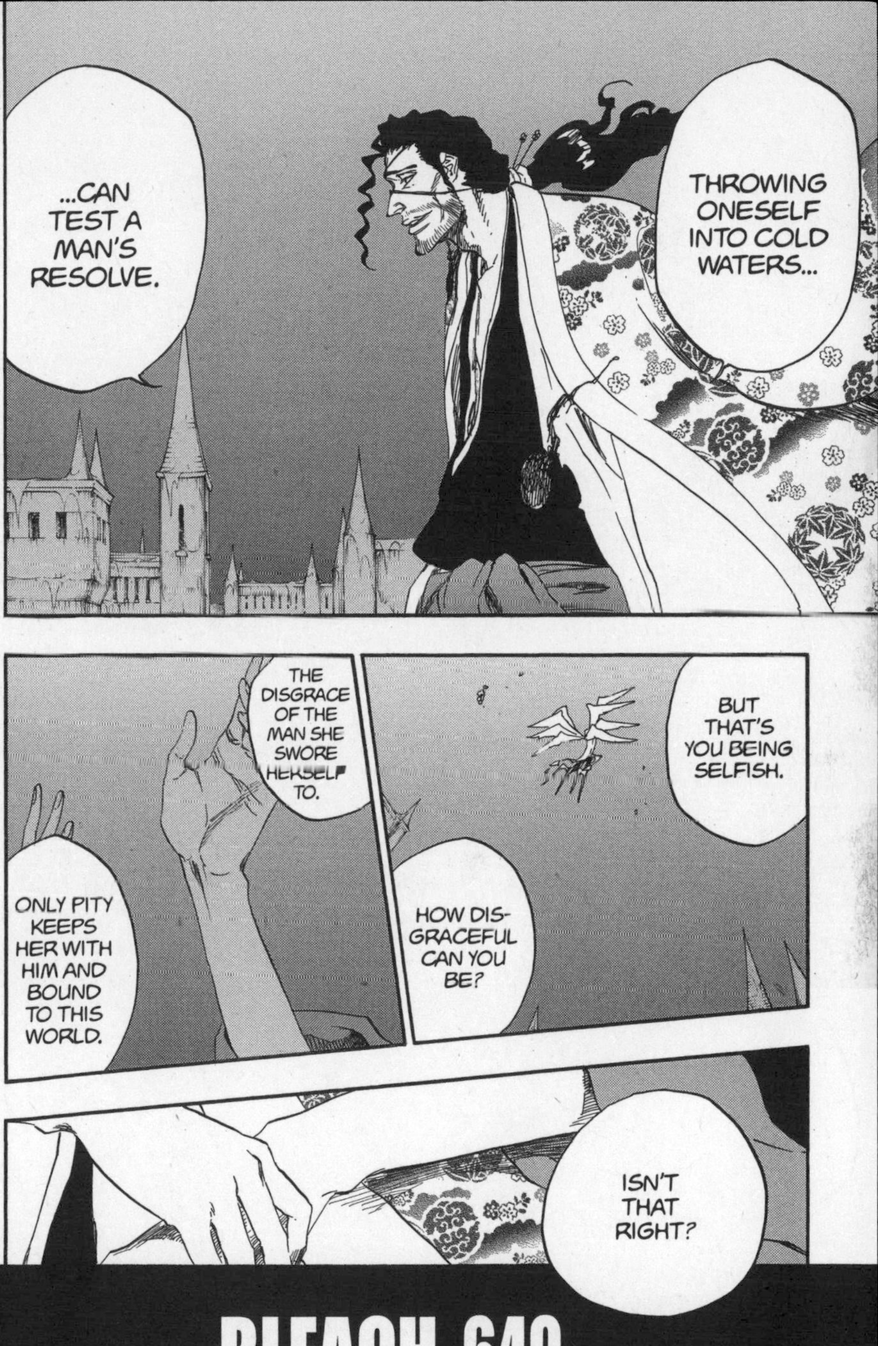
THROWING ONESELF INTO COLD WATERS...
...CAN TEST A MAN'S RESOLVE.
BUT THAT'S YOU BEING SELFISH.
HOW DIS-GRACEFUL CAN YOU BE?
THE DISGRACE OF THE MAN SHE SWORE HERSELF TO.
ONLY PITY KEEPS HER WITH HIM AND BOUND TO THIS WORLD.
ISN'T THAT RIGHT?

BLEACH 649.

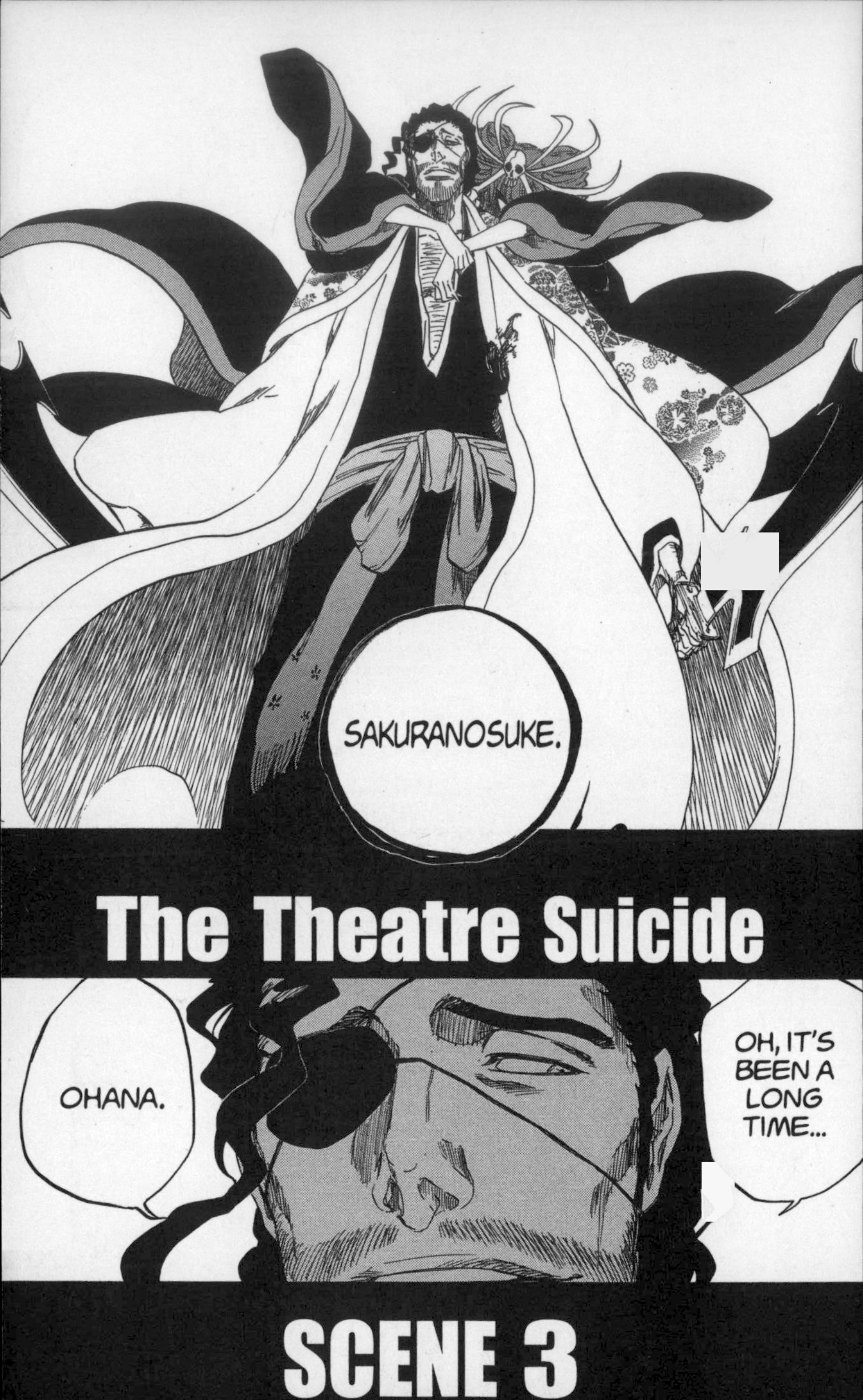
SAKURANOSUKE.
The Theatre Suicide
OH, IT'S BEEN A LONG TIME...
OHANA.
SCENE 3

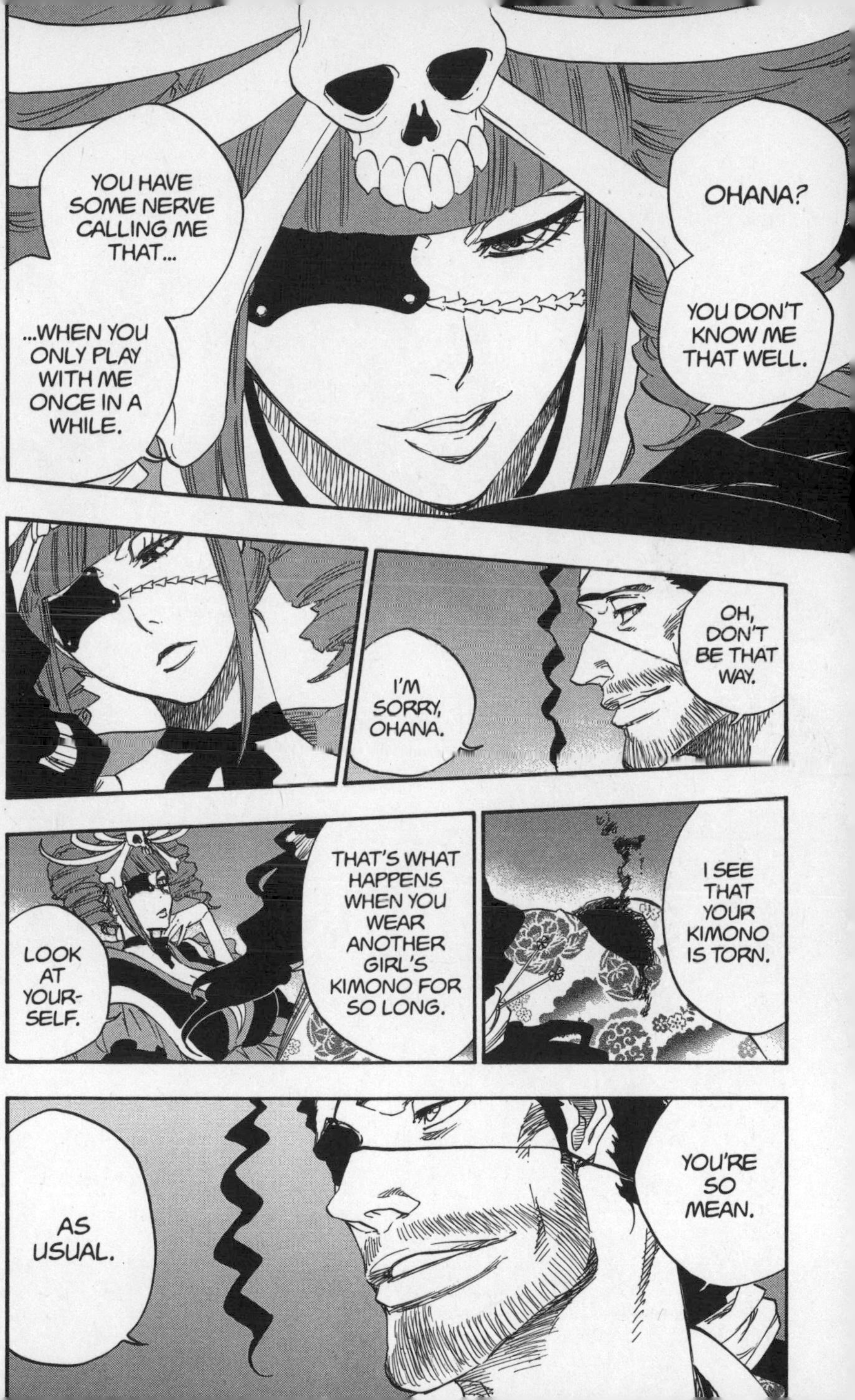
OHANA?
YOU DON'T KNOW ME THAT WELL.
YOU HAVE SOME NERVE CALLING ME THAT...
...WHEN YOU ONLY PLAY WITH ME ONCE IN A WHILE.
OH, DON'T BE THAT WAY.
I'M SORRY, OHANA.
I SEE THAT YOUR KIMONO IS TORN.
THAT'S WHAT HAPPENS WHEN YOU WEAR ANOTHER GIRL'S KIMONO FOR SO LONG.
LOOK AT YOURSELF.
YOU'RE SO MEAN.
AS USUAL.

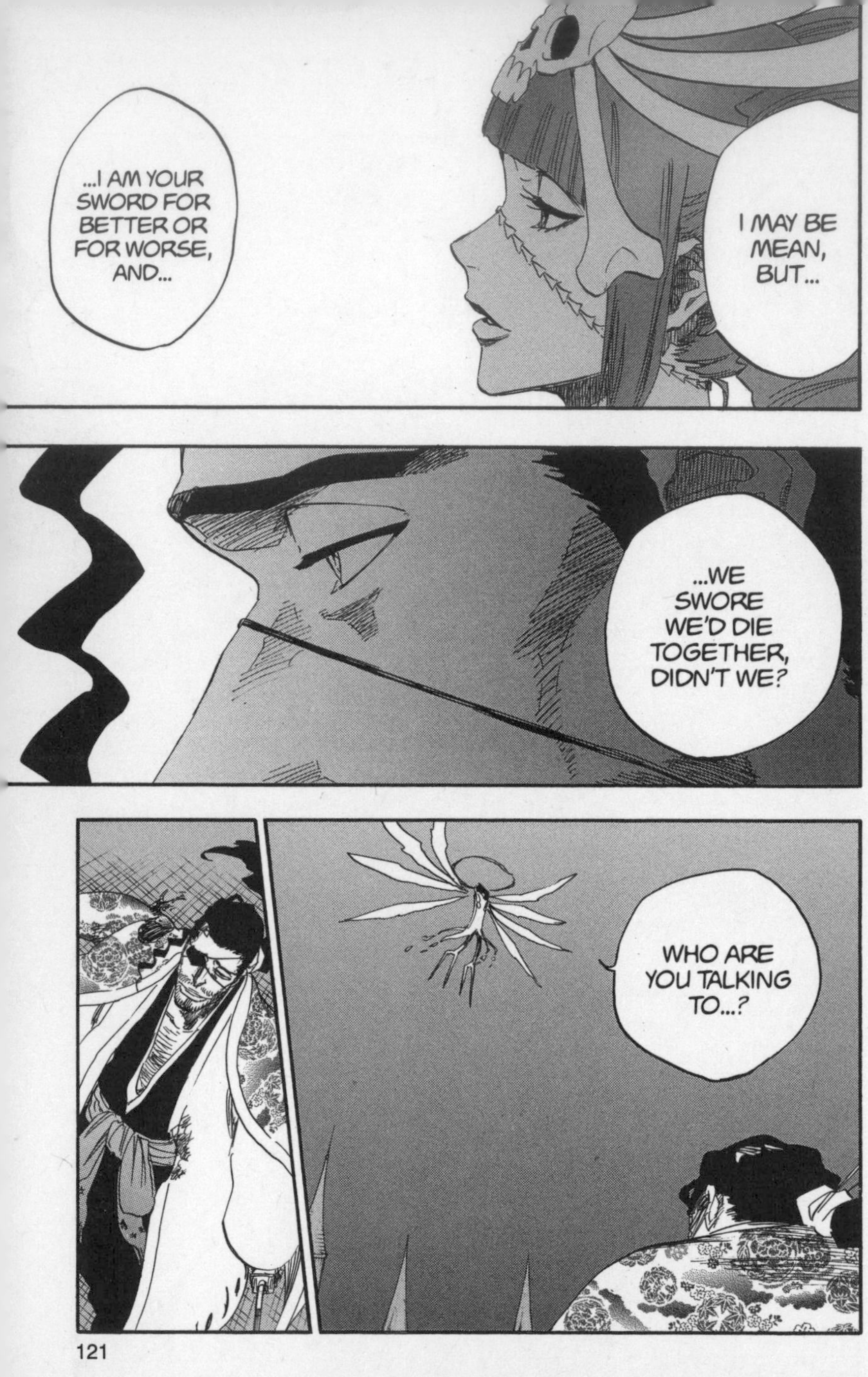
I MAY BE MEAN, BUT...
...I AM YOUR SWORD FOR BETTER OR FOR WORSE, AND...
...WE SWORE WE'D DIE TOGETHER, DIDN'T WE?
WHO ARE YOU TALKING TO...?

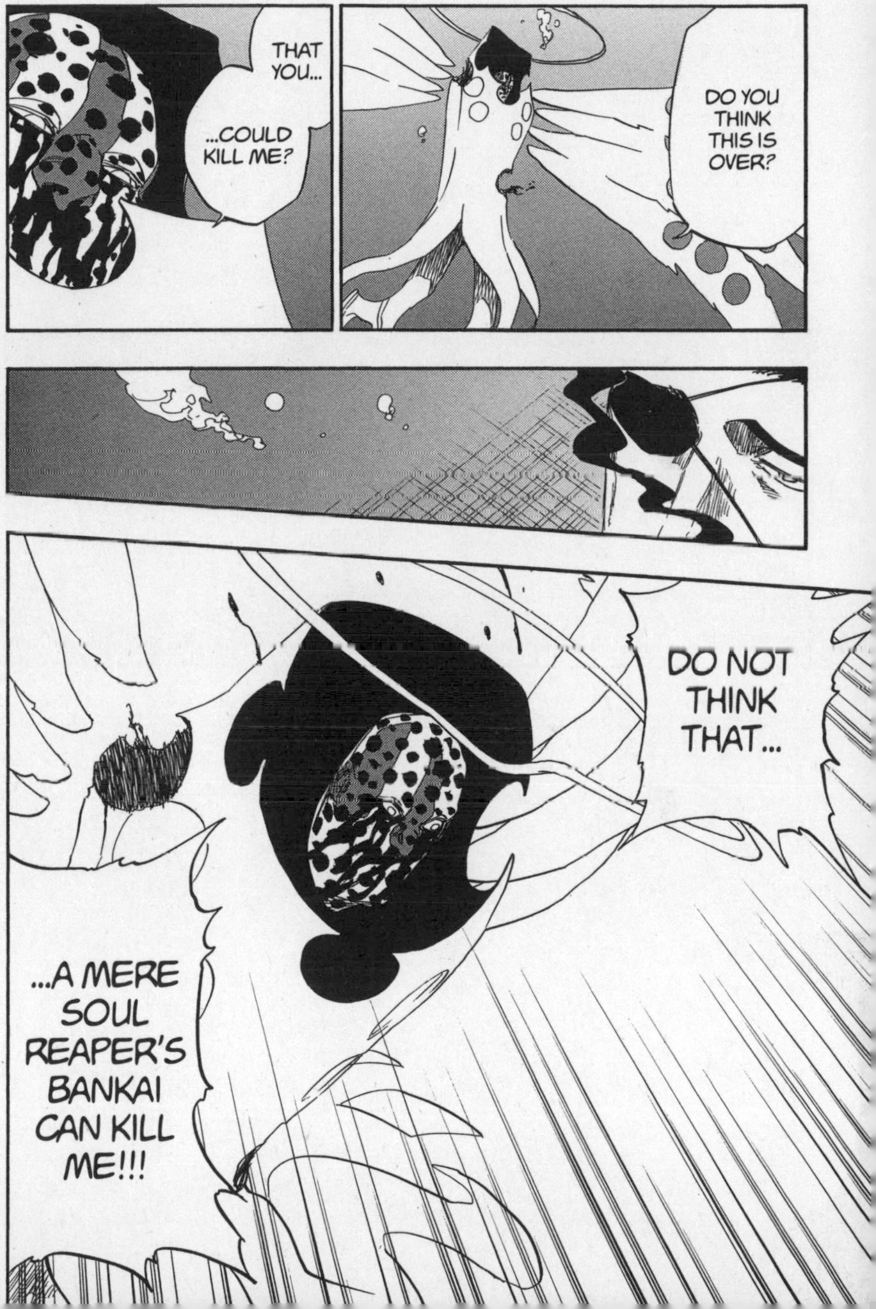
DO YOU THINK THIS IS OVER?
THAT YOU...
...COULD KILL ME?
DO NOT THINK THAT...
...A MERE SOUL REAPER'S BANKAI CAN KILL ME!!!

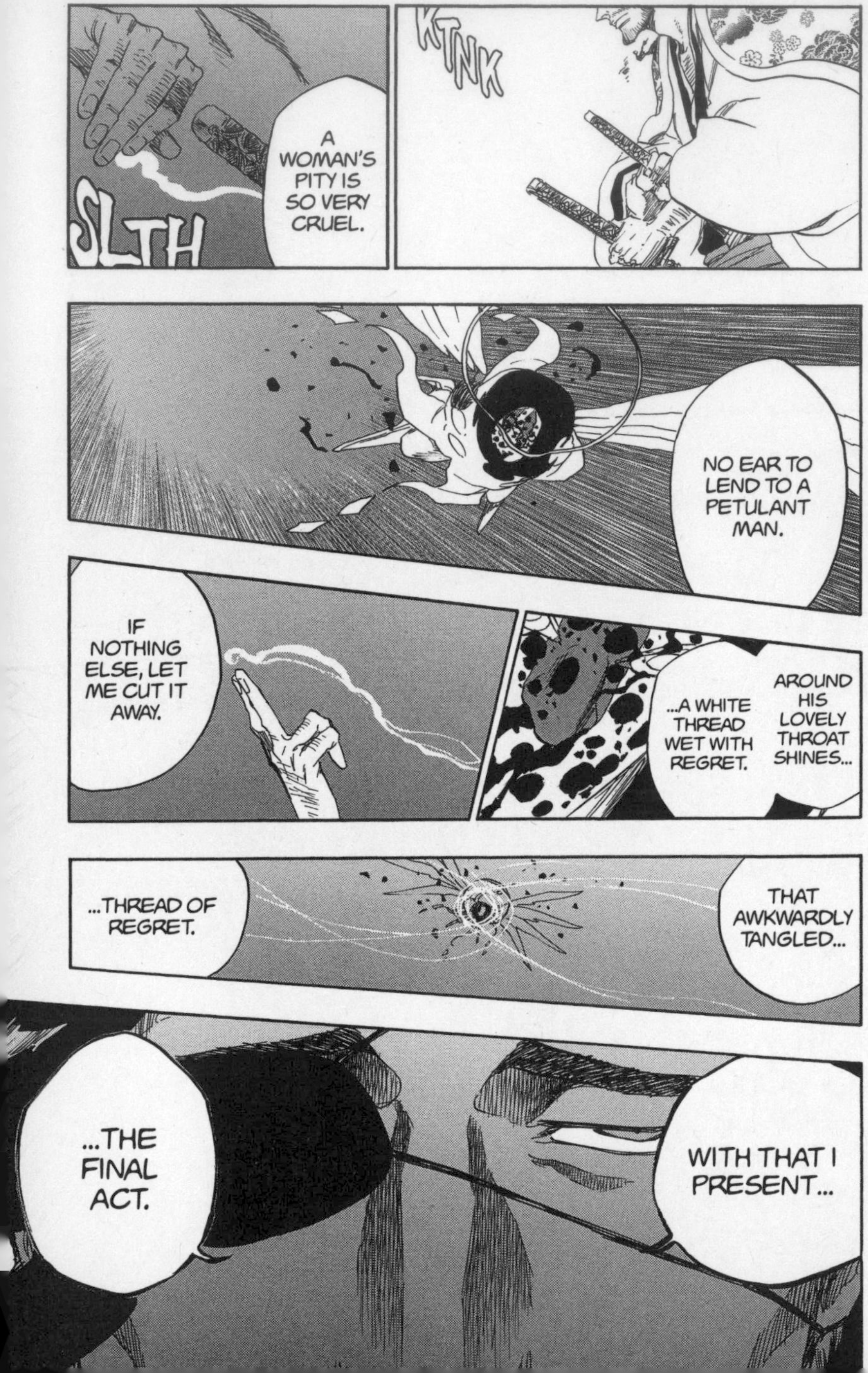
KTNK
A WOMAN'S PITY IS SO VERY CRUEL.
SLTH
NO EAR TO LEND TO A PETULANT MAN.
AROUND HIS LOVELY THROAT SHINES...
...A WHITE THREAD WET WITH REGRET.
IF NOTHING ELSE, LET ME CUT IT AWAY.
THAT AWKWARDLY TANGLED...
...THREAD OF REGRET.
WITH THAT I PRESENT...
...THE FINAL ACT.

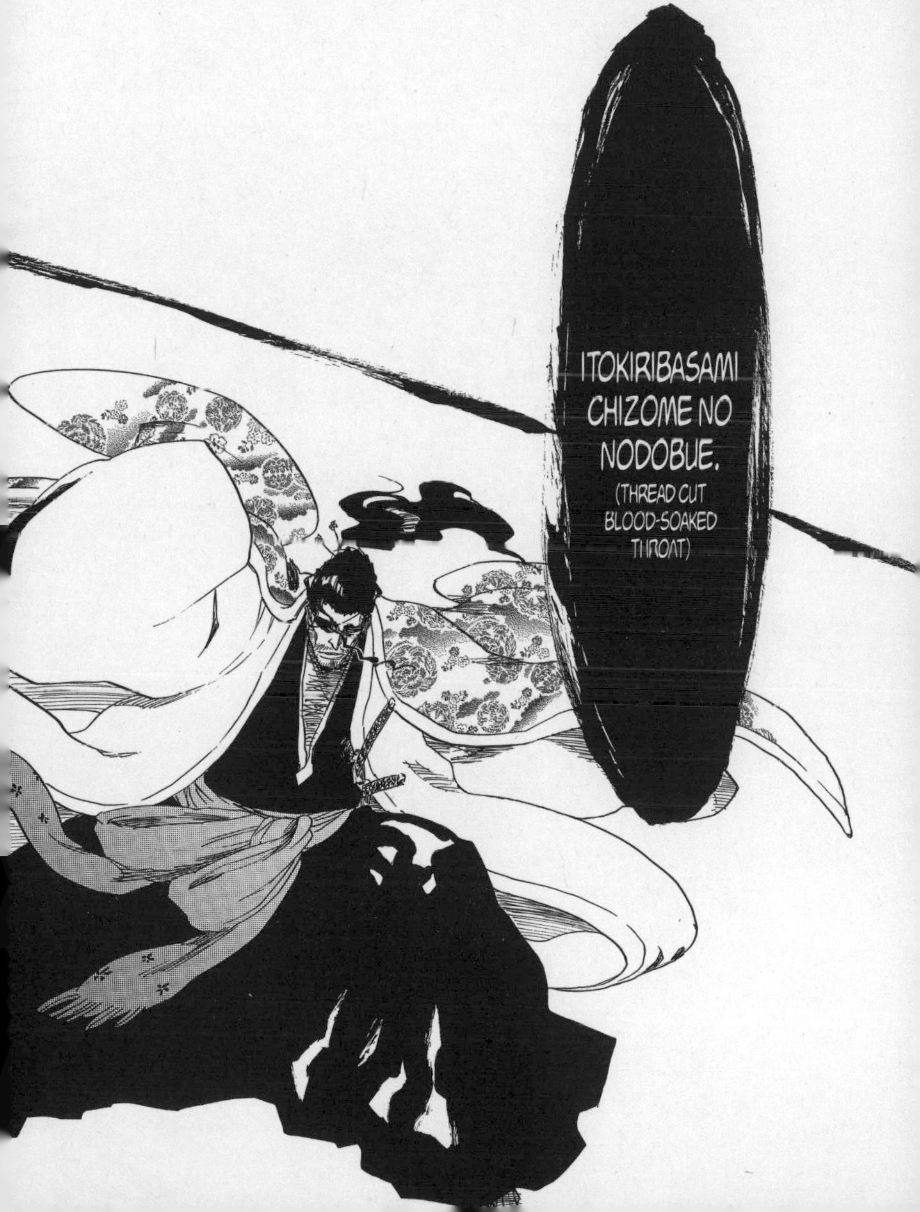
ITOKIRIBASAMI CHIZOME NO NODOBUE.
(THREAD CUT BLOOD-SOAKED THROAT)

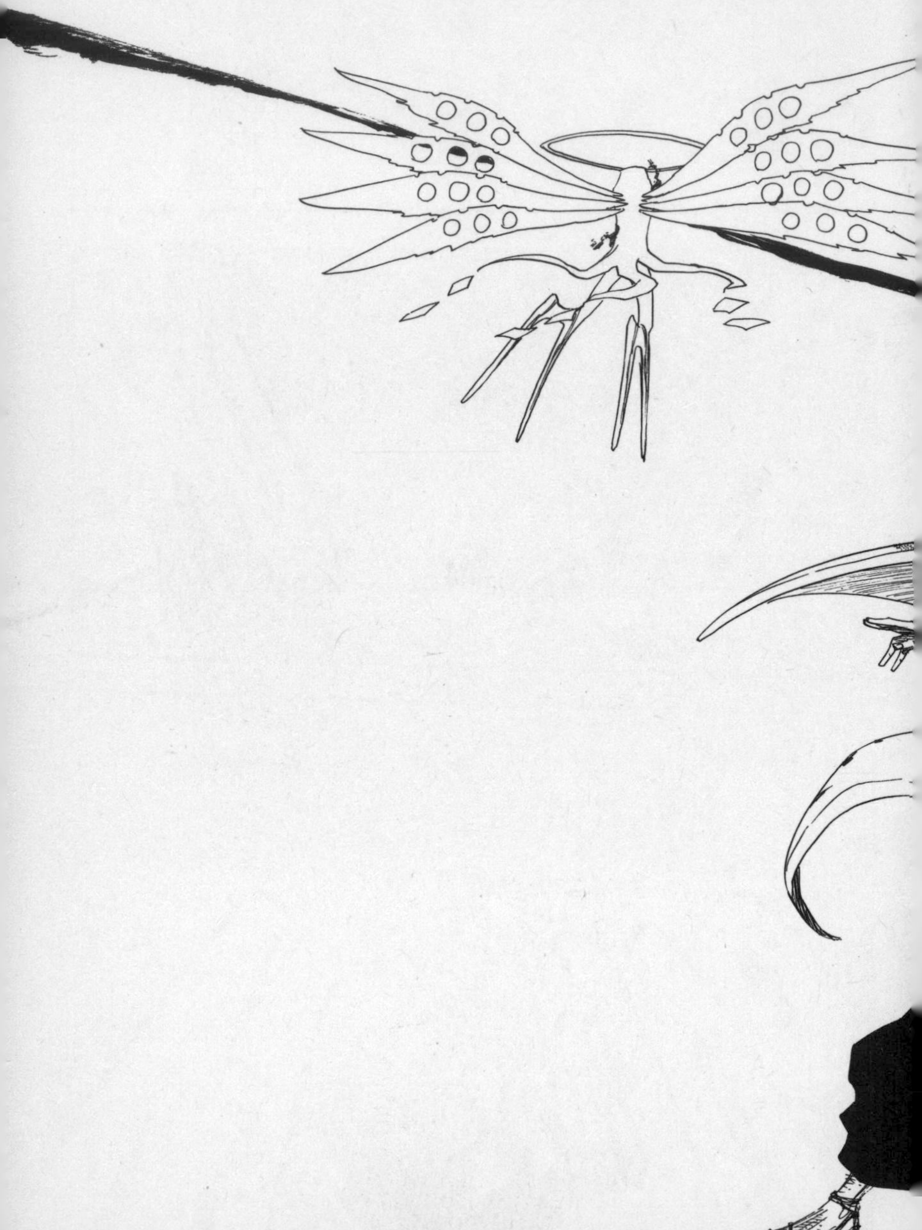

BLURP
BOOM

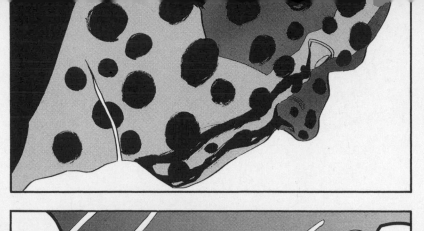

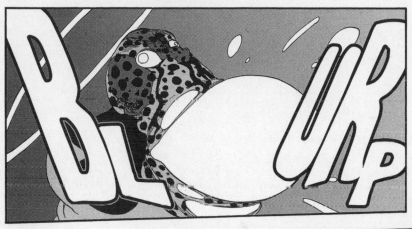

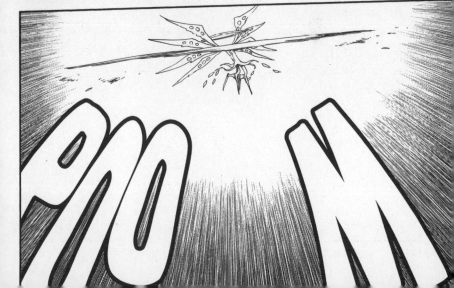

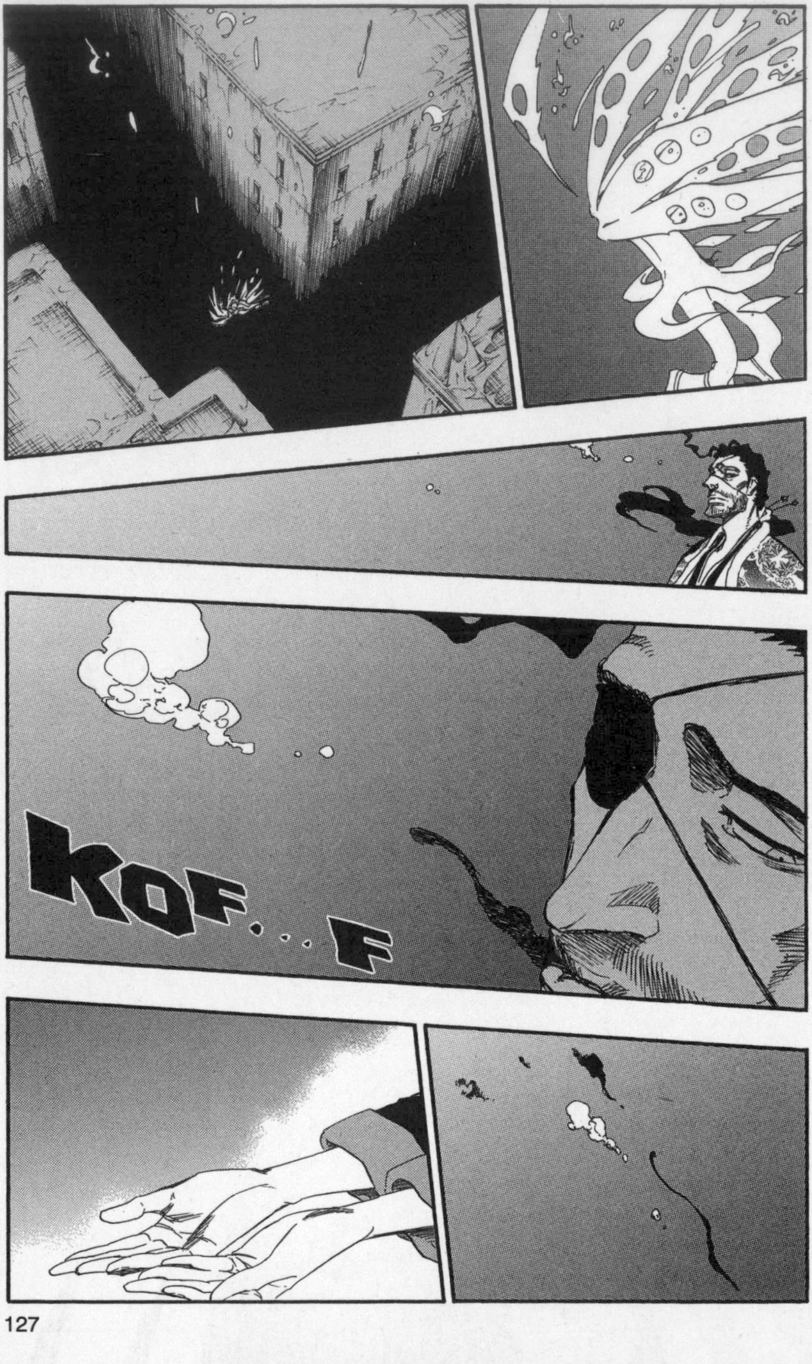
KOF...F

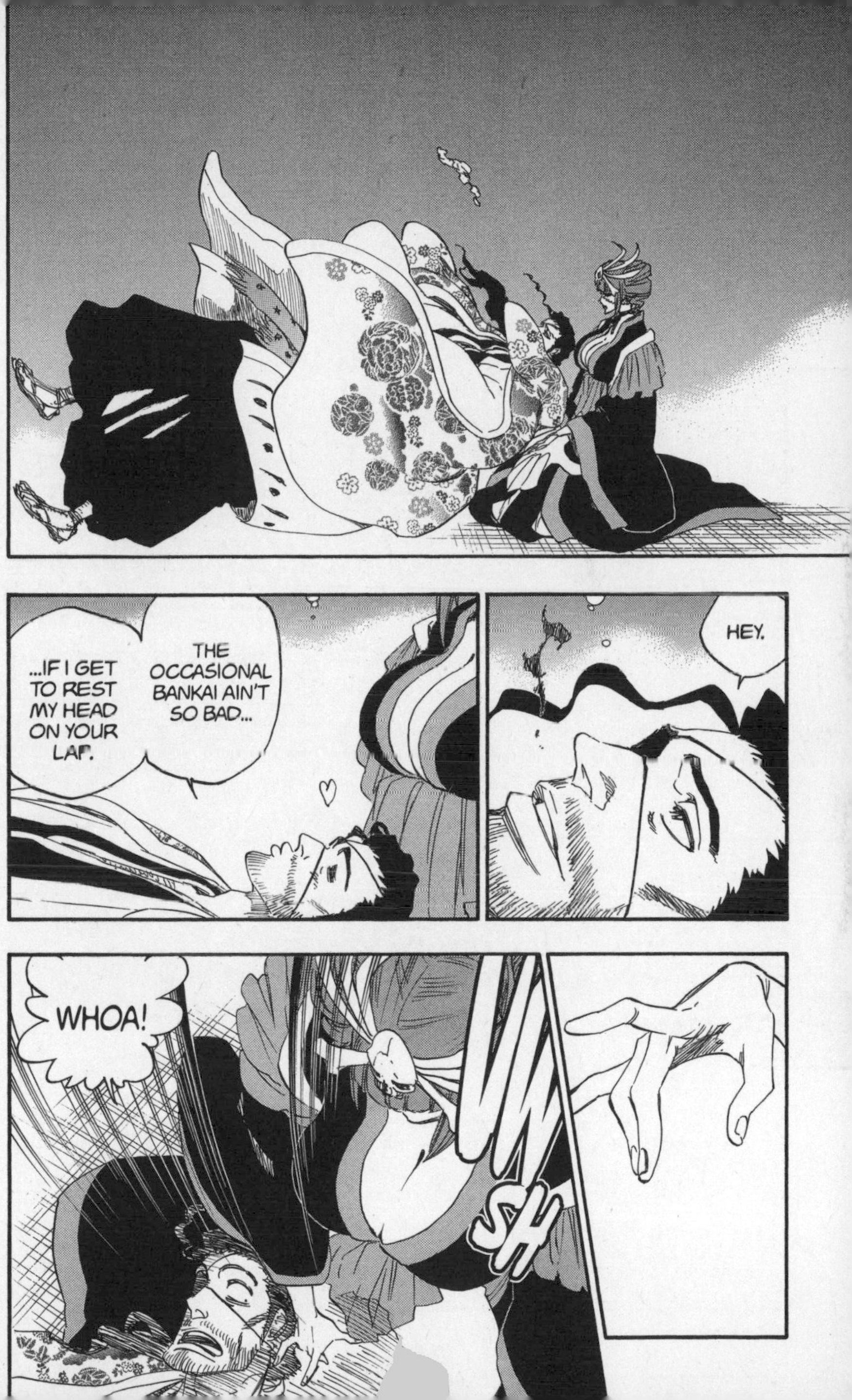
HEY.
THE OCCASIONAL BANKAI AIN'T SO BAD...
...IF I GET TO REST MY HEAD ON YOUR LAP.
WHOA!

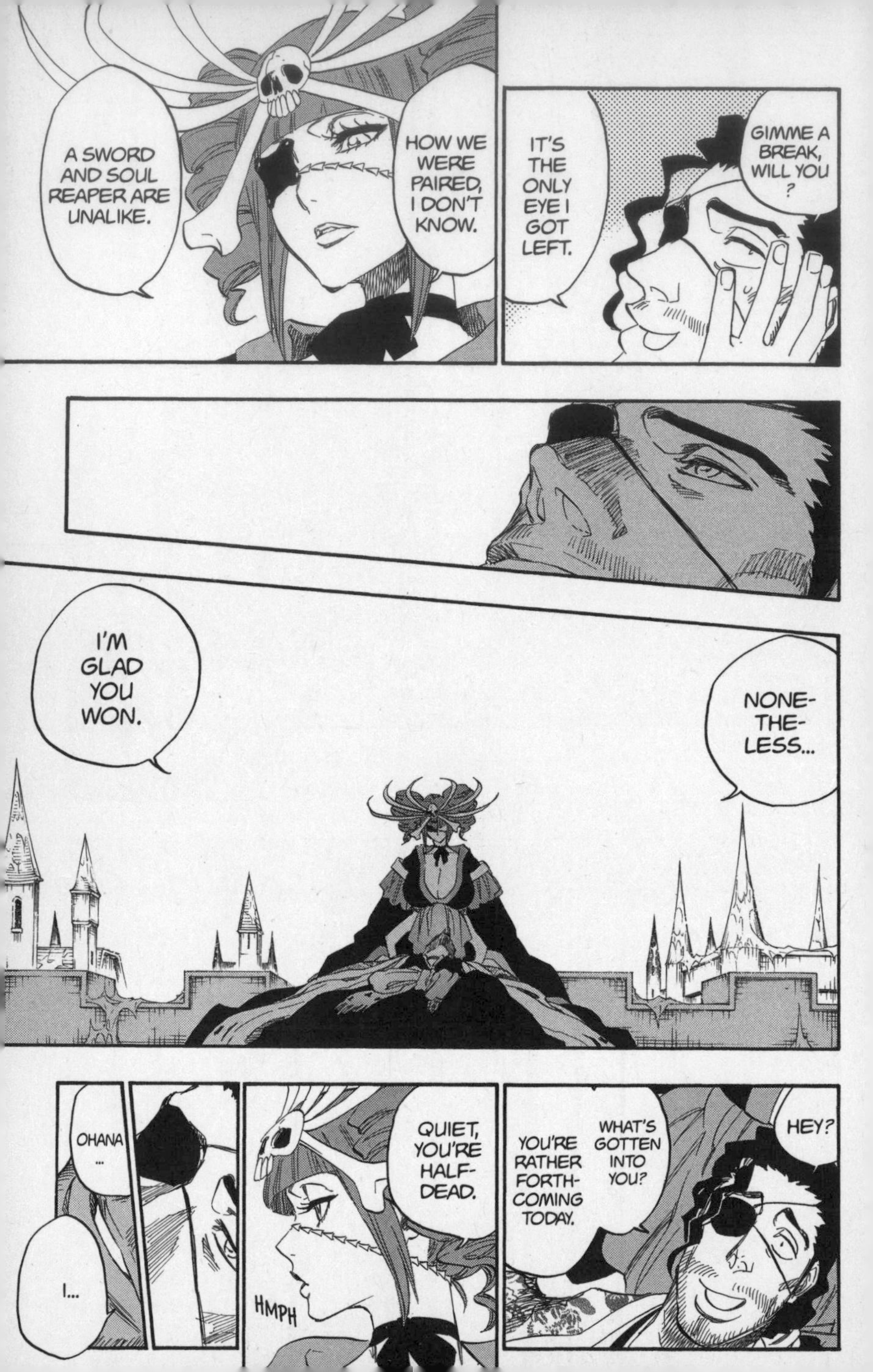
GIMME A BREAK, WILL YOU?
IT'S THE ONLY EYE I GOT LEFT.
HOW WE WERE PAIRED, I DON'T KNOW.
A SWORD AND SOUL REAPER ARE UNALIKE.
NONE-THE-LESS...
I'M GLAD YOU WON.
HEY?
WHAT'S GOTTEN INTO YOU?
YOU'RE RATHER FORTH-COMING TODAY.
QUIET, YOU'RE HALF-DEAD.
HMPH
OHANA...
I...

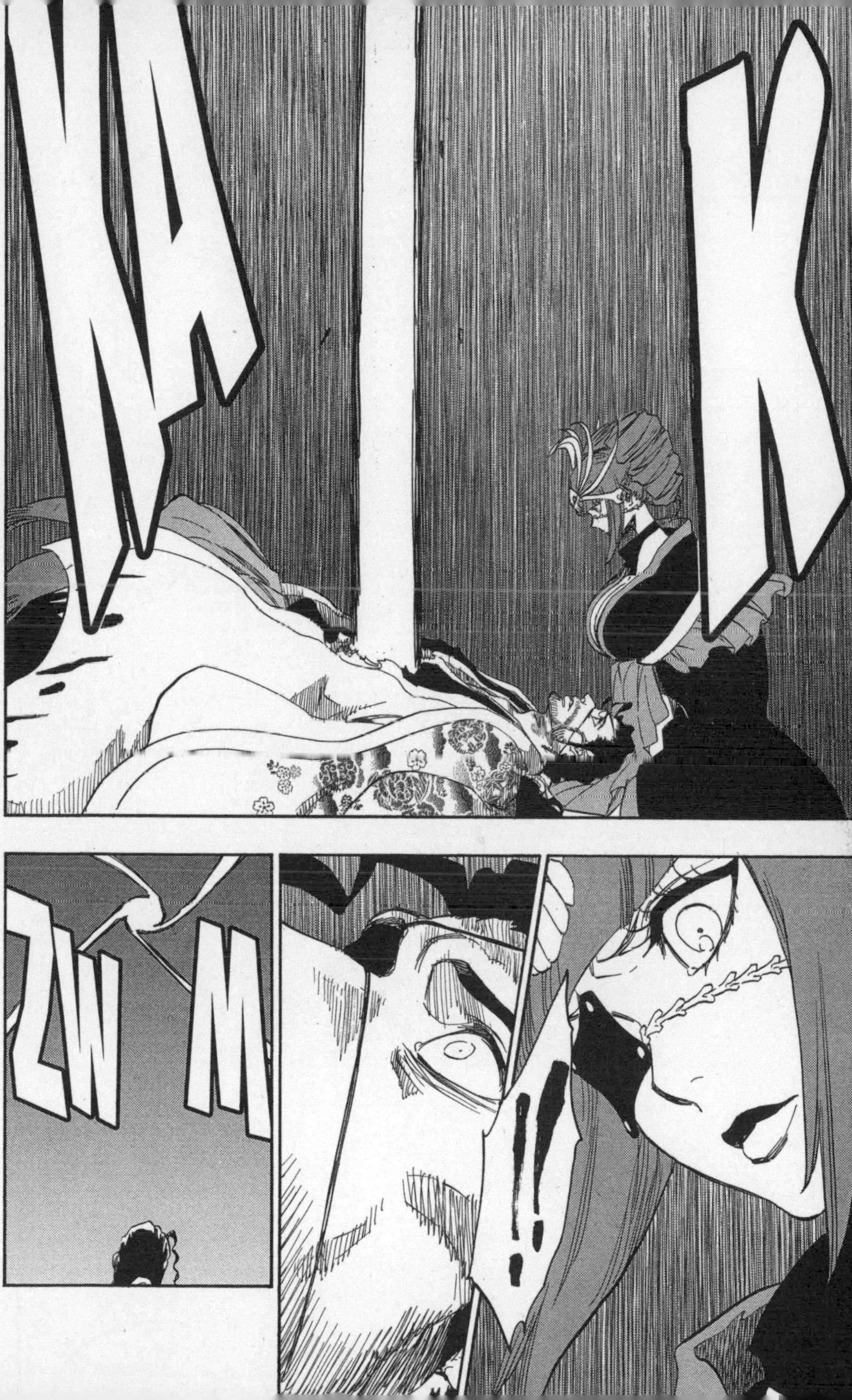
!!

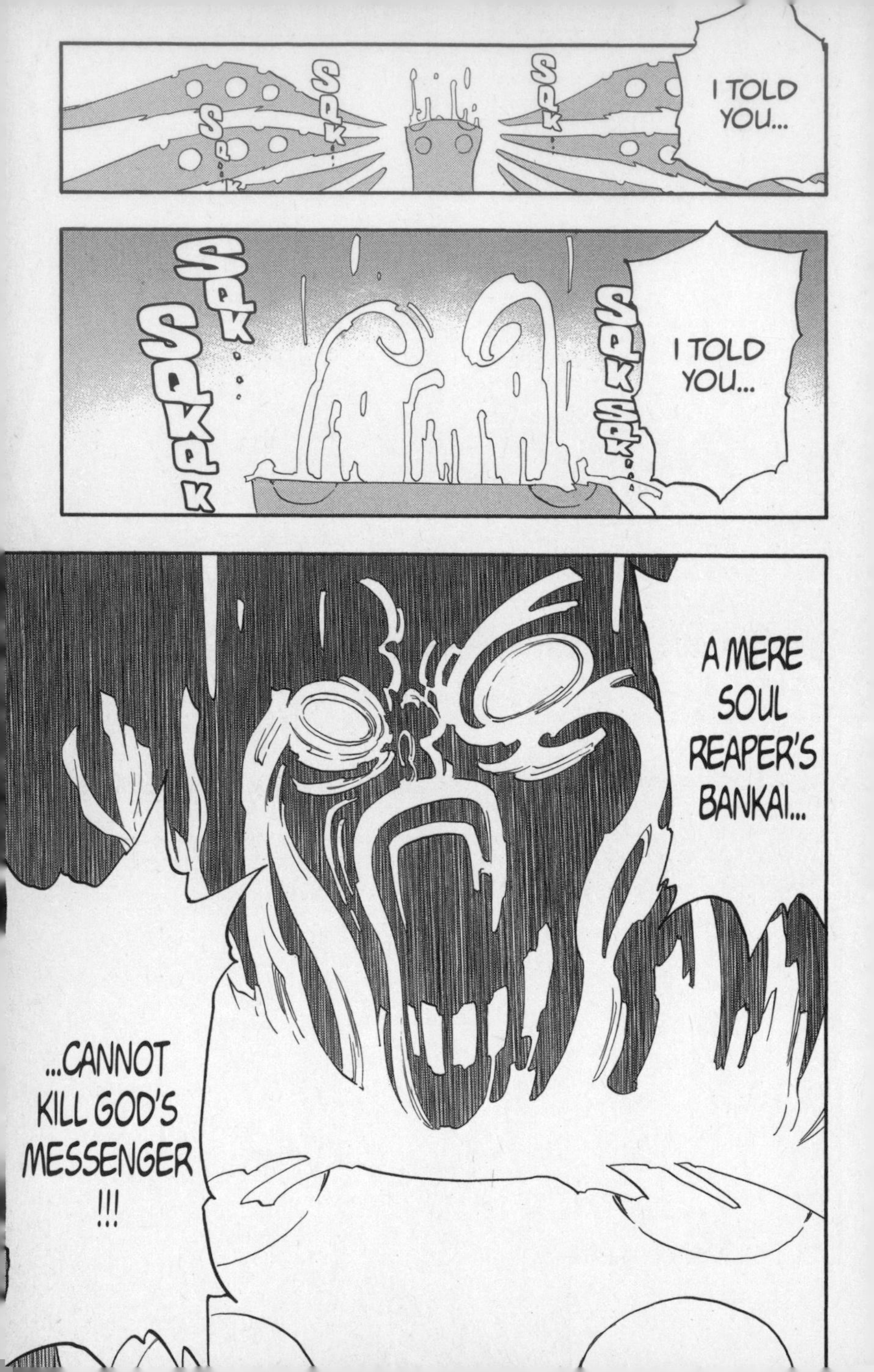
I TOLD YOU...
SQK
SQK
SQK
I TOLD YOU...
SQK
SQK
SQK
SQKQK
A MERE SOUL REAPER'S BANKAI...
...CANNOT KILL GOD'S MESSENGER!!!

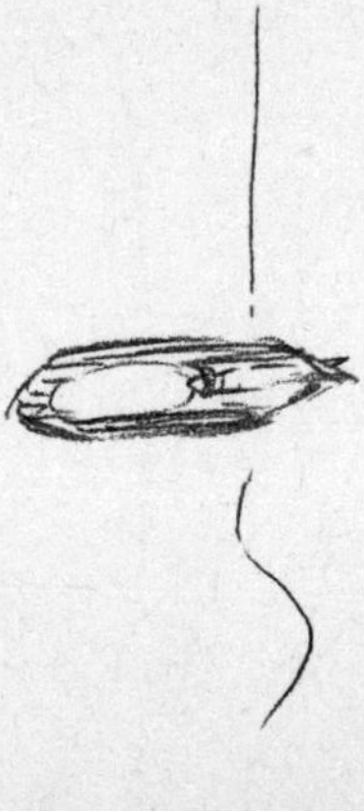

650.THE THEATRE SUICIDE SCENE 4

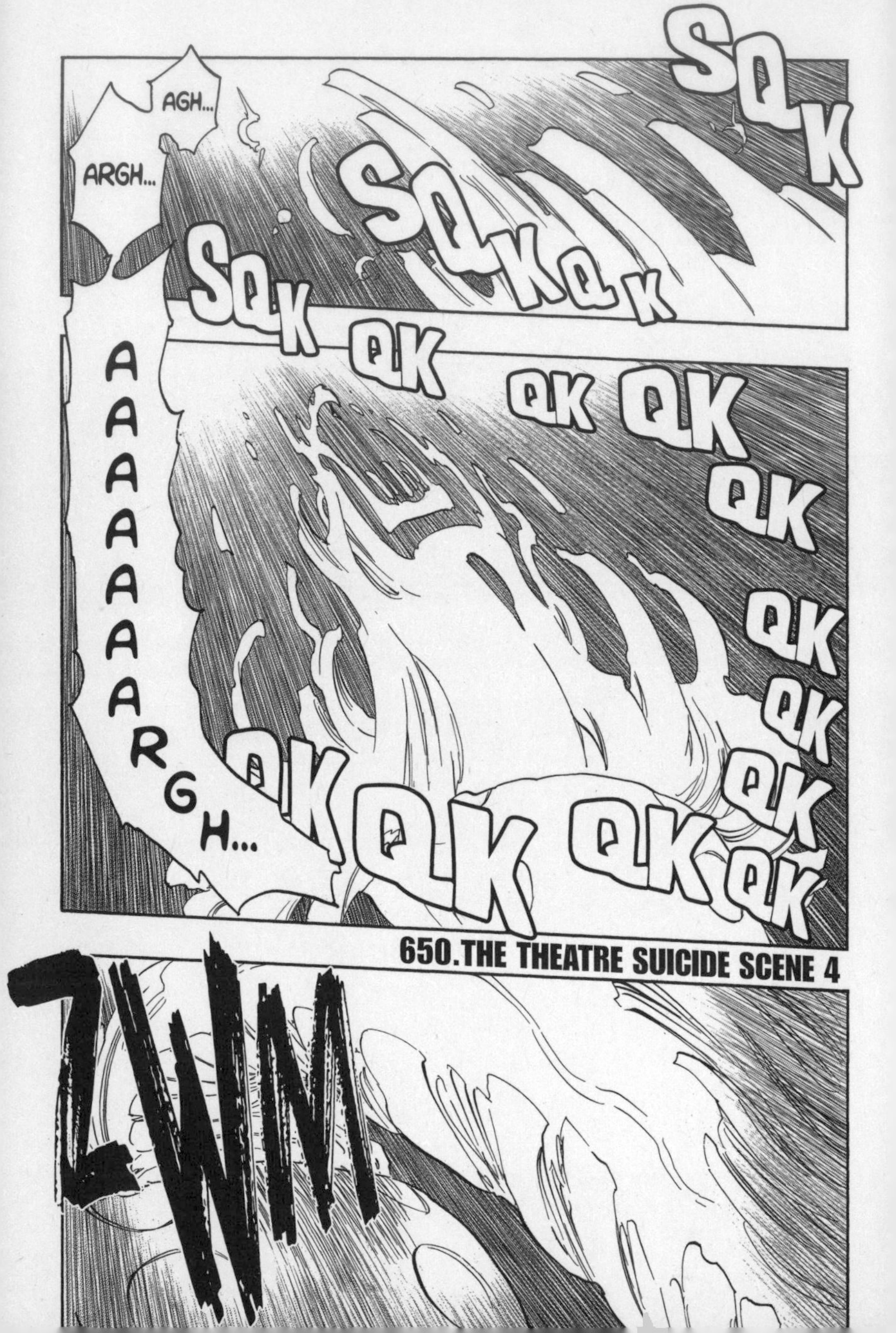
SQK
SQKQK
AGH...
ARGH...
SQK
QK
QK QK
QK
QK
QK
QK
QK
QK
QK QK
AAAAAAARGH...
ZWM

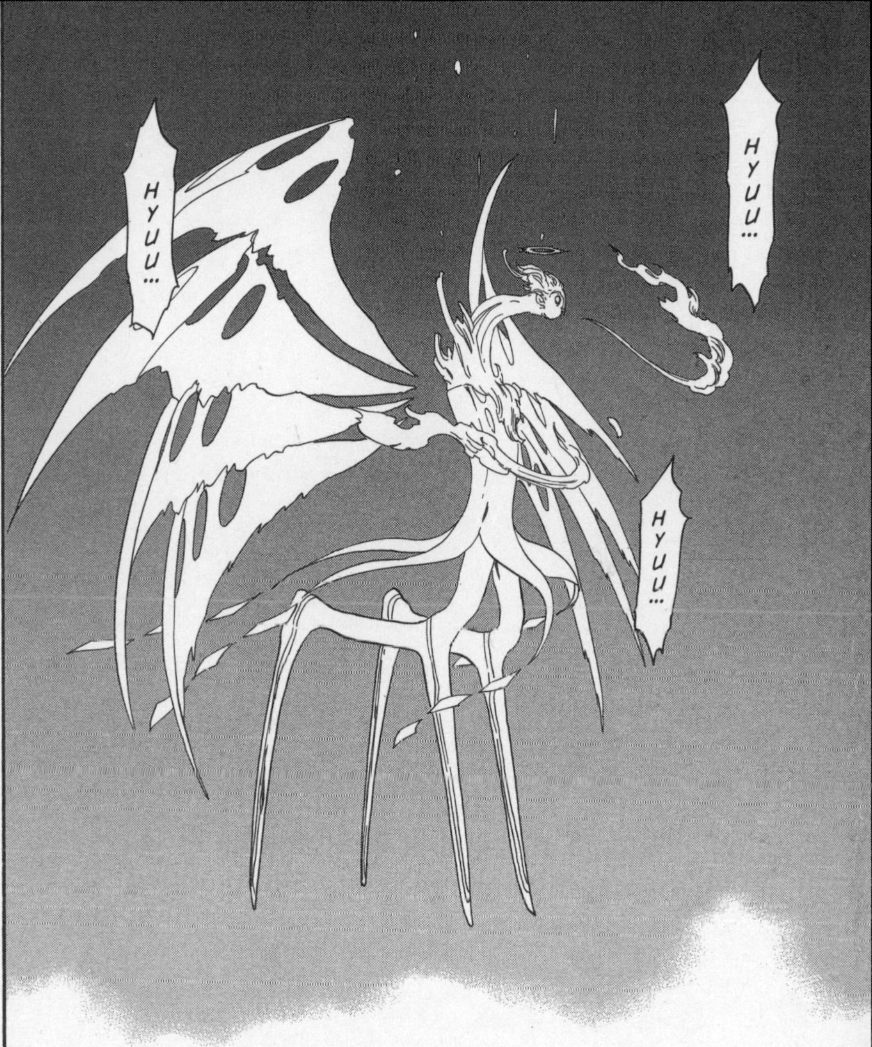
HYUU...
HYUU...
HYUU...

BLEACH 650.

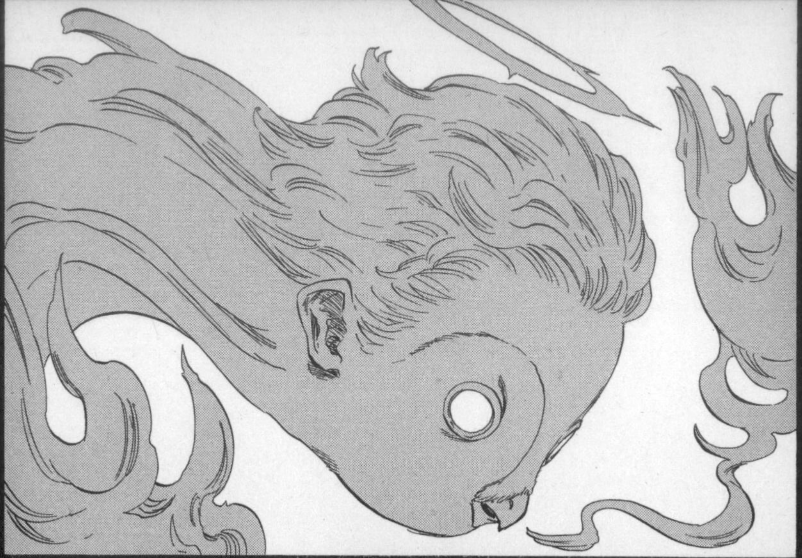

THE THEATRE SUICIDE SCENE4

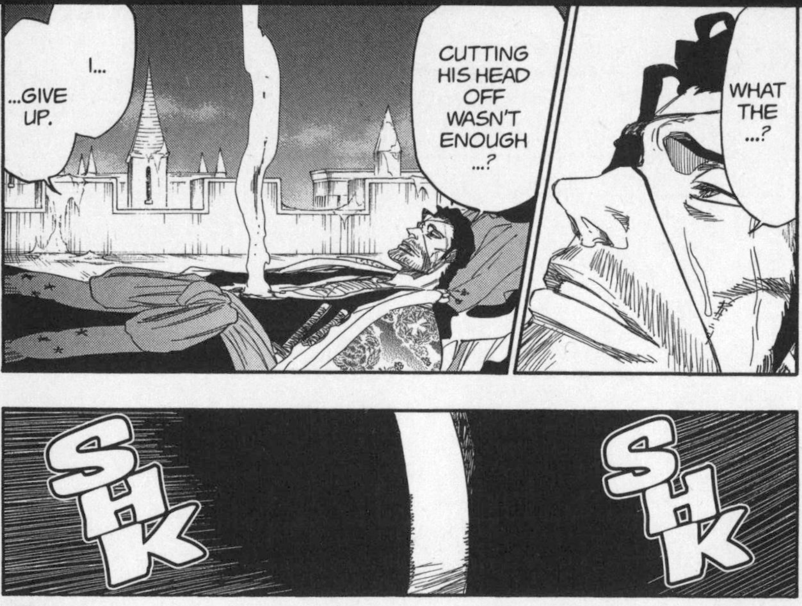
WHAT THE ...?
CUTTING HIS HEAD OFF WASN'T ENOUGH ...?
I...
...GIVE UP.
SHK
SHK

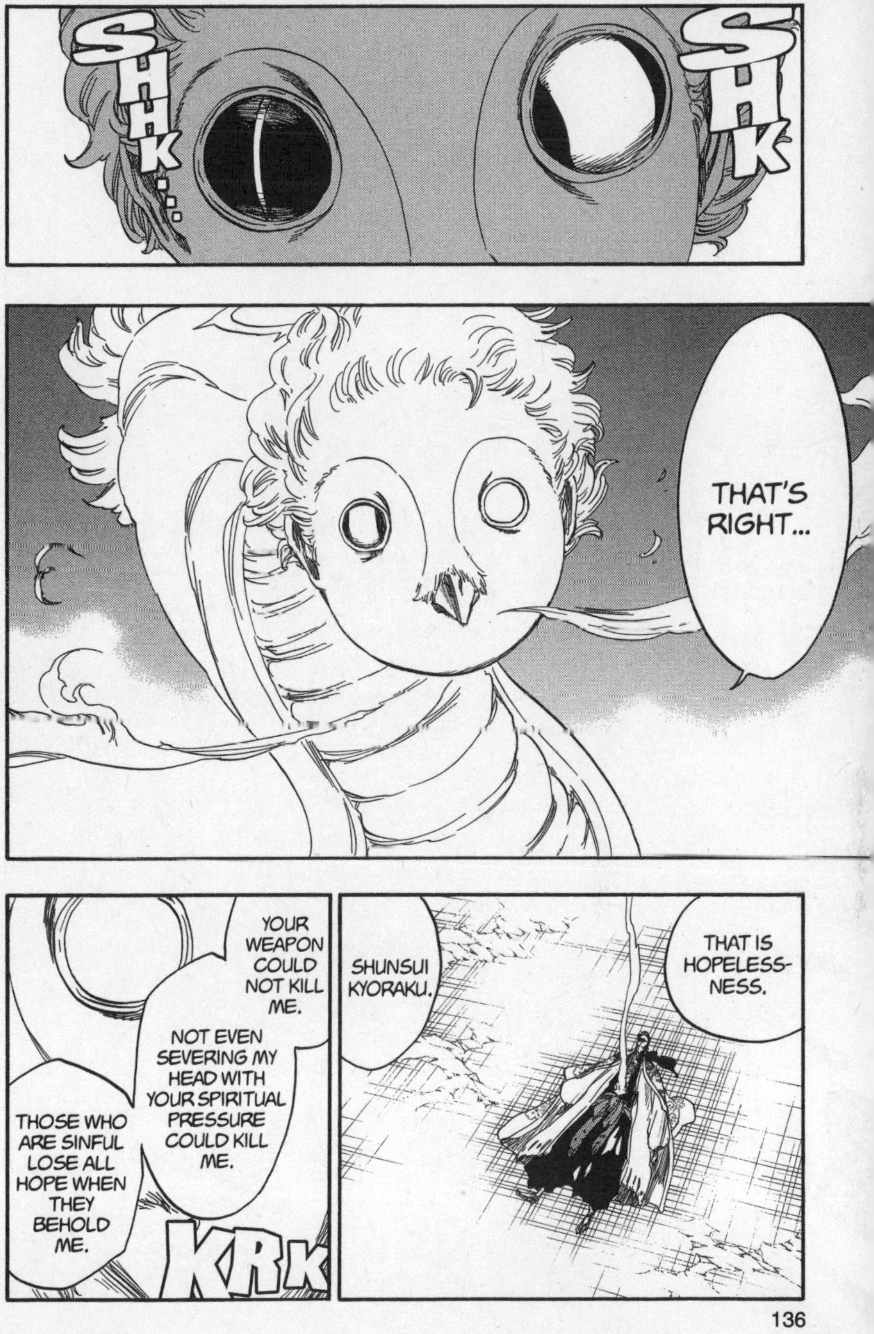
SHK
SHHK...
THAT'S RIGHT...
THAT IS HOPELESSNESS.
SHUNSUI KYORAKU.
YOUR WEAPON COULD NOT KILL ME.
NOT EVEN SEVERING MY HEAD WITH YOUR SPIRITUAL PRESSURE COULD KILL ME.
THOSE WHO ARE SINFUL LOSE ALL HOPE WHEN THEY BEHOLD ME.
KRK

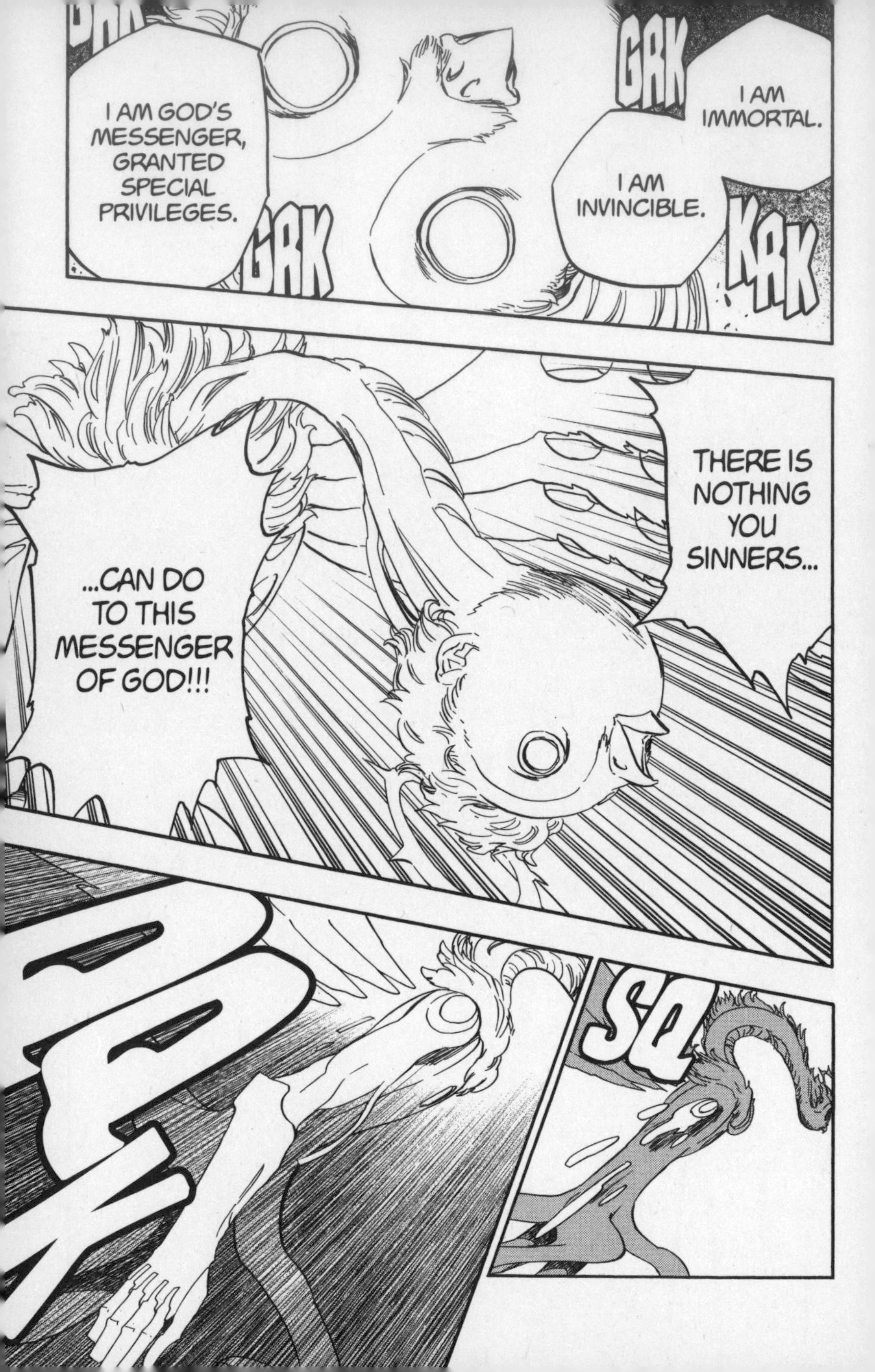
GRK
I AM IMMORTAL.
I AM INVINCIBLE.
KRK
I AM GOD'S MESSENGER, GRANTED SPECIAL PRIVILEGES.
GRK
THERE IS NOTHING YOU SINNERS...
...CAN DO TO THIS MESSENGER OF GOD!!!
SQ

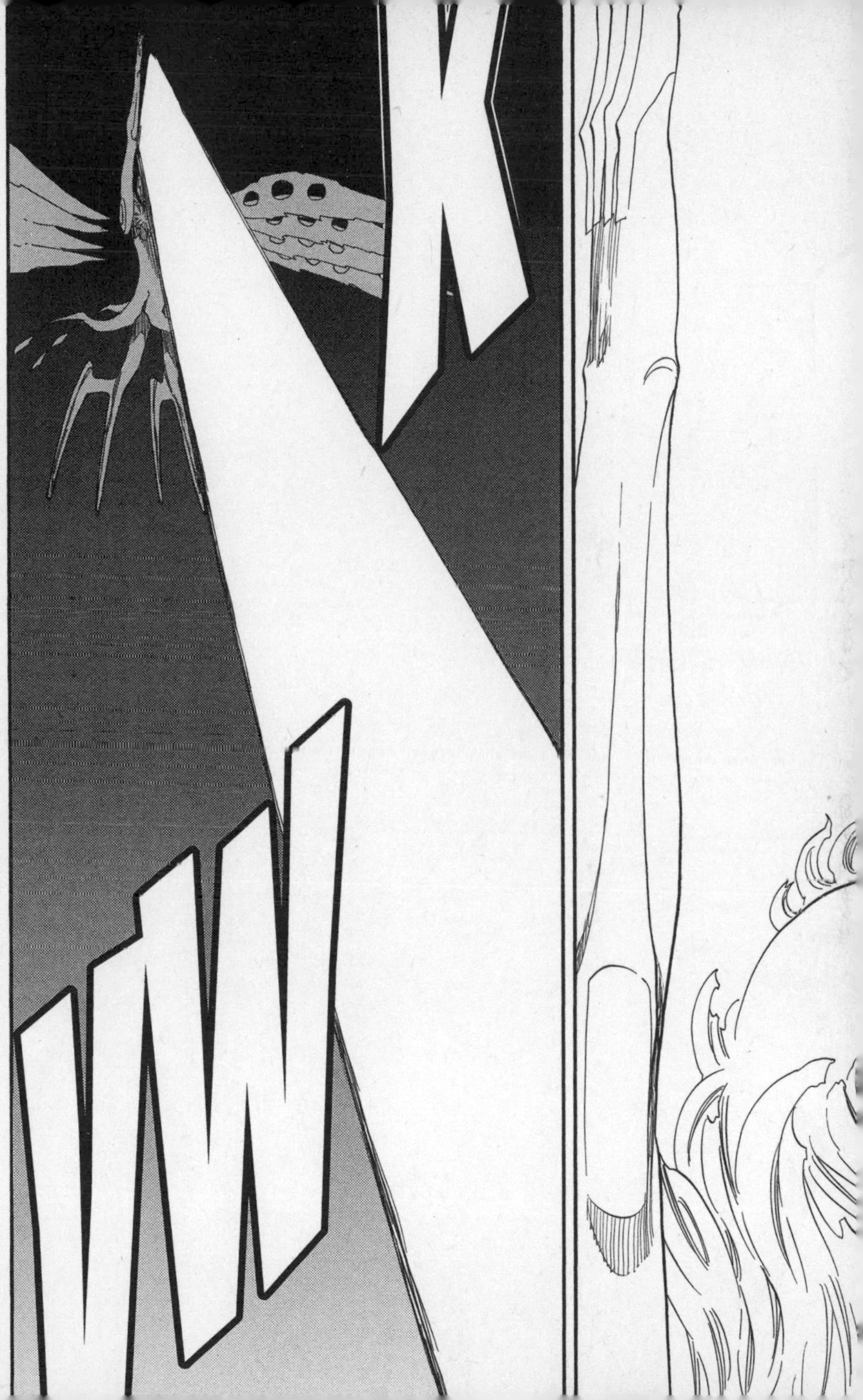

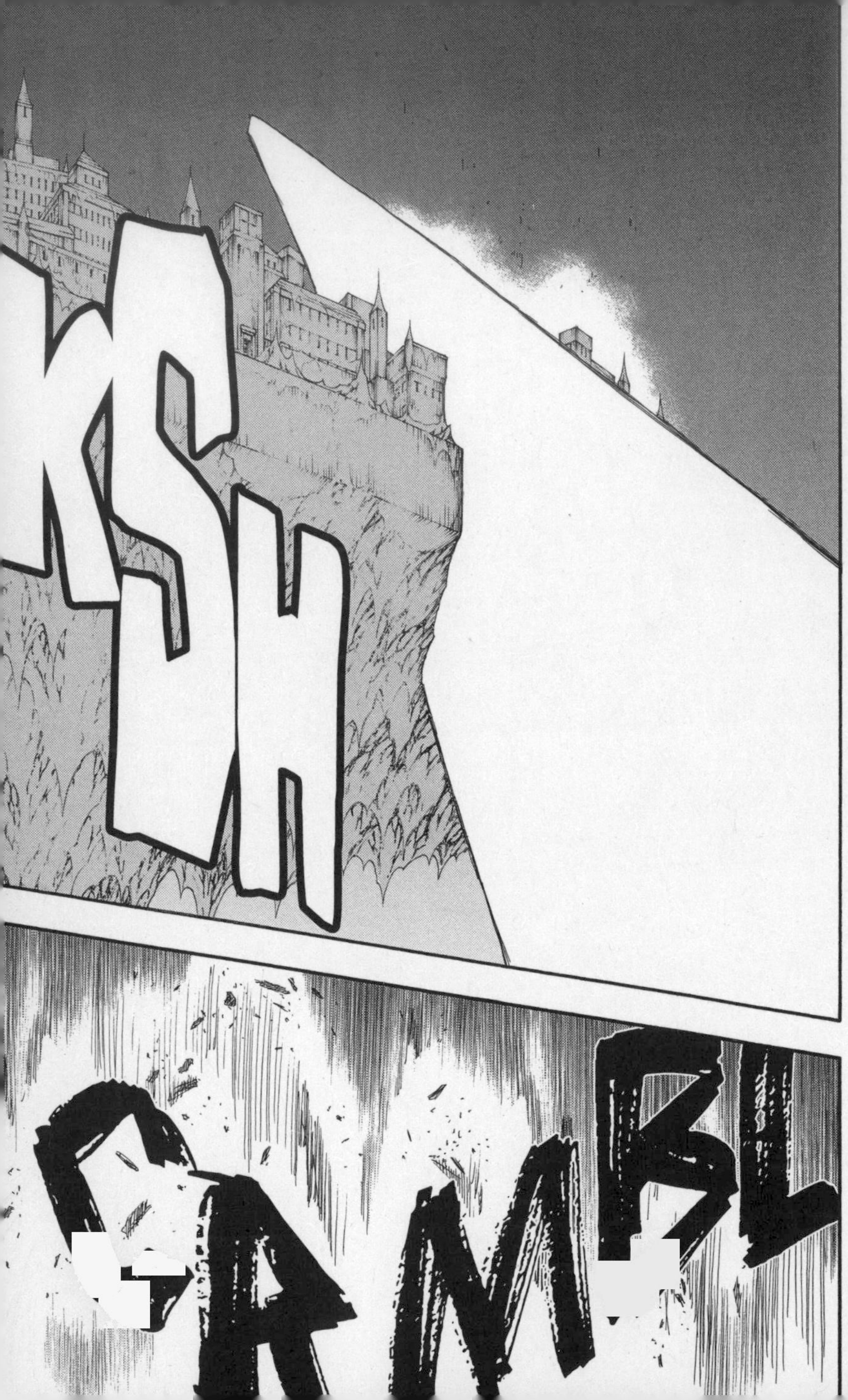
SH
AMBL

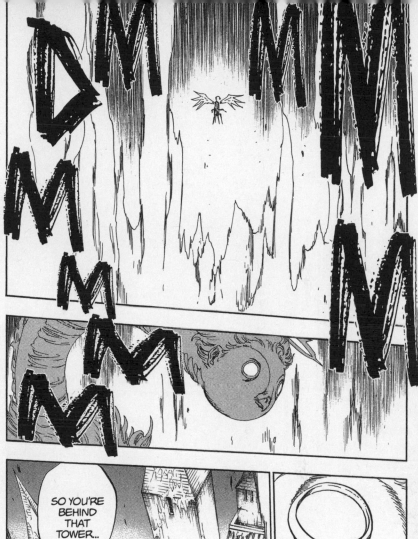

SO YOU'RE
BEHIND
THAT
TOWER...

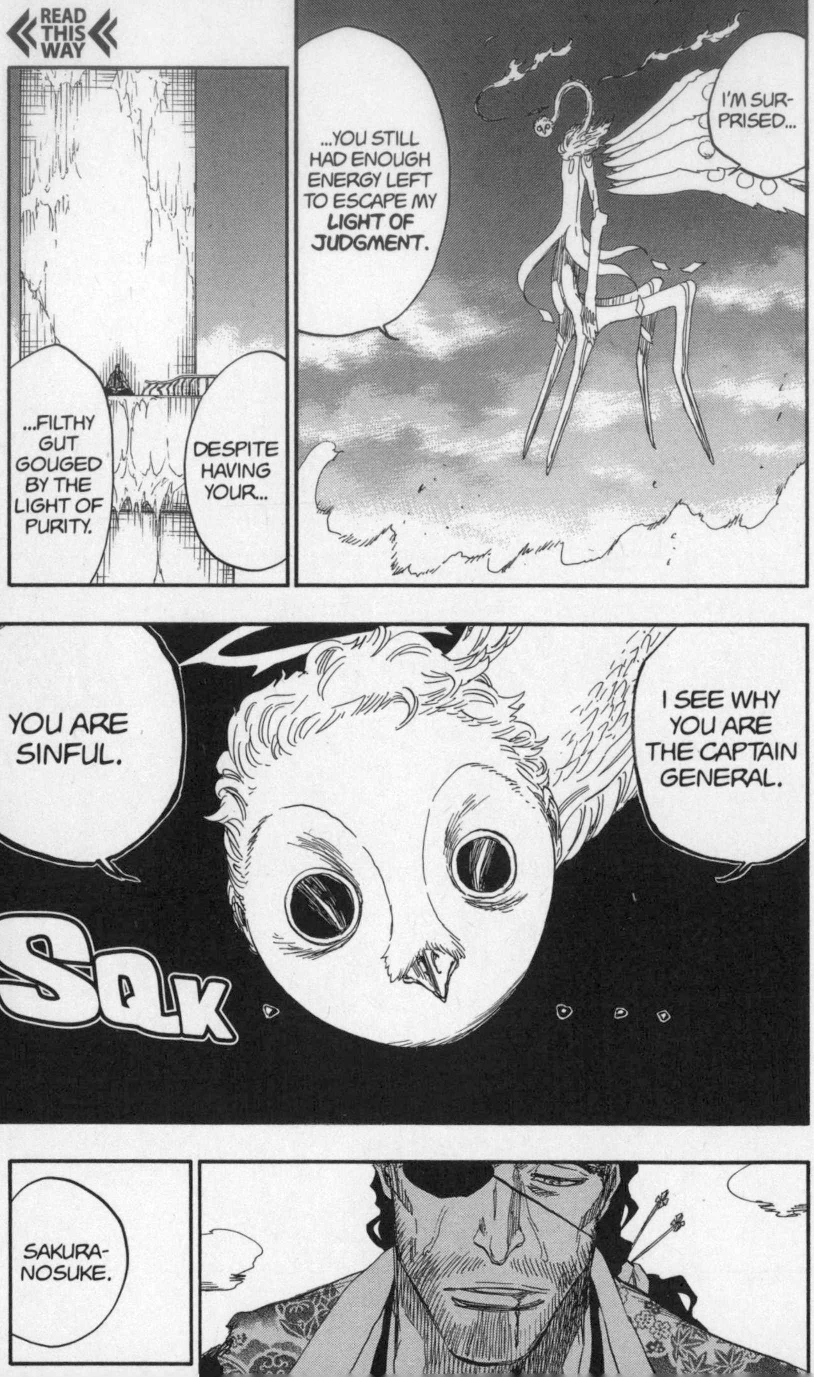
READ THIS WAY
I'M SURPRISED...
...YOU STILL HAD ENOUGH ENERGY LEFT TO ESCAPE MY LIGHT OF JUDGMENT.
DESPITE HAVING YOUR...
...FILTHY GUT GOUGED BY THE LIGHT OF PURITY.
I SEE WHY YOU ARE THE CAPTAIN GENERAL.
YOU ARE SINFUL.
SQK
SAKURA-NOSUKE.

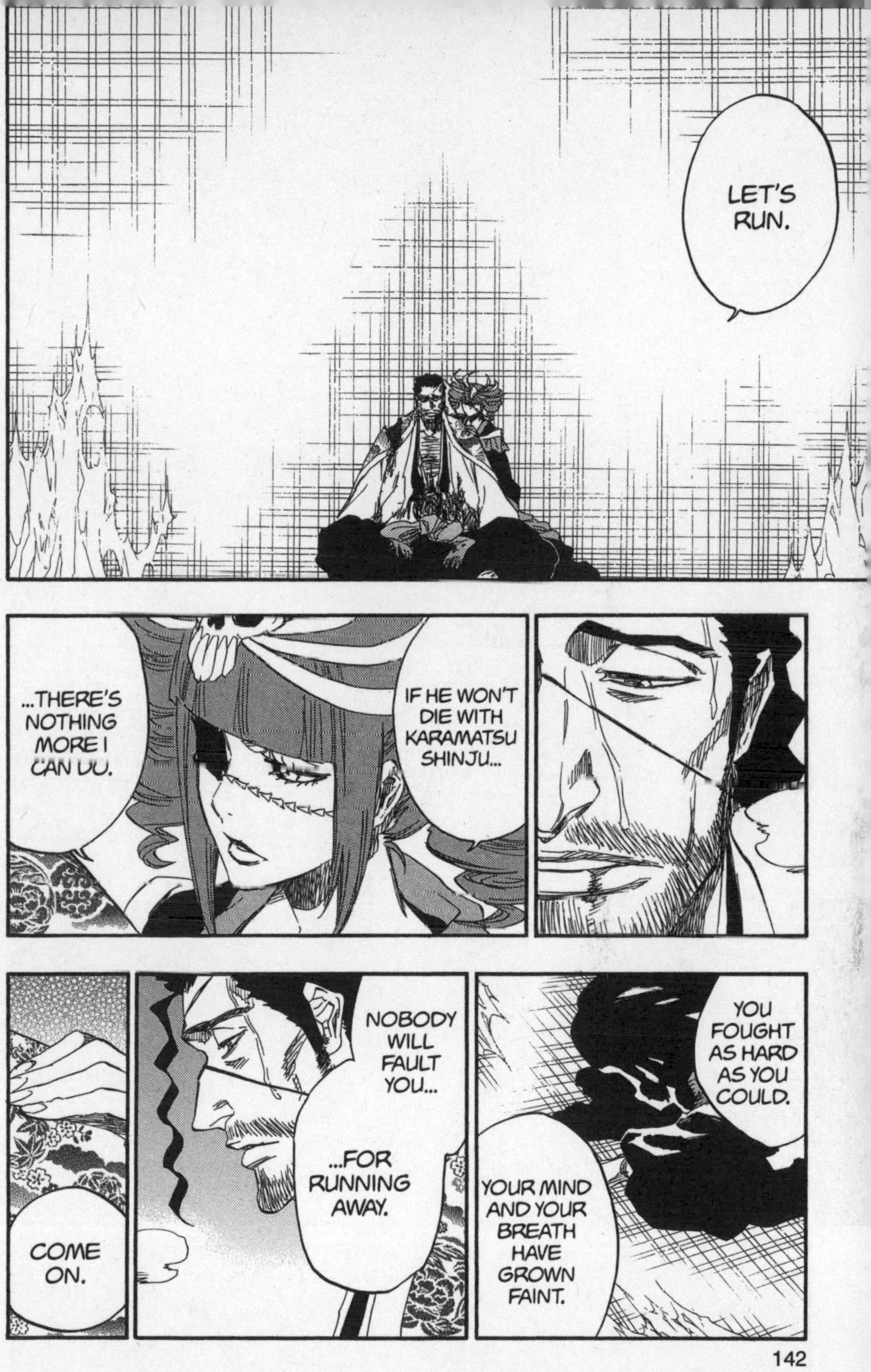
LET'S RUN.
IF HE WON'T DIE WITH KARAMATSU SHINJU...
...THERE'S NOTHING MORE I CAN DO.
YOU FOUGHT AS HARD AS YOU COULD.
YOUR MIND AND YOUR BREATH HAVE GROWN FAINT.
NOBODY WILL FAULT YOU...
...FOR RUNNING AWAY.
COME ON.

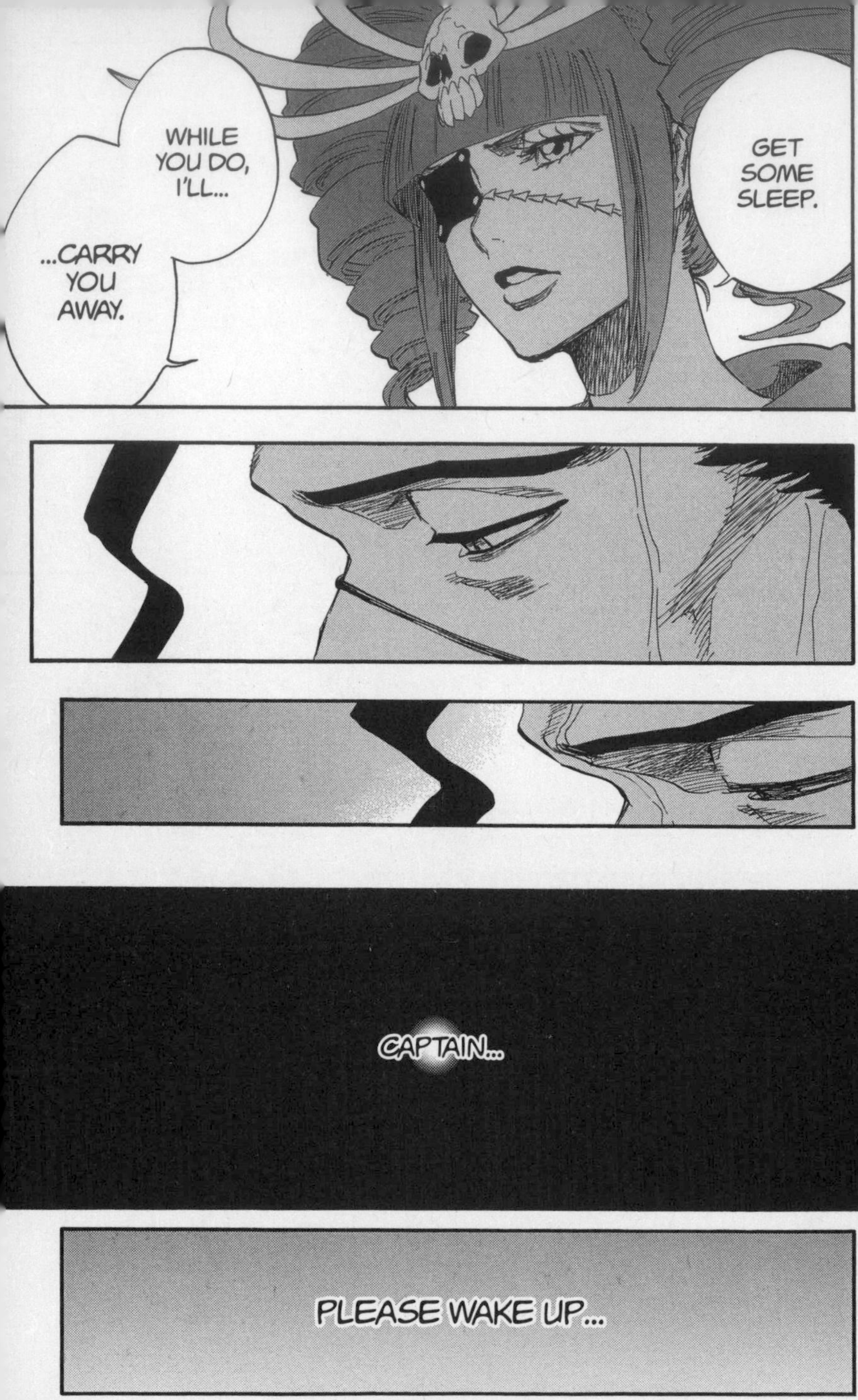
GET SOME SLEEP.
WHILE YOU DO, I'LL...
...CARRY YOU AWAY.
CAPTAIN...
PLEASE WAKE UP...

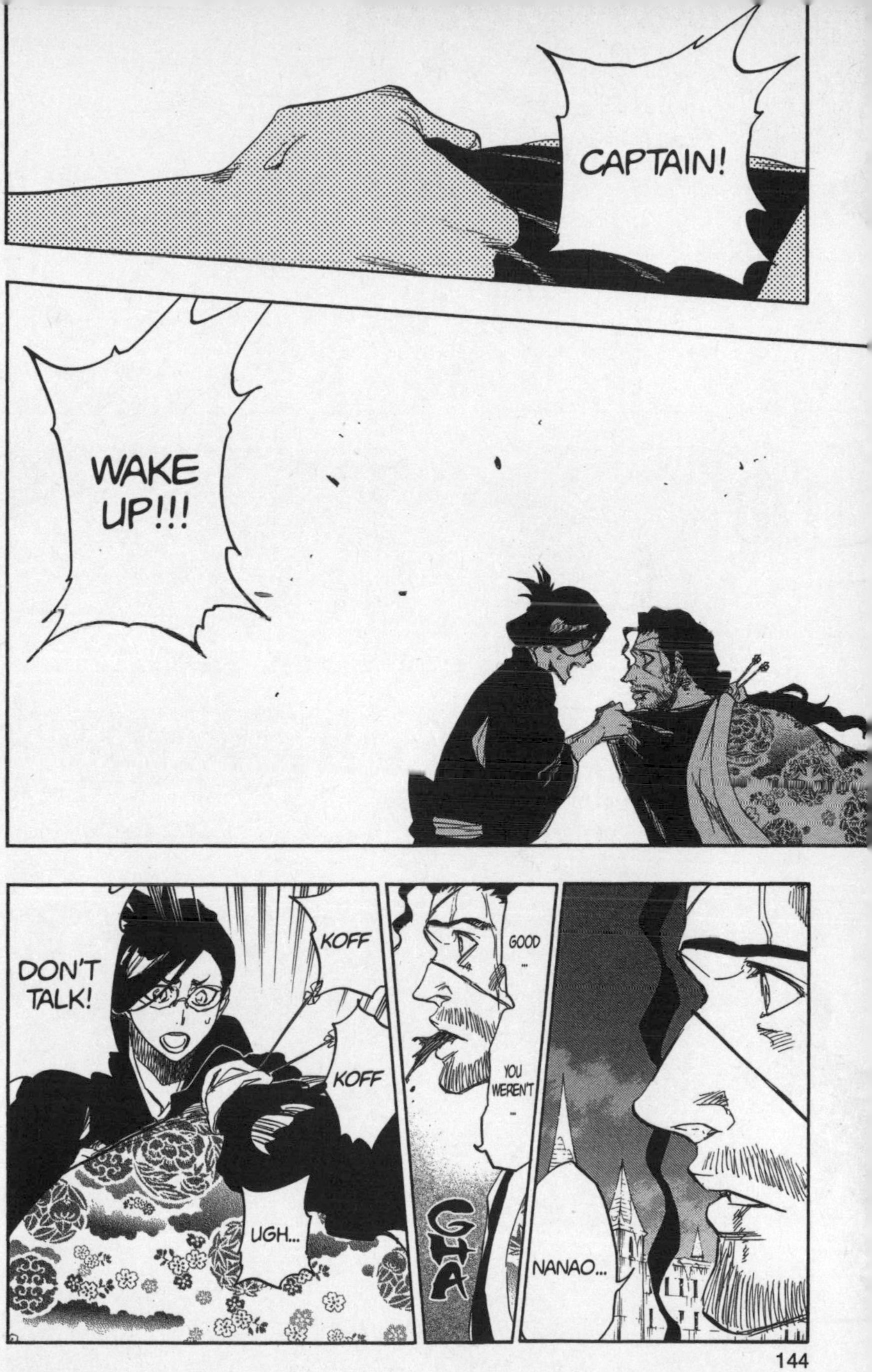
CAPTAIN!
WAKE UP!!!
NANAO...
GOOD...
YOU WEREN'T...
GHA
KOFF
KOFF
DON'T TALK!
UGH...

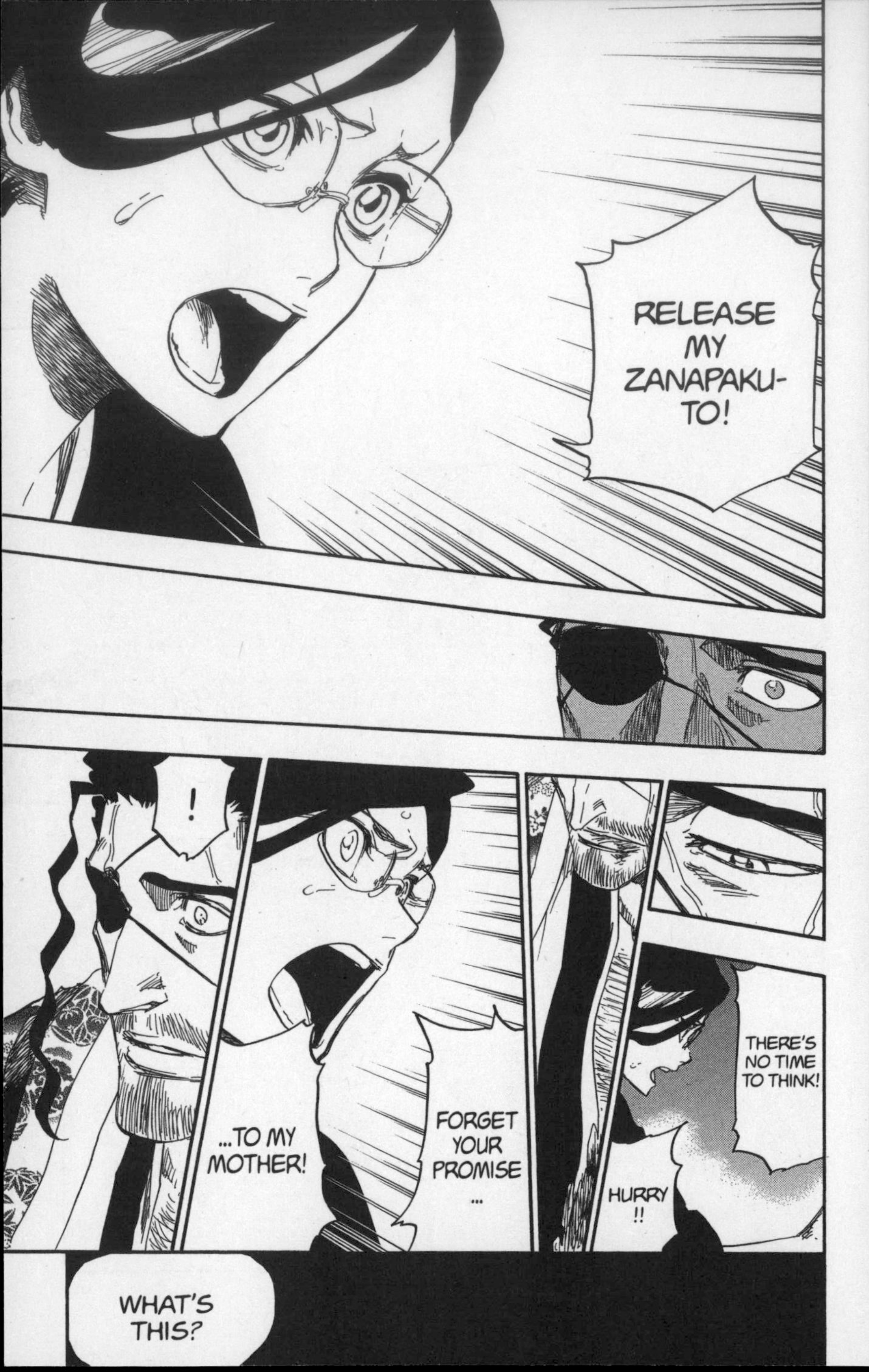
RELEASE MY ZANAPAKU-TO!
THERE'S NO TIME TO THINK!
HURRY!!
FORGET YOUR PROMISE...
...TO MY MOTHER!
!
WHAT'S THIS?

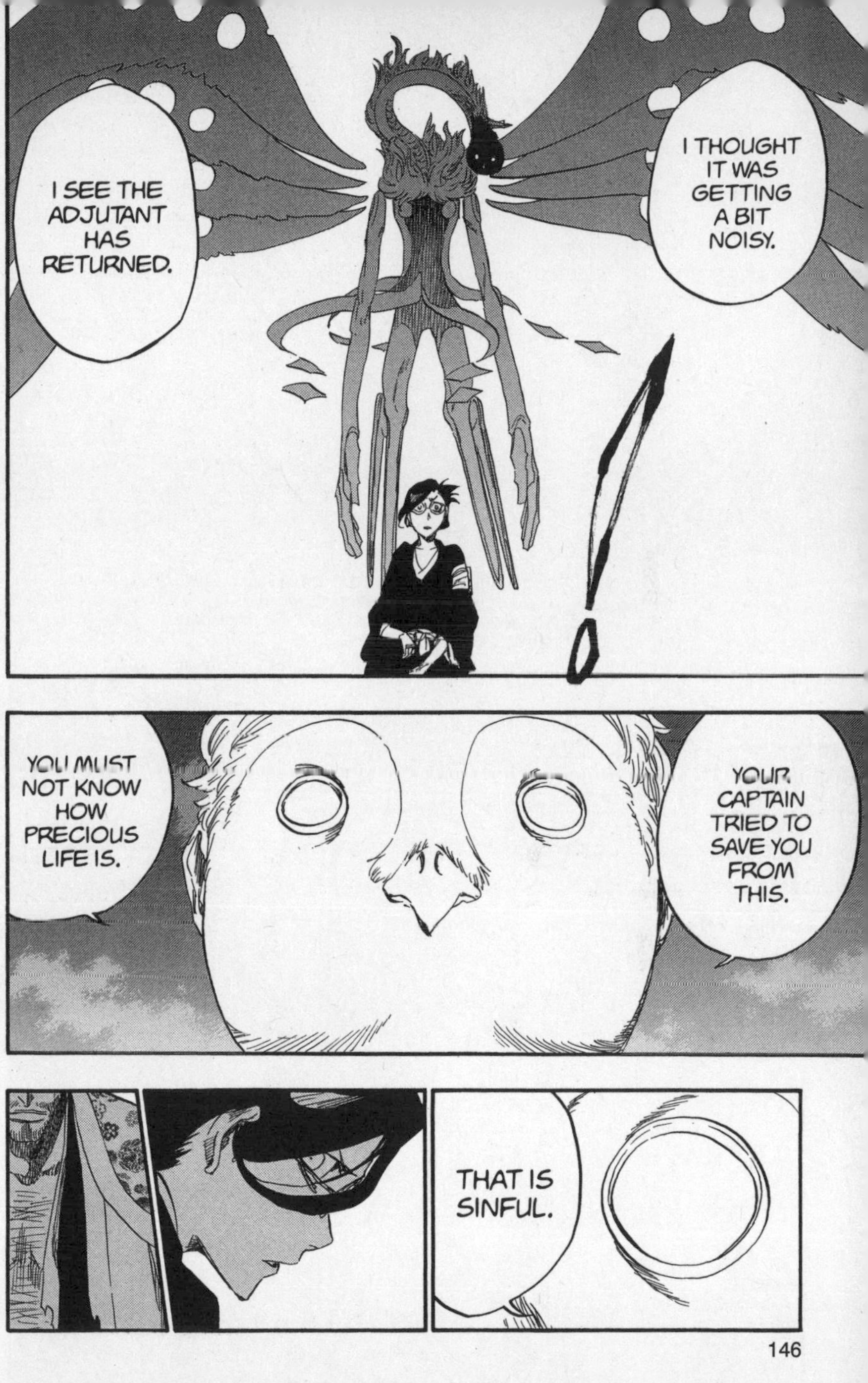
I THOUGHT IT WAS GETTING A BIT NOISY.
I SEE THE ADJUTANT HAS RETURNED.
YOUR CAPTAIN TRIED TO SAVE YOU FROM THIS.
YOU MUST NOT KNOW HOW PRECIOUS LIFE IS.
THAT IS SINFUL.

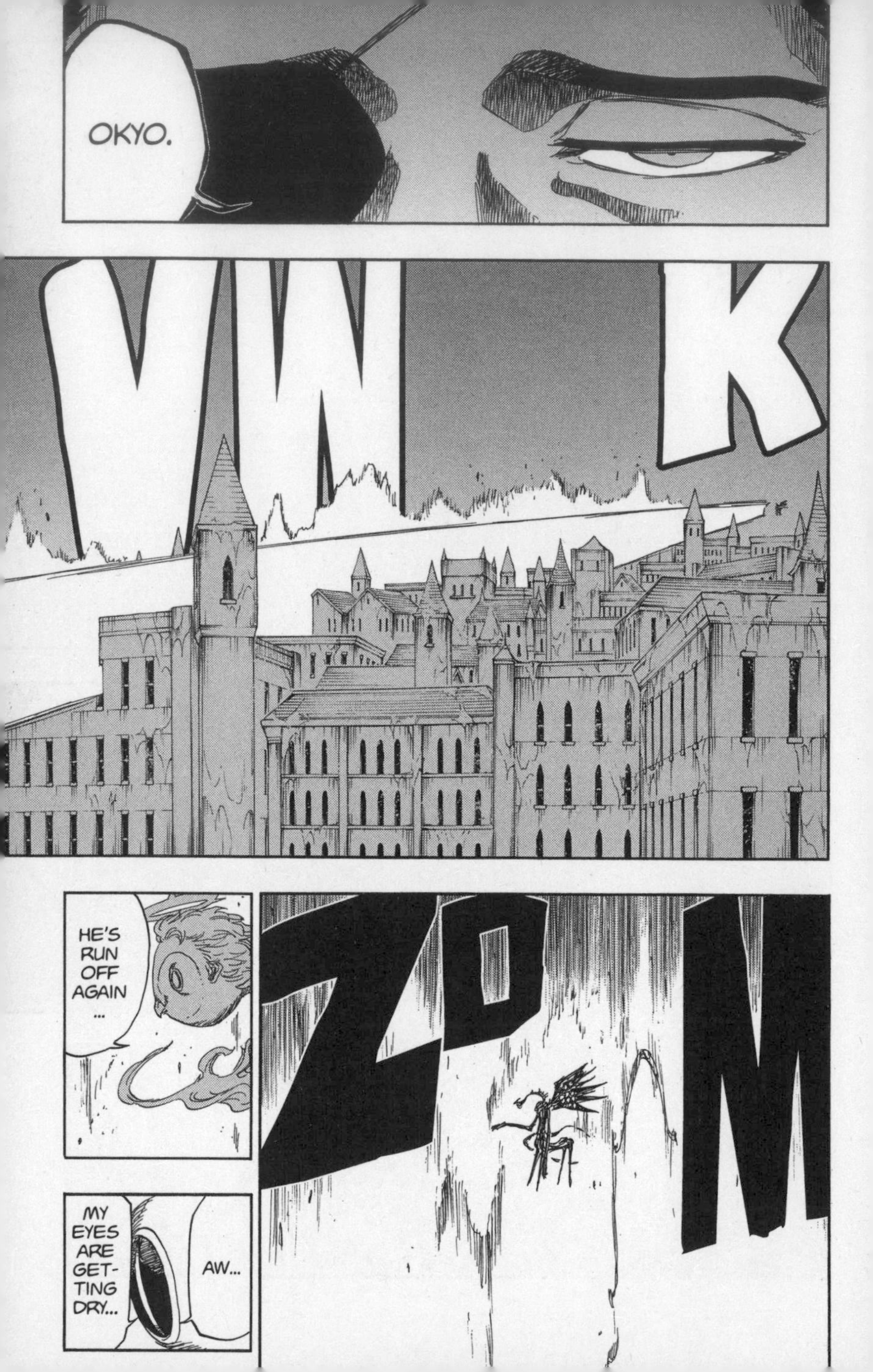
OKYO.
VNK
ZOM
HE'S RUN OFF AGAIN ...
AW...
MY EYES ARE GET-TING DRY...

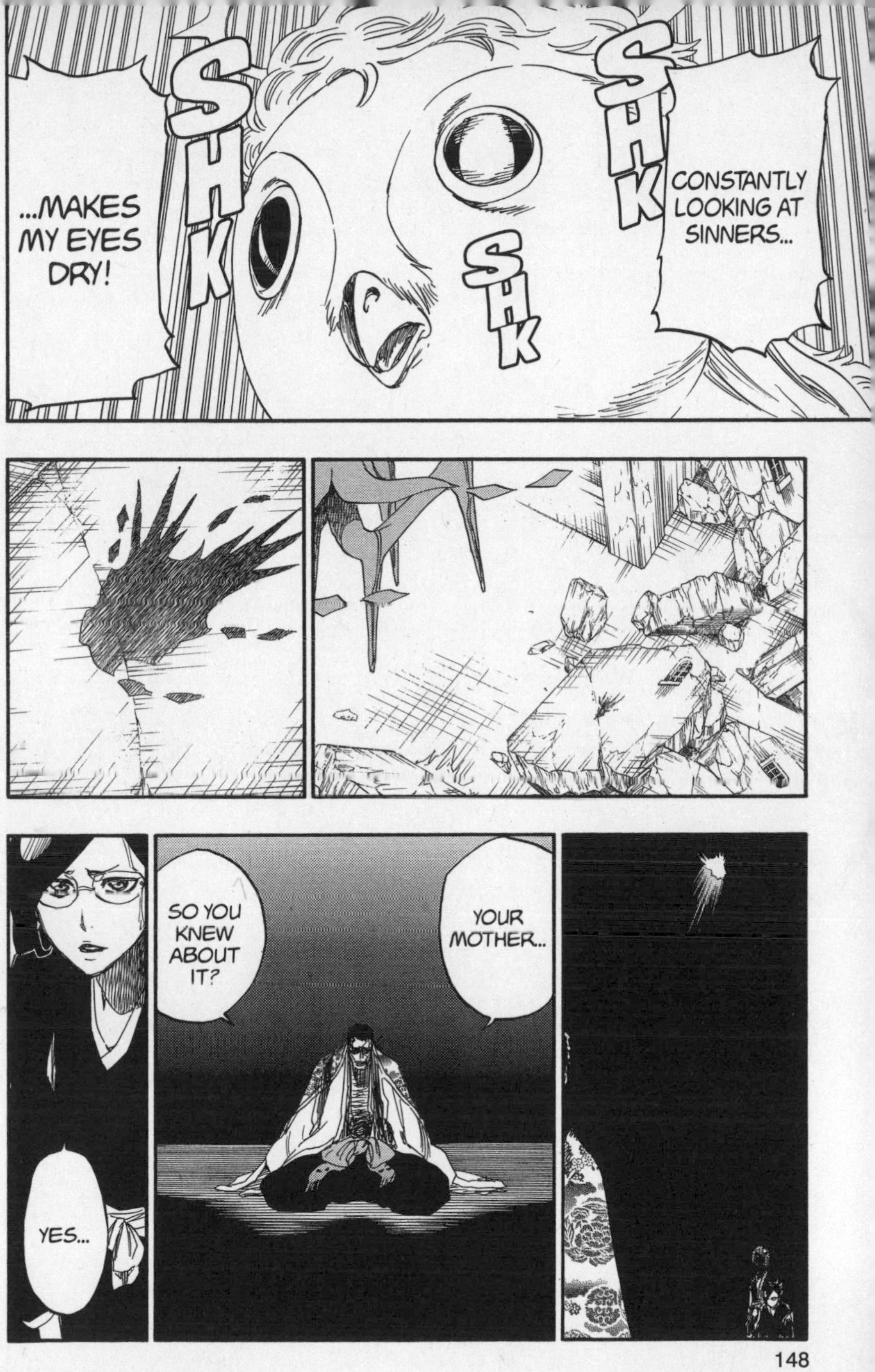
CONSTANTLY LOOKING AT SINNERS...
SHK
SHK
SHK
...MAKES MY EYES DRY!
YOUR MOTHER...
SO YOU KNEW ABOUT IT?
YES...

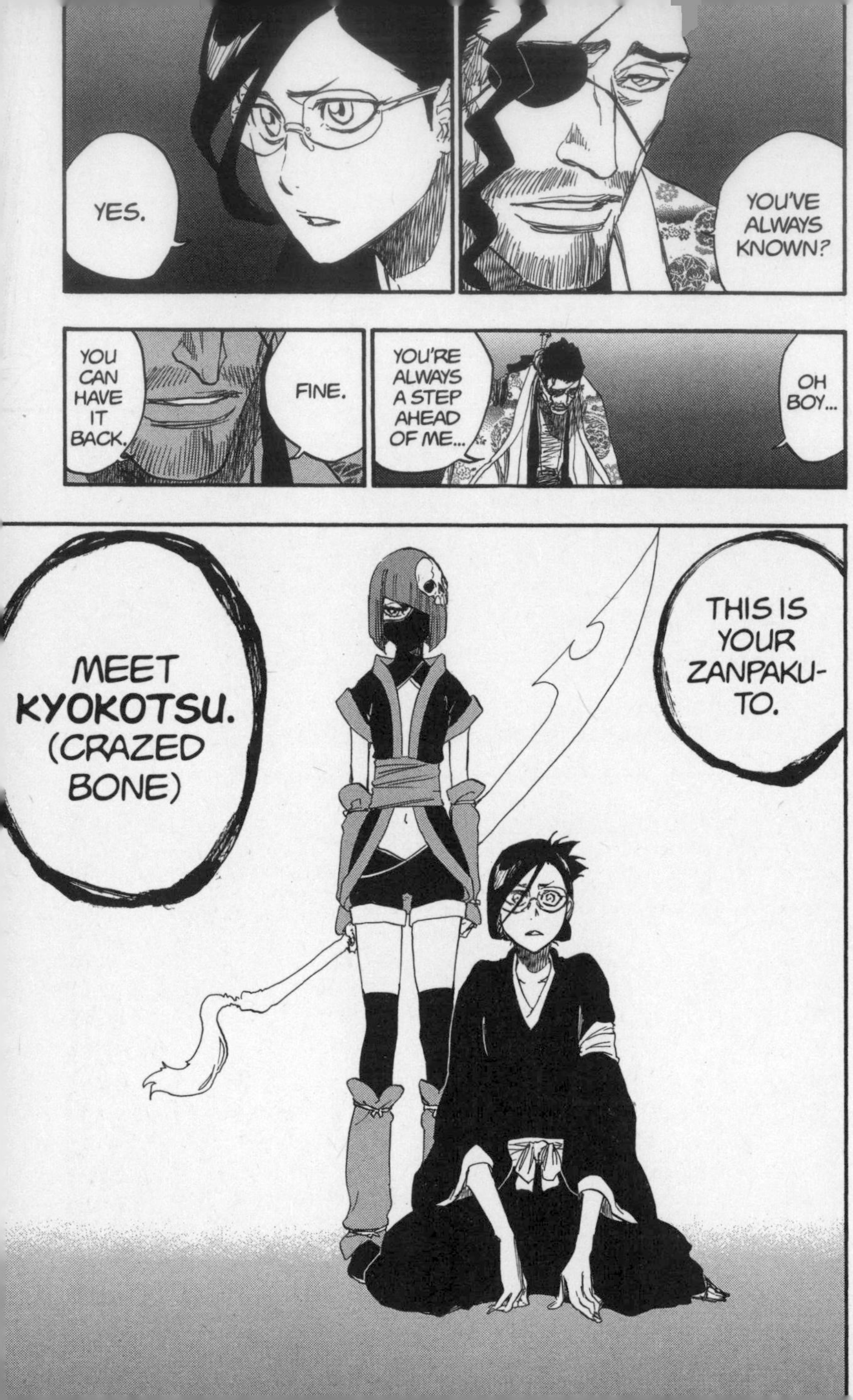
YOU'VE ALWAYS KNOWN?
YES.
OH BOY...
YOU'RE ALWAYS A STEP AHEAD OF ME...
FINE.
YOU CAN HAVE IT BACK.
THIS IS YOUR ZANPAKU-TO.
MEET KYOKOTSU. (CRAZED BONE)

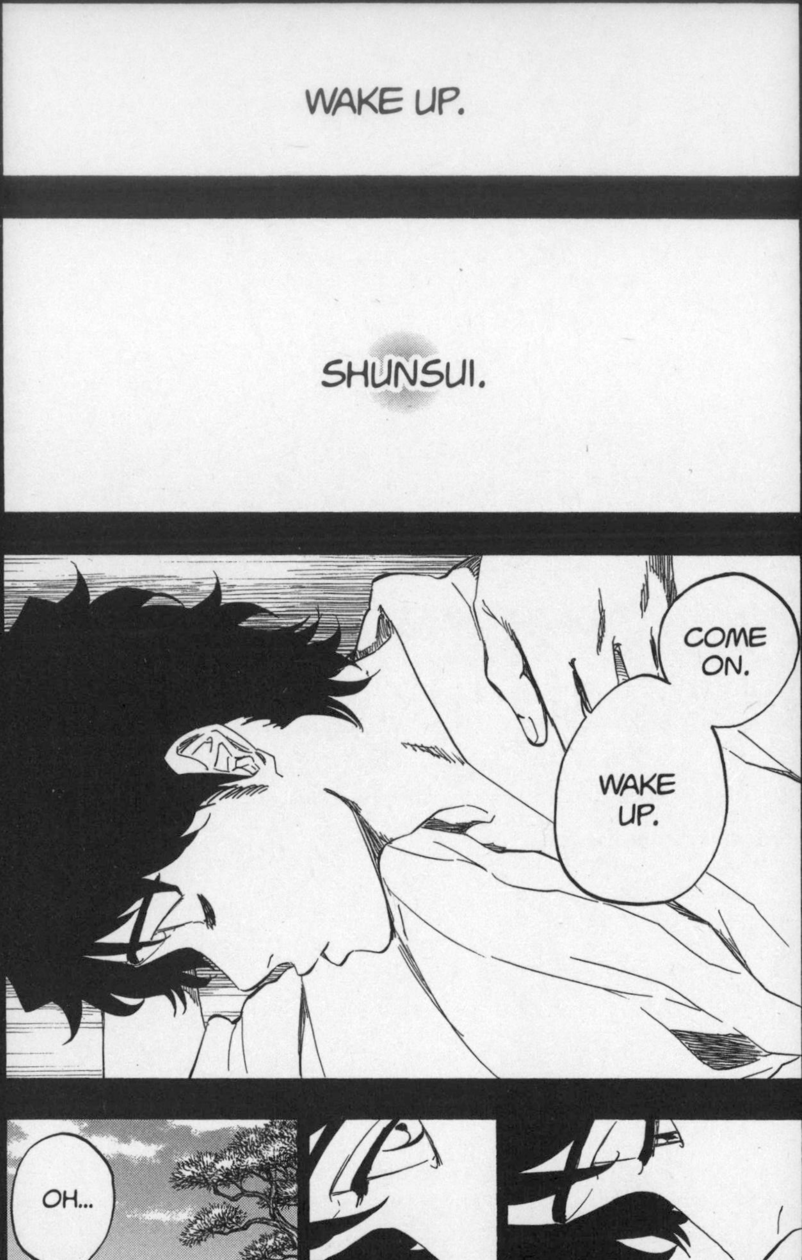
WAKE UP.
SHUNSUI.
COME ON.
WAKE UP.
OH...

651.THE THEATRE SUICIDE SCENE 5

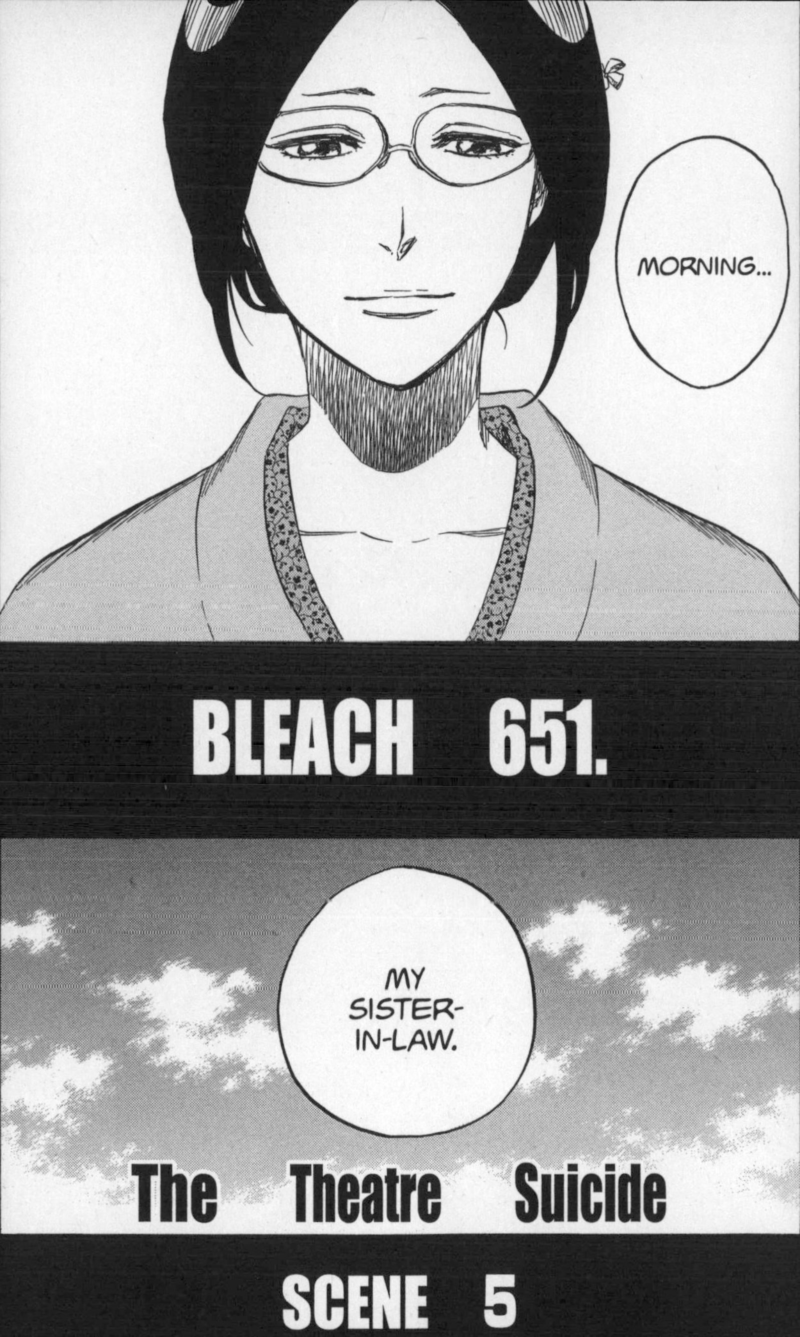
MORNING...
BLEACH 651.
MY SISTER-IN-LAW.
The Theatre Suicide
SCENE 5

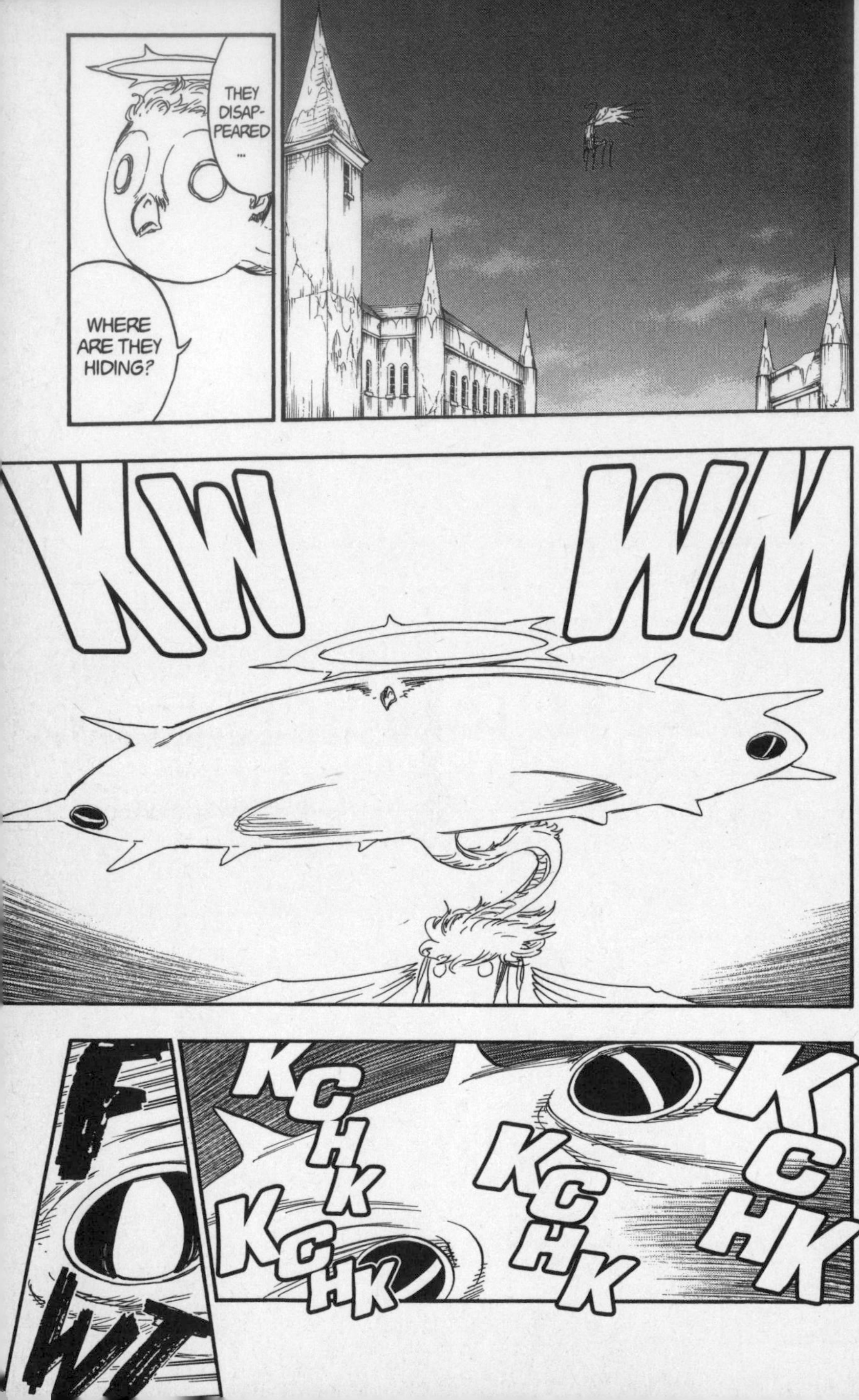
THEY DISAP-PEARED ...
WHERE ARE THEY HIDING?
KWWM
KCHK
KCHK
KCHK
KCHK
FWT

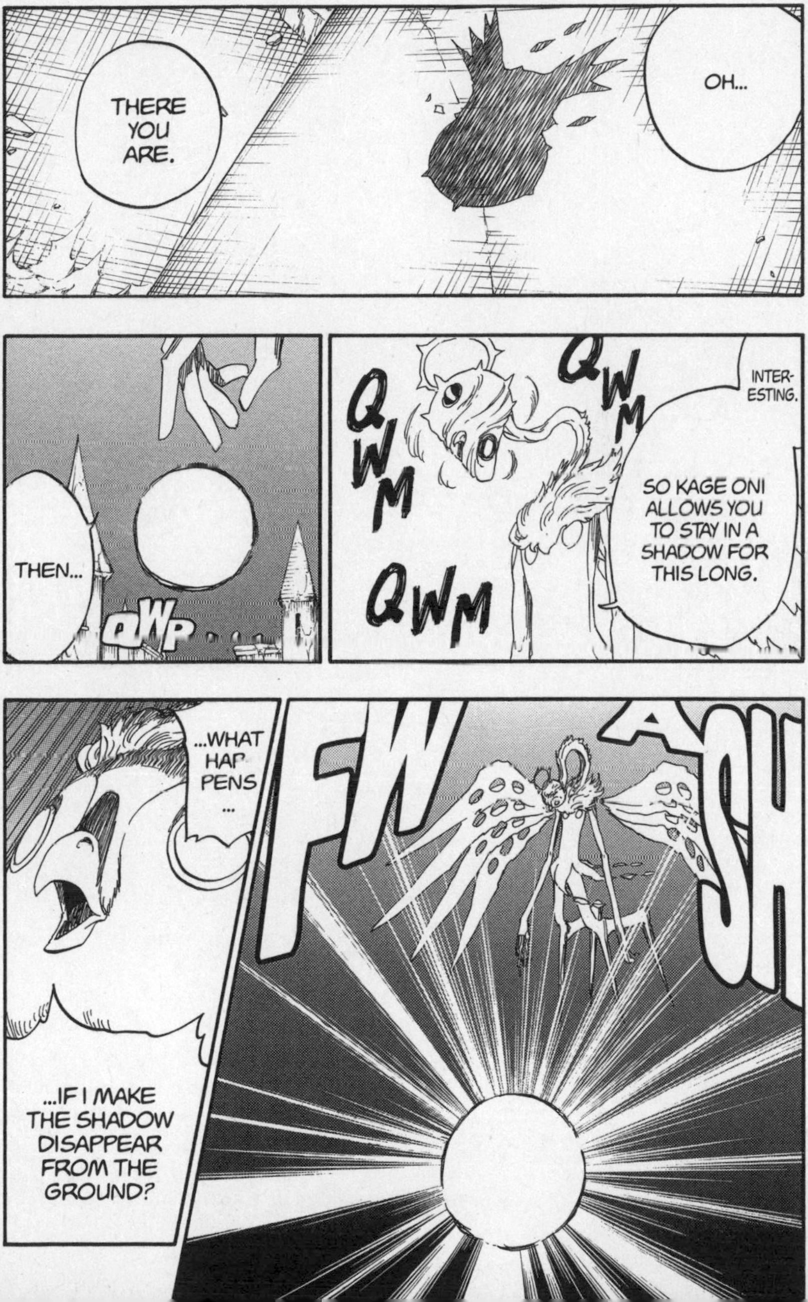
OH...
THERE YOU ARE.
INTER-ESTING.
SO KAGE ONI ALLOWS YOU TO STAY IN A SHADOW FOR THIS LONG.
QWM QWM QWM
THEN...
QWP
FWASH
...WHAT HAP PENS ...
...IF I MAKE THE SHADOW DISAPPEAR FROM THE GROUND?

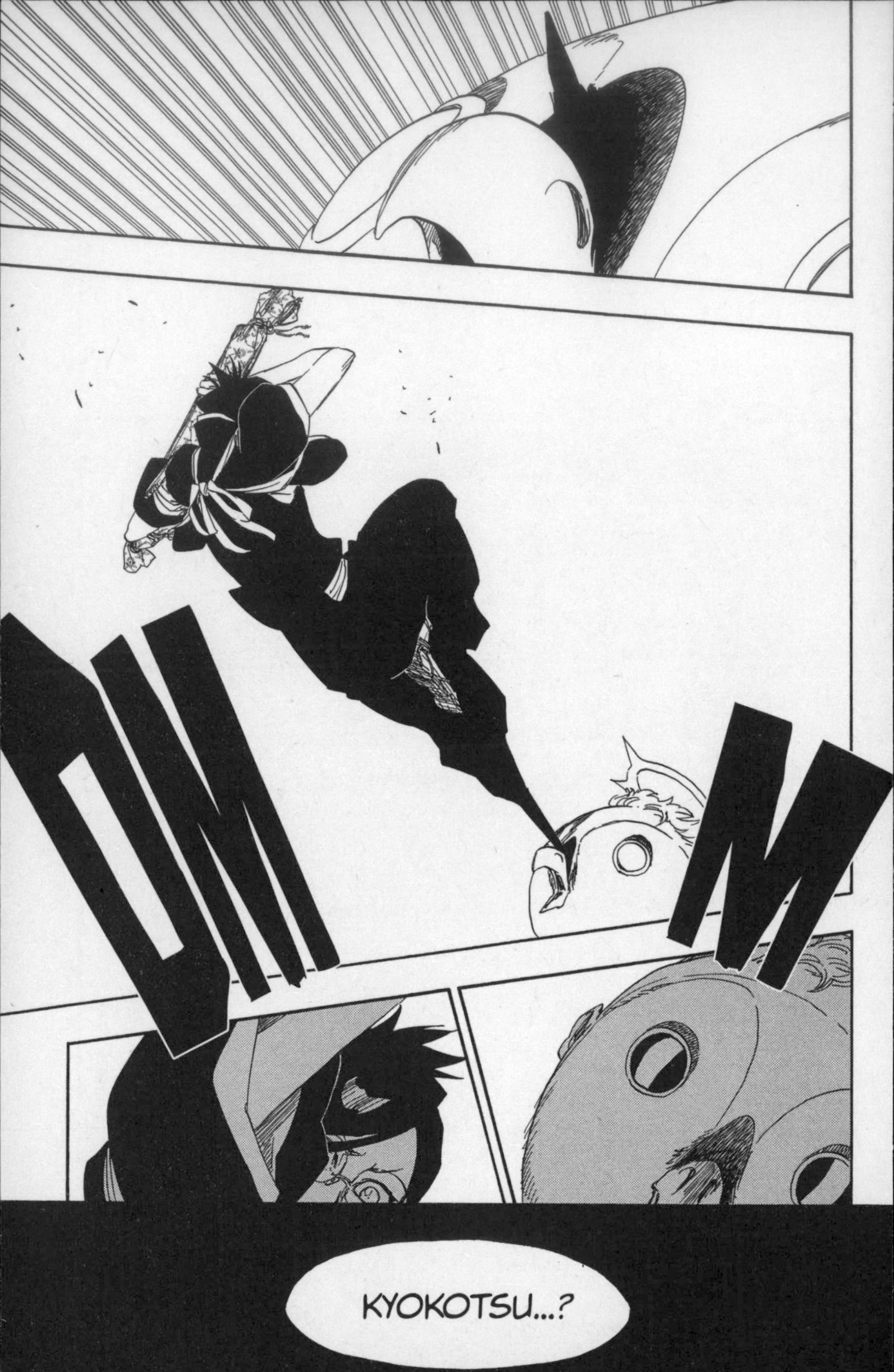
KYOKOTSU...?

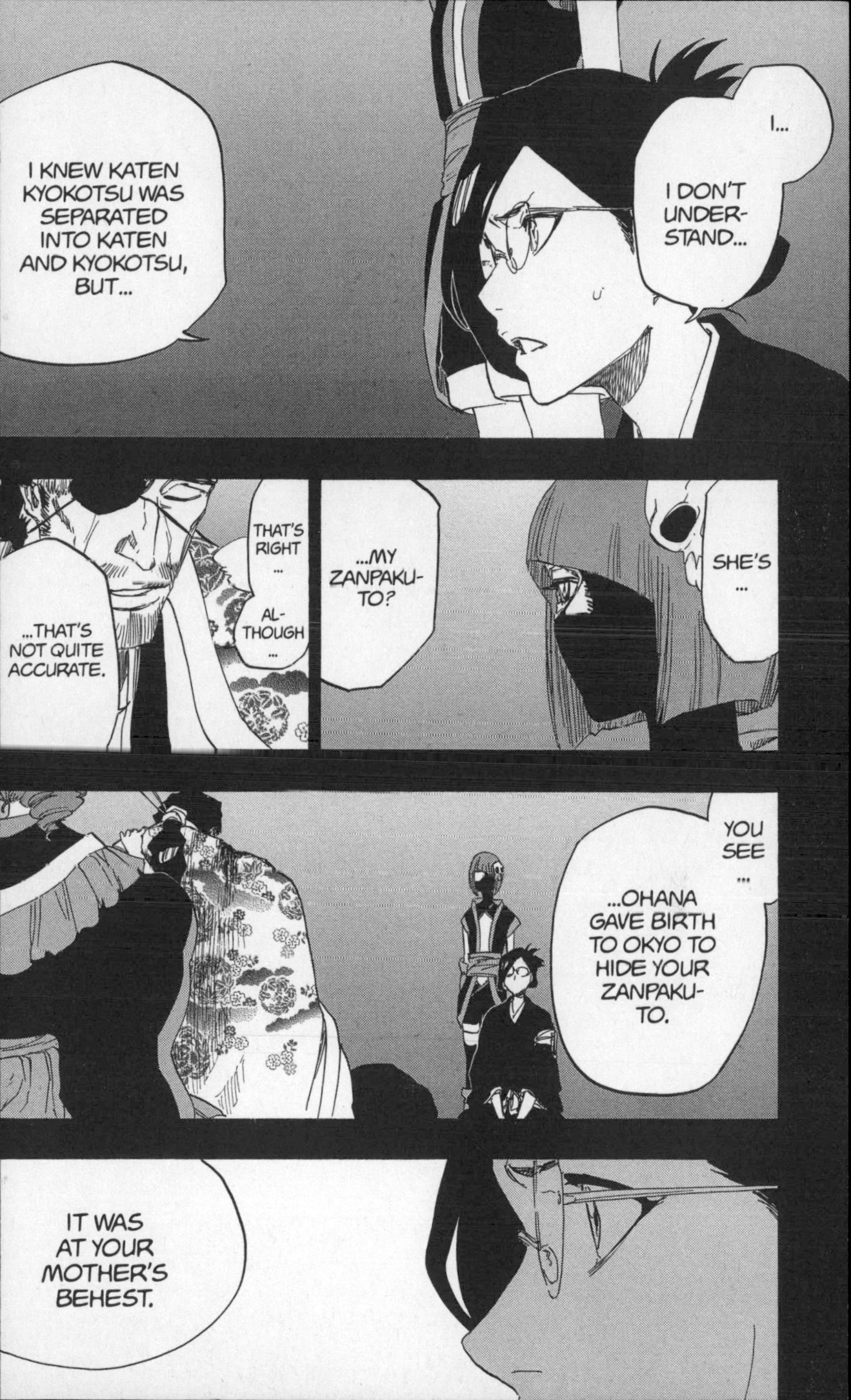
I...
I DON'T UNDER-STAND...
I KNEW KATEN KYOKOTSU WAS SEPARATED INTO KATEN AND KYOKOTSU, BUT...
SHE'S...
...MY ZANPAKU-TO?
THAT'S RIGHT...
AL-THOUGH...
...THAT'S NOT QUITE ACCURATE.
YOU SEE...
...OHANA GAVE BIRTH TO OKYO TO HIDE YOUR ZANPAKU-TO.
IT WAS AT YOUR MOTHER'S BEHEST.

READ THIS WAY

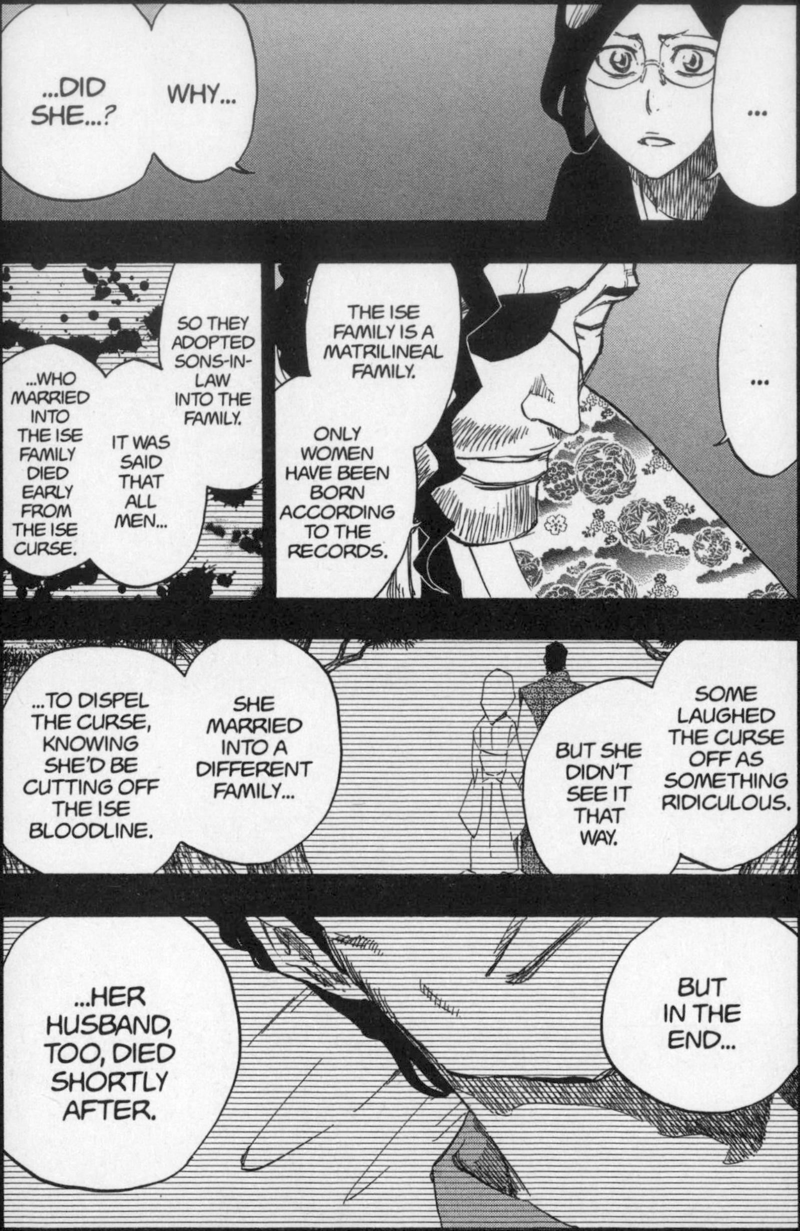
...
WHY...
...DID SHE...?
...
THE ISE FAMILY IS A MATRILINEAL FAMILY.
ONLY WOMEN HAVE BEEN BORN ACCORDING TO THE RECORDS.
SO THEY ADOPTED SONS-IN-LAW INTO THE FAMILY.
IT WAS SAID THAT ALL MEN...
...WHO MARRIED INTO THE ISE FAMILY DIED EARLY FROM THE ISE CURSE.
SOME LAUGHED THE CURSE OFF AS SOMETHING RIDICULOUS.
BUT SHE DIDN'T SEE IT THAT WAY.
SHE MARRIED INTO A DIFFERENT FAMILY...
...TO DISPEL THE CURSE, KNOWING SHE'D BE CUTTING OFF THE ISE BLOODLINE.
BUT IN THE END...
...HER HUSBAND, TOO, DIED SHORTLY AFTER.

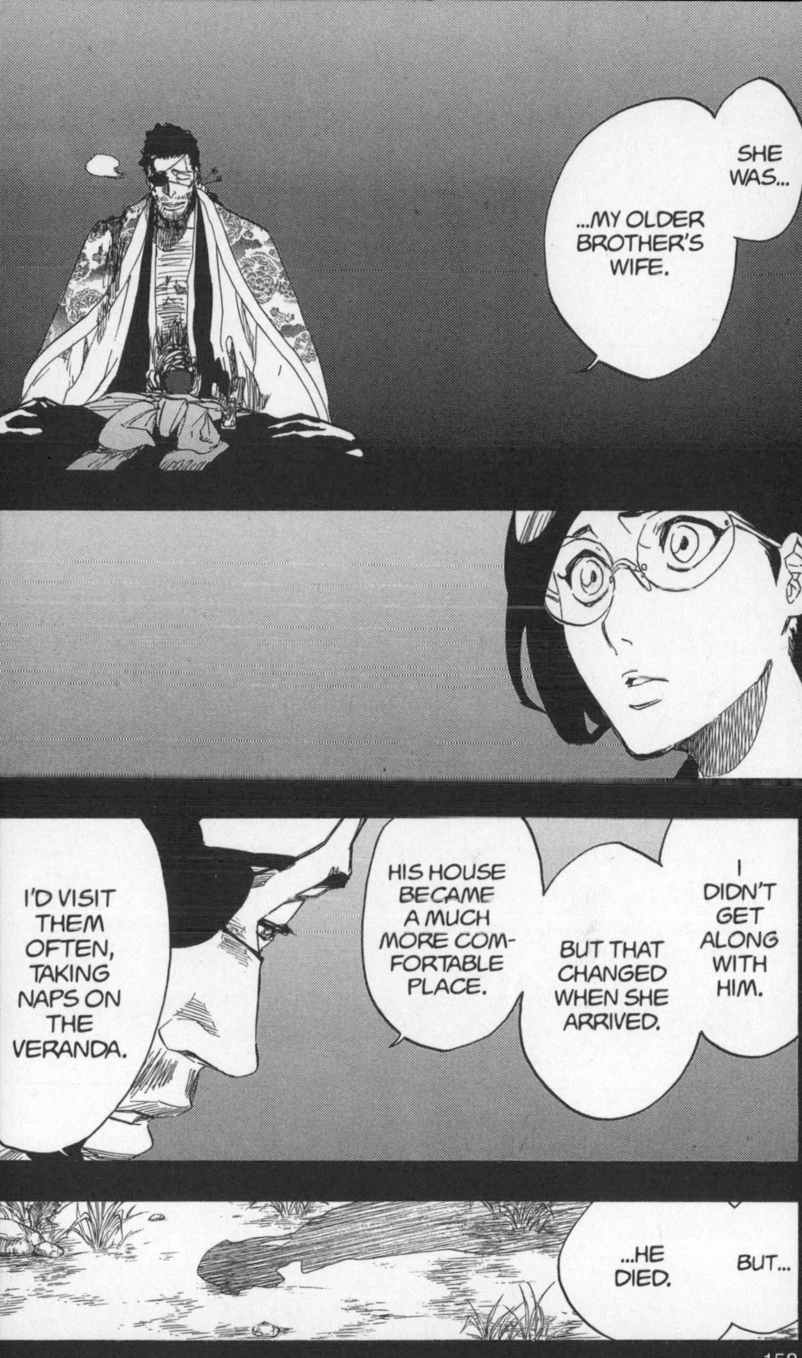
SHE WAS...
...MY OLDER BROTHER'S WIFE.
I DIDN'T GET ALONG WITH HIM.
BUT THAT CHANGED WHEN SHE ARRIVED.
HIS HOUSE BECAME A MUCH MORE COM-FORTABLE PLACE.
I'D VISIT THEM OFTEN, TAKING NAPS ON THE VERANDA.
BUT...
...HE DIED.

READ THIS WAY

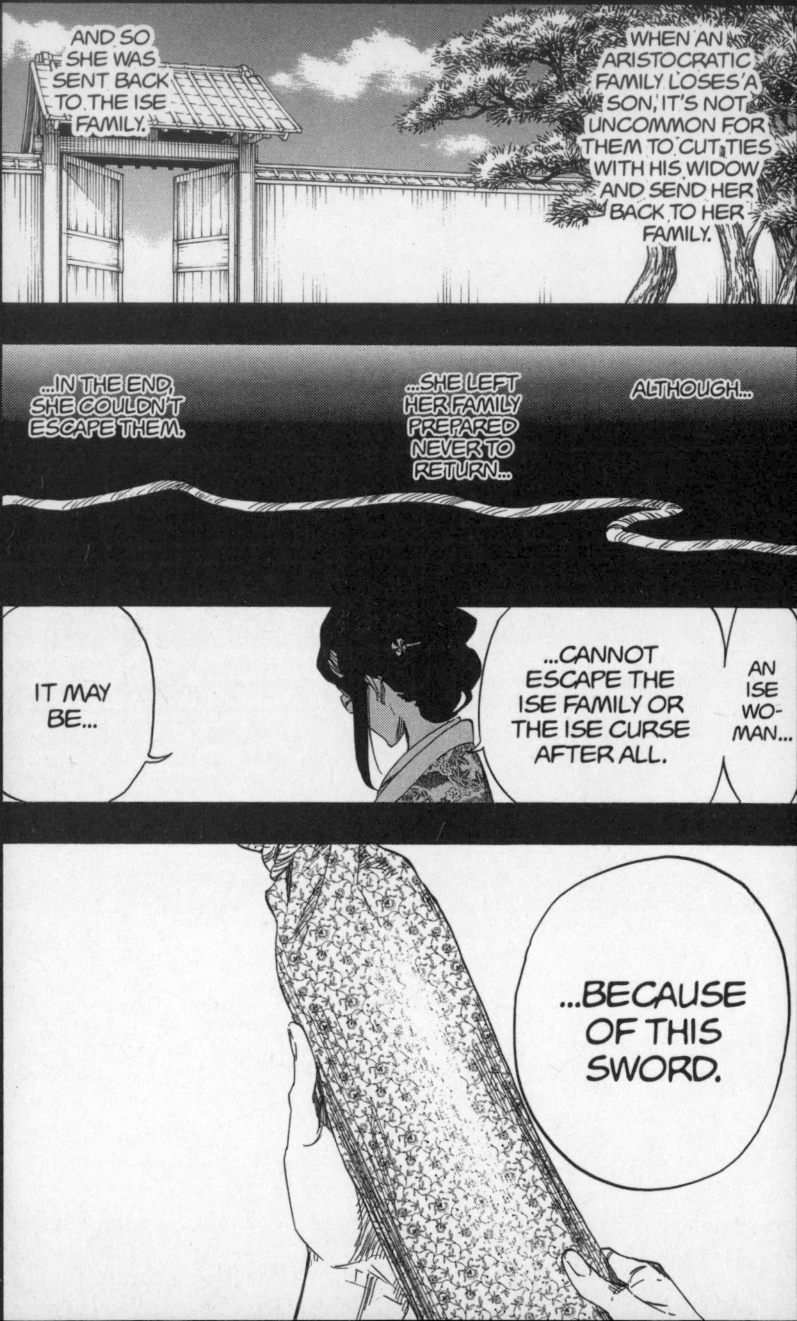
WHEN AN ARISTOCRATIC FAMILY LOSES A SON, IT'S NOT UNCOMMON FOR THEM TO CUT TIES WITH HIS WIDOW AND SEND HER BACK TO HER FAMILY.
AND SO SHE WAS SENT BACK TO THE ISE FAMILY.
ALTHOUGH...
...SHE LEFT HER FAMILY PREPARED NEVER TO RETURN...
...IN THE END, SHE COULDN'T ESCAPE THEM.
AN ISE WO- MAN...
...CANNOT ESCAPE THE ISE FAMILY OR THE ISE CURSE AFTER ALL.
IT MAY BE...
...BECAUSE OF THIS SWORD.

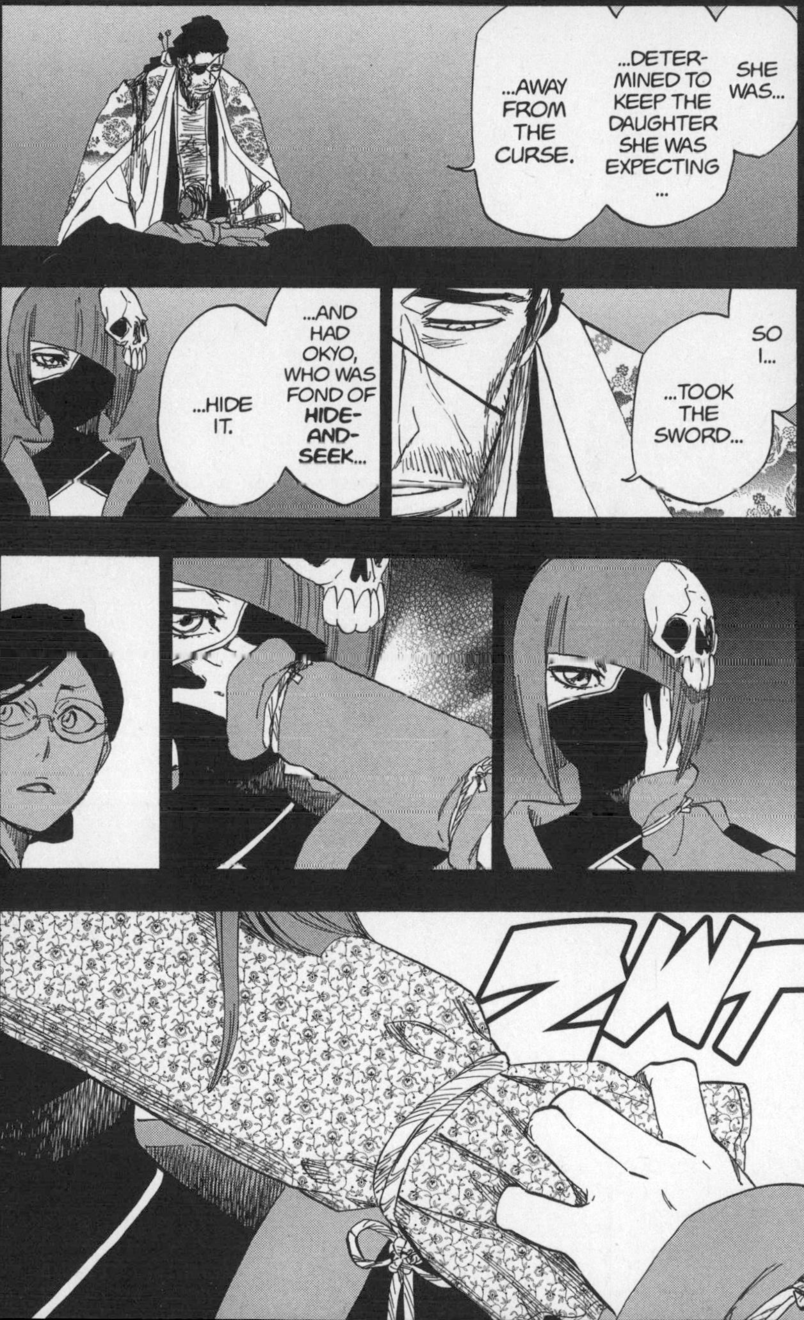
SHE WAS...
...DETER-MINED TO KEEP THE DAUGHTER SHE WAS EXPECTING ...
...AWAY FROM THE CURSE.
SO I...
...TOOK THE SWORD...
...AND HAD OKYO, WHO WAS FOND OF HIDE-AND-SEEK...
...HIDE IT.
ZWT

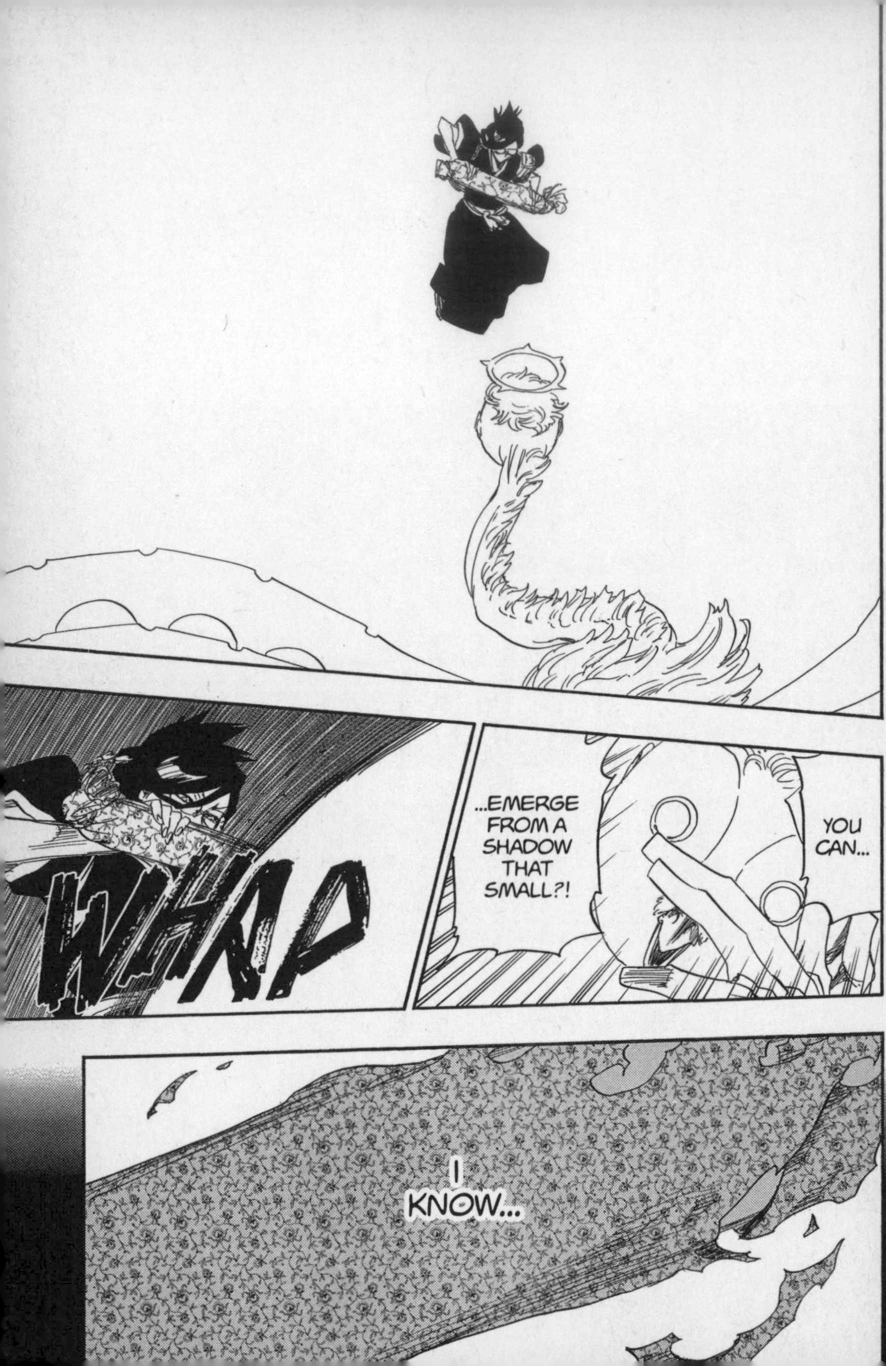
YOU CAN...
...EMERGE FROM A SHADOW THAT SMALL?!
WHAP
I KNOW...

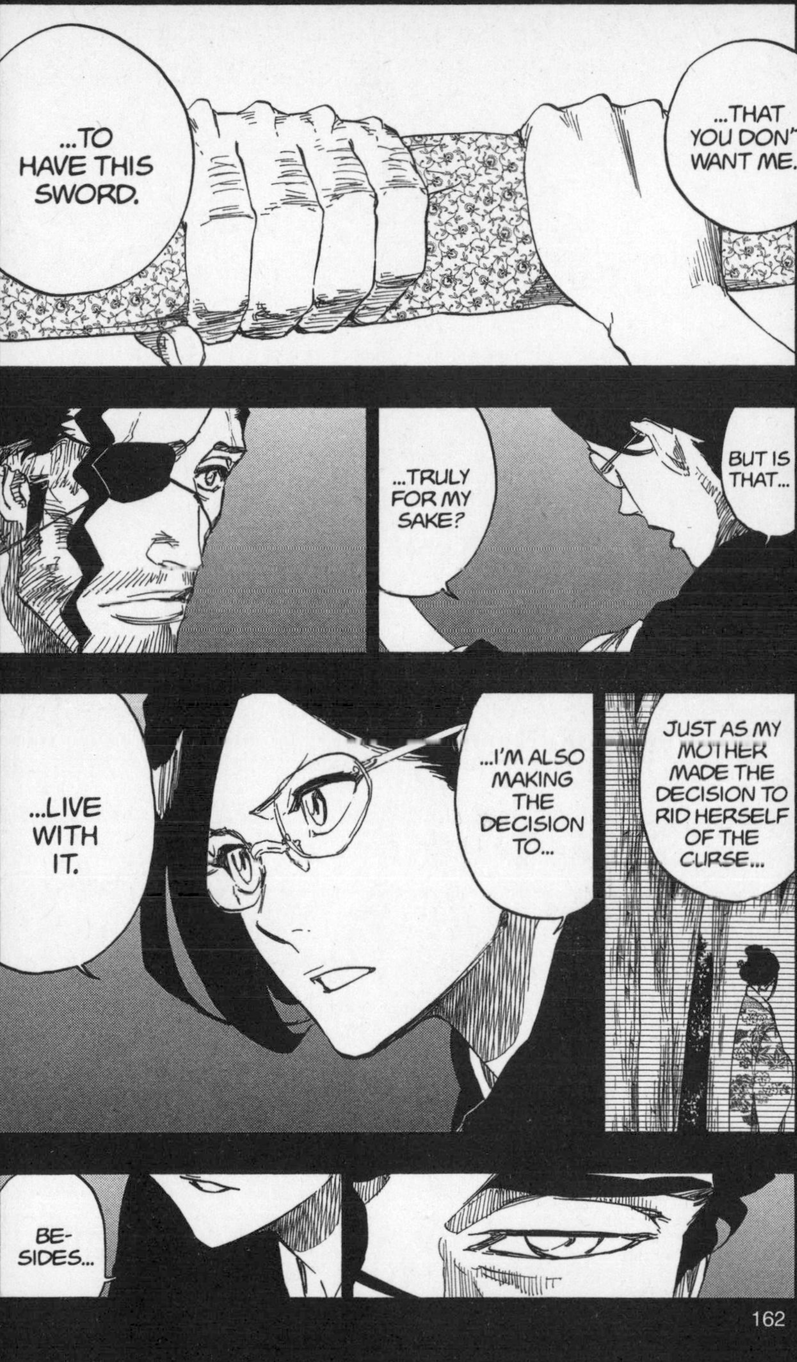
...THAT YOU DON'T WANT ME...
...TO HAVE THIS SWORD.
BUT IS THAT...
...TRULY FOR MY SAKE?
JUST AS MY MOTHER MADE THE DECISION TO RID HERSELF OF THE CURSE...
...I'M ALSO MAKING THE DECISION TO...
...LIVE WITH IT.
BE-SIDES...

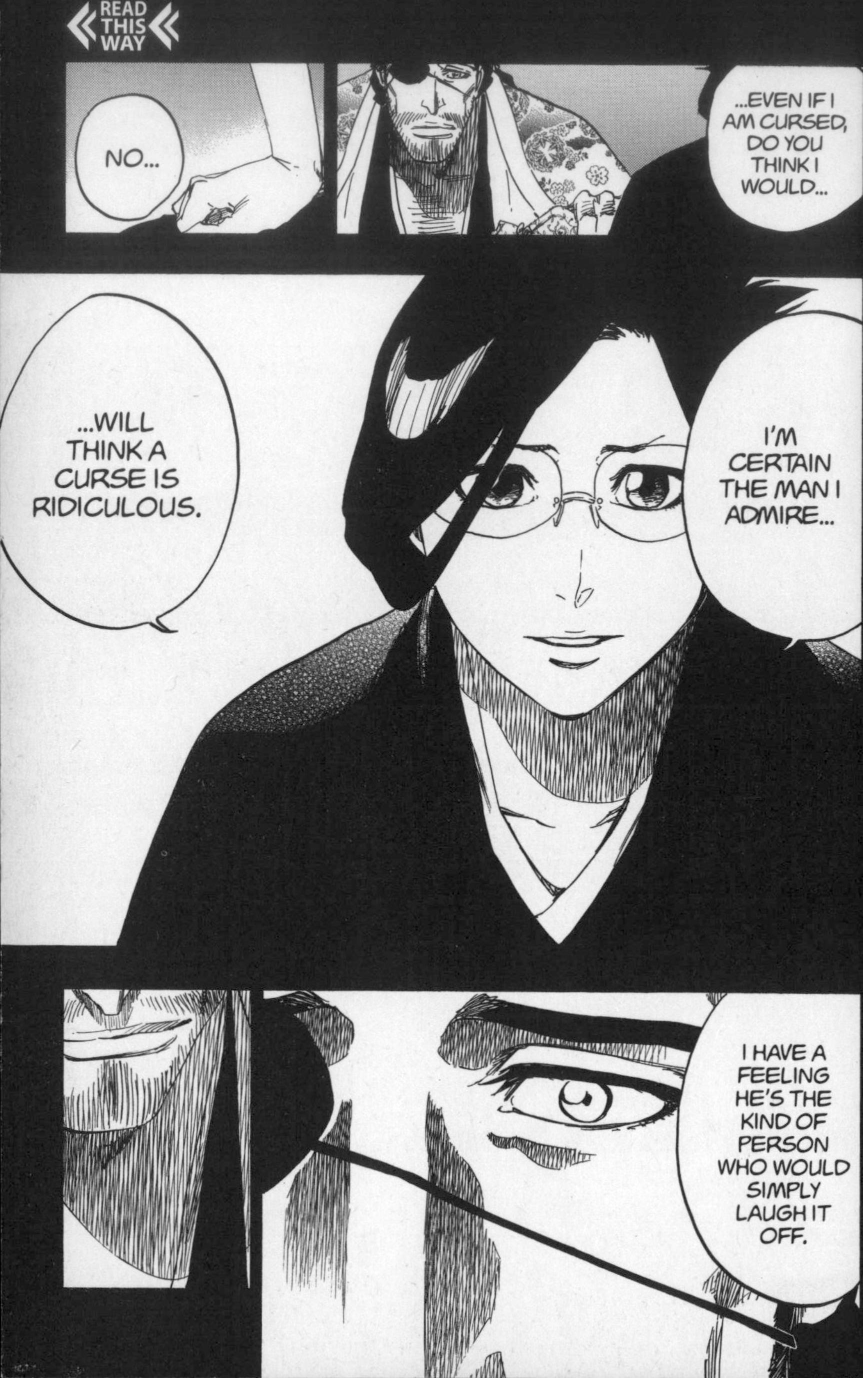
READ THIS WAY
...EVEN IF I AM CURSED, DO YOU THINK I WOULD...
NO...
I'M CERTAIN THE MAN I ADMIRE...
...WILL THINK A CURSE IS RIDICULOUS.
I HAVE A FEELING HE'S THE KIND OF PERSON WHO WOULD SIMPLY LAUGH IT OFF.

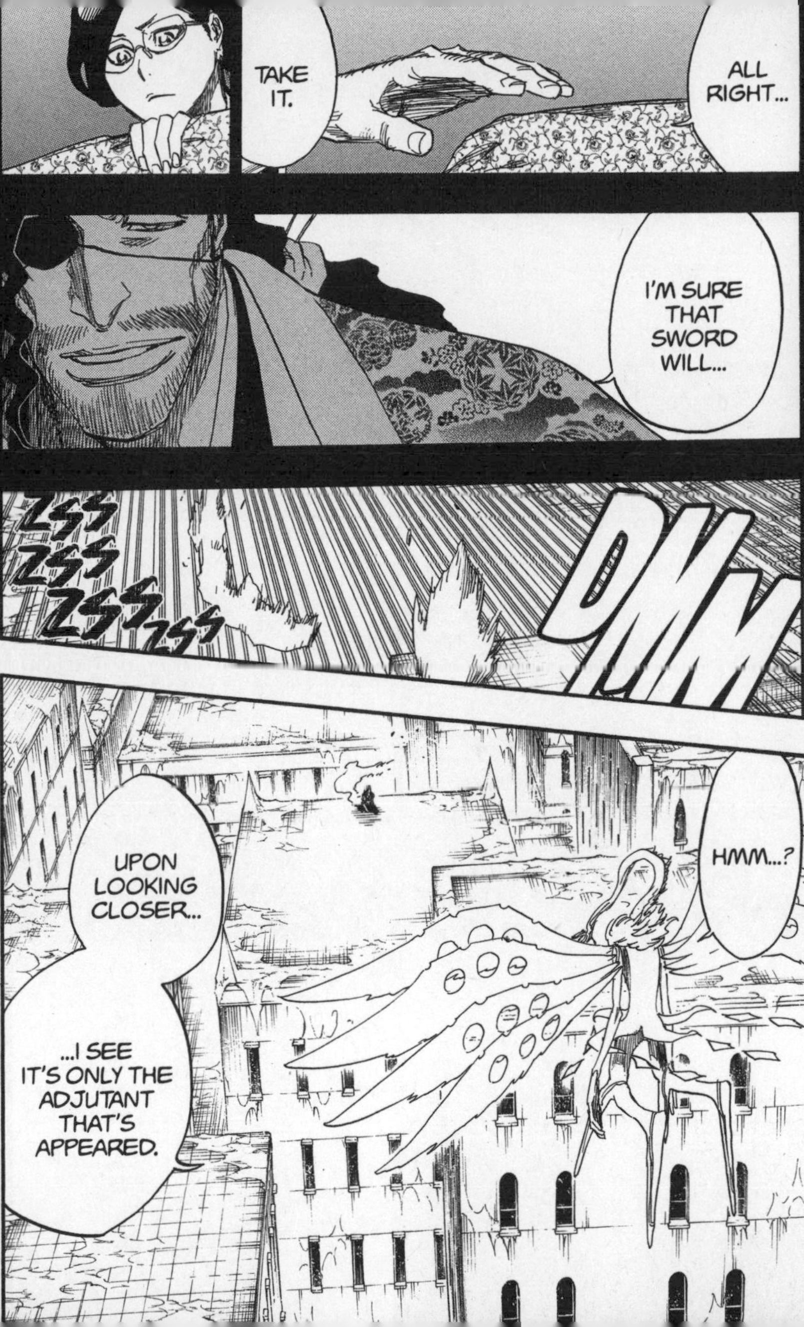
ALL RIGHT...
TAKE IT.
I'M SURE THAT SWORD WILL...
DMM
ZSS ZSS ZSS ZSS
HMM...?
UPON LOOKING CLOSER...
...I SEE IT'S ONLY THE ADJUTANT THAT'S APPEARED.

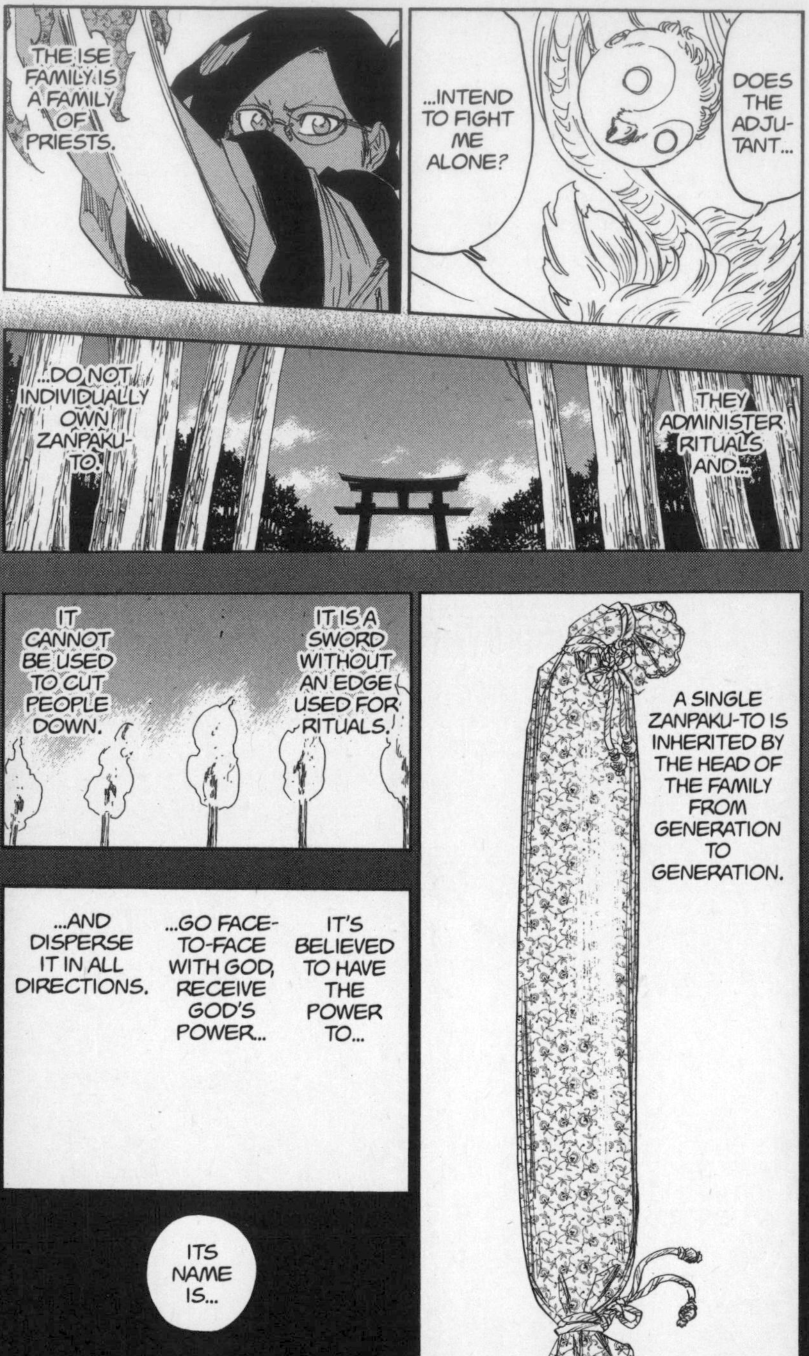
DOES THE ADJUTANT...
...INTEND TO FIGHT ME ALONE?
THE ISE FAMILY IS A FAMILY OF PRIESTS.
THEY ADMINISTER RITUALS AND...
...DO NOT INDIVIDUALLY OWN ZANPAKU-TO.
A SINGLE ZANPAKU-TO IS INHERITED BY THE HEAD OF THE FAMILY FROM GENERATION TO GENERATION.
IT IS A SWORD WITHOUT AN EDGE USED FOR RITUALS.
IT CANNOT BE USED TO CUT PEOPLE DOWN.
IT'S BELIEVED TO HAVE THE POWER TO...
...GO FACE-TO-FACE WITH GOD, RECEIVE GOD'S POWER...
...AND DISPERSE IT IN ALL DIRECTIONS.
ITS NAME IS...

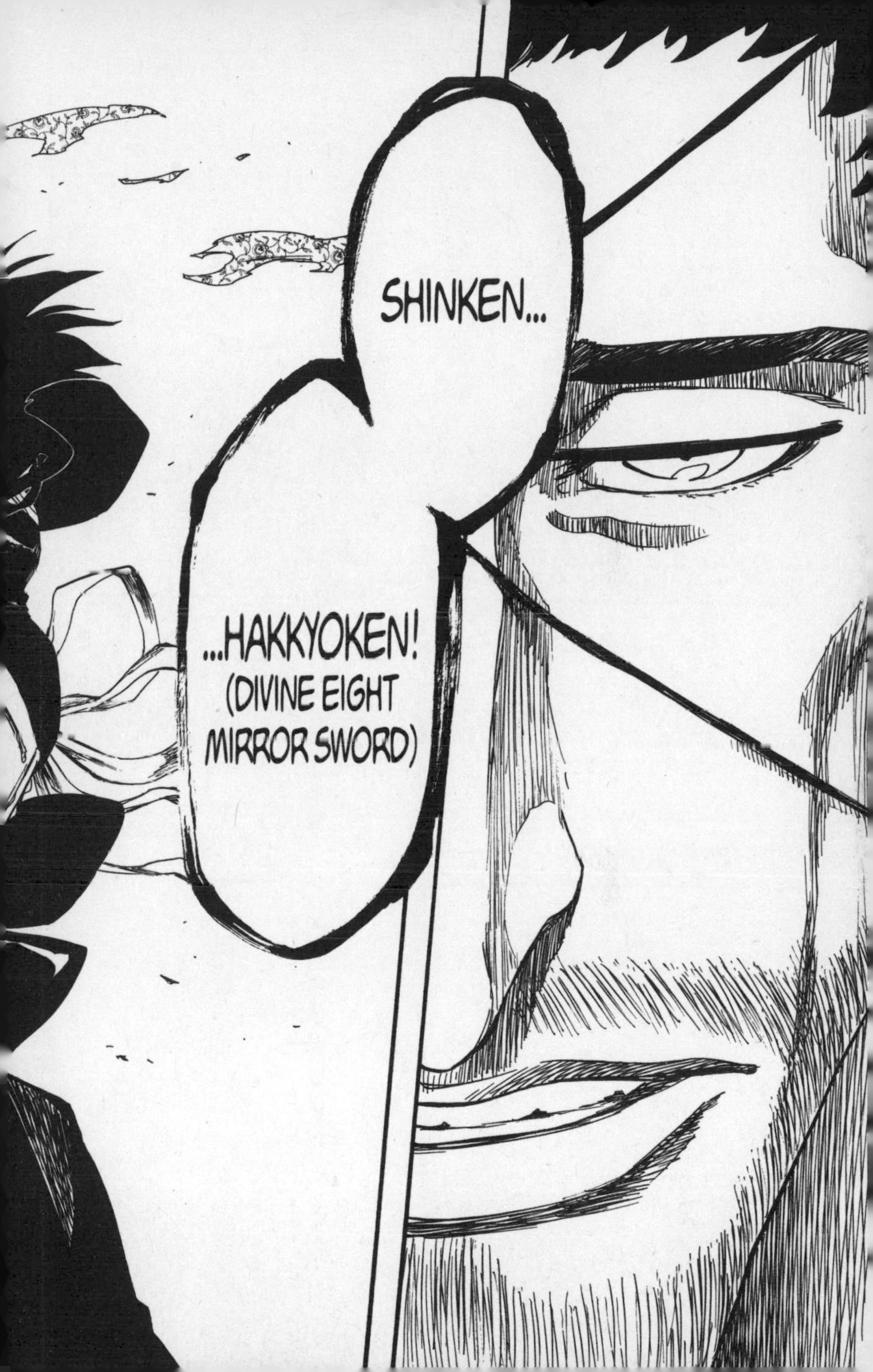
SHINKEN...
...HAKKYOKEN! (DIVINE EIGHT MIRROR SWORD)

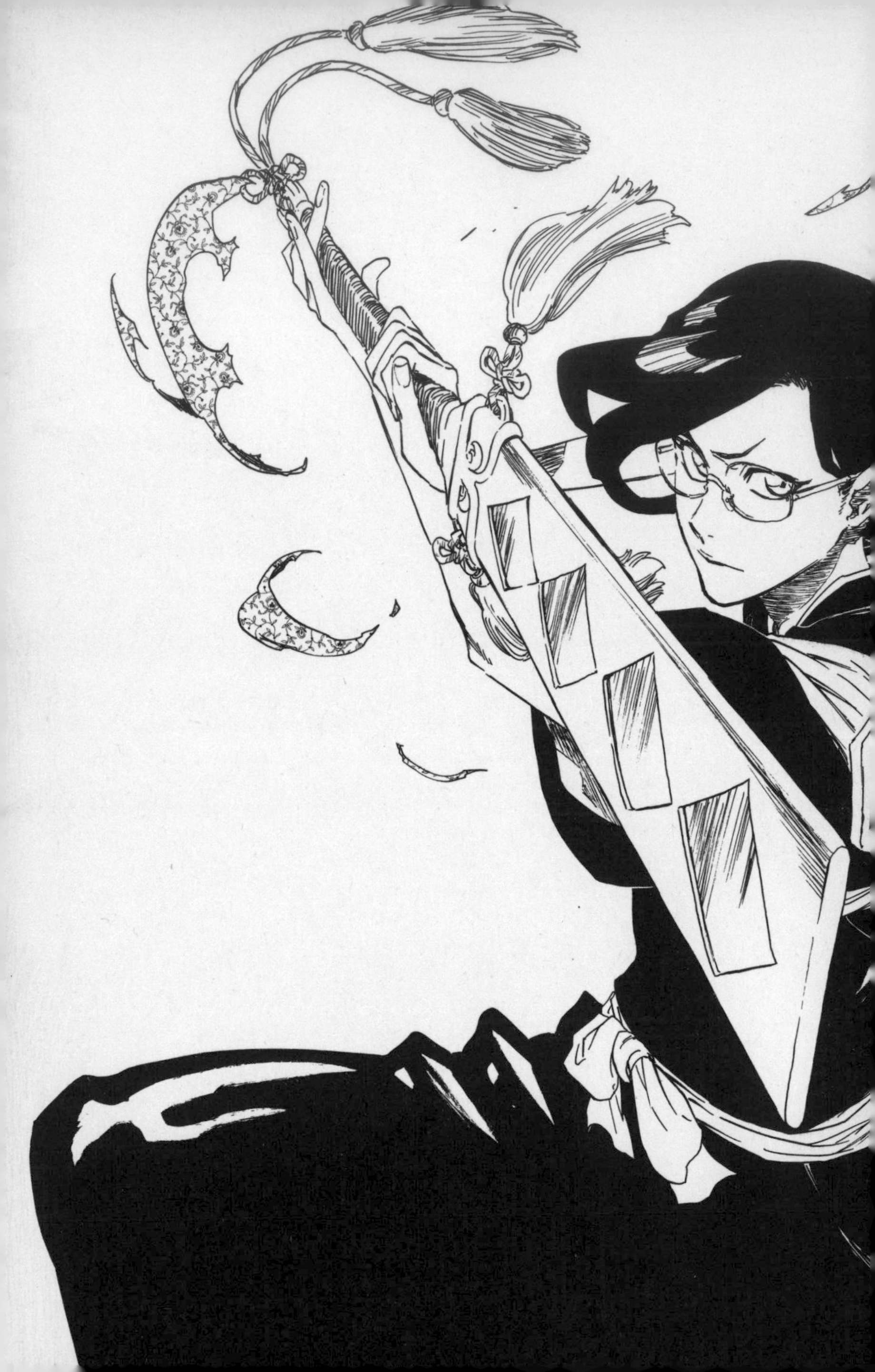

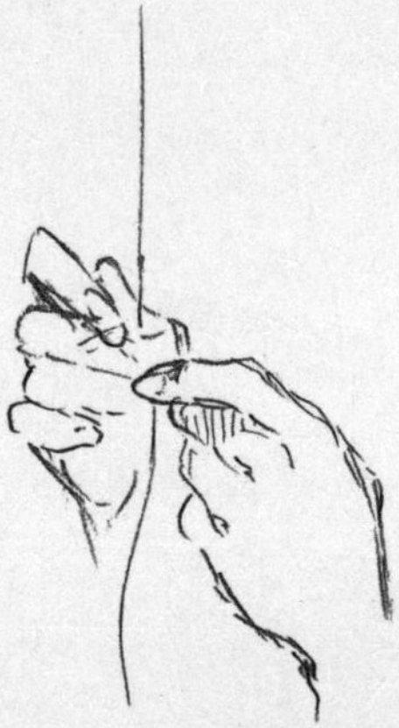

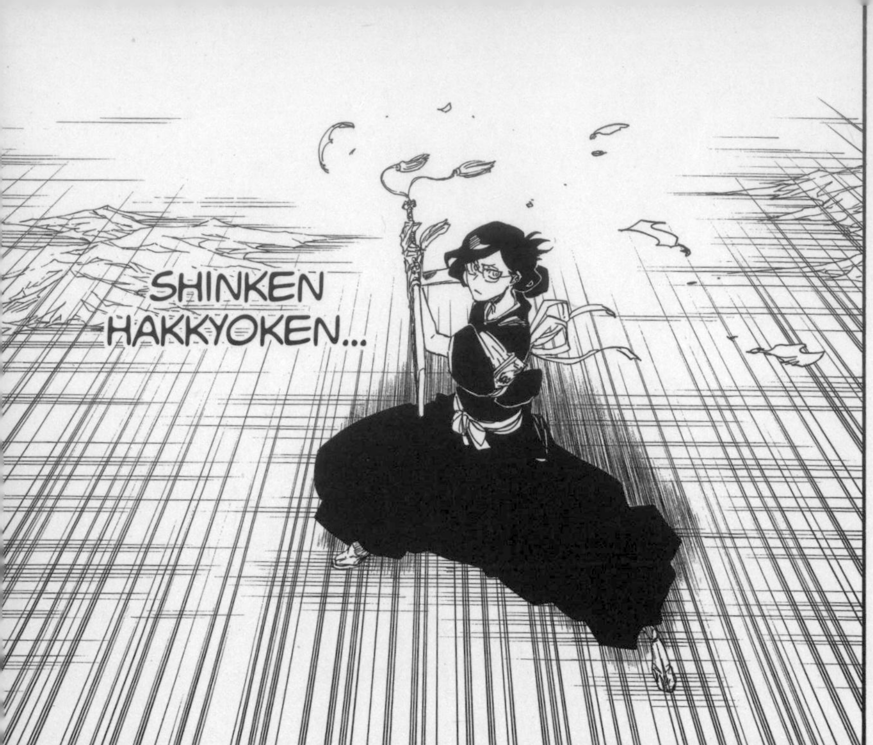
SHINKEN HAKKYOKEN...

652. THE THEATRE SUICIDE SCENE 6

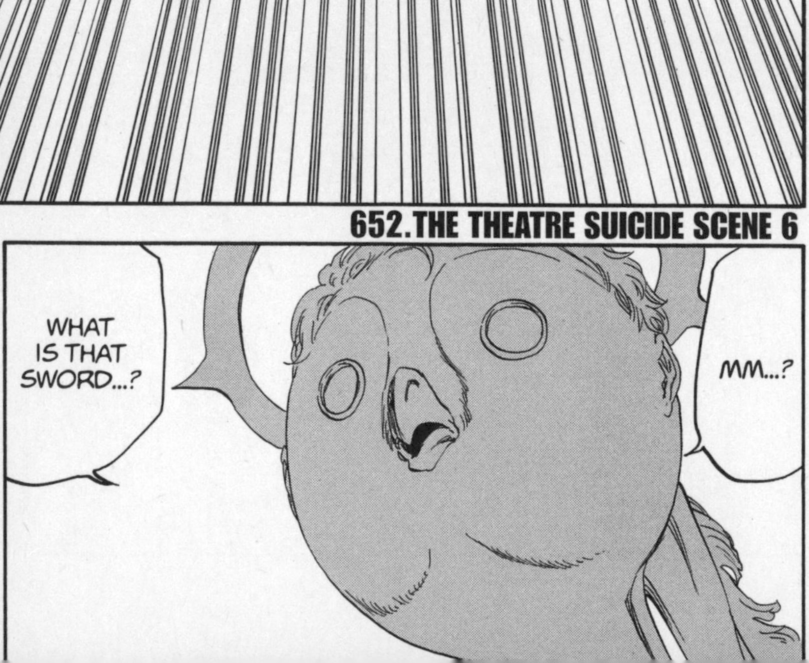
MM...?
WHAT IS THAT SWORD...?

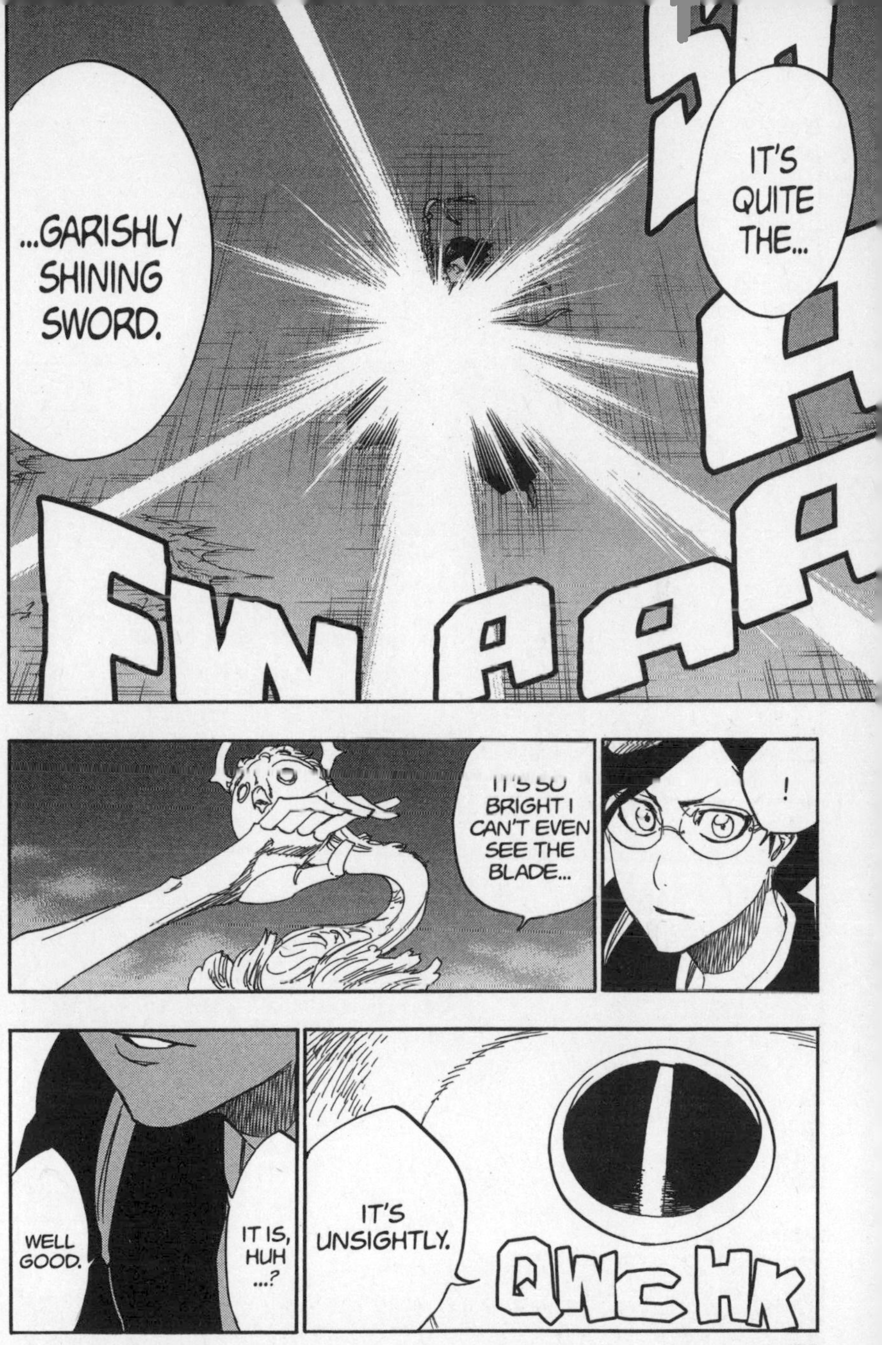
IT'S QUITE THE...
...GARISHLY SHINING SWORD.
!
IT'S SO BRIGHT I CAN'T EVEN SEE THE BLADE...
IT'S UNSIGHTLY.
QWCHK
IT IS, HUH ...?
WELL GOOD.

READ THIS WAY

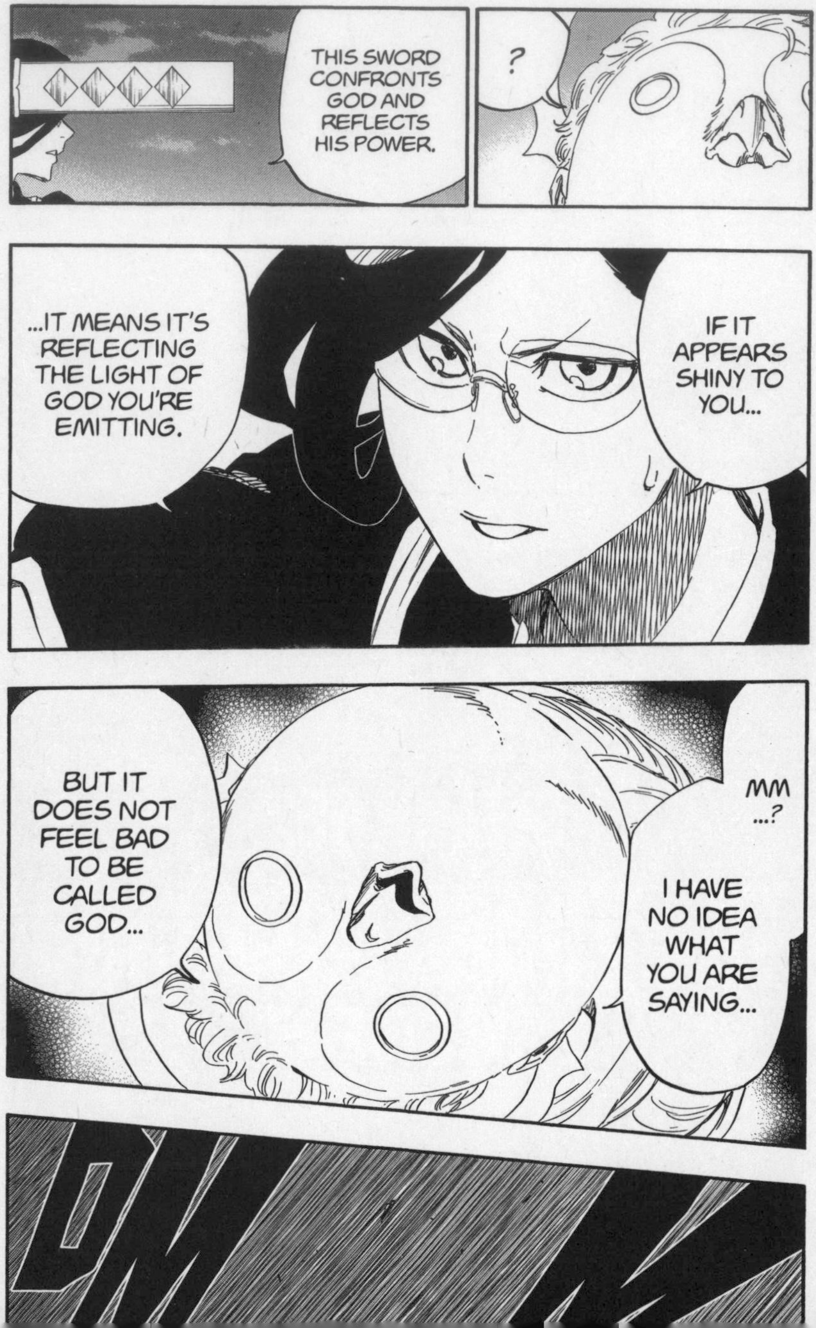
?
THIS SWORD CONFRONTS GOD AND REFLECTS HIS POWER.
IF IT APPEARS SHINY TO YOU...
...IT MEANS IT'S REFLECTING THE LIGHT OF GOD YOU'RE EMITTING.
MM ...?
I HAVE NO IDEA WHAT YOU ARE SAYING...
BUT IT DOES NOT FEEL BAD TO BE CALLED GOD...

BLEACH 652.
The Theatre Suicide
SCENE 6

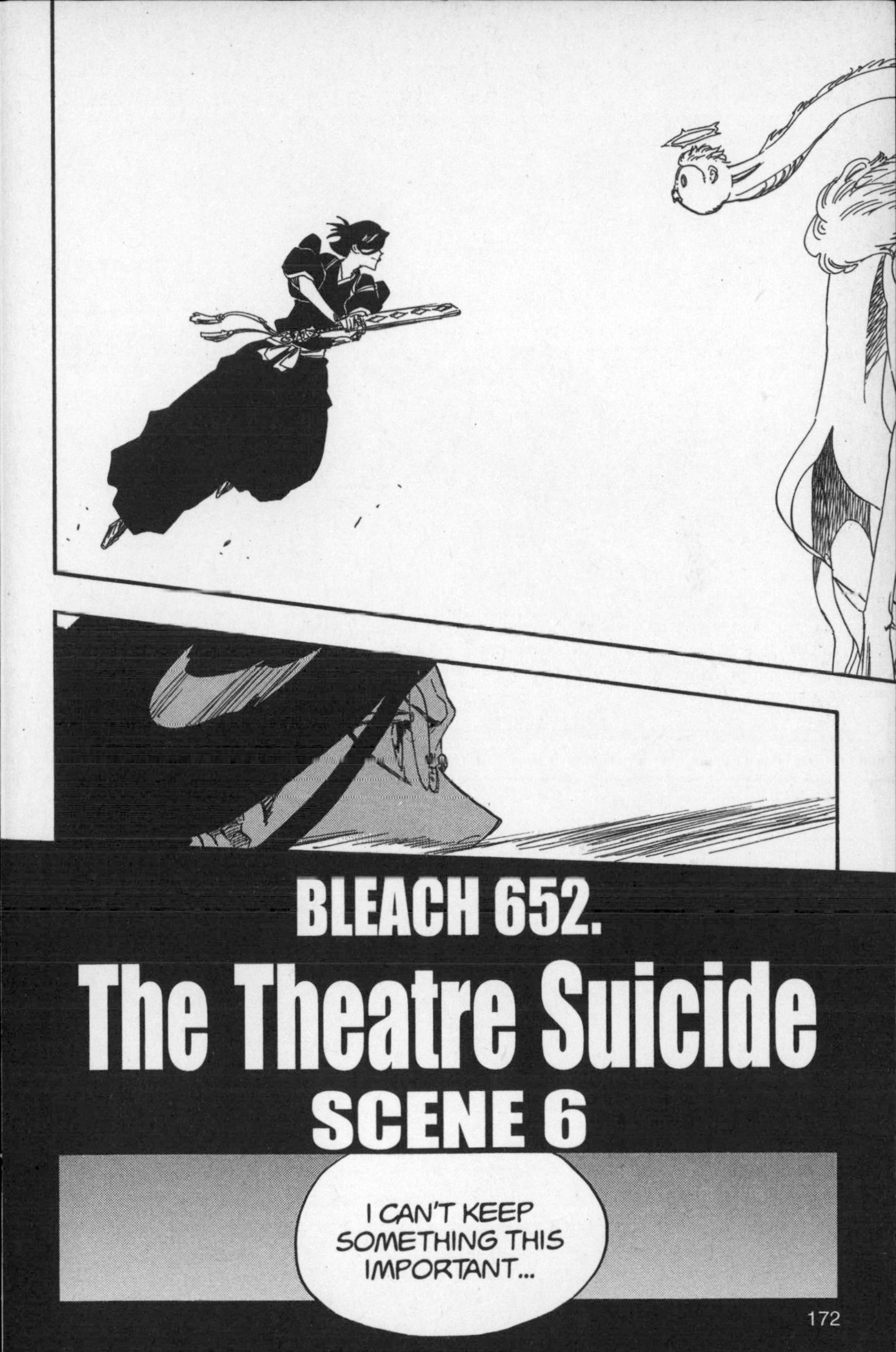
I CAN'T KEEP SOMETHING THIS IMPORTANT...

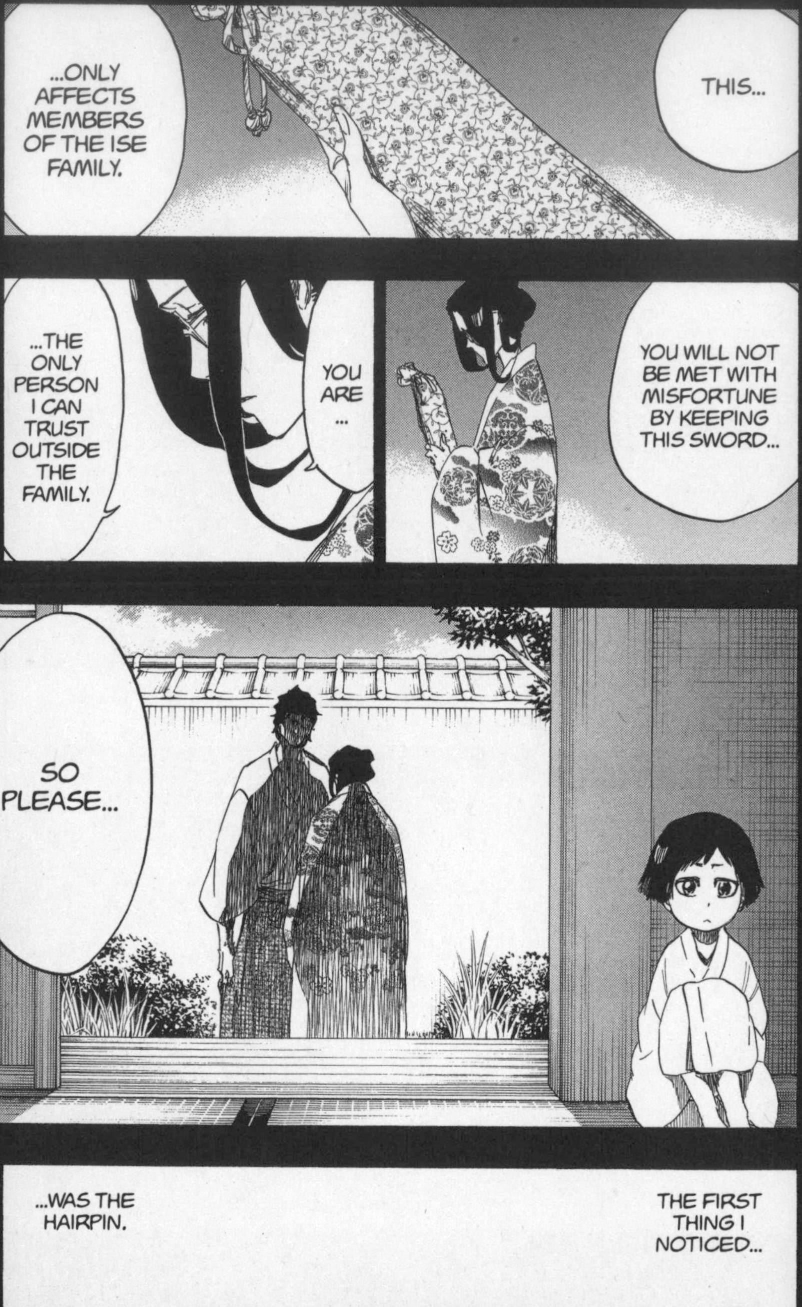
THIS...
...ONLY AFFECTS MEMBERS OF THE ISE FAMILY.
YOU WILL NOT BE MET WITH MISFORTUNE BY KEEPING THIS SWORD...
YOU ARE ...
...THE ONLY PERSON I CAN TRUST OUTSIDE THE FAMILY.
SO PLEASE...
THE FIRST THING I NOTICED...
...WAS THE HAIRPIN.

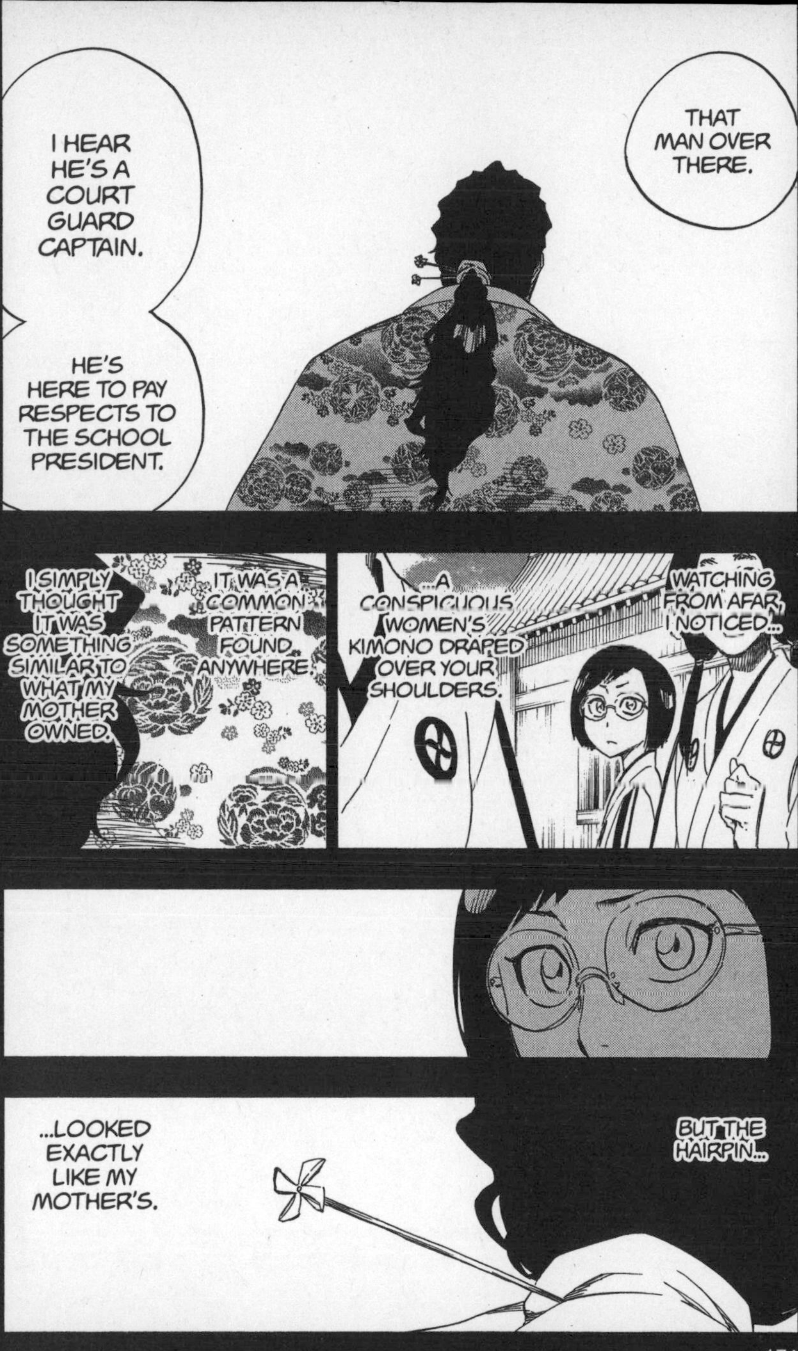
THAT MAN OVER THERE.
I HEAR HE'S A COURT GUARD CAPTAIN.
HE'S HERE TO PAY RESPECTS TO THE SCHOOL PRESIDENT.
WATCHING FROM AFAR, I NOTICED...
...A CONSPICUOUS WOMEN'S KIMONO DRAPED OVER YOUR SHOULDERS.
IT WAS A COMMON PATTERN FOUND ANYWHERE.
I SIMPLY THOUGHT IT WAS SOMETHING SIMILAR TO WHAT MY MOTHER OWNED.
BUT THE HAIRPIN...
...LOOKED EXACTLY LIKE MY MOTHER'S.

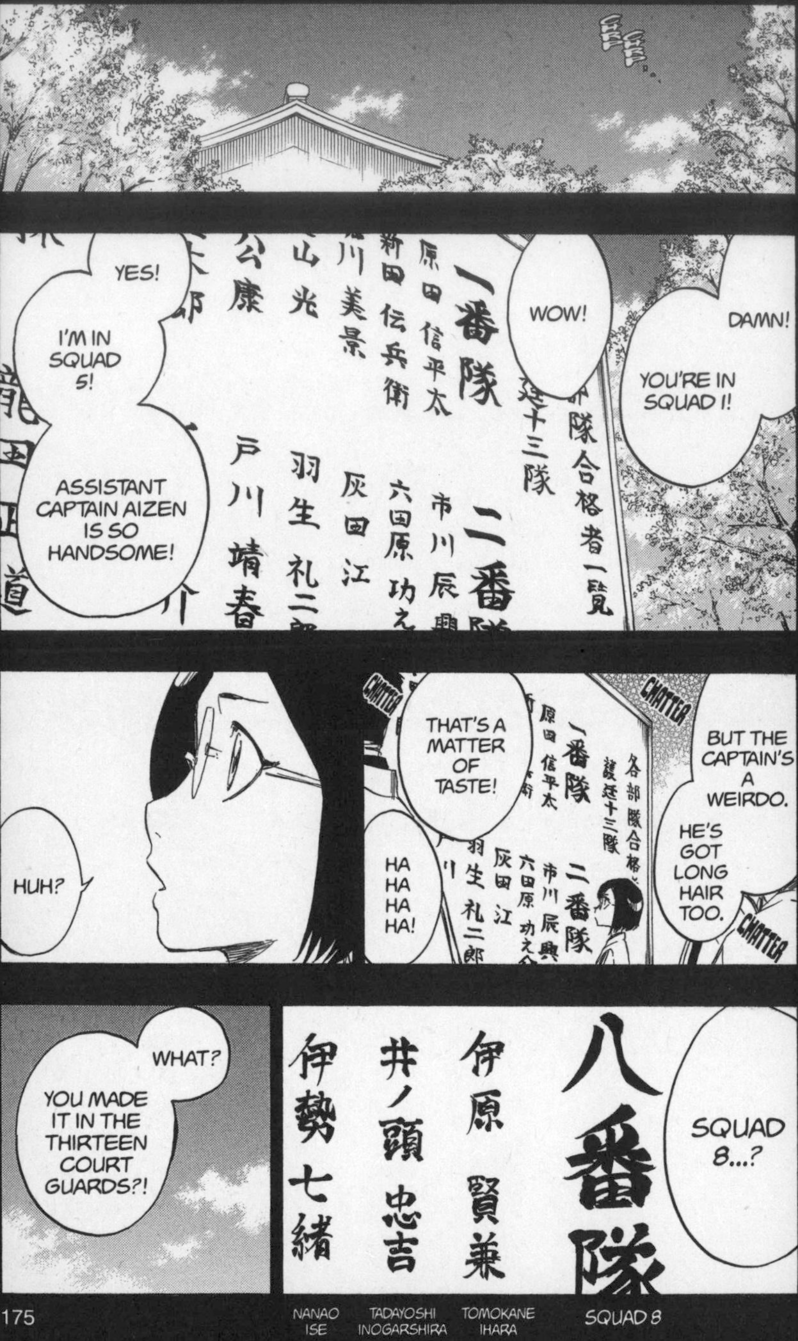

DAMN!
YOU'RE IN SQUAD 1!
WOW!
YES!
I'M IN SQUAD 5!
ASSISTANT CAPTAIN AIZEN IS SO HANDSOME!
CHATTER
BUT THE CAPTAIN'S A WEIRDO.
HE'S GOT LONG HAIR TOO.
CHATTER
THAT'S A MATTER OF TASTE!
HA HA HA HA!
CHATTER
HUH?
SQUAD 8...?
八番隊
伊原賢兼
井ノ頭忠吉
伊勢七緒
WHAT?
YOU MADE IT IN THE THIRTEEN COURT GUARDS?!

SQUAD 8 TOMOKANE IHARA TADAYOSHI INOGARSHIRA NANAO ISE

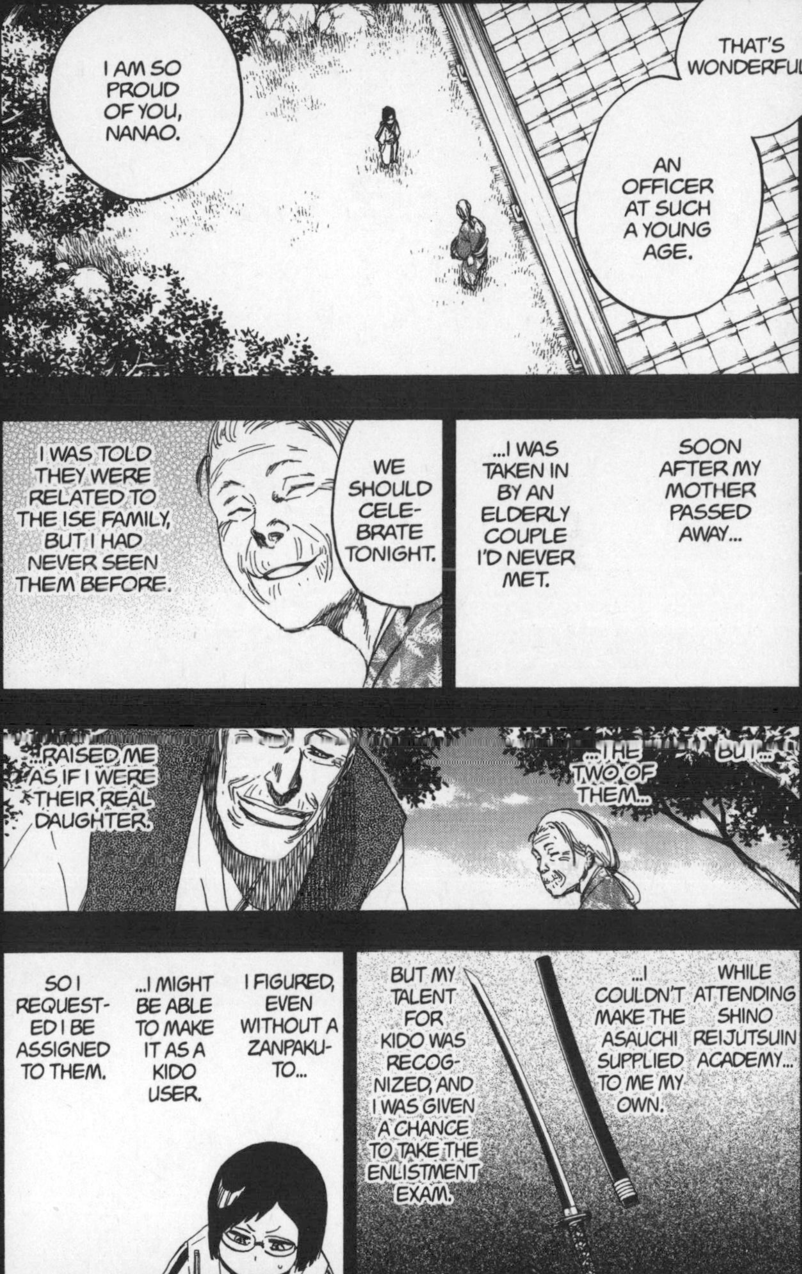
THAT'S WONDERFUL!
AN OFFICER AT SUCH A YOUNG AGE.
I AM SO PROUD OF YOU, NANAO.
SOON AFTER MY MOTHER PASSED AWAY...
...I WAS TAKEN IN BY AN ELDERLY COUPLE I'D NEVER MET.
WE SHOULD CELE-BRATE TONIGHT.
I WAS TOLD THEY WERE RELATED TO THE ISE FAMILY, BUT I HAD NEVER SEEN THEM BEFORE.
BUT I...
...THE TWO OF THEM...
...RAISED ME AS IF I WERE THEIR REAL DAUGHTER.
WHILE ATTENDING SHINO REIJUTSUIN ACADEMY...
...I COULDN'T MAKE THE ASAUCHI SUPPLIED TO ME MY OWN.
BUT MY TALENT FOR KIDO WAS RECOG-NIZED, AND I WAS GIVEN A CHANCE TO TAKE THE ENLISTMENT EXAM.
I FIGURED, EVEN WITHOUT A ZANPAKU-TO...
...I MIGHT BE ABLE TO MAKE IT AS A KIDO USER.
SO I REQUEST-ED I BE ASSIGNED TO THEM.

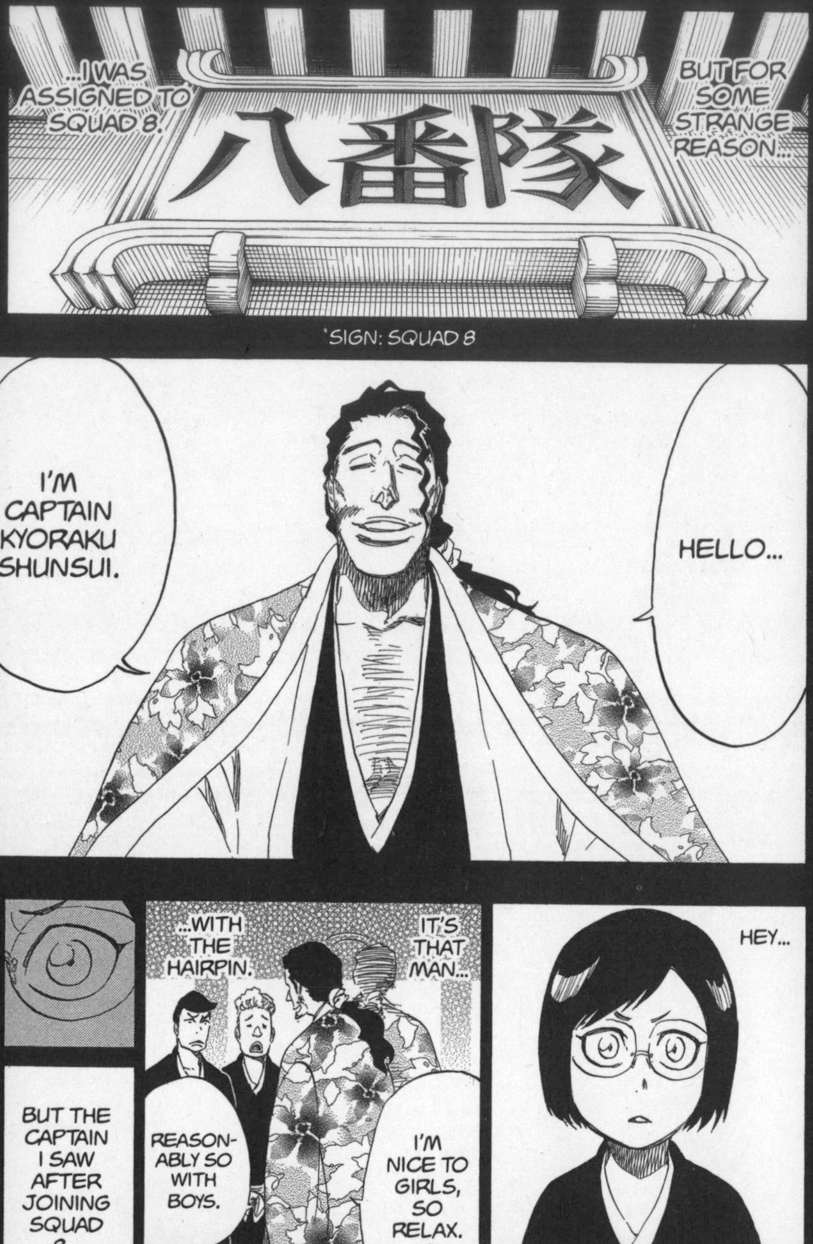
BUT FOR SOME STRANGE REASON...
...I WAS ASSIGNED TO SQUAD 8.
八番隊
*SIGN: SQUAD 8
HELLO...
I'M CAPTAIN KYORAKU SHUNSUI.
HEY...
IT'S THAT MAN...
...WITH THE HAIRPIN.
I'M NICE TO GIRLS, SO RELAX. ♪
REASON-ABLY SO WITH BOYS.
BUT THE CAPTAIN I SAW AFTER JOINING SQUAD 8...

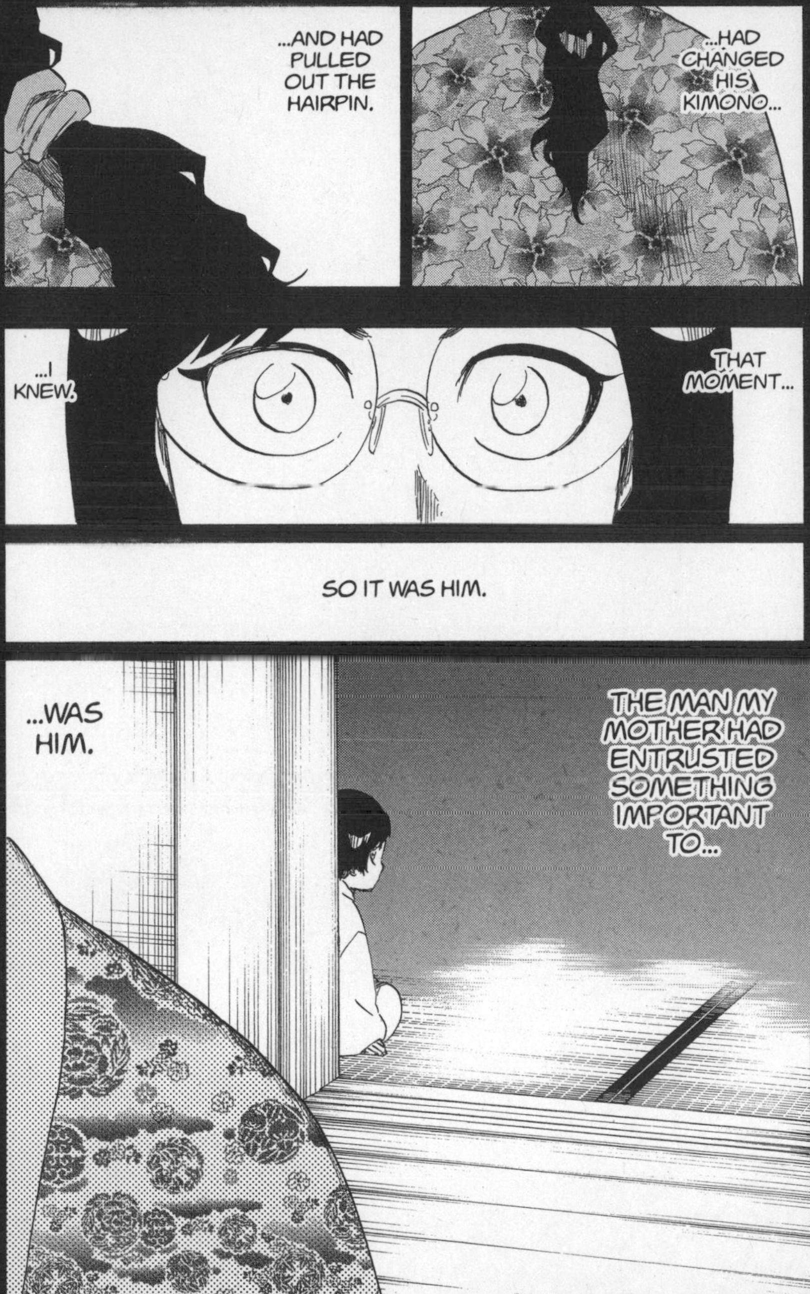
...HAD CHANGED HIS KIMONO...
...AND HAD PULLED OUT THE HAIRPIN.
THAT MOMENT...
...I KNEW.
SO IT WAS HIM.
THE MAN MY MOTHER HAD ENTRUSTED SOMETHING IMPORTANT TO...
...WAS HIM.

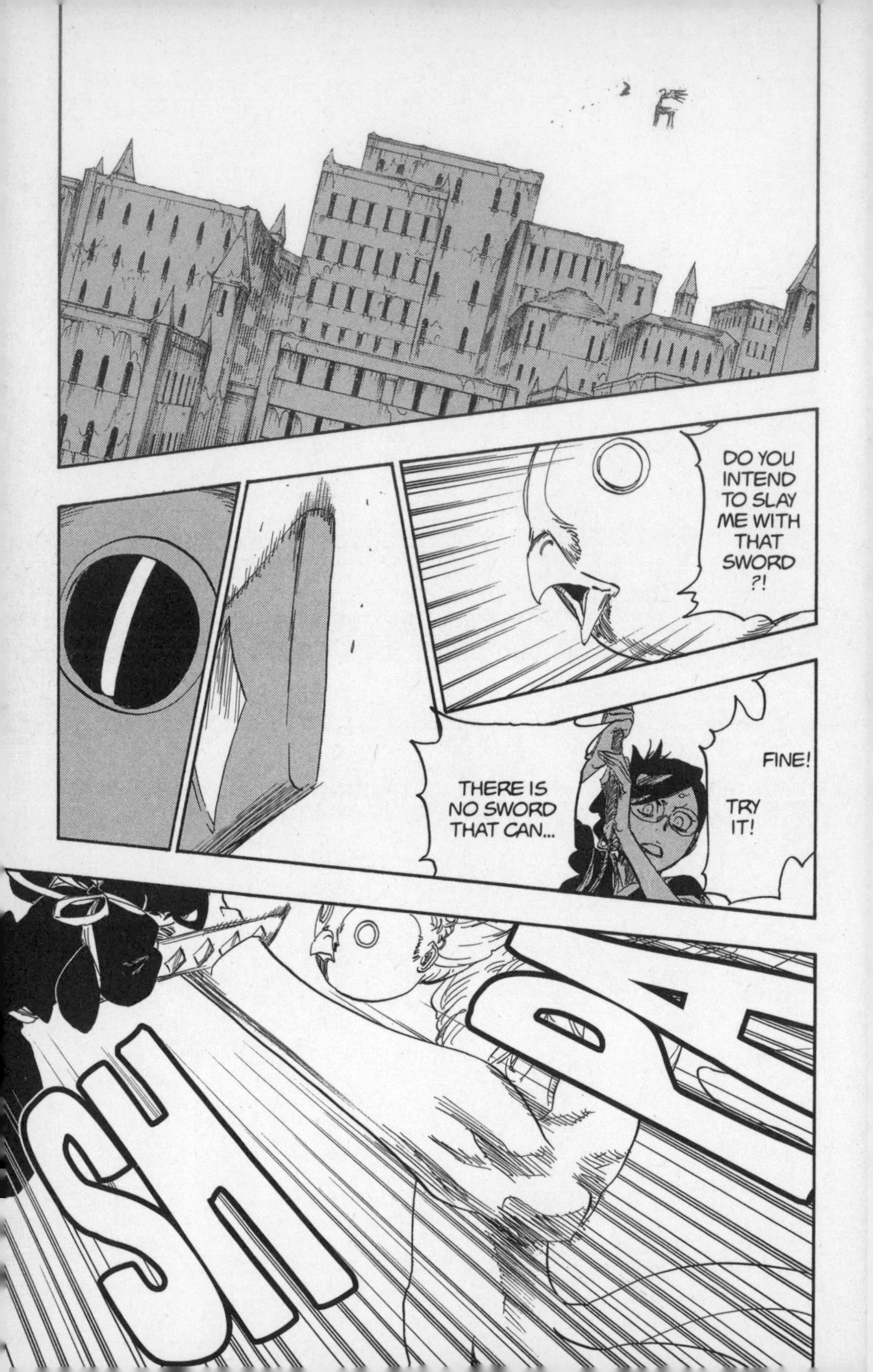
DO YOU INTEND TO SLAY ME WITH THAT SWORD ?!
FINE!
TRY IT!
THERE IS NO SWORD THAT CAN...

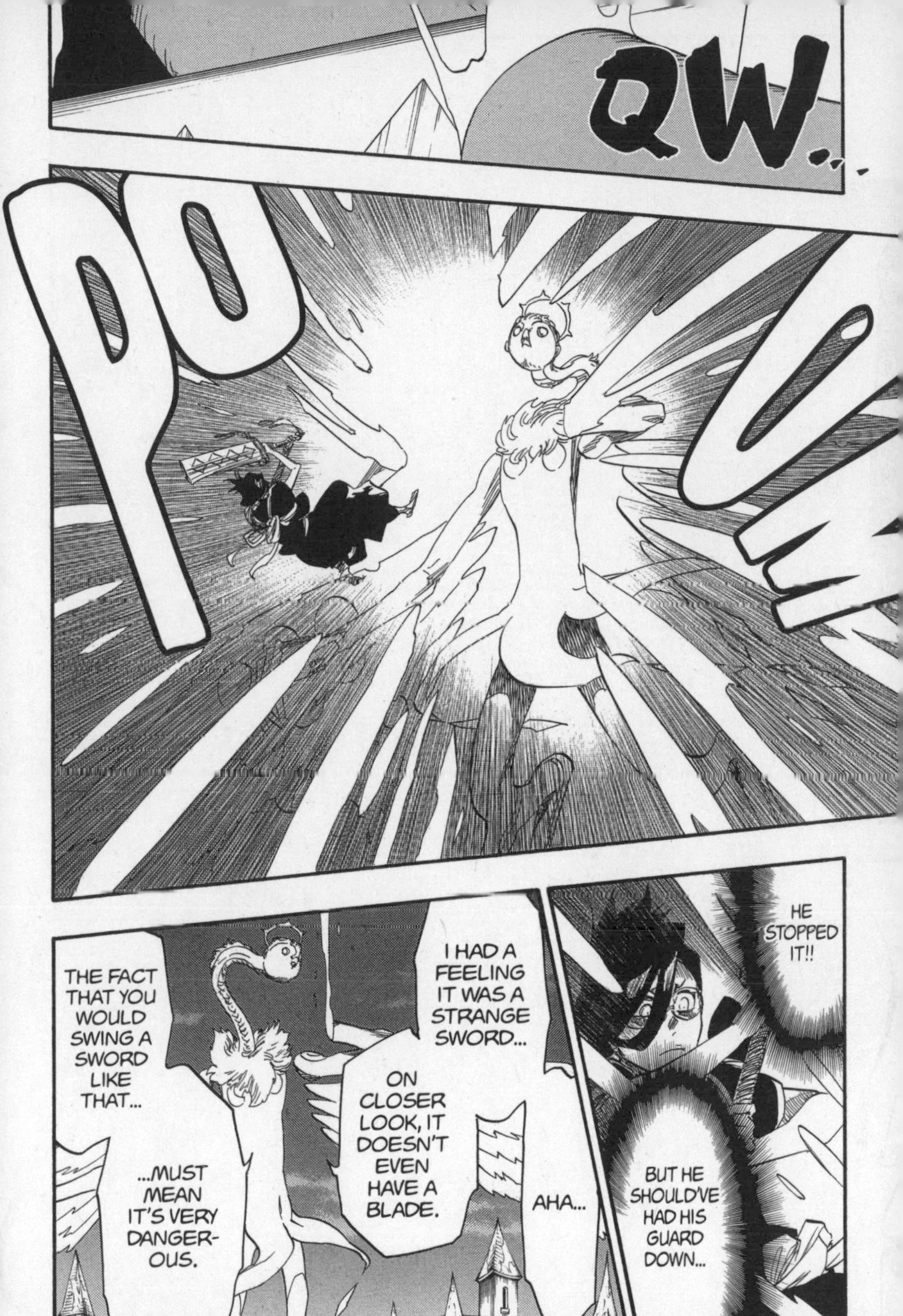
QW...
DOOM!!
HE STOPPED IT!!
BUT HE SHOULD'VE HAD HIS GUARD DOWN...
I HAD A FEELING IT WAS A STRANGE SWORD...
ON CLOSER LOOK, IT DOESN'T EVEN HAVE A BLADE.
AHA...
THE FACT THAT YOU WOULD SWING A SWORD LIKE THAT...
...MUST MEAN IT'S VERY DANGER-OUS.

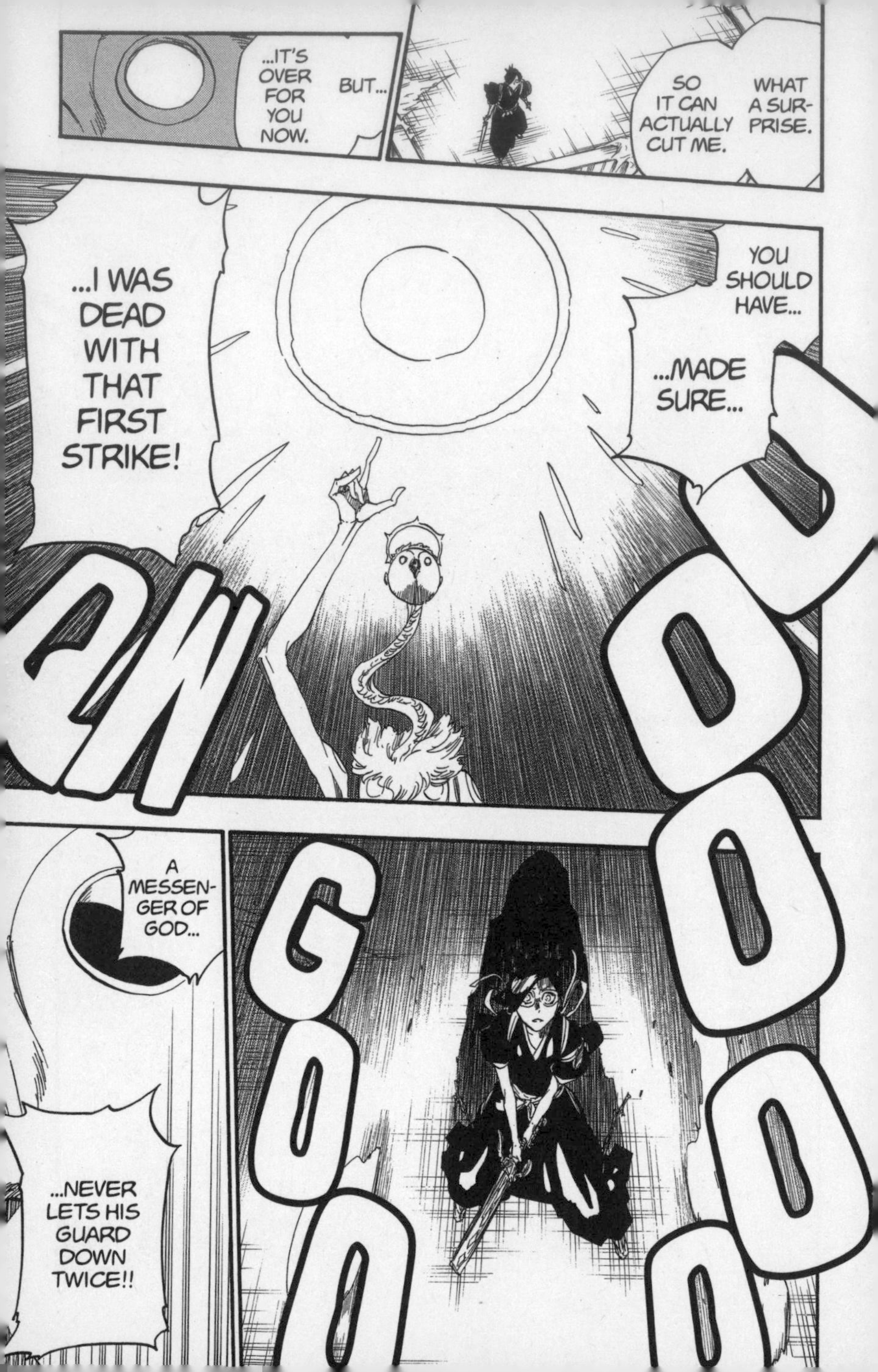
WHAT A SURPRISE.
SO IT CAN ACTUALLY CUT ME.
BUT...
...IT'S OVER FOR YOU NOW.
YOU SHOULD HAVE...
...MADE SURE...
...I WAS DEAD WITH THAT FIRST STRIKE!
DOOOOO
GOOO
A MESSENGER OF GOD...
...NEVER LETS HIS GUARD DOWN TWICE!!

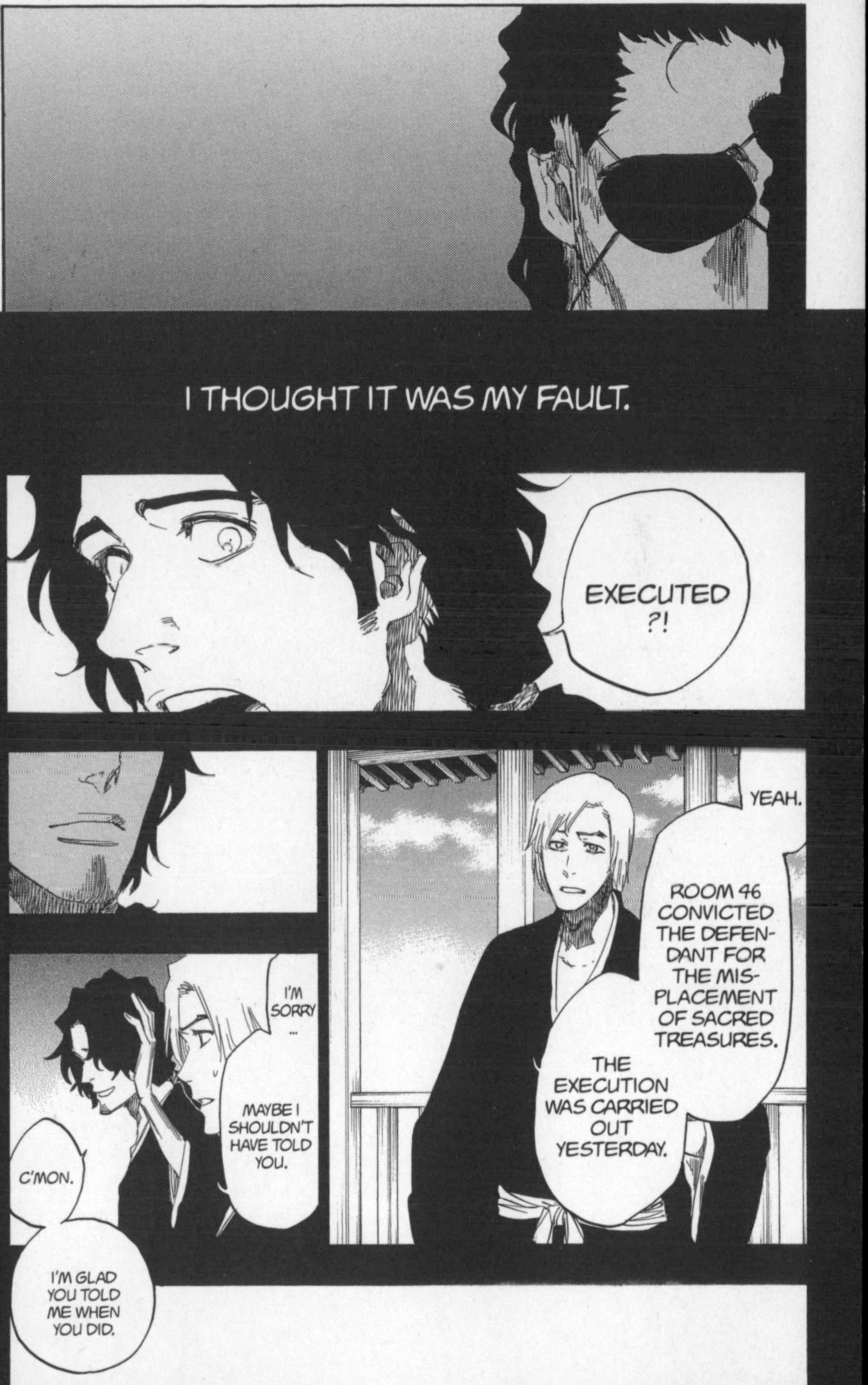
I THOUGHT IT WAS MY FAULT.
EXECUTED ?!
YEAH.
ROOM 46 CONVICTED THE DEFEN- DANT FOR THE MIS- PLACEMENT OF SACRED TREASURES.
THE EXECUTION WAS CARRIED OUT YESTERDAY.
I'M SORRY ...
MAYBE I SHOULDN'T HAVE TOLD YOU.
C'MON.
I'M GLAD YOU TOLD ME WHEN YOU DID.

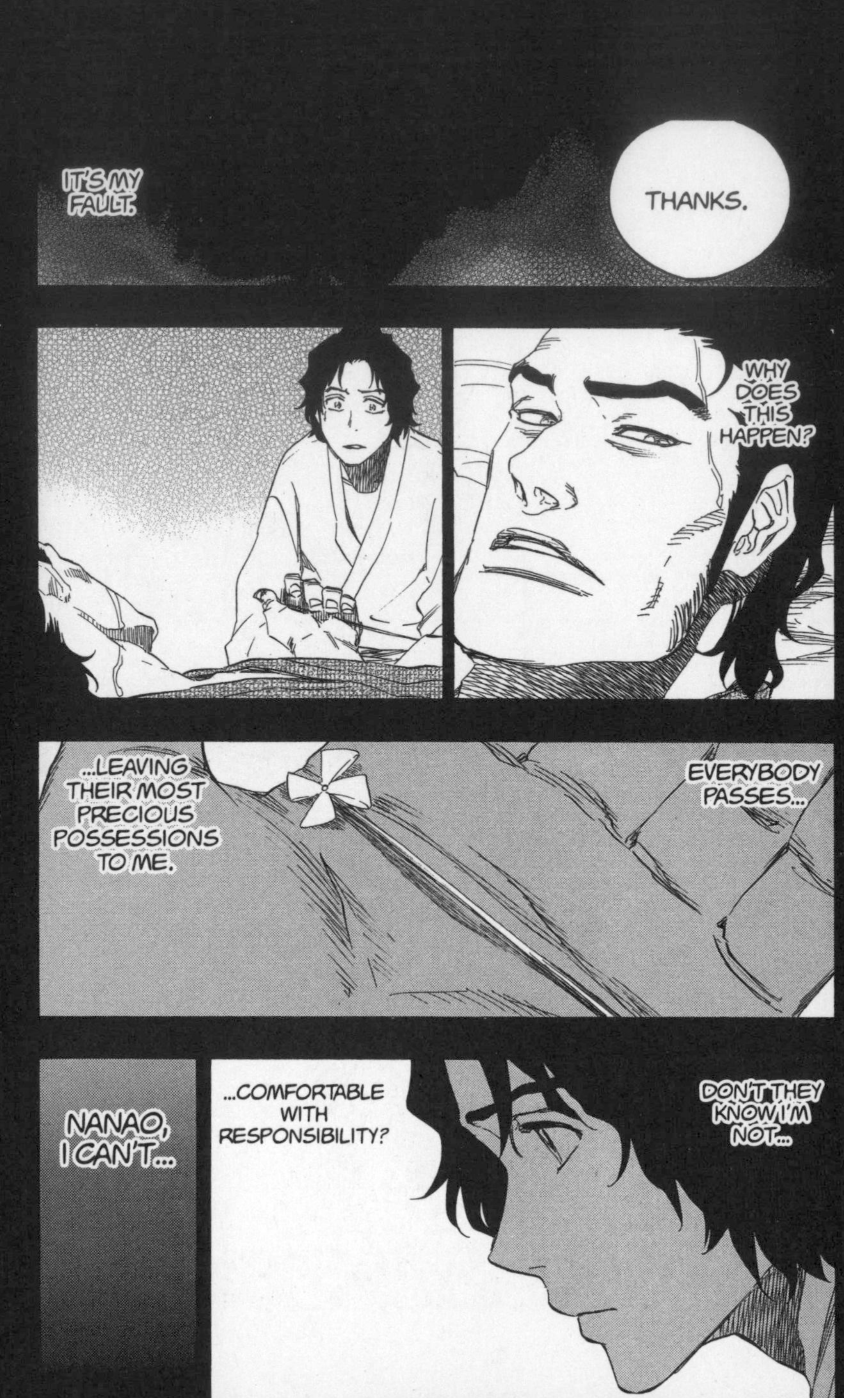
THANKS.
IT'S MY FAULT.
WHY DOES THIS HAPPEN?
EVERYBODY PASSES...
...LEAVING THEIR MOST PRECIOUS POSSESSIONS TO ME.
DON'T THEY KNOW I'M NOT...
...COMFORTABLE WITH RESPONSIBILITY?
NANAO, I CAN'T...

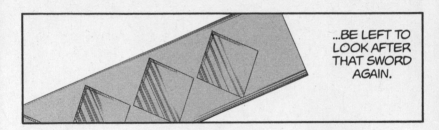

...BE LEFT TO LOOK AFTER THAT SWORD AGAIN.

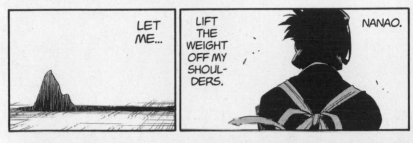

LET ME...

LIFT THE WEIGHT OFF MY SHOUL- DERS.

NANAO.

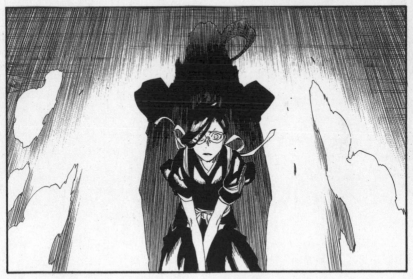

LET ME PROTECT YOU.

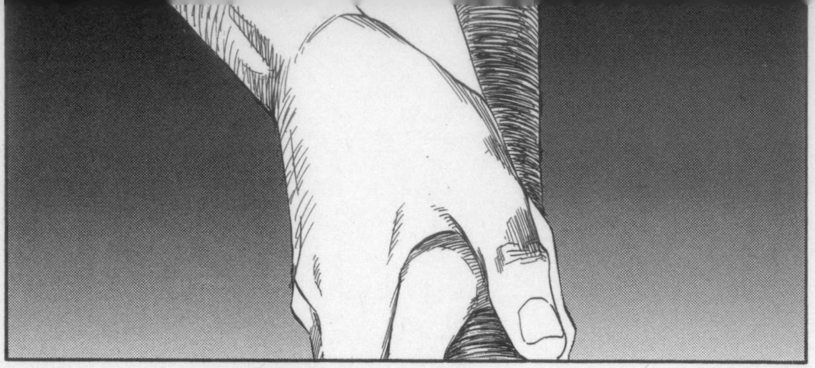
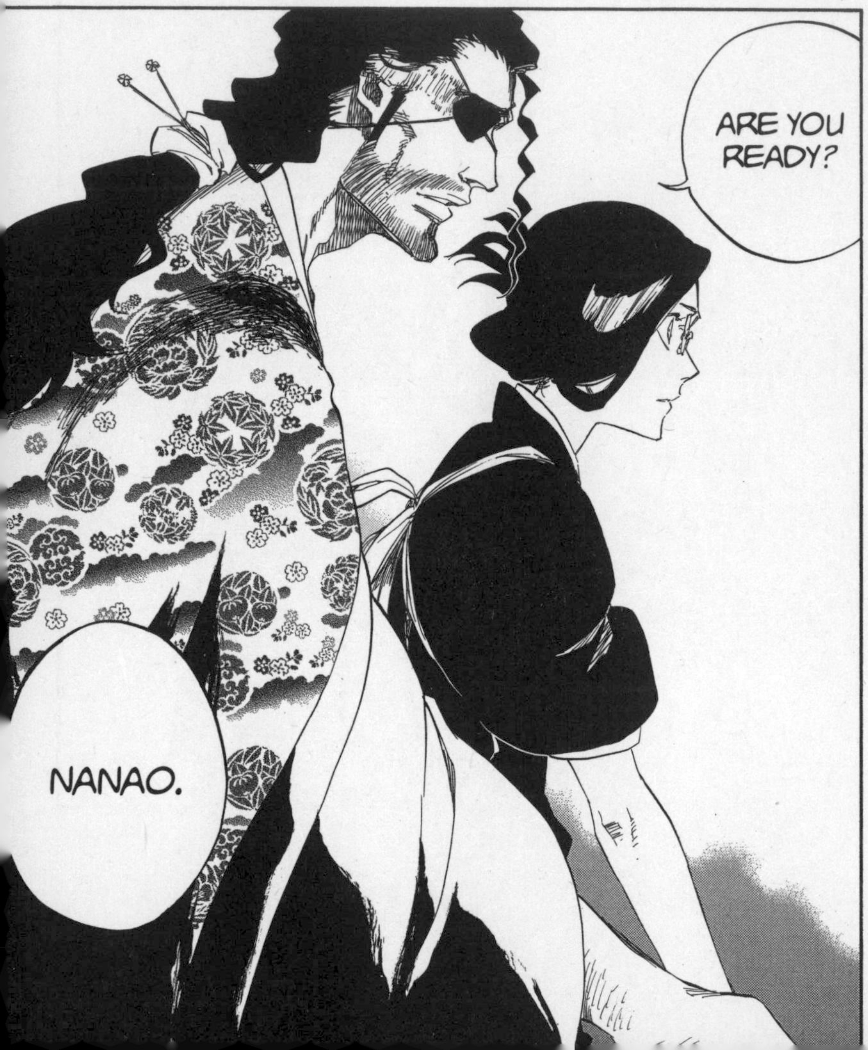
ARE YOU READY?
NANAO.

CONTI
NUED
IN
BLEACH
72

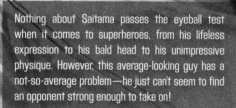
  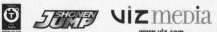

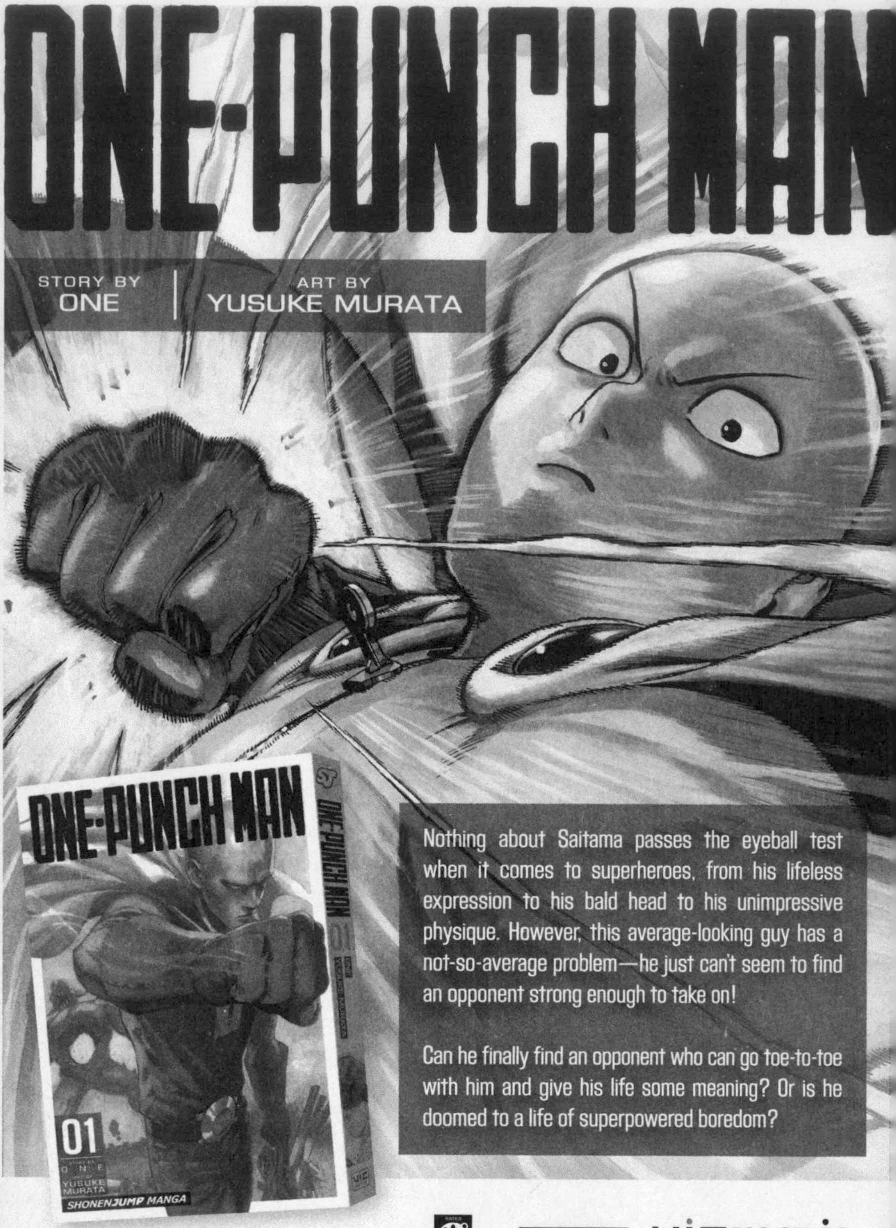

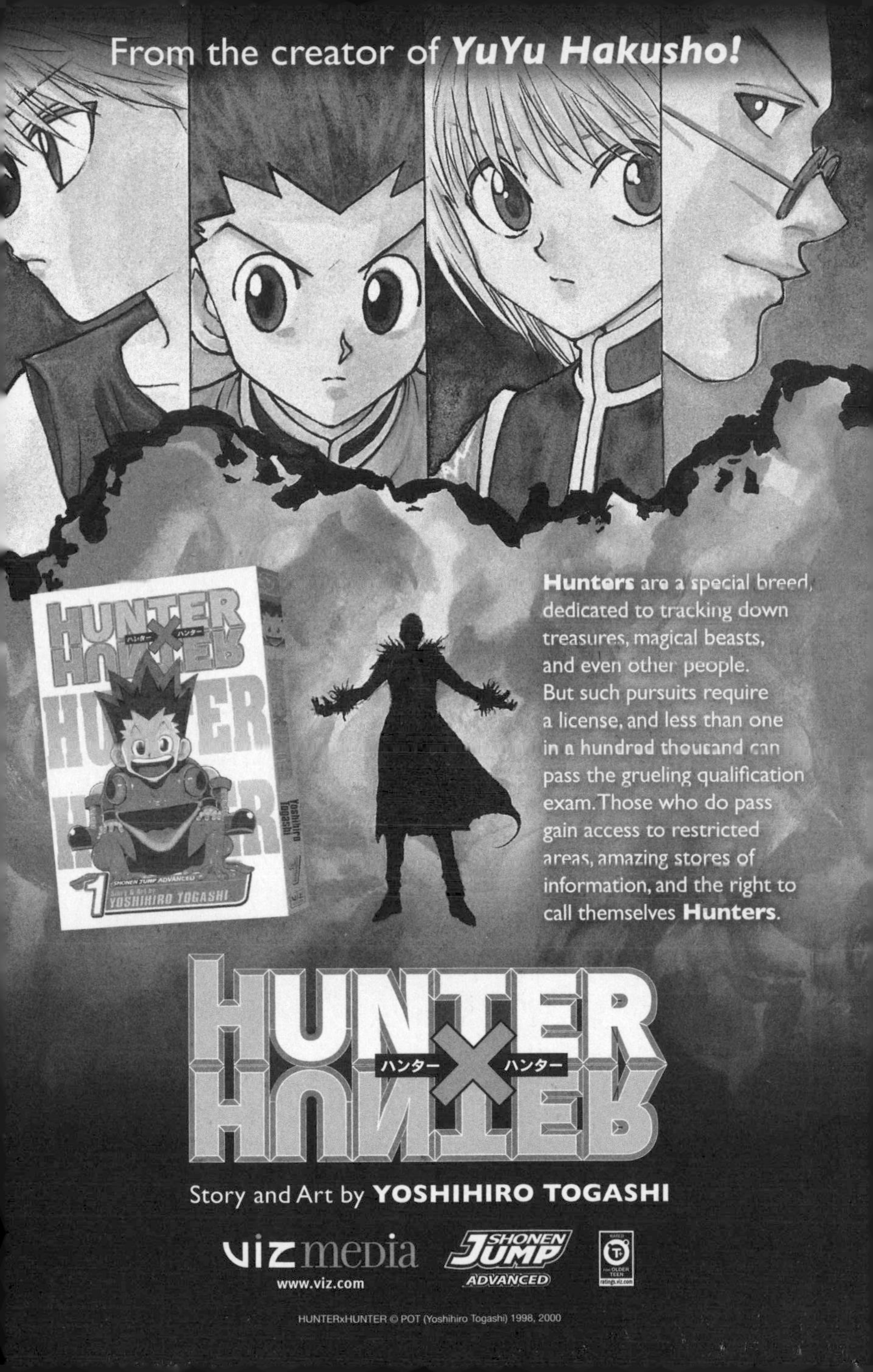
From the creator of *YuYu Hakusho!*
HUNTER × HUNTER
ハンター ハンター
SHONEN JUMP ADVANCED
1
YOSHIHIRO TOGASHI
Hunters are a special breed, dedicated to tracking down treasures, magical beasts, and even other people. But such pursuits require a license, and less than one in a hundred thousand can pass the grueling qualification exam. Those who do pass gain access to restricted areas, amazing stores of information, and the right to call themselves **Hunters**.
HUNTER × HUNTER
ハンター ハンター
Story and Art by YOSHIHIRO TOGASHI
viz media
www.viz.com
SHONEN JUMP ADVANCED
ratings.viz.com
HUNTERxHUNTER © POT (Yoshihiro Togashi) 1998, 2000

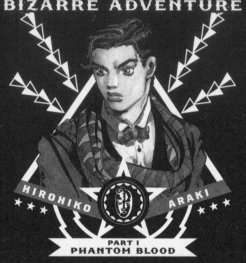
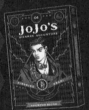
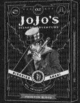
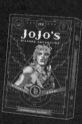

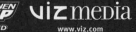

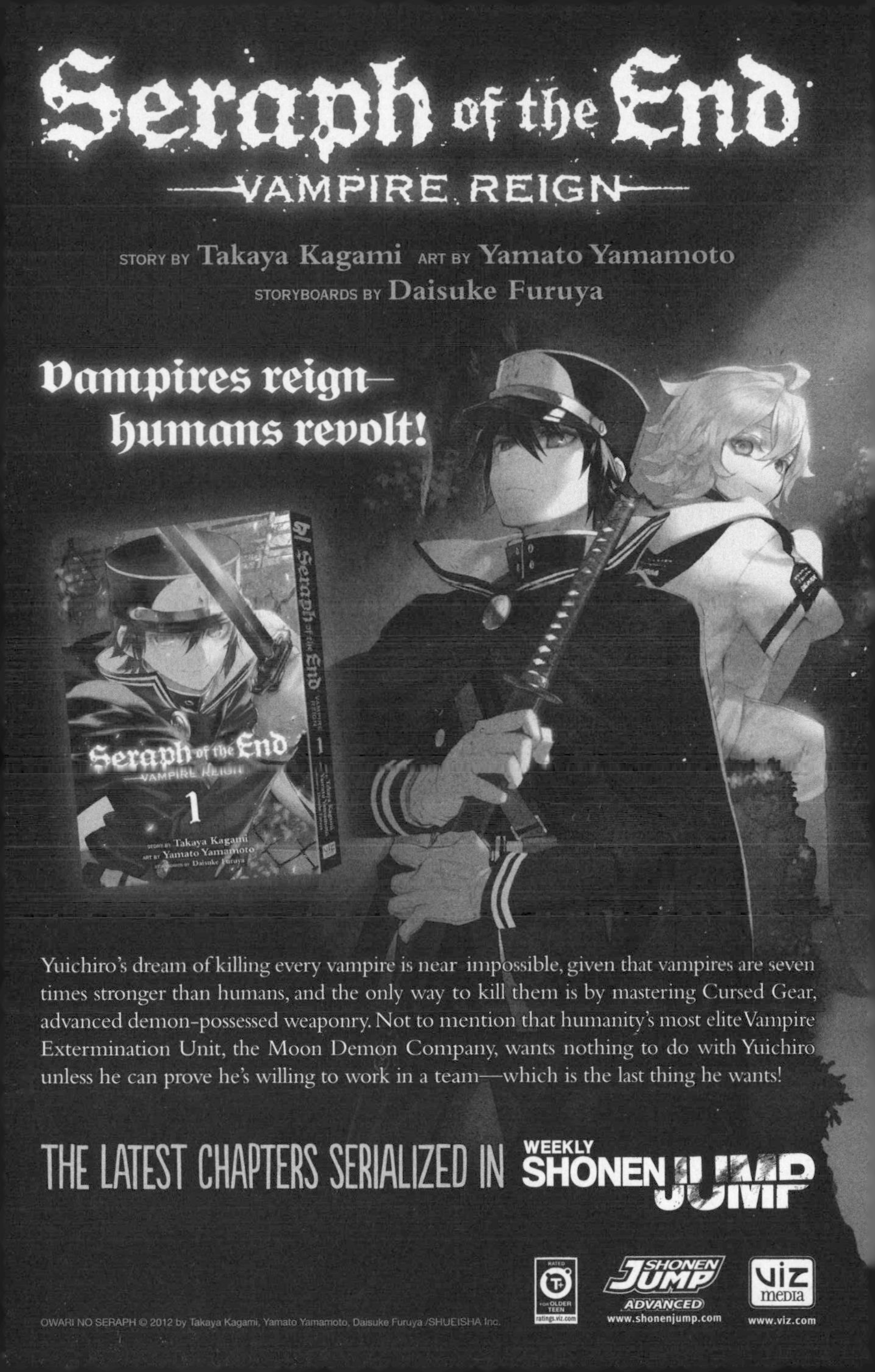
Seraph of the End
VAMPIRE REIGN
STORY BY Takaya Kagami ART BY Yamato Yamamoto
STORYBOARDS BY Daisuke Furuya
Vampires reign—
humans revolt!
Seraph of the End
VAMPIRE REIGN
1
STORY BY Takaya Kagami
ART BY Yamato Yamamoto
Yuichiro's dream of killing every vampire is near impossible, given that vampires are seven times stronger than humans, and the only way to kill them is by mastering Cursed Gear, advanced demon-possessed weaponry. Not to mention that humanity's most elite Vampire Extermination Unit, the Moon Demon Company, wants nothing to do with Yuichiro unless he can prove he's willing to work in a team—which is the last thing he wants!
THE LATEST CHAPTERS SERIALIZED IN WEEKLY SHONEN JUMP
RATED T+ FOR OLDER TEEN
ratings.viz.com
SHONEN JUMP ADVANCED
www.shonenjump.com
viz media
www.viz.com
OWARI NO SERAPH © 2012 by Takaya Kagami, Yamato Yamamoto, Daisuke Furuya /SHUEISHA Inc.

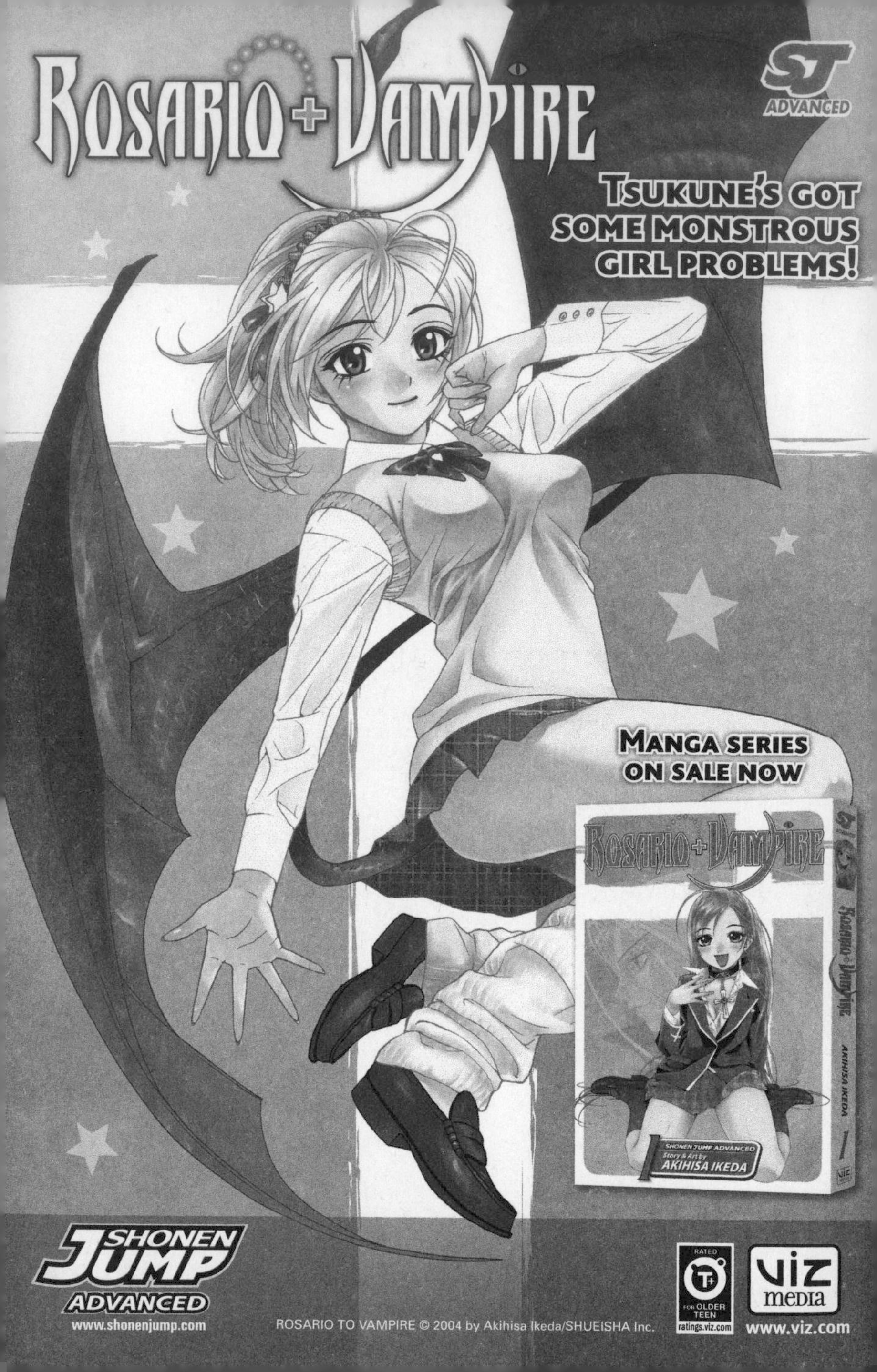

You're Reading in the Wrong Direction!!

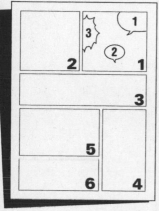

Whoops! Guess what? You're starting at the wrong end of the comic!

…It's true! In keeping with the original Japanese format, **Bleach** is meant to be read from right to left, starting in the upper-right corner.

Unlike English, which is read from left to right, Japanese is read from right to left, meaning that action, sound effects and word balloon order are completely reversed… something which can make readers unfamiliar with Japanese feel pretty backwards themselves. For this reason, manga or Japanese comics published in the U.S. in English have sometimes been published "flopped"—that is, printed in exact reverse order, as though seen from the other side of a mirror.

By flopping pages, U.S. publishers can avoid confusing readers, but the compromise is not without its downside. For one thing, a character in a flopped manga series who once wore in the original Japanese version a T-shirt emblazoned with "M A Y" (as in "the merry month of") now wears one which reads "Y A M"! Additionally, many manga creators in Japan are themselves unhappy with the process, as some feel the mirror-imaging of their art skews their original intentions.

We are proud to bring you Tite Kubo's **Bleach** in the original unflopped format. For now, though, turn to the other side of the book and let the adventure begin…!

—Editor

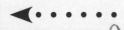

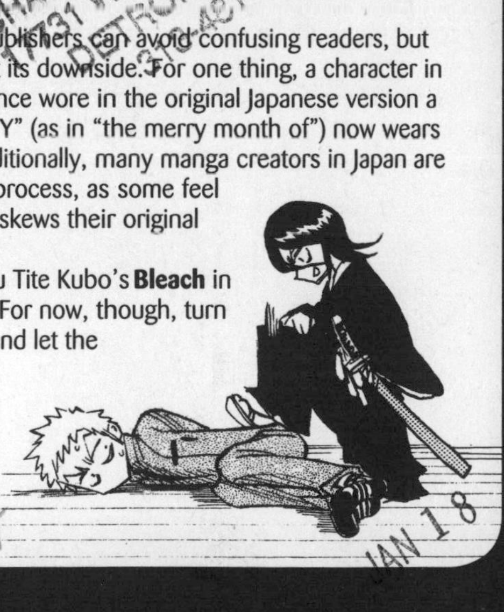